Design Governance

Design Governance focuses on how we design the built environment where most of us live, work, and play and the role of government in that process. To do so, it draws on the experience of the Commission for Architecture and the Built Environment (CABE), a decade-long, globally unique experiment in the governance of design. This book theorises design governance as an arm and aspiration of the state; tells the story of CABE, warts and all, and what came before and after; unpacks CABE's 'informal' toolbox: its methods and processes of design governance; and reflects on the effectiveness and legitimacy of design as a tool of modern-day government. The result is a new set of concepts through which to understand the governance of design as a distinct and important sub-field of urban design.

Matthew Carmona is a Professor of Planning and Urban Design at University College London's (UCL) Bartlett School of Planning, UK. His research has concentrated on urban design, processes of design governance, and the design and management of public space. He is an architect, planner, and chairs the Place Alliance.

Claudio de Magalhães is a Reader of Urban Regeneration and Management at UCL's Bartlett School of Planning, UK. His interests have been in planning and the governance of the built environment, the provision and governance of public space, property development processes, and urban regeneration policy.

Lucy Natarajan is an experienced researcher at UCL's Bartlett School of Planning, UK, where she did her PhD. Her core areas of concern are urban policy, knowledge in decision-making, public participation, spatial strategy, and new technologies of governing.

Design Governance

The CABE Experiment

Matthew Carmona,
Claudio de Magalhães,
and Lucy Natarajan

Routledge
Taylor & Francis Group

NEW YORK AND LONDON

First published 2017
by Routledge
711 Third Avenue, New York, NY 10017

and by Routledge
2 Park Square, Milton Park, Abingdon, Oxon, OX14 4RN

Routledge is an imprint of the Taylor & Francis Group, an informa business

Library of Congress Cataloging in Publication Data
Names: Carmona, Matthew, author. | Magalhäaes, Claudio de, author. | Natarajan, Lucy, author.
Title: Design governance : the CABE experiment / Matthew Carmona, Claudio de Magalhäaes, Lucy Natarajan.
Description: New York, NY : Routledge, 2017.
Identifiers: LCCN 2016025160 | ISBN 9781138812147 (hardback) | ISBN 9781138812154 (pbk.)
Subjects: LCSH: Great Britain. Commission for Architecture and the Built Environment. | Architectural design—Great Britain. | City planning—Great Britain.
Classification: LCC NA9185 .C37 2017 | DDC 307.1/2—dc23
LC record available at https://lccn.loc.gov/2016025160

ISBN: 978-1-138-81214-7 (hbk)
ISBN: 978-1-138-81215-4 (pbk)
ISBN: 978-1-315-74897-9 (ebk)

Typeset in Adobe Caslon
by Apex CoVantage, LLC

Printed and bound in India by Replika Press Pvt. Ltd.

Contents

A Personal Acknowledgement

The governance of design has been a personal interest and passion of mine since I first registered to do a PhD at the University of Nottingham in 1992. In many respects, this book represents the culmination of those efforts (so far) as it brings together much of that thinking and applies it to a particular and unique episode of design governance with far-reaching and important lessons for us all.

I would like to thank my fellow authors, Dr Claudio de Magalhães and Dr Lucy Natarajan, whose contribution to the empirical elements of this project has been invaluable. At the start this seemed like a mammoth, almost insurmountable task, but their on-going support, good sense, and encouragement have brought us through.

Helping us throughout the study were two researchers without whom we could not have completed this project: Wendy Clarke and Valentina Giordano. Many, many thanks to you both!

I also thank Andrew Renninger for all his work with me gathering the material underpinning Chapter 3.

Over the years, thousands of people were directly involved in the CABE experiment, as CABE staff, as commissioners, within or responsible for its sponsoring government departments, or as part of what became known as the wider 'CABE family'. Many millions were impacted indirectly as a result of its various programmes and projects, and this impact continues to be felt throughout England, but also elsewhere across the United Kingdom and even internationally.

I am indebted to those who were part of this unique experiment, so many of whom generously gave up their time to speak and engage with us simply because they felt it was important that the story should be properly told for our future learning and for posterity. Many (the majority) felt positively about the experience of CABE, although a substantial minority was critical, and for us it was vital to record and reflect both perspectives. We have made every attempt to faithfully, accurately, and fairly report on what we heard and read, and if any errors have crept in, I apologise. My only excuse is the sheer volume of materials we collected—written, visual, and aural—and my own limitations in understanding it.

I also gratefully acknowledge Dr Richard Simmons and Dr Elanor Warwick, who, in the dying days of a publicly funded CABE, had the foresight to grant access to the CABE archiving process and to financially support me in preparing an application for the Arts and Humanities Research Council (AHRC). Finally, I should thank the AHRC itself, a grant from whom—Evaluating the Governance of Design in the Built Environment[1]—enabled the project to commence, and five years after the demise of CABE, for this book to be completed.

Matthew Carmona
London
April 2016

Note

1. Principal Investigator, Prof Matthew Carmona, see: www.researchperspectives.org/rcuk/8C846D2D-E672–40B1-B00B-511B65A9B9C2_Evaluating-The-Governance-Of-Design-In-The-Built-Environment-The-CABE-Experiment-And-Beyond.

FOREWORD

Exploring Design Governance

Put simply, this book focuses on how we design the built environment where most of us live, work, and play and the role of the state (government) in that process. We can christen this activity 'design governance' and define it as:

> The process of state-sanctioned intervention in the means and processes of designing the built environment in order to shape both processes and outcomes in a defined public interest.
>
> (Carmona 2013a)

In this foreword the aims and intention of this book are set out and briefly discussed alongside an overview of the book's structure.

Design Governance through the CABE Lens

Whilst much has been written over the years about aspects of this subject, *Design Governance: The CABE Experiment* attempts a comprehensive re-evaluation of the subject and its constituent processes by drawing on the experience of a unique experiment in the governance of design—conducted in England between 1999 and 2011 at the level of the nation-state.

The New Labour government of Tony Blair and Gordon Brown was tracked for most of its period in power by a second smaller-scale experiment, an experience with potentially longer-lasting impacts as enshrined in the fabric of England's towns and cities. This was the attempt to address questions of design in the built environment through systematic government action. The most significant expression of this was the work of the Commission for Architecture and the Built Environment (CABE), which on a largely informal (non-statutory) basis,[1] sought to understand, campaign for, and prescribe solutions to the delivery of better architectural, urban, and public space design to the nation at large.

From its creation in 1999 to its demise as a government-funded organisation in 2011, CABE fronted a national drive in England for better design in the built environment. Whilst not universally supported at home, its scope, ambition, and impact were certainly impressive, and as an organisation it was unique on a global scale. As such the study of this exceptional experiment offers an unparalleled opportunity to shine a light on the often unfathomable processes of governing the design of development. Through these means, this book unearths a range of important conceptual and tangible lessons about how we govern design in the built environment, and these are of relevance far beyond English shores.

The Aims and Structure of This Book

This book is structured into three main parts and an afterword, each of which addresses a different primary aim:

1. To theorise design governance as an arm and aspiration of modern-day government.
2. To tell the story of CABE, warts and all, and to set it in the context of the work of the Royal Fine Art Commission (RFAC) that came before, and the market in design governance that came after.
3. To unpack CABE's 'informal' toolbox: its methods and processes of design governance.
4. To conclude by drawing from the research to reflect on the effectiveness and legitimacy of design as a tool of government.

Part I contains the key theoretical chapters. In Chapter 1, the subject of design governance is unpacked and then re-formulated in a manner that offers a comprehensive theory of its scope, purpose, and challenges. Chapter 2 then focuses on the 'tools' of design governance, and in so doing establishes a framework for thinking about the full range of approaches to design governance—nationally and locally.

Part II examines the story of national-level design governance in England through a historical lens. The three chapters in this section deal, respectively, with the pre-CABE, CABE, and post-CABE design governance environments and situate each story in relation to the prevailing political economy, processes of governance, and changing national narrative around design in the built environment.

Part III focuses firmly on practice. Whilst the predominance of discussion in this field so far (and in Chapter 2) has tended to be on the statutory or 'formal' approaches governments use to 'regulate' design, the five chapters in this part focus on how CABE used other, more 'informal' tools to steer a national design agenda. Each of these chapters follows the same simple structure, addressing the 'why', 'how', and 'when' of the tools that CABE used.

This book closes with an afterword in which overarching conclusions are drawn out. Here the opportunity is taken to reflect back on the research and to evaluate the CABE experiment. First, this is done in its own terms, as regards how impactful was the organisation and the range of 'informal' tools it adopted as means to deliver on the design aspirations set by government. Second what this suggests about the legitimacy of design governance generally is explored, and about the moral/societal case for such intervention?

The research employed an inductive research methodology to journey from the specifics of practice to a broad theory of design governance as laid out in this book. The research methods are briefly set out in the Appendix.

Note

1. Throughout this book, references to and discussion of 'CABE' relate *only* to the government-funded body that existed from August 1999 to April 2011, and not to 'Design Council CABE' that inherited some of CABE's functions and that is always referred to in this book with its full, correct title (see Chapter 5).

PART I

The Governance of Design

CHAPTER 1

Design Governance (Why, What, and How—in Theory)

This introductory chapter sets the scene by introducing the notion of design governance[1] in the built environment, and exploring why the public sector should seek to intervene in design. This chapter is in three parts. The first addresses the motivation for design governance through examining why our design, development, and management processes continually give rise to sub-standard outcomes, and whether we can conceptualise an alternative view of design in the built environment, one based on different notions of quality. The second and third parts, respectively, address the 'what' and 'how' questions. They do this through dissecting the concept of design governance and investigating a number of recurring debates in the literature that reveal key conceptual threads and problematics that run through the subject. The issues and ideas explored in this chapter provide the underpinning theory for the experiences and practices that the remainder of this book goes on to explore.

Why Do We Design Sub-standard Places?

Design Knowledge

In Europe we are spoiled. Our rich urban history has given rise to an equally rich and varied urban heritage right across the continent. Tourists travel from around the world to enjoy and experience our historic urban centres, and we care for them (typically) with great dedication. They have character and coherence; they

Figure 1.1 Central Copenhagen, a place of character and coherence

Source: Matthew Carmona

feel comfortable and engaging; typically they are mixed, dense, and walkable; and often they are loved and valued by inhabitants and visitors alike. They are 'places' of character and coherence (1.1).

Yet beyond these centres and the often leafy, medium-density, nineteenth- and early-twentieth-century districts that typically surround them, the picture is not so rosy. Instead it mirrors the sorts of sub-urbanism found around the world. Indeed an EU-funded project conducted to explore housing design and development processes across the continent concluded:

It seems that whatever the system, whatever the governance, no matter what our rules and regulations, however we organise our professions, and no matter what our histories, placeless design seems to be the inevitable consequence of development processes outside our historic city centres. Moreover, this is despite the ubiquitous condemnation of such environments as sub-standard by almost every built environment professional you ever meet.

(Carmona 2010: 14)

Such critiques are broad indeed. They apply to the majority of our planned post-war suburbs and contemporary urban extensions; to most peripheral office, retail, and leisure parks; to our inner-urban estates; to peri-urban areas in general, including the large swathes of land along our urban arterial corridors and around our ring roads; and to new settlements (where they exist) in their entirety; to almost anywhere a coherent and unifying human-centred urban structure has been allowed to break down or where one never existed in the first place. These sorts of environments are what some have termed 'placeless', and they are certainly global: they are the parts of cities to which tourists never venture (at least not on purpose); are unremarkable, incoherent, and often unloved; and typically require inhabitants to adopt carbon-intensive lifestyles simply to get around. We all know such environments and likely as not will live or work in one. Increasingly they have become the urban norm rather than the exception across much of the world, and in the not too distant past even threatened to overwhelm and replace many of the historic centres we now so jealously guard.

So why do such places come about? Looking at the question through a design lens, we can logically postulate a number of possible reasons.

We Don't 'Design' Places at All

Some places are clearly shaped by a network of ad hoc uncoordinated hands, where individual physical interventions—for example a building or a piece of infrastructure—may be designed, but only in relation to narrow functional requirements and not in terms of a contribution to a coherent greater whole. The whole, in this sense, is not designed and is arrived at unintentionally. Whilst this mirrors the way that many of our most cherished historic urban fabrics grew—incrementally and without a 'grand plan', yet giving rise to a strong sense of internal coherence—today the

scale, rate, and complexity of change has hugely increased, as has the range of building technologies available to us, our infrastructure needs, and a preference amongst many development, political, professional, and individual interests for drivable as opposed to walkable urban form. All this makes unintentional coherence far less likely to occur and may give rise to the question: are the resulting built environments designed in any real sense at all?

We Don't Know How to Design 'Good' Places

Today, of course, few developed societies rely on such uncoordinated incremental development to meet their development needs. Instead, places are shaped by highly trained professionals from a variety of background disciplines, most notably architects, planners, civil engineers, landscape architects, and developers, and this work is coordinated through a plan or strategy to ensure that individual interventions contribute to something larger such as a neighbourhood. Yet despite our undoubted 'expertise', the education of traditional disciplines has often omitted to cover the key urban design knowledge and skills required to shape places holistically and in a coordinated manner. As a consequence the skills and knowledge needed to guarantee that the place in its entirety is well designed and coherent may be (and often is) sub-standard; places are designed, but not very well. As the adage goes, 'a little knowledge can be a dangerous thing,' and in this field, sub-standard skills and knowledge poorly applied has the potential to do profound and long-lasting damage.

We Know How to Design 'Good' Places, Yet We Fail to Do So

A final cause of poor place design might be our inability to deliver good design despite having carefully constructed normative frameworks and clear visions for what places should be like. In such circumstances, it is not our design skills or knowledge that is lacking, but instead a host of other local contextual factors that have the potential to frustrate implementation and defeat even the most noble of design propositions. These might include economic barriers to change; insensitive and overbearing regulatory processes; land-ownership or land availability barriers; lack of political leadership; NIMBY pressures; or perhaps differential aspirations about what should be built between key development actors: developers, politicians, communities, and the range of built environment professionals.

Simplistically we can summarise this trinity of barriers as: no design knowledge, poor design knowledge, and ineffective design knowledge, and today, one or more of these states is likely to explain most substandard place design. This raises three further questions: (i) what do we mean by 'design' in the context of urban places; (ii) if design processes are sub-standard, what is filling the gap; and (iii) what anyway do we mean by design 'quality' in such circumstances?

What Do We Mean by 'Design'?

For many, the term 'design' will often have narrow associations with the creative activity of drawing or otherwise conceptualising a particular object that is being 'designed'. When used in the context of designing the built environment, for many, this will conjure associations with the creation of plans and propositions to demonstrate how particular buildings, landscapes, or

urban townscapes might look—in other words, a demonstration of their aesthetic qualities. In this book, however, 'design' has a broader meaning in two senses.

First, design concerns all the elements of place—land uses, activities, environmental resources, and physical elements (buildings, spaces, infrastructure, and landscape)—that constitute urban environments and that transcend the professional remits of architecture, urban planning, landscape architecture, and urban engineering. In short, urban design. Second, design in this sense does not just refer to the activities of the 'designer', from whichever profession, but instead encompasses the sum of all the activities that together shape the built environment (intentional and unintentional)—a metaprocess that has been characterised as a place-shaping continuum (Carmona 2014b).

The place-shaping continuum (1.2) hypothesises that the process of shaping places cannot be grasped (and thereby steered) without understanding the full range of influences that act together to shape the process and thereby the outcomes of urban change. This implies a process: informed by historically defined norms and practices of development that vary from

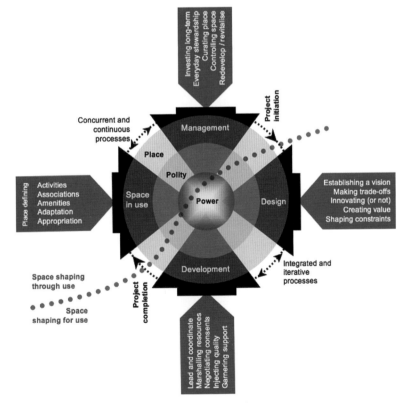

Figure 1.2   The place-shaping continuum (adapted from Carmona 2014b)

place to place; set within and modified by the local contemporary political economic context, or 'polity'; and defined by a particular set of stakeholder power relationships that again will vary from place to place and even from development to development.

Within this macro-context, there is also the need to understand the creation, re-creation, and performance of the built environment across the four interrelated process dimensions represented in 1.2. Thus it is not just design, or even development processes that shape the experience of space, but instead the combined outcomes and interactions between:

- Design—the key aspirations and vision, and local contextual and stakeholder influences on a particular project or set of proposals.
- Development—the power relationships, and processes of negotiation, regulation, and delivery for a particular project or set of proposals.
- Space in use—who uses a particular place, how, why, when, and with what consequences and conflicts.
- Management—the responsibilities for stewardship, security, maintenance, and on-going funding of place.

This is not a series of discrete episodes and activities, but instead a continuous integrated process or continuum; sometimes focussed on particular projects or sets of interventions (design and development) to shape the physical environment for use; and sometimes on the everyday 'processes of place' (use and management), shaping the social environment through the manner in which places are actually used and looked after. We can conclude from this that the design of the built environment at large represents an on-going journey through which places are continuously shaped and re-shaped— physically, socially, and economically—through periodic planned intervention, day-to-day occupation, and the long-term guardianship of space. As a process, it is multidimensional, multi-actor, and often poorly understood, and this inherent complexity forms an important context for all the discussion that follows in this book.

What Do Sub-standard Places Have in Common?

Whilst a complete absence of self-conscious design processes—'no design knowledge'—would be extremely rare in the developed world, arguably 'poor design knowledge' and 'ineffective design knowledge' are the norm. Take Rome, for example, perhaps the most historic of Europe's capital cities, and boasting an enviable urban heritage with the likes of Piazza Novona, Via del Corso, Piazza del Campidoglio, Piazza della Rotonda, and Via Vento. But move beyond the ancient city and into its expanding suburbs and we find very little evidence of a carefully considered urban design process. Instead, in these areas developers and their architects focus on the buildings (typically standard building types repeated from place to place), whilst urban planning focuses on the production of two-dimensional zoning plans. No one focuses on the bit in the middle, the public realm, which remains largely un-designed. As a result, instead of being linked by a coherent and connected urban fabric that encourages walking and social and economic exchange, we see buildings constructed in unrelated plots with the spaces between dominated by parking and roads, and by very little else (1.3). Instead of a corner shop or café, these new suburbs rely on their privatised malls to serve their low-density 'edge city' communities.

In Rome, the results are all the more surprising given the historic context, but perhaps they shouldn't be. This is simply the global norm that UN Habitat tells us is fast engulfing many developing as well as developed nations "as real estate developers promote the image of a 'world-class lifestyle' outside the city" (2010:10). They report, for example, that between 1970 and the year 2000, the surface area of Guadalajara in Mexico grew 1.6 times faster than the population

Figure 1.3   Edge city, Roman style
Source: Matthew Carmona

whilst similar urban sprawl is consuming considerable amounts of land in cities as diverse as Antananarivo, Beijing, Johannesburg, Cairo, and Mexico City, to name just a few.

Regulations as a Substitute for Design

What unites all these places, as well as their counterparts in developed Europe, North America, Australasia, and the Far East? A major factor seems to be the shaping of cities through crude standards and regulations as a substitute for actually engaging in a place-centred design process. As a consequence, regulations prescribe parking norms, road widths and hierarchies, land uses, density requirements, health and safety issues, construction and space standards, and so forth. Typically, these forms of control are limited in their scope, technical in their aspiration, not generated out of a place-based vision, and are imposed on projects without regard to outcomes (Carmona 2009b: 2649). Moreover, once adopted, there is a tendency for such standards to become the norms that are then applied everywhere, even in the historic city cores (1.4).

Eran Ben-Joseph traces the evolution across North American cities of what he refers to as these 'hidden codes' (2005a). In doing so, he argues that too often the original purpose and value of the codes are forgotten as the bureaucracies put in place to implement them do so in a manner that has little regard for their actual rationale, and even less for the knock-on effects of their

Figure 1.4 Suburban-style developments located on Liverpool's historic Pier Head, complete with standard parking requirements, road splays, and buffer planting

Source: Matthew Carmona

existence. Emily Talen agrees, arguing that worthy social purposes such as the pursuit of public health are all too quickly buried under the weight of successive technical amendments (2012: 28). Instead, these forms of standards are about achieving minimum requirements across the board (regardless of site context), whilst in many cases the slavish adherence to standards has led to the creation of bland and unattractive places.

In the United Kingdom, such critiques go back at least as far as the 1950s and to the emergence of the townscape movement with its concerns for the sorts of 'prairie planning' that standards-based housing layouts were giving rise to (Cullen 1961: 133–137). Arguably this represents a classic case of regulatory (rather than market) failure, but the failure extends well beyond the suburbs and beyond the sorts of standards imposed by the public sector. The little Thames-side town of Erith on London's eastern fringes represents a case in point.

Erith has medieval roots and grew up as a port, serving at various times as a naval dockyard, general anchorage, riverside resort, and locus for industry. The town was heavily bombed in the Second World War, but it was the peace that so comprehensively and systematically ripped the heart out of this community through incremental episodes of development made in the absence of a coherent design framework and little concern for place quality (1.5). Instead, the town saw:

- Insensitive public development: the imposition of alien Modernist design visions from 1966 onwards through the comprehensive redevelopment of the town centre and nearby residential areas, in the process sweeping away the tight knit urban grain and complex mix of uses and replacing it with large mono-use blocks and high-rise residential towers to the latest standards as laid down in the national 'Design Bulletins' of the era (Carmona 1999).
- Poorly directed market opportunism: not least through the imposition in 1998 of a 'big-box' out-of-town-style supermarket close to, but detached from exiting shopping areas which, over time, it has almost completely usurped.
- Infrastructure prioritised over people: the insensitive imposition of highways infrastructure at strategic and local scales, including the upgrading of the A2016 in the 1970s to trunk road standard, in the process cutting off the town centre from its residential hinterland.

• Bad management: typified by moving the market to an edge-of-town car park in order to safeguard a route for emergency vehicles through the main shopping street (Pier Road), whilst in the process killing off both the market and much of the retail along Pier Road with which it had a symbiotic relationship.

The Tyrannies of Practice

In common with so many other towns and cities worldwide, in Erith nobody was consciously designing the place, just the parts, driven on by three dominant tyrannies of practice: creative, market, and regulatory (Carmona 2009b: 2645–2647). The tyrannies stem from the very different sets of aspirations of the three key classes of built environment actors who shape such places—architects, development professionals, and regulators—each of whom has a very different set of motivations underpinning their actions. Typically, and respectively, these motivations include peer approval, profit, and a narrowly defined view of the public interest. They are in turn informed by very different modes of working and associated professional knowledge fields, respectively: design, management/finance, and social/technical expertise. In Erith the placeless public design prescriptions of the 1960s (1.5i), the market opportunism of the 1990s and 2000s (1.5ii), the intensive infrastructure of the town's post-war history (1.5iii), and the insensitive management approaches of today (1.5iv) perfectly encapsulate the tyrannies.

Today, places are shaped to greater or lesser degrees by the interplay between these creative, market-driven, and regulatory modes of practice and arguably, too

Figures 1.5i–iv   Erith (London), shaped and destroyed by the tyrannies of practice

Source: Matthew Carmona

Figures 1.6i–iii   In Japanese cities, different tyrannies predominate in different places

Source: Matthew Carmona

often by the failure to strike an appropriate balance between those forces. This can lead, as often in the United Kingdom, to profound and ingrained conflict between the different professionals who encapsulate each culture. The danger is then that places are shaped by development solutions based on the conflict, compromise, and delay that result from the friction between contrasting perspectives on the city rather than on what is right for a particular locality.

Particular tyrannies predominate to different degrees in different places, and this is 'written' into the urban fabric of our cities, as famously illustrated by the sequence of drawings by Hugh Ferris (1929) depicting the implications of the 1916 Zoning Ordinance on New York's buildings, where simple regulatory formulae crossed

with developers' desire to maximise development, led directly to the characteristic stepped skyscraper designs of the 1920s and 1930s. In Japanese cities, the impact of the tyrannies can be particularly striking (Carmona & Sakai 2014). In Tokyo, for example, a lack of visual controls of any form gives architects a free hand to create wild and extravagant architectural gestures that in some parts of the city result in an architectural zoo of competing visions (1.6i). Elsewhere it is the forces of commerce that dominate, with the centres of many Japanese cities, including Osaka (1.6ii), festooned with gaudy signs and lights competing for the attention of customers. There is also a more restrained side that is most obvious in the ordinary streets of Japanese cities, particularly in historic cities such as Kyoto (1.6iii), where rigid zoning and building regulations dominate, leading to some very regimented and ultimately uncomfortable relationships between buildings.

Yet whilst undoubtedly visually chaotic, Japanese urban landscapes are also amongst the most vibrant and stimulating in the world. This invites the thorny question: what exactly do we mean by design quality in the built environment? 'Design quality' is invariably a problematic concept that will mean different things to different people, not least to the different professionals involved in a development project, as well as to the many individuals who make up the community affected by it.

What Do We Mean by 'Quality' in Design?

As has already been touched on, discussion of design immediately raises issues of visual appearance in many minds. In the United Kingdom, for example, prior to the 1990s the regulation of design through the planning process was known as aesthetic control, largely because 'design' was seen as largely an aesthetic concern. Indeed, for many years, and in particular in the 1980s, the design agenda of national government was largely limited to telling local government to steer clear from 'meddling' (as they saw it) in such concerns. Yet, as the Japanese case suggests, quality in the built environment is not just a visual concern, as even the most visually chaotic of city spaces can work in a whole host of other ways: they might be comfortable, engaging, safe, social, efficient, sustainable, and so forth. Even in aesthetic terms, what for one person may be a satisfying visual harmony for another may be simply boring. In this respect, as has already been argued, we are better off thinking about 'places' in the round rather than about particular more limited notions of quality.

Conceptually unpacking this, it is possible to conceive of four levels of design quality relating to the built environment, each more complex than the last:

1. Aesthetic quality: Which is the most limited conceptualisation of design, yet is also often the 'headline' consideration when architectural, urban, or landscape design is debated, not least because of the overriding preoccupation in the training of architects and other design professionals with the physical 'vision' as something to be understood and critiqued first and foremost on an artistic/aesthetic level.

2. Project quality: Takes a larger perspective on design encompassing the Vitruvian principles of firmness, commodity, and delight (aka: soundly built, fit for purpose, and attractive). This notion thereby encompasses important aspects of functionality alongside aesthetic concerns, but in a different way is also limited. Thus whether the project is a building, a bridge, or a piece of green infrastructure, the emphasis will tend to be on the project in isolation and therefore on an object-based assessment of quality within the boundaries of a clearly defined site.

3. Place quality: Again enlarges the plane of concern, this time beyond the project and its site to the larger place in the sense already discussed and incorporating all the complex interacting dimensions of the use, activity, resources, and physical components of place. This notion encompasses how particular interventions (e.g. individual projects) interact with and impact the whole as well as the parts of the complex contexts in which they are situated.

4. Process quality: The final type is quite different from the previous conceptualisations as it is concerned with the 'why', 'how', and 'when' of design as much as with the 'what'. In other words, with how the place, project, or vision is shaped or created, for what purpose, and by who; with why an intervention is right in the context of all the other processes of change that impact that place; and with when change occurs and how processes facilitate or undermine that. This notion of process quality structures the discussion in Part III of this book.

Ultimately, whilst judgement about design quality in any given circumstance will never elicit unanimity from one individual or organisation to the next, each notion of quality is perfectly capable of being defined in normative terms depending on the exact nature of the aesthetic vision, project, place, or process. In England, the Royal Fine Art Commission (RFAC) defined six criteria for *What makes a good building* in order to guide its design review activities. These were: order and unity, expression (of the function of a building), integrity (in design), plan and section (an honest three-dimensional construction), detail (to delight and hold the eye), and integration (with the surroundings). Whilst admitting that a building could embody every criterion and still not be a 'good' building and, conversely, could be a 'good' building without complying with any of the criteria, underpinning the principles was an overriding concern with the aesthetic consequences of development (Cantacuzino 1994).

In 2001 and again in 2006, the Commission for Architecture and the Built Environment (CABE) updated the criteria for design review, this time with an emphasis on *What makes a good project*. The new broader criteria encompassed: clarity of organisation (site and building planning), order, expression and representation, appropriateness of architectural ambition, integrity and honesty, architectural language (coherent and compelling, rather than arbitrary), scale, conformity and contrast, orientation prospect and aspect, detailing and materials, structure environmental services and energy use, flexibility and adaptability, sustainability, inclusive design, and aesthetics (CABE 2006a). Whilst this advice also outlined the importance of context and how to understand the project in its context and in relation to planning a site, the overriding emphasis remained on the various complex, interweaving dimensions of the project rather than the larger place.

Moving to the broader notion of place rather than project quality, a wide range of normative frameworks summarise the desirable components of place. The Place Diagram of the Project for Public Spaces, for example, defines four 'key attributes' of successful places: sociability, access and linkages, uses and activities, and comfort and image;[2] whilst the UK Government's guidance on design and the planning system that heavily influenced English urban design policy and practice throughout the 2000s promoted a seven-part agenda of: character, continuity and enclosure, quality of the public realm, ease of movement, legibility, adaptability, and diversity. Such frameworks demonstrate that the concern for place extends from the physical reality and qualities of space to the actual experience of and practicalities inherent in its use.

Above and beyond such normative conceptualisations of design outcomes is the idea that the processes of design also have quality dimensions that ultimately influence how places are shaped. This notion of 'process' as something that can be influenced goes to the heart of the discussion in this book, as does the idea that process is continuous and not just concerned with the act of designing. Critically, it also encompasses processes of development, long-term management, and even the use of place; in other words, with what has already been described as the place-shaping continuum. Thus these processes relate not only to the sorts of self-consciously designed schemes that catch the eye of the press, but also to the un-self-conscious processes of urban adaptation and change that continuously shape and reshape the built environment all around.

Tridib Banerjee and Anastasia Loukaitou-Sideris observe that "Not much literature has focused on the process of urban design and its relationship to the final design outcome" (2011: 275). They argue that whilst some see design as a 'glass box' process, completely explicable and capable of understanding and refinement, more often it is viewed as a 'black box' phenomenon, obscured by the fathomless complexities and depths of the design imagination. They conclude that the reality is likely to lay somewhere between; in other

words, explicable but fathomless. To understand this process certainly requires an integrative understanding of the politically defined historic and contemporary processes of change, and a long-term view of all the processes that shape place and how they are moulded through the complex and changing power relationships between stakeholders. This is unlikely to be easy to grasp, let alone influence, perhaps explaining why normative models of the qualities of design process are less abundant than those relating to design outcomes.

In sum, many sets of 'quality' principles could be listed here, but the important point to take away is the need to understand the limits of any conceptualisation and how judgement and interpretation will always be a factor in assessments about what is good and what is not. When such judgements are being made in the public interest, then a process will be required to do this (part of the larger place-shaping process), and it is to this that discussion now turns.

Conceptualising the Governance of Design: What Is It?

The Governance Turn

Whilst 'governance' as a concept remains slippery and the subject of much heated debate amongst political scientists, from the 1990s onwards the term has increasingly been associated with a shift in our understanding of how society manages its affairs. So whilst the traditional view of public power was one of command and control where authority was centralised and exercised hierarchically, governance starts from the notion that power is typically dispersed and governments are severely limited in their ability to effect change when acting alone. Instead, public power acts through different tiers of government, through a wide range of governmental and pseudo-governmental agencies, and through the resources and activities of the private sector. In this respect, "effective power is shared, bartered and struggled over by diverse forces and agencies" (Held et al. 1999: 447).

Contemporary discussions of governance cover many variants: global, corporate, project, environmental, regulatory, participatory, urban, and so on. Focussing on the last of these, the urban governance cake may be sliced and understood in multiple ways: in terms of the formal overlapping tiers of government, supranational to local; relating to places as geographically defined units such as cities, districts, neighbourhoods, etc.; as regards particular types of area, for instance places of rapid change, areas of environmental or historical sensitivity, areas of multiple deprivation, etc.; in relation to the particular challenges of service provision in different policy arenas, including the governance of planning, highways maintenance, parks management, and so on; or even as regards particular sub-areas of service provision, like the governance of tall buildings as a subset of planning. Governance has been discussed in all these ways and many more, it is often set within larger discussions of political economy, and has spawned a huge and growing literature as a result.

Jon Pierre holds that urban governance should be understood "as a process blending and coordinating public and private interests" and references regime theorists who contend that: "governing the city and its exchange with private actors is a task that is too overwhelming for public organisations to handle alone" (1999: 374). Instead, urban governance quite simply represents all the diverse processes through which public bodies in concert with private interests and civil society seek to enhance collective goals: "a process shaped by those systems of political, economic and social values from which the urban regime derives its legitimacy" (Pierre 1999: 375). Likewise, David Adams and Steve Tiesdell have argued that "successful places come about through effective coordination between the many different actors involved in their production and consumption" and that "this task is essentially one of governance" (2013: 106). They distinguish three commonly recognised modes:

- First, governance through hierarchies, where power is concentrated in the public sector and at the top (in government) and those further down the hierarchy, for example local government, abide by the rules set further up.
- Second, governance through markets where the state is tasked to enable the market, and a shrunken state apparatus gives way to the private sector wherever possible to actually deliver urban services and amenities.
- Third, governance through networks, where collaborative and partnership arrangements between public, private, and voluntary sectors attempt a middle

way that avoids the 'big government' of hierarchies and the fragmentation of markets; although with the additional layers of complexity born of seeking network solutions to complex urban problems.

Broadly these three modes of governance equate to the periods of post-war government epitomised in the United Kingdom and elsewhere by (i) the welfare state; (ii) Thatcherite or Reaganomics-inspired neoliberalism from the 1980s onwards; and (iii) its modification through 'third-way' politics epitomised by New Labour in the United Kingdom and the administration of Bill Clinton in the United States. Pierre (1999) usefully digs a little deeper and defines four different 'ideal' models of urban governance according to their prevailing characteristics:

1. Managerial governance: where, rather than viewing government as a conduit for resolving political conflict, the emphasis is instead on the efficient, cost-effective, and professional delivery of public services, often by arms-length organisations of government. Arguably this model has come to dominate government in the neoliberal era from the 1980s onwards and reflects an ideology that market-like mechanisms of supply and demand should dictate the relationship between consumers and producers of public services, rather than political preferences and accountability.
2. Corporatist governance: by contrast, gives primacy to the ideals of participatory democracy through collectives, with the discussion and settlement of policy dependant on bargaining processes between interested parties directed at achieving consensus and coordinated public/private action. In this model, decision-making is collective and inclusive, but also often slow, and can be limited to those organisations and individuals that are politically engaged.
3. Pro-growth governance: is characterised by close interaction between public and private parties with a particular view to strengthening the economy. These forms of governance are rarely participatory, but instead engage political elites directly with their business counterparts with the objective of boosting growth rather than redistributing it. In this model, public/private partnership is institutionalised and the resulting organisations enjoy considerable operational discretion.

4. Welfare governance: predominates in cities in which economic growth is limited and the major source of income to inhabitants flows through welfare spending leading to a particular dependency on the state and to the predominant position of the state as the key provider or enabler within the territory. Typically such regimes are hostile to the private sector as a supplier of services, whilst the main participants in delivering this governance are the government officials themselves.

In reality, different forms of governance can exist simultaneously, even in the same territory, as different problems and different contexts will give rise to different local relationships and therefore to varied forms of governance. As recent research taking a comparative perspective on urban governance concludes: "No one model of governance stands above the rest. The wide variety of governance institutions and decision-making models reflects both the local context and history and the complexity of the issues to be resolved" (Slack & Côté 2014: 5).

Deconstructing these various models and cutting through the politics of provision, it is possible to identify a triad of fundamental characteristics within whose parameters urban governance of all types will sit. These are: the mode of operation, whether ideological (directed at particular political objectives) or managerial in style; the relative concentration of public authority, whether centralised or disaggregated, including to arm's-length agencies; and the power to deliver, whether public or market-oriented. These are represented as three continua in 1.7 because in reality urban

governance will rarely sit at the extremes, for example wholly market or wholly public provision, but will instead, on each axis, sit somewhere in between. The framework will be returned to throughout Part II of this book.

Why Design Governance?

Human beliefs and philosophies have, since ancient times, been reflected in a diverse range of local codes that dictate the form and layout of buildings, monuments, and settlements, whether related to natural phenomenon (on earth or in the stars) or to superstitions, creeds, and practices of human and/or spiritual origin. The use of Feng Shui from 4000 BC onwards in China; the layout of ritual landscapes such as Stonehenge in England from 3000 BC; the design of religious buildings across today's Christian, Islamic, and Hindu worlds; and the layout of sacred sites in the great civilisations of the past, in ancient Egypt, Greece, or the Andean civilisations, for example, each share in common the use of prescribed design codes to give meaning and narrative to devotional practices, whether of monarch or deity.

Beyond the laws of religious authorities, design has also long been a subject for governmental activity, and societies through the ages have regulated aspects of design for many reasons. In ancient China, for example, the colour yellow was associated with imperial dignity, and for many centuries its use on buildings was restricted to the emperors. In medieval England, the right to use crenellations on a building was controlled by the king because of their association with the building of fortifications, and those wishing to use crenellations had to obtain a licence to crenellate from the twelfth century onwards. From the thirteenth century, the development of Siena was regulated by controls on building heights, materials, window shape, and building line established by the then Nova Government of the Republic of Siena. Following the great fire of 1666, a series of building and urban codes were laid down in the Rebuilding Act of 1667 for the reconstructing of the City of London. This was the first time that such comprehensive design regulations had been set down in England and included seven types of street, four types of house, and a range of approved construction types (1.8). Much later, height restrictions were enacted

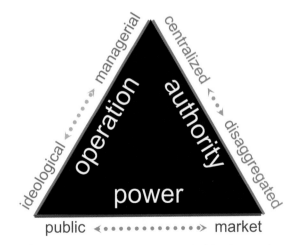

Figure 1.7 Urban governance, a triad of fundamental characteristics

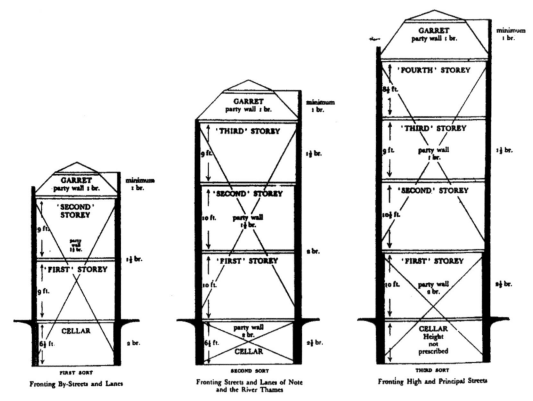

Figure 1.8   Codes from the Rebuilding Act of 1667 following the great fire of London the previous year, building types giving rise to a street typology

for the first time in America through the Washington, DC, height regulations of 1899 following hot on the heels of an 1894 act that set an eighty-foot height limit in London. Additionally in Washington, DC, from 1910 (and still in operation today), Congress set up a Commission of Fine Arts to advise on the location of statues, fountains, and monuments, and later on the design of all public buildings in the District of Columbia. It was this that provided the model for the Royal Fine Art Commission for England and Wales, established in 1924 (see Chapter 3), whilst the development and spread of planning and zoning systems during the twentieth century all had at their heart control of land use mix and development quantum, both fundamental aspects of what we have come to know as urban design.

These examples represent just a tiny sample of state interventions in design that in modern times have become increasingly extensive as societies and their administrations attempt to intervene and shape the public and private built environment for a range of

predominantly 'public interest' motivations. Prominent amongst these are:

- Welfare motivations: At their most basic, many design regulations simply attempt to protect the public and individuals from a host of health and safety concerns, both manmade and natural. These range from fire transmission, to structural stability, to access to light and air, to road safety, to avoiding pollution and disease, and so on.

- Functional motivations: These concern the fitness for purpose and everyday efficiency with which the built environment operates, for example encouraging the free movement of pedestrians and vehicles, the conduct of different uses and activities simultaneously, the provision of the infrastructure and amenities that make life possible, and the facilitation of the day-to-day management of buildings and space.

- Economic motivations: Economic outcomes are always a key political concern and there are strong bodies of opinion that see controls of any sort as inhibitors to economic activity and to the natural operation of the market. Careful control of design is nevertheless also seen as a means to stimulate local economic growth by facilitating particular types, forms, and densities of development in particular localities and as a means to deliver the economic dividend that evidence suggests well-designed developments can command (Carmona et al. 2002).

- Projection motivations: Which relate to the desire amongst leaders to project a particular image of place, perhaps in order to encourage investment or attract particular sorts of companies and/or individuals to a city or locality, but also to establish and project a clear identity for places that users can identify with and that reflect the worldview (good or ill) and ultimately the power and legacy of those responsible.

- Fairness motivations: Individuals or companies acting alone are likely to attempt to maximise their own benefit, and this may be at the expense of others or of resources held in common (sometimes known as the tragedy of the commons; see Webster 2007). Regulation can attempt to guarantee private property rights in a manner that doesn't unduly impact the rights of others or resources held in common.

- Protection motivations: Conservation of important historic and natural assets and environments is a key concern that has become all the more prominent in recent years in the face of large-scale rapid change. It encompasses not only protection, but also enhancement of the positive distinctive qualities of place, whether historic or contemporary.

- Societal motivations: These rationales (arguably) encompass all the other categories, but more specifically include the range of liveability, improved amenity, civic pride and engagement, crime reduction, inclusivenesss, and health and social benefits that a better-designed public environment can bring. Such concerns amount to perhaps the most compelling set of reasons for the state to be interested in design.

- Environmental motivations: Such arguments are increasingly central to urban governance agendas, and the design of the built environment has a potentially large part to play in delivering this agenda through designing for adaptability, energy reduction/efficiency, public transport, mix and intensity of use, greening, and so forth (Carmona 2009c).

- Aesthetic motivations: Whilst visual concerns are often the headline factors when 'design' is discussed, because of their somewhat intangible nature they are also amongst the most difficult to evaluate. Despite this, aesthetic concerns remain vitally important (albeit often controversial) for reasons relating to how developments integrate into their surroundings, because of the desire amongst many architects to innovate and build something 'of today', and as a consequence of the basic human sensibility to beauty (CABE 2010d).

Reflecting these diverse motivations and the widely held belief (already articulated) that many environments produced in the modern and postmodern eras have been sub-standard, the extent and nature of attempts to influence design outcomes have also increased through time. Despite suggestions that such controls on design are partly complicit in this general deterioration, one of the few international studies of the use of urban codes demonstrates that they are now universal. It also argues that when used in a manner sympathetic to their original local forms and contexts, they are just as likely to be viewed positively as negatively (Marshall 2011). The term 'design governance' captures all such state-sanctioned interventions in the design of development. Later in this chapter the scope of this activity is discussed; before then some of the challenges and contradictions such processes throw up are examined.

The Problematics of Design and Its Governance

Despite its pedigree and the wide range of motivations driving public authorities to engage in the governance of design, design as a subject for state action is inherently problematic. The international literature on urban governance, for example, establishes a number of normative principles associated with 'good urban governance'. These include positive aspirations such as: the need to be accountable and transparent, to encourage participation and consensus building, to be responsive to changing need whilst also being efficient, and to be both effective and equitable. Yet design, as a subject for governmental activity, has long suffered from a range of inherent challenges that reveal something of how design is profoundly different from many of the 'big ticket' policy realms such as health, defence, welfare, or policing (Carmona 2001: 58–68). These can be boiled down to eight core problematics that reveal how design fails to conveniently tick the boxes of good governance in that it is open to challenge and debate, to quite different professional perspectives and priorities (the tyrannies), and does not easily divide into neat, efficient, and predictable considerations for decision-makers.

A Fragmented Responsibility and Built-in Dissensus

In most countries, the design/development arena is split in three senses, first between public and private interests, as already alluded to; second between numerous professional specialisations represented by their professional membership organisations; and third in the responsibility for such concerns within government, across the spatial scales. As such it typically doesn't have the sort of strong unified sectoral voice that is more common in other policy arenas; in health, law, or business, for example. Instead, the field is fragmented and can be highly contested along the sorts of 'tyrannical' lines already described, where agreement on what constitutes 'good' design will depend more on the primary motivations of key players—for example to make a profit, garner political support, get published in architectural journals, and so forth—than on how to deliver the optimum place quality within the given resources and constraints. This is certainly the case within local government, about which Ethan Kent (n.d.) has argued: "the fractured, siloed structure of contemporary government, with its myriad departments and bureaucratic processes, often directly impedes the creation of successful public spaces." The inevitable result is that dissensus is built in from the start, and, even if it is not, responsibility is often so fragmented that coordinated action over design is difficult to achieve.

The Marginalisation of 'Expert' Judgement

A dimension of the dissensus relates to the particular role of non-experts in making public interest judgements on design in a manner that would not normally be allowed in other areas of professional endeavour (Imrie & Street 2009: 2514). Thus whilst architects, landscape architects, and urban designers typically train for many years with design as the core focus of their attentions, others with little or no design training are empowered to pass judgement on their designs. These include: planners, whose engagement with design is often just a small part of the multiplicity of factors covered in their training; engineers, for whom design is a more limited technical activity; developers, for whom design is inevitably a subset of the profit equation; and politicians, often with no design training at all. Each will instead seek to balance their 'non-expert' judgement against other public and private objectives, including weighing up the costs (financially and in time) of hiring design expertise. Conflict between expert and non-expert is perhaps inevitable in such circumstances where non-experts may have a greater impact on outcomes than the experts themselves, and where lay and expert tastes will often diverge (Hubbard 1994).

The Debatable Concept of 'Good Design'

Despite the sorts of normative frameworks discussed earlier and widely used to evaluate development proposals, the notion that transferable and easily identifiable characteristics of good design exist remains a debatable contention. Certainly some dimensions of design in the built environment will always be more subjective than others. Thus whilst technical issues such as energy rating or inclusive access will be objectively verifiable (albeit debatable in terms of what standard is deliverable), other concerns such as architectural style and aesthetics will be far less so. Moreover, urban design solutions will vary from place to place, will depend on the sorts of varying aspirations of stakeholders already discussed, and are not amenable to easy one-size-fits-all prescriptions. In such a context, informed and skilled design judgement and a careful understanding of the local development context are likely to be key to making judgements about design quality, whilst there will always be multiple possible (and acceptable) solutions to most urban design problems. Equally there will always be many solutions that are clearly not right or simply sub-standard, and whilst it may be challenging to agree on what is the 'right' solution to any given design problem, agreeing on what is not right will often be more straightforward.

The Intangible Nature of Design and Design Value

Related to the difficulties in defining what is good design is the conceptually challenging and somewhat intangible nature of design that means it is poorly understood by many decision-makers (and some professionals) who continue to equate design with narrow aesthetic debates or with a sense that design is a luxury that can be cut in bad times. Equally, many design objectives (and processes) are difficult to measure and impacts are difficult to attribute, and are therefore not amenable to centrally driven performance management approaches or targets, or to specification in policy or guidance. To use an example quoted elsewhere (Carmona 2014c: 6), investing in an anti-obesity pill would seem to deliver a tangible and direct benefit from a single, clearly defined product with clear, knock-on commercial benefits. By contrast, designing the built environment to encourage users to do more exercise and not to get fat in the first place, seems infinitely more complex, involving numerous interconnecting elements, diffused responsibilities, and difficult-to-trace impacts. Similarly, the pursuit of better design in the built environment will be a long-term project, requiring many years before tangible impacts can be felt from policy decisions or from innovations in design process, and requiring long-term commitment and dedicated resources that do not naturally fit with short-term political priorities. As such, design is difficult to debate or to prescribe in policy, let alone to encourage concerted action to address such complex intangible concerns.

The Appropriate Limits of Power

In the neoliberal era, increasingly the state has pulled out of directly developing projects. Even where the ultimate responsibility remains public, for example for the provision of prisons, schools, hospitals, and much large-scale infrastructure, increasingly the private sector provides and operates these facilities whilst the public sector pays for them over time. In such a context, the public policy aspirations for design that involve new development need largely to be delivered through the auspices of the private sector acting in the market, and in this respect are outside the direct ability of the public sector to deliver particular outcomes. The issue brings into focus a long-held concern regarding the appropriate limits of state power over private property rights, and whether attempts to control design (in the absence of direct delivery) amount to undue interference or the legitimate pursuit of the public interest (Case Scheer 1994). It raises the uncomfortable issue that for the state to influence design quality in such circumstances, it needs to do so through indirect means (directing the actions of others) with all the limits on state authority that this implies. By implication, this also limits the ability of communities both to hold their public representatives to account and to directly engage in such matters themselves.

Market Realities and the Detached State

In a related category falls the issue that public design requirements may add to the costs of development, either by extending and elaborating the development process itself (e.g. requiring more detailed design proposals early on in the process) or in the build-out costs of development (e.g. a higher public realm specification or greater energy efficiency). Because these costs may or may not be recoverable by developers, they will directly impact the viability of schemes in the market. Whilst there is plenty of evidence that public design requirements can equally reduce build-out costs (e.g. replacing expensive impermeable surfaces with cheaper porous permeable ones) or generate a design premium on sales or rental values (Carmona 2009b: 2664), the question of cost and the detached nature of the state from these market realities will loom large in the considerations of many private development actors as they engage with public design aspirations.

How Much Intervention?

The issue of intervention versus interference also leads to another problematic: if intervention is deemed appropriate, how much intervention is the right amount and when is it too much; or in other words, how prescriptive should the requirements of the state be? Ultimately this is a matter for political and democratic judgement and will vary from place to place, although it has both policy and process ramifications. In policy terms, questions of over-prescription versus under-prescription in design policy and guidance can dominate debates on the legitimacy or otherwise of the public sector engaging in design; especially when this is seen to impact the ability of architects (in particular) to creatively innovate in design (Imrie & Street 2011: 85). Equally processes that involve too many parties in decision-making and lead to lowest common denominator 'design by committee' or compromise solutions as a substitute for clear vision and a creative design process can be equally destructive. Whilst there can be no right or wrong answer to such issues, to some degree the legitimacy of greater or lesser intervention will depend on the quality of that intervention and whether, as a result, it carries public support.

Balancing Certainty with Flexibility?

There is also a related issue around the certainty and consistency of decisions, with much criticism reserved in systems where such decisions involve a greater degree of discretionary power, such as in the United Kingdom (see Chapter 2), for the seemingly arbitrary decision-making that can result when there is an absence of clear policy or guidance on which to base decisions. For market actors, this has a decisive impact on the certainly with which they can plan their operations. Equally these same actors may quickly object if their flexibility to operate in a changing market is unduly impaired, for example by (for them) the over-prescriptive imposition of public design requirements on their projects. This question of how much or how little intervention on design is right represents a problem that is unlikely to have a simple or consistent answer.

Together, the problematics mean that design does not lend itself naturally to public debate, to easy national or local policy solutions, or to the constraints of short-term political cycles. Design has also, at different times and in different contexts, been critiqued from both sides of the political spectrum. From the right have come concerns that giving undue consideration to design can undermine the operation of the free market, tying up local initiative and creativity with unnecessary delays and 'red tape'. Campaigners Mantownhuman, for example, have argued, "we must seek a new humanist sensibility within

Figure 1.9 This space on the Thames riverside in Greenwich was of appropriate quality to get planning permission, but has little social (it is fenced in), economic (it is an on-going management problem), or aesthetic value (it is crudely constructed of cheap materials)

Source: Matthew Carmona

architecture—one that refuses to bow to preservation, regulation and mediation—but instead sets out to win support for the ambitious human-centred goals of discovery, experimentation and innovation" (2008: 3). From the left have come critiques that design quality is an elitist concern and is largely a preoccupation of property owners seeking to protect their asset values or developers wishing to enhance theirs, and that reducing socio-economic inequality rather than improving local environmental quality should be the priority. As Alexander Cuthbert has commented with regard to public sector attempts to influence design outcomes: "At best they look to the past and, in the process, seek to conserve property values . . . self-interest and autonomy of control over the design process" (2011: 224).

Both perspectives are based on the same fundamental misconception that good design is a narrow concern primarily in the interests of one side of the public/private divide at the expense of the other, be that society or particular private interests. In fact, good urban design is fundamentally in the interests of society at large by avoiding the problems of the sorts of substandard places already described, and instead aspiring to the creation of what Alan Rowley has characterised as 'sustainable quality' rather than 'appropriate quality' (1998: 172) (1.9). In other words, development that returns long-term social, economic, and environmental value and looks beyond short-termism, whether based on economic opportunity or social need.

The Design Governance Conundrum

Many approaches to design governance ultimately operate by, on one hand, restricting private property rights and, on the other, granting development rights. The former (restricting property rights) constrains the freedom of key stakeholders to design and those who perceive themselves to be most directly affected—designers and developers—are likely to resist such intervention the hardest. David Walters even argues that, faced with such circumstances, "Many architects are guilty of knee-jerk reactions to design standards, preferring the 'freedom' to produce poor buildings rather than be required to improve standards of design to meet mandated criteria" (2007: 132–133). The latter (granting development rights) has equally often been criticised for sanctioning developments that are quite simply not up to standard, and some have suggested that it is planners' inability to define and deliver a public design agenda that is the problem here: "Vision is something that your average planner simply does not have" (Building Design 2013).

More positively Witold Rybczynski has argued: "Cities as disparate as Sienna, Jerusalem, Berlin, and Washington DC, suggest that the public discipline of building design does not necessarily inhibit creativity—far from it. What it does have the potential to achieve . . . is a greater quality in the urban environment as a whole" (1994: 211). Certainly the public resources devoted to such activities in countries around the world can be taken as a reflection of the public endorsement that processes of design governance command, and that these processes are largely apolitical. In the United Kingdom, for example, polling revealed that only 2 per cent of people on the right of the political spectrum, 4 per cent on the left, and 3 per cent in 'other' categories had no interest in what buildings, streets, parks, and public spaces look or feel like to use (CABE 2009c). Yet perhaps such a result is inevitable. It certainly does not represent a carte blanche to the public sector in this sphere.

Kelvin Campbell and Rob Cowan (2002), for example, have argued that 'rulebooks' (by which they mean the various design standards and the bureaucracies that go with them) are too often crude and therefore too unresponsive to local circumstances to positively shape place quality. Despite this, once a system of regulation is in place, it becomes very difficult to change, as it quickly generates large numbers of vested interests whose primary concern (arguably) is with maintaining the system as it is rather than with dismantling or changing it. A case in point are the legions of zoning officials charged to create and manage ever more complex zoning ordinances in the United States. Set against them, and with an equal stake in maintaining the status quo, are the legions of land use zoning lawyers whose job it is to challenge the rules and find ways around them (Carmona 2012).

Although the inherent value of such systems is often asserted, just as they are contested, few would dispute that once they are in place, public authorities are often highly adept at applying the 'technical' standards and regulations that result. In England, for example, almost half a million planning applications are received and decided each year, most of which are known as 'minor' for household alterations and the like, the large majority of which (around 75 per cent) are decided efficiently and effectively within eight weeks.[3] Given that this is the case, it is reasonable to question whether it might be possible to raise the bar to, instead, focus these sorts of bureaucratic efforts more concertedly on securing higher-order urban design outcomes. This is the design governance conundrum:

Can state intervention in processes of designing the built environment positively shape design processes and outcomes, and if so, how?

Nan Ellin puts it another way: "Should we step aside and allow the city to grow and change without any guidance whatsoever? No [she says] that would simply allow market forces to drive urban development. Markets are only designed to allocate resources in the short term and without regard for things that do not have obvious financial value like the purity of our air and water or the quality of our communities" (2006: 102). Design of the built environment falls into this category. Many have a potential hand in its delivery, but market forces acting in a vacuum will tend to lead to competition between players based around securing

Figure 1.10   Design as market failure, impermeable loop-and-lollipop landscapes (looking from one across a fence into another)

Source: Matthew Carmona

narrow market advantage rather than to collaboration focussed on creating something greater than the sum of the parts. The 'loop-and-lollipop' landscapes of suburban retail and business parks represent a case in point where in order to compete with their neighbours, operators are typically concerned with maximising unit attraction within their site (e.g. large and obvious parking and highly visible signage) rather than with connecting to their competitors. The result is that travel between adjacent plots is often impossible by foot and instead requires a roundabout journey by car. Examples of such layouts are globally ubiquitous (1.10) and a clear case of market failure.

In such circumstances, state intervention may seem justified in order to correct the failure, yet we also need to be careful not to fall foul of the 'nirvana fallacy' that the solution to imperfect markets is necessarily more government; as Bradley Hansen has argued, "Because governments are run by imperfect people, government regulation is unlikely to be perfect" (2006: 117). Thus, just as markets fail, so do governments, and whilst public intervention might be seen as an appropriate response to poor place-making, for a variety of reasons the assertion that more intervention will necessarily deliver better design, or the presumption that 'good' design guidance and control will, ipso facto, create good places, should be treated with extreme caution:

- There may be no market failure in the first place: most historic towns and cities, for example, grew

up organically with very little regulation dictating where and how buildings, uses, and public spaces should be located, and yet formed some of the most celebrated and humane of today's urban landscapes.

- The solution may be worse than the problem: Arguing against zoning, for example, Bernard Siegan (2005) suggests that such practices increase the price of homes by limiting supply; encourage sprawl by imposing restrictions on uses, densities, and height; and are exclusionary because zoning acts against the needs of disadvantaged groups by distorting the market from meeting their needs.

- It may create barriers to change and innovation: Architects, for example, have long argued that processes of design control favour 'safe', even historicist, design solutions and undermine the creation of places resonant of their time, both aesthetically and in terms of the construction technologies that are thereby favoured (Cuthbert 2006: 193–194).

- Perverse outcomes may result: Stories of unintended outcomes from overly crude design regulations are not uncommon and famously include the creation of a generation of poor-quality Publicly Owned Public Spaces as a result of incentive zoning practices in New York during the first few decades following the introduction of these new rights in 1961 (Kayden 2000). Less famously, in the United Kingdom, the removal of street trees from residential schemes has sometimes occurred when, following marketing and sales, it has transpired that the relevant local authorities have been unwilling to 'adopt'[4] roads with street trees because of the ongoing maintenance liability.

- The risk of discrimination: Processes of controlling design may support the tastes and values of certain cultural groups over others and (unintentionally or not) discriminate against those with different cultural values or who simply wish to use space differently. A documented case in point has been the development of 'McMansions'[5] in suburban North America. These developments have typically been criticised by commentators and campaigners for their crass, showy, and uncontextual 'bigness', but Willow Lung-Amam (2013) argues that they simply reflect the different cultural norms of their owners—typically affluent immigrant groups—and that policies to control them reinforce elitist, white, middle-class perceptions of good design held by residents of longer standing (and city officials) and unduly discriminate against those with a different view.

Regulatory economists argue that regulation is inherently costly and inefficient, but difficult to challenge because of what Peter van Doren of the right-wing CATO Institute calls 'Bootleggers' (special interests who gain economically from the existence of regulation) and 'Baptists' (those who don't like the behaviour of others and want government to restrict it) (2005: 45, 64). For such commentators, the market, rather than state regulation, is the proper mechanism through which optimum development outcomes can be achieved and through which individuals can best express, meet, and protect their interests. In support of these arguments, Houston in the United States is often cited as a city in which communities have been able to meet their needs despite being the only major US city without a system of zoning. Houston, however, has adopted other sorts of ordinances to alleviate the land use problems that result, including banning nuisances, imposing off-street parking, and regulating minimum lot, density, and land use requirements (Siegan 2005: 227). Thus even the least regulated cities in the developed world impose controls of some sort or other on the development and use of space.

Although, as we will see, privatised alternatives do exist and have gained some traction in the United States, for most urban areas, public sector intervention of some sort or other seems inevitable. Equally there will always be both good and bad intervention. Consequently, rather than the fault of intervention per se, problems associated with perverse outcomes may simply be a consequence of bad intervention. Two key questions arise from this. First, not 'if', but instead 'how' should intervention in design occur? And second, at what point—'when'—will intervention be most effective?

The 'When' Question

The first question will be determined by the choice of 'tools' available and our ability to use them, but taking the second question first, to ask 'when' it is important to make a key conceptual distinction about the nature of public sector design governance as opposed to private sector project design. On this issue Varkki George (1997) has made an important division between first- and second-order design processes: "In first-order design, the designer usually has control over, is involved in, or is directly responsible for all design decisions. . . . Second-order design [by contrast] is appropriate to a situation characterised by distributed decision-making because the design solution is specified at a more abstract level and is, therefore, applicable across a wider range of situations." He argues that most urban design falls into the latter category—characterised by distributed decision-making. This contrasts with architecture, which is typically in the former camp.

Because of the long-term horizons over which it operates, design at any scale beyond that of the individual building typically needs to deal with shifting and complex economic, social, political, legal, and stakeholder environments, and with how these adapt and change over sometimes very long time horizons. Second-order design is particularly suited to such turbulent decision-making environments because it is more strategic in nature, ideally specifying what is critical to define and ignoring what is not. In some respects, therefore, the distinction between first and second order is confusing because if urban design is about setting the framework within which other more detailed design occurs—architectural, engineering, and the local landscape—then it should come first.

The Decision-Making Environment

Setting this potential confusion aside, Jon Lang (2005) distinguishes between four key types of design process at the urban scale:

- Total urban design: complete control by a single design team over the design of a large area—buildings, public space, and implementation.
- All-of-a-piece urban design: where schemes are parcelled out to different development/design teams following an overall masterplan that acts to coordinate the pieces.
- Piece-by-piece urban design: the process of single uncoordinated developments coming forward as and when opportunities or the market allows, although guided by area objectives and policies.

- Plug-in urban design: where infrastructure is designed and built in new or existing areas, into which individual development projects can be later plugged in.

All but the first of these are second-order activities, and even in scenarios of 'total design' the framework urban design provides will come before the detailed design of individual buildings or spaces. At this level, design can be as much about shaping the environment within which decisions occur as with the process of designing; or, to put it another way, the more one moves away from designing actual things (buildings, roads, landscape features, etc.), the more considerations are with the way decisions are made than with the making of design decisions. The challenge is to design a decision-making environment that in its turn positively influences how decisions about design are made and ultimately how outcomes are shaped. But rather than seeing this as second-order design, we might see it instead as the governance of the design process, or, in other words, as design governance.

As a consequence, design governance should not be time limited as the design of a project would be, but should instead be continuous, journeying around the place-shaping continuum (as already described, see 1.2) in a never-ending cycle of stewardship and change. Seen in this way, design governance has the potential to shape all stages of the journey of projects from inception to completion: shaping the decision-making environment within which they are conceived, influencing their passage through design and development processes, and guiding how they continue to mature after they are completed.[6]

Therefore, to directly answer the second question posed earlier—when should intervention occur?—the answer is continually in that the shaping of the design decision-making environment will be an on-going process. At the same time, for any given project the critical and most effective interventions are likely to come early, before key decisions about the design of development have been firmed up. This will also help to avoid conflicts, tensions, delays, and abortive work by ensuring that public aspirations are clearly known prior, during, and after the design process, and can thereby be factored into the development process (Carmona 2009b: 2665). Design process quality, in this

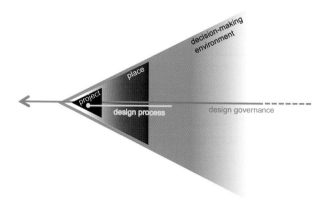

Figure 1.11 The design governance field of action

sense, is critical to optimising each of the other forms of design quality—aesthetic, project, and place. The key relationships, as theorised earlier, are represented graphically in 1.11.

Unpacking Design Governance

How Should Intervention Occur?

Returning to the 'how' question posed earlier—How should intervention occur?—this question goes to the heart of this book, and it is not possible to give an easy answer. As a first step on the road towards its resolution it is useful to revisit and unpack the definition of design governance given earlier in this chapter in order to better understand the scope of the concern and the menu of interventions available.

In the Foreword to this book, design governance was defined as: *"The process of state-sanctioned intervention in the means and processes of designing the built environment in order to shape both processes and outcomes in a defined public interest"* (Carmona 2013a). Mapping onto the triad of fundamental urban governance traits represented in 1.7—operation, authority, and power—the definition implies that design governance operates: (i) in the public interest; (ii) through multiple means and processes of design; and (iii) as, ultimately, a responsibility of the state.

Operation

Taking each in turn, beginning with the 'operation' of design governance. The governance of design, to some degree, will always be ideological in that it aims at achieving a set of aspirational public interest outcomes, namely, 'better design' than would otherwise be achieved without it. But because it is very difficult to secure design quality without expert judgement, which is in turn an expensive commodity, and because good design is anyway intangible and debatable and potentially fraught with 'tyrannical' discord (see earlier), it is likely that authorities with less commitment to design will orientate themselves away from the ideological and proactive and more towards the managerial and reactive end of the operations spectrum. They might, for example, choose to use as-of-right control against fixed and inflexible criteria, as opposed to discretionary negotiation against a flexible design framework or set of policies (see Chapter 2). Design governance clearly shifts up and down the operation axis.

Authority

On the question of 'authority' (the second axis), in a neoliberal political economy this will rarely be concentrated in a single place. Instead, as the definition implies, by recognising multiple processes of design, responsibility is likely to be dispersed through many hands, all of which form part of the decision-making environment that design governance is helping to shape. Critically, however, given variations in the range of actors and their power relationships from one place to another, and variations in the dominance or otherwise of a central public agency, the extent to which public authority is centralised or disaggregated will also vary significantly, ranging from, on one hand, a concentration of power in areas of significant heritage value, to, on the other hand, the multiple overlapping regimes that characterise many local mixed streets (Carmona 2014d: 18–19). Design governance will shift accordingly along the authority axis.

Power

Finally, regarding the 'power' axis, design governance will almost always be operated as a formal activity of the state, and ultimately the state will choose how much and what responsibilities it wishes to take in this regard, and what it wishes to avoid or give away. In some circumstances, private corporations have taken on the function, sometimes partially and sometimes

wholesale, effectively privatising it in the process. The case of Canary Wharf in London is well known in this regard where the original developers, operating in a policy vacuum (an Enterprise Zone), effectively imposed detailed codes upon themselves in order to build London's new business district in a manner that would, through its quality, safeguard their long-term investment (Carmona 2009a: 105). Today, local government control has been reasserted in the area. In Lebanon, following the civil war that ended in 1991, the government established the private company Solidere to rebuild central Beirut. In effect the company has complete control over the historic centre of the city and is responsible for administering all of its planning and development regulations (Carmona 2013a: 126–127) (1.12). In the United States, nearly 15 per cent of the housing stock has been provided using the Common Interest Development (CIDs) model where large urban areas and all their social infrastructure are developed privately before being handed over to community Homeowner Associations (HOA) for long-term management. Whilst the powers of HOAs vary, in the largest cases, such as Irvine in California, they are responsible for the full range of regulatory responsibilities normally associated with a municipality (Punter 1999: 144–160).

Figure 1.12 The private company Solidere not only controls the planning of downtown Beirut, but was effectively given ownership of the land on behalf of the original landowners, giving it an unprecedented power to shape design and development outcomes that go far beyond normal state powers and that have profound implications for local accountability and democracy

Source: Matthew Carmona

Some argue that such 'voluntary' arrangements between landowners "are capable of producing a host of so-called public goods, including aesthetic and functional zoning, roads, planning, and other aspects of physical urban infrastructure," and will do so more efficiently and effectively than the state (Gordon et al. 2005: 199), at least if viewed from the narrow perspective of property owners. Whether this is the case is open to debate, and that falls outside of the scope of this book. Perceptions of design governance, and what is acceptable in any given context will certainly depend on the underlying values on which any system is built, and this will vary between jurisdictions, both public and private. In general terms, however, those where the market represents the primary arbiter of social relationships based on efficiency will tend to eschew processes that unduly intrude on market relationships, whilst those where distributive justice is seen as a legitimate political objective will tend to view regulation aimed towards such ends—for example the improvement of design in the public interest—as an appropriate aim (Elkin 1986). The expectation in such places will be that processes of design governance remain largely the responsibility of the state.

Despite this, for the purpose of theorising design governance, it can be assumed that in many of their essentials, private organisations engaged in such processes effectively assume the role of a pseudo-public authority within their realms of influence and can be treated in the same way. In reality, the state's resources and authority is always limited, often severely, and responsibility for the success or otherwise of design governance will depend on various mixes of public and private influence. The balance between the two will therefore vary significantly along this third axis, from a relative absence of state control within, for example, an Enterprise Zone, to a very prominent position within a state-led new town or major infrastructure project, to various sorts of partnership arrangement in between.

The Spectrum of Design Governance

This discussion suggests that whilst maintaining the essential characteristics encompassed in the definition, as an activity design governance can potentially exist within a wide spectrum of urban governance contexts:

ideological to managerial, centralised to disaggregated and with various degrees of public and private influence. Even within the same jurisdiction, different development processes can lead to quite different relationships along the three axes. Take two examples from the United Kingdom. First, the regulatory design process to agree the masterplan for a new privately led urban extension (a. in 1.13). Typically this involves a disaggregated decision-making process, encompassing planning and highways consents (often across different tiers of local government), and inputs from higher-level sub-regional (economic development) or even national actors (conservation, environmental management, affordable housing, and planning). Assuming a design code is in place alongside any adopted highways design standards, the decision-making process in such a case is likely to sit towards the managerial end of the operations spectrum, particularly if there is no firm political direction regarding what should be achieved. In such circumstances, the ultimate responsibility for delivery will rest with the housebuilder (most likely a large-volume builder), who will wield considerable power and resources to ensure that the outcomes reflect their development model.

Compare this with governance processes associated with the design of a major public project such as London's Olympic Park in the run-up to the 2012 Olympics (b in 1.13). In this example, the whole project was firmly in the hands of a single dedicated public authority set up to oversee delivery of the event, including its planning and design. In this process, every element was 'special' and subject to discretionary negotiation against clear nationally imposed

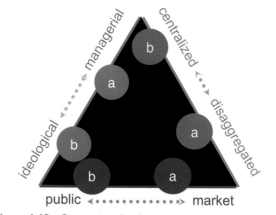

Figure 1.13 Contrasting development processes and their urban governance

political objectives to showcase the best of British design within the constraints of the budget. A dedicated design review panel was established which operated with clear high-level design aspirations laid down in a detailed masterplan and accompanying development guidelines. The result was a public, centralised, and ideological process directed at securing high-quality design outcomes through the dedication of considerable public sector resources. As such, this latter model, in the United Kingdom at least, represents the exception rather than the rule, and when used does not always achieve optimal outcomes, as some of the British new towns of the 1960s demonstrate.

Key Conceptual Distinctions

In a purely governance sense, the treatment of design can clearly take many paths, and there is little evidence to suggest that one path is necessarily superior to another. Recent research examining the creation and recreation of public spaces in London, for example, concluded that "there was no common process. In each [development] the line-up of stakeholders, the leadership, and the power relationships were different" (Carmona & Wunderlich 2012: 254), and yet many delivered outcomes that were of high quality. Equally, on the face of it, very similar urban governance processes can deliver quite different design quality outcomes, suggesting that it is not fundamentally whether a process is centralised or disaggregated, ideological or managerial, public or private that is at the heart of good design governance, but other factors. Indeed, given the increasing proliferation of different urban governance structures and practices, a recent report from the Royal Town Planning Institute (2014) has argued that we spend too much time making the case for theoretical or generalised preferences for particular forms of governance when what is more important is to be pragmatic about what works best, when, and where, and how we should join up the various contributions.

With this in mind, it is beneficial to further unpack the definition of design governance given earlier in order to understand the key components of those varied practices. Four additional conceptual distinctions can be made.

The Tools and Administration of Design Governance

First, the definition encompasses the full range of instruments and techniques available to those charged with the governance of design, referred to throughout this book as the 'tools' of design governance. The tools are classified in Chapter 2, discussed at length throughout Part III of this book, and range from research to design review, and from design competitions to hands-on propositional design. Their use encompasses the administrative infrastructures and procedures and the full range of human, financial, and skills resources necessary to utilise the tools and fully realise their potential. Rather than the meta-system of urban governance, it is most likely this detailed delivery of design governance—the tools that are chosen and how they are administered—that will be key to shaping a positive and effective decision-making environment.

Process and Product as a Focus of Intervention

Second, the definition concerns the pursuit of good design process—the place-shaping continuum in all its complexity—as much as it does good design outcomes, as ultimately outcomes are shaped by the processes of their creation, whilst any state intervention in design takes place within a process. It may be, for example, that the absence of design capacity within a system stems from a lack of design awareness and skills amongst key stakeholders, an absence of high-level policy, or from a general lack of demand for good design. As such this should be the appropriate focus for state-led intervention, not just the direct regulation of particular design proposals.

Formal and Informal Tools and Processes

Third, as well as any formal 'systems' sanctioned by legislation (national or local), the definition also embraces the full range of informal or non-statutory processes that can either supplement or enhance the formal ones, or that exist altogether outside of any formal system. The former, for example, would include processes of public policy making or zoning control and the latter design competitions, design awards, or educational initiatives to raise design skills. In this regard, different jurisdictions present different balances of formal and informal processes. In Germany, the system of local planning through Bebauungspläne (B-Plans) results in legally binding plans that define the detailed urban form of new development (Stille 2007); by contrast, in China, the processes of large-scale urban design that have developed since the country's rapid urbanisation of the 1990s operate in an entirely non-statutory manner, feeding ideas into the layers of statutory planning above and below, but unencumbered by their strictures (Tang 2014). In the United Kingdom, the picture is mixed. Whilst regulation of design happens within the legislative frameworks for planning and highways, the work of CABE from 1999 to 2011 took place almost entirely within the informal realm and therefore at the discretion of national government (see Chapter 4).

Direct and Indirect Modes of Design

Finally, design governance will encompass both direct and indirect forms of urban design. Thus, whilst much intervention will focus on shaping the decision-making environment within which better-quality design outcomes are articulated, encouraged, and regulated, and are therefore indirect processes detached from actually designing projects, other tools will deal with projects and sites directly. The commissioning of exemplar projects, establishing design parameters for sites through site-specific design codes, or even the preparation and adoption of masterplans are all forms of direct design, albeit that most remain second- rather than first-order design processes in the terms discussed earlier.

The combination of everything encompassed within and across these various categories covers a very wide range of practices, from high-level policy to hands-on delivery through direct action, and involving a broad range of actors, both public and private. This smorgasbord of approaches is returned to in subsequent chapters and contrasts strongly with how the subject is dealt with in much of the literature where discussion tends to be framed in more limiting ways, seeing the state's involvement in design through the narrow lens of public policy or regulation/control. This preoccupation is discussed now before this chapter is brought to a close.

Beyond Design as Public Policy, Regulation, and Control

In his seminal book *Urban Design as Public Policy*, Jonathan Barnett explores the experience of New York in the late 1960s and early 1970s, a period in which the city embraced urban design through aspects of its zoning, neighbourhood, and infrastructure planning practices, and through design review of public projects (1.14) (1974: 6). He argues that "instead of handing over city designs as an ostensibly finished product, from a position outside the decision-making process, designers of cities should seek to write the rules for the significant choices that shape the city, within an institutional framework." His call for design influence and expertise to sit as an integral part of the formal functions of urban authorities is a powerful one and expresses a need that is just as significant today as it was forty years ago: that government functions with a direct impact on how urban areas are shaped should be

Figure 1.14 The distinctive forms of New York's buildings and streets have been shaped by its zoning practices since 1916

Source: Matthew Carmona

operated by appropriately skilled staff in the clear knowledge of how their decisions will impact upon local place. The fact that often this does not happen is strongly implicated in why we continue to create substandard places.

So too has a tendency to place too much faith in the role of such public sector urban design via policy and regulation. As Barnett concludes, "In the end, better urban design will be achieved by a partnership between private investment and government, and between the design professional and the concerned decision-maker in either private or public life" (1974: 192); in other words, cities cannot solve their problems by policy and regulation alone. In fact, as Part III of this book demonstrates, there are many more possibilities to influence design quality outside of formal regulatory systems than is generally recognised, although they get relatively little attention in the urban design literature where a recurrent theme focuses on the interrelationship between urbanism and the formal regulation of development practices (Imrie & Street 2009: 2510).

This is unsurprising when, as John Punter (2007) notes, the notion of design as public policy has continued to develop over recent decades with agendas of urban regeneration, local distinctiveness, environmental sustainability, economic development, liveability, and urban competitiveness all, at various times and for better or worse, being loaded into the space that design is being asked to address. Architects in particular have become increasingly concerned about the range of new agendas with accompanying spatial controls that they need to concern themselves with and which "many architects consider to be outside the boundaries of what design should reasonably be asked to respond to" (Imrie & Street 2011: 279). These include, but are not limited to, terror threats, climate change, and international migration.

It is perhaps for these reasons, as well as for the widespread condemnation of the failures of crude design regulation and its tendency towards mediocrity, that Eran Ben-Joseph and Terry Szold conclude their compilation on *Regulating Place* with a call for innovation in such regulation: "There must be a willingness to test standards, not just in relation to preventing harm or preserving property value, but in relation to their impact on the form of communities. In essence rules must be place tested" (Szold 2005: 370).

Looking beyond narrow regulatory perspectives, the notion of design governance is broader than design as either public policy or design regulation/control— two perspectives that (arguably) place too much emphasis on the formal roles of the state to influence design outcomes. Instead, the notion of governance has at its heart the idea of complex, shared responsibilities for delivery that transcend the simple public/private binary and the limitations of the state's statutory responsibilities.

To a Governance of Constructive Engagement

This notion of a set of external state requirements that are simply imposed on private actors gives succour to the three tyrannies already described and recalls Ian Bentley's favoured 'battlefield' metaphor for a typical development process in which actors negotiate, scheme, and plot with and against each other in order to achieve their individual design/development outcomes (1999: 42). He argues that all development actors have 'resources' (finance, expertise, ideas, interpersonal skills, etc.) and 'rules' by which they operate, and these various webs of rules and resources create 'fields of opportunity' within which actors necessarily operate. Developing the concept of 'opportunity space', Steve Tiesdell and David Adams (2004), for example, suggest that the boundaries or 'frontiers' of the opportunity space are best conceived as fuzzy and ambiguous rather than hard-edged and clear-cut, as while they may be relatively fixed at any particular moment in time, they are dynamic and open to transformation over time as factors such as the policy context or the property market(s) change. In such a context, certain state actions can enlarge the designer or developer's opportunity space. Financial subsidies and grants, for example, give the developer more scope to respond to a particular market context; a less constraining regulatory context might encourage design innovation; while infrastructure improvements on or near a development site can make a location more attractive in the market and therefore less risky to develop.

Typically developers will seek to enlarge their opportunity space by opposing externally imposed design constraints on their sites as these may limit their options and potential (as they see it) to make a good profit. Likewise, designers will seek to enlarge their opportunity space by negotiating with developers in order for developers to yield the necessary scope for them to achieve, in their own terms, good design (Carmona et al. 2010: 290–291). Even the public sector will seek greater opportunity space from the other actors by seeking the space within a still viable development to achieve their own design (and other) aspirations. But these are not simple two-way processes. A process of design review, for instance, might reduce the developer's opportunity space from the outside but also compel the developer to yield opportunity space to the designer, thus enlarging the opportunity space for design. At the same time, other regulations may pull in the opposite direction, for example the imposition of rigid highways standards leading to regimented and standardised housing layouts with far less opportunity for urban, architectural, or landscape design.

All this suggests that a battle over opportunity space will only go so far, and ultimately a process that constructively engages all parties in the process of optimising outcomes for all may deliver a more fruitful and profitable process for all. Design governance, as opposed to policy or regulation, offers this possibility by accepting that the governance of design quality—aesthetic, project, place, and even process quality—can be an inclusive process, led by the state, but reaching out to all parties with a stake in shaping places for the better. In this context, David Adams and Steve Tiesdell have argued that "Since the governance of place rarely involves a wholesale state takeover of the real estate development process, but is normally characterised by specific interventions within it, governments must wrestle with the inherent tension between what they might ideally want to achieve and what they actually can achieve without taking over development projects directly" (2013: 105). This brings us full circle back to the design governance conundrum set out earlier, which will be addressed again in the final chapter of this book.

Conclusion

This chapter has explored the rationale for state intervention in design, rooted in the sub-standard quality of many of our urban areas, as well as the nature, purpose, and problematics of design governance as a response to such concerns. In doing so, a rich conceptual tapestry of issues has been revealed concerning: why we design sub-standard places in the first place; the aspirations that underpin our subsequent societal attempts to intervene in and improve quality; the challenges this presents the state, whose role has become increasingly detached from actually designing itself; the nature of design quality and its key relationships to both process and place; how governance provides a useful framework within which to explore our approaches to design; that design governance is as much concerned with designing the environment within which design decisions occur as with shaping actual design outcomes; that this process is continuous, diverse, and shared across stakeholder groups, both public and private; and that finally it reaches well beyond the imposition of statutory formal instruments on market actors and instead, through constructive engagement, seeks to extend (rather than restrict) the opportunity space within which profitable, creative, and socially useful design can occur.

In the end, all forms of design governance are essentially political and part of a political process that sits in judgement over the nature of 'good' design. Through their forensic study of *Architectural Design Regulation* Rob Imrie and Emma Street confirm that such actions are "ultimately, part of a broader system of social and moral governance that seeks to (re) produce places consistent with normative considerations of what the good city is, or ought to be" (2011: 284). Arguably, this is a process in which there is a moral 'ethic of responsibility' on those involved to engage in the shaping of such practices and not simply to complain if and when they fail to come up to the mark. This driving idea 'that we can do better' underpinned much of the practice that this book, in subsequent chapters, goes on to explore. This book itself also seeks to learn from practices of the recent past in order that they should not be forgotten but instead remembered and applied or rejected in a better future.

Notes

1. The ideas underpinning Part I of this book were first put together for a lecture to celebrate the work of Prof John Punter on the occasion of his retirement in 2013. They were further developed for the Bartlett School of Planning Centenary Lecture: *The Design Dimension of*

Planning (20 Years On) given by Matthew Carmona in February 2014. See: www.bartlett.ucl.ac.uk/planning/centenary.

2. www.pps.org/reference/what_is_placemaking/
3. www.gov.uk/government/collections/planning-applications-statistics
4. The process of roads and footpaths adoption transfers ownership and long-term responsibility for maintenance from developers to the relevant highways authority (see Chapter 2). In the absence of adoption, liability remains with the developer, something few are willing to retain.
5. The practice of tearing down or significantly remodelling existing homes to build much larger homes.
6. For example, through the restrictions that regulatory approvals processes impose on the future development and use of completed projects.

CHAPTER 2

The Tools of Design Governance (Formal and Informal)

In this chapter, discussion moves from a broad theory of design governance to a typological exploration of its 'tools'. This chapter begins by exploring the generic literature that focuses on the range of instruments, approaches, and actions that policy makers deploy in order to steer public and private actors towards particular policy outcomes. In this context, how the notion of tools relates to the design governance agenda will be examined, first, through studying three 'formal' categories of design governance tools—guidance, incentive, and control—and second, through introducing the five categories of 'informal' design governance used by the Commission for Architecture and the Built Environment (CABE) to deliver its core business. As the chapters in Part III of this book go on to investigate the informal tools in some depth, the preponderance of discussion in this chapter is on the formal tools, as these (and the sorts of statutory frameworks within which they exist), form a key context within which informal tools and indirect design governance operate.

A Tools-Based Approach

The Tools of Government

An important strand of public policy focuses on the tools of government. Its accompanying literature concentrates on the range of instruments, approaches, and actions policy makers deploy in order to steer the contexts, actors, and organisations for which they are responsible towards particular policy outcomes. These are what Steve Tiesdell and David Adams describe as the means rather than the ends of government (2011: 11). Their classification and analysis is valuable for the clues it gives about both the effective working of government and the range of alternate mechanisms that might be used to deliver defined ends.

Lester Salamon, often regarded as the godfather of tools-based approaches to understanding government, argues that in recent years, there has been a proliferation of tools in government, driven on by a newfound faith in liberal economic theories and frustration at the cost and effectiveness of government. "As a consequence, governments from the United States and Canada to Malaysia and New Zealand are being challenged to reinvent, downsize, privatize, devolve, decentralize, deregulate and de-layer themselves, subject themselves to performance tests, and contract themselves out" (Salamon 2000: 1612). Many such approaches see government as a problem to be solved by making it: more efficient and less costly; more responsive to the needs of its constituents (those individuals and organisations it seeks to govern); more effective at achieving clearly defined ends; and less self-serving (of the bureaucracy itself). But Salamon argues that modern government has in fact already come a huge distance to address these concerns, although this journey often remains unrecognised. "At the heart of this revolution", he contends, "has been a fundamental transformation not just in the scope and scale of government action, but in its basic forms" (Salamon 2000: 1612).

Underpinning this has been a rapid proliferation in the tools of public action, in other words, in the instruments or means used to address public policy concerns. Whereas earlier government activity was largely restricted to the direct delivery of goods or services by government bureaucrats, now it embraces a dizzying array of approaches: direct government; government corporations and government-sponsored enterprises; economic regulation; social regulation; government insurance; public information; corrective taxes, charges, and tradable permits; contracting for things; contracting for services; grants; loans and loan guarantees; tax expenditures; and vouchers (Salamon 2002). Moreover, as new tools have been invented, so, by necessity, have new sets of operating procedures, skills requirements, delivery mechanisms, even professions, dedicated to their development and use.

Over the years, a number of approaches have been developed to interrogate and classify the tools now available to government. Such attempts quickly discover that this cake can be cut in many different ways. Christopher Hood (1983), for example, sorts tools in terms of the role of government for which they are used (e.g. for detecting information or effecting behaviours) and as regards the governmental resource they utilise, namely: nodality (government information), treasure (public resources), authority (legal power), or organisation (ability to action change). This, he christens the NATO framework. McDonnell and Elmore focus instead on the strategy of intervention: mandates, inducements, capacity-building, and system-changing (1987: 133). Schneider and Ingram classify against the behaviours government action seeks to change: authority tools, incentive tools, capacity tools, symbolic or hortatory tools, and learning tools (1990: 513–522); and Evert Vedung (1998) explores the extent of force that different tools involve: carrots, sticks, and sermons. Salamon (2000) himself offers a classification against dimensions of governmental utility: degree of coerciveness, directness, automaticity, and visibility; whilst Lascoumes and Le Gales classify according to the

political relations and forms of legitimacy that tools represent (2007: 12). Finally, Vabo and Røisland (2009) return to the NATO framework and (echoing the 'authority' dimension in 1.7) distinguish according to whether government is delivering 'directly' or 'indirectly'; the latter via the network of associations, partnerships, and agencies that defines the new landscape of 'governance'.

Individually such frameworks are valuable in helping to understand and classify governmental activity in the round, even though collectively they overlap and may seem confusing. Underpinning all are the larger processes of urban governance as defined by the triad of fundamental characteristics explored in Chapter 1. This relationship will be returned to in Part II of the book, but first, how does a tools-based approach relate to the governance of design?

Tools in Public Sector Urban Design

When one focuses on particular public policy remits, the specifics of the actual tools for directing and influencing change are quickly discussed. On the question of what type of tools are appropriate for the governance of design, whilst the literature on this front is far more limited than that relating to government at large, a number of frameworks have been proposed that together reveal that a sophisticated toolkit is available.

Stemming from a focus on built heritage, Schuster and colleagues (1997) identify five categories of tool that Mark Schuster subsequently argues represent "the fundamental building blocks with which a government's urban design policy is implemented" (2005: 357). He contends that these can be used to map all urban design actions of the state and therefore need to be fully understood in order that—in any given context—the best choice can be made among them. They are:

- Ownership and operation, the public sector may choose direct provision by owning land and building itself (the state will do X).
- Regulation, by intervening directly in the actions of others who seek to develop (you must or must not do X).
- Incentives (and disincentives), offered to encourage certain behaviours, for example grants, land

transfer, or enhanced development rights (if you do X, the state will do Y).

- Establishment, allocation, and enforcement of property rights, for example through zoning or re-zoning land uses (you have the right to do X, and the state will enforce that right).
- Information, by collecting and distributing information intended to influence the actions of other actors, such as the production of guidance on desirable design attributes (you should do X or you need to know Y in order to do X).

None of these are exclusively the province of design, and in fact relate to the full range of place-shaping disciplines from urban planning to urban management. They confirm that the aspirations of governmental bodies may be implemented through direct action by government agencies or through the various ways and means of influencing the decisions of private actors such as the creation of policy and legal frameworks or through fiscal measures such as the imposition of taxes or tax breaks and subsidies. In the United Kingdom, for example, conservationists have long argued that a perverse incentive exists to demolish historic buildings and build from scratch because, whilst renovation and refurbishment typically attracts VAT (value added tax) at 20 per cent, new build is zero-rated. All but the first of Schuster's categories thereby shape the decision-making environment within which design occurs (see Chapter 1) rather than specific design solutions, and all except (in some circumstances) the last are typically part of formal processes through which powers granted by statute are used to direct, cajole, or encourage other parties towards particular ends in the public interest.

Focussing specifically on the role of the urban designer acting in the public sector, Carmona and colleagues offer a simplified three-part framework—'guidance, incentive, and control'—on the basis that, in the neoliberal age, the state rarely builds non-infrastructure-related development beyond the scale of the individual building (a school, a hospital, etc.) and (in Schuster's terms) regulation typically flows from establishment rights (201: 298). Therefore the day-to-day practice of urban design in the public sector predominantly focuses around three key categories of tool:

- Guidance equates to the 'positive' encouraging of appropriate development by producing plans and guides ranging from simple 'information' tools to 'establishment and allocation' devices guiding the distribution and redistribution of land uses.
- Incentive processes, by contrast, encompass proactive means of enabling development that is in the public interest by actively contributing public sector land or resources to the development process or otherwise making the prospect of development more attractive to landowners.
- Control processes give public authorities direct power over the development process through the ability to refuse development via regulation and enforcement. Typically this occurs care of a series of overlapping regulatory regimes.

Rather than a top-down command-and-control activity, this framework posits that a better way of understanding the role of urban design in the public sector is as a means of positively shaping the production of higher design quality and better places where processes of control are moulded by allied processes of guidance and incentive. And ideally these should precede the act of control (Carmona et al. 2010: 298–299). All three actions are typically governed by statute and are often highly directive in that proposals are ultimately judged on the degree to which they meet the quality thresholds laid down in guidance or by the prerequisites for releasing public sector funding, for example for new infrastructure.

Steve Tiesdell and Phil Allmendinger (2005) argue that how tools affect the decision-making environment, and hence the behaviour of key development actors, is vital to understand, not least because in utilising the set of available tools, the public sector also make some actions more likely than others. The first three of their categories relate well to the trilogy of guidance incentive and control, but the fourth takes a new direction. For them, tools:

- Shape behaviours, by setting the context for market decisions and transactions through shaping the decision environment.
- Stimulate behaviours, by lubricating market actions and transactions, through restructuring the contours of the decision environment.

- Regulate behaviours, by controlling and regulating market actions through defining the parameters of the decision environment.
- Develop the capacity of development actors/organisations, by enhancing the ability of actors to operate more effectively within a particular opportunity space through, for example, developing human capital (skills, knowledge, and attitudes) and/or enhancing organisational networks.

This last category, when applied to the built environment, is particularly important because it recognises a role for the public sector that goes beyond a focus on particular development outcomes and relates instead to shaping the process that leads to those outcomes. Implicitly it suggests that there is little point in having sophisticated governance infrastructure in place if those tasked with its operation lack the necessary competence, confidence, information, alliances, or resources to manage it effectively. These sorts of concerns are likely to exist outside of any formal or statutory systems of governance and instead fall within that extensive group of activities and services that can be called informal or discretionary.

Carmona and colleagues (2010: 297) also recognise this distinction, and draw on Kevin Lynch's (1976: 41–55) modes of urban design action—diagnosis, policy, design, and regulation—supplemented by Alan Rowley's (1994: 189) two additional modes—education and participation and management—to establish a second larger framework for understanding how the public sector shapes the nature of place beyond that associated with guiding and controlling development. This framework reflects the idea that shaping the built environment in the public interest starts by: understanding it as a complex local context, through diagnosis/appraisal; moves on to define key aspirations through policy and design (guidance); enforces these through regulation (control); and concludes with the long-term challenges of, first, education (to develop capacity and raise aspirations over time), second, participation (to engage all those with a stake in local places), and, third, management of the resulting built environments (reflecting the public sector's responsibility for a huge estate of buildings, streets, and spaces).

The framework reflects a simplistic notion of urban design as a linear process to be shaped via public sector intervention using different tools along its length.[1] Adding to the complexity, however, tools operate neither in isolation nor in a vacuum, and may exist within very crowded governance contexts with single tools variously impacting on a range of different behaviours. Design guidance, for example, is typically a bundle of shaping, regulating, and stimulus instruments (Carmona et al. 2010: 65).

Towards a Typology for Design Governance

Reflecting the discussion so far, it is possible to suggest a typology of tools to aid analysis and the understanding of design governance. In Chapter 1, the nature of design governance was unpacked and four key conceptual distinctions were made. The first, between tools and administration, will be returned to later; the other three (formal and informal, process and product, direct and indirect) can usefully form the skeleton for such a typology.

First, there is a major distinction between formal and informal tools, in other words, between those that are legally defined in statutes as 'required' roles of the state (typically tied to defined regulatory responsibilities) and those that are discretionary and therefore optional. This is the major distinction that determines where tools fall in the typology. Second, we can combine the important conceptual division relating to the focus for governance, whether product and process, and between direct and indirect processes of urban design, into a second major distinguishing characteristic of tools. This one focuses on the degree of intervention. Thus a focus on process and on indirectly shaping the decision-making environment is likely to be more long-term and diffuse in its impact, whereas a focus on product—on particular projects and/or places—is likely to be more immediate and clear-cut in its impact on shaping outcomes.

A multi-levelled typology flows from this, one in which, first, formal and, second, informal processes of design governance are distinguished. The sections that follow discuss these meta-categories in turn, and within each identify tools representing the gradation from lesser to greater intervention as represented diagrammatically in 2.1.

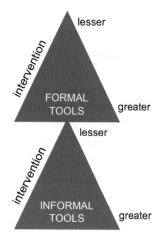

Figure 2.1 Design governance tools, framework for a typology

Formal Tools, the Tried and Tested Approach

A Basis in Legislation

Following on from discussion in Chapter 1 that charted the common reliance (perhaps overreliance) on formal regulatory tools in the practice of design governance, discussion begins here with formal tools. To a large degree, such tools represent the tried and tested approach to the public sector's engagement with design in that they stem from very clear state powers sanctioned in legislation or binding national/state policy that typically places a responsibility on local government to deliver these functions, as well as the specifics of the tools they should use to do the job. In the United Kingdom, for example, national legislation since 1909 has permitted the creation of plans that over the years have gone by various titles and that were given teeth with the nationalisation of the right to develop land in 1947, after which 'planning permission' was required in order to actually develop land.

Over the past century, a huge body of legislation (hundreds of pieces) has been enacted either to directly shape the planning system in the United Kingdom (or within its constituent countries) or that has significant indirect consequences on how it operates, for example legislation dealing with environmental protection or human rights. In 2015, sixteen separate pieces of primary legislation were of direct relevance to planning in England,[2] and eighteen pieces of secondary legislation

were also in force.[3] Furthermore, before 2012 (when it was consolidated), these were accompanied by more than 1,000 pages of policy and 7,000 pages of guidance interpreting how the powers should be used (see later).[4] Whilst only a small proportion of this national planning legislation, policy, and guidance related centrally to design, much of it concerned the context within which design was governed through planning, and planning remains just one of the legislative regimes that impact how places are shaped. Others include legislation dealing with highways, housing, economic development, conservation, the environment, wildlife and countryside, local government, building control, public procurement, parks and open spaces, and so forth.

As each legislative or policy intervention carries with it obligations for the state operating at its various scales, it also carries significant resourcing consequences (ultimately with tax-and-spend implications). In the case of design, this also impacts property rights, freedoms, and collective public interests, as discussed in Chapter 1. It is perhaps for these reasons that the concern for design as an interest of government so overwhelmingly focuses on the formal tools of government, and why informal tools are, by contrast, hardly dealt with at all in the academic literature. The discussion that follows adopts Carmona and colleagues' simplified three-part framework—guidance, incentive, and control—to structure the discussion of formal tools for design governance (2010: 298). In doing so, it moves from advice through to compulsion, or from lesser to greater intervention (2.2).

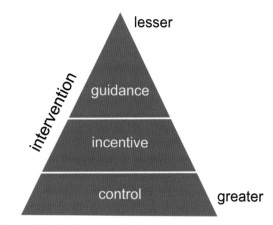

Figure 2.2 The formal tools, by level of intervention

Guidance

William Baer observes that "There are a number of words that mean approximately the same thing relating to devices to guide human behaviour," and identifies customs, norms, rules, regulations, and standards; using rules as the generic catch-all within which regulations ("government-issued rules") and standards ("a profession's internally devised rules") can be located (2011: 277). These terms, and a wide range of others, are often used indiscriminately (or at least interchangeably), and no agreed set of definitions exists. Jon Lang distinguishes between objectives, principles, and guidelines when exploring public sector urban design, describing 'objectives' as the broad "statements of what a design is to achieve", 'principles' as "the link between a desired design objective and a particular pattern or layout of the environment", and 'guidelines' as "a statement which specifies (for uninformed people) how to meet a design objective" (1996: 9). In this conception, the 'guideline' or 'guidance'[5] becomes the operational definition of the broad objective. In a similar vein, 'design guidance' is also favoured here as the generic term for the range of tools that set out operational design parameters with the intention of better directing the design of development.

Matthew Carmona argues that different countries have different traditions in this regard and use different forms of guidance to greater or lesser degrees (2011a: 288). He recalls the British situation where "if one asked 'what is design guidance?' the detailed and unwieldy residential design guides produced by local authorities up and down the country since the 1970s would come to mind; the Essex Design guide being the most famous." He notes that these forms of guidance were, and still are, produced by the public sector to guide the design of (predominantly) housing developments across entire local authority areas. Yet design guidance does not have to take this form, it does not have to be produced by the public sector, it can relate to all types of development, and rather than broad guidance for all locations within a municipality, it can be customised to guide development for specific areas or sites.

Within this broad remit, Carmona nevertheless places an important limit on what can be included in the category of guidance, suggesting that design guidance does not encompass fixed legally binding design requirements, as are found in some forms of zoning, because this would imply an element of enforceability that guidance does not possess (2011a: 289). This, he suggests, "is critical because the very term 'guidance' suggests recommendation rather than compulsion and this represents a critical distinction between processes of guidance and those of control". Yet, despite the restriction, there has been a proliferation of types of design guidance, amongst which are: local design guides, design strategies, design frameworks, design briefs, development standards, spatial masterplans, design codes, design protocols, and design charters. These terms are often confusing, poorly defined and overlapping, and despite attempts to classify them in relation to one another (e.g. Carmona 1996), their sheer variety only helps to illustrate the ambiguity of design guidance as a design/development tool, and the confusion that can too easily result from its use.

Carmona goes on to argue that design guidance can be classified in many ways: according to its subject matter (type of land use or development); the type of context to which it applies; its scale of application (strategic to local); level of governance; whether generic or specific (the latter relating to a particular place or project); by level of detail or prescription; ownership (publicly or privately commissioned); whether focussed on process or product; by the medium of representation (e.g. printed or online); and even by the degree of design ambition (2011a: 289–291). The goals envisaged for design guidance, for example, may vary depending on the ambitions of its instigators and the nature of the development context; particularly whether the intention is to establish minimum desirable thresholds for quality or to raise the bar and strive for a superior quality of design. The former—a 'safety net' approach—may be the limited ambition of an area beset by poor quality development. The latter—a 'springboard to excellence'—would apply in an area where the ambition to achieve better-quality design is widely shared amongst key actors and the skills exist to do so. Although not mutually exclusive, these aspirations would depend on the nature of likely users of the guidance, on the extent to which they are receptive to its content, and on the balance of power between the various players within the development process (Bentley 1999: 28–43).

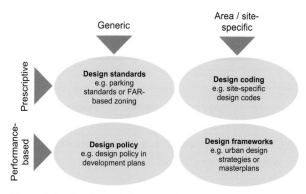

Figure 2.3 Typology of design guidance

At this point, two fundamental qualities are singled out to underpin a simple four-part typology of design guidance as expressed in 2.3. These concern:

- The degree of locational specificity, whether generic (for example applying to a whole municipality) or relating to a particular locality (for example a defined neighbourhood or site).
- The degree of interpretation that guidance requires,[6] specifically whether performance-based or prescriptive.

The first part of this conceptualisation is self-explanatory whilst the second part reflects a distinction made by John Punter and Matthew Carmona (1997: 93–94).[7] Whereas performance requirements establish the broad design objectives of a public authority through the 'performance' expected of projects or places, or aspects of them (e.g. that it should be accessible to all), they do not specify how that performance should be met. Prescriptive criteria, by contrast, 'prescribe' what exactly this requires, in other words, how the desired performance should be met in the end product or place (e.g. step-free access to buildings). The former will be open to a good degree of interpretation when applied whilst the latter will be closely defined and, typically, inflexible.

Design Standards

Perhaps the most consistently problematic of tools are generic design standards, a typology that dominates the sorts of critiques of design regulation that featured so strongly in Chapter 1. This category is typified by the forms of standards that apply to projects and places

but which, because they are generic, apply at the scale of a whole municipality or beyond, and therefore have little regard for the peculiarities of individual projects or places. Typically they are crude, inflexible, and non-contextual as instruments for encouraging 'good' design. Technically and bureaucratically, however, these are the easiest and cheapest of tools to implement because there is little need for interpretation or negotiation in relation to particular projects. They are also very blunt tools if the intention is to deliver responsive, creative, or even optimal design solutions.

In the United Kingdom, for example, the use of rigid highways standards that prioritise vehicle flow efficiency over other factors and that take an approach to road safety based on separation of vehicles and pedestrians, have long been criticised as unresponsive to local place and the achievement of high-quality urban design. In planning, generic prescriptive guidelines are less often used in the United Kingdom today, although in the past, standards setting out 'space between dwellings' were often used and frequently criticised for producing the sorts of regimented suburban landscapes that emerged from the 1950s onwards. Designed to safeguard privacy and 'amenity' through specifying frontage-to-frontage distances, such standards have largely been abandoned as planners have come to realise their harmful side effects and that privacy can be designed in through other means. Parking standards, which can be equally damaging if over-generous, are still widely used (2.4).

Figure 2.4 High parking and rigid highways standards at the expense of place quality

Source: Matthew Carmona

Practice in the United States and elsewhere is often similarly indicted, with 'Euclidean' zoning (based on separating uses from each other) still the dominant practice in the United States and leading, according to Christopher Leinberger, to sprawl based on a driveable-urbanism model (2008: 10). An alternative commercial zoning model based on control of floor area ratio (FAR), as opposed to the sorts of controls on building form that have typically accompanied Euclidean zoning, have equally led to unintended consequences with building forms morphing into towers that eschew the traditional street frontage and consequently undermine the street as a unifying force in the design of cities (Barnett 2011: 209). Whilst some qualities clearly lend themselves to fixed prescriptive guidelines, including the more technical aspects of building design and technology (e.g. energy efficiency), when taken to the urban scale, the substitution of subtlety and flexibility for certainty and efficiency can come at a very high cost for the quality of place.

Design Coding

Design codes share the fixed immutable qualities of design standards, but relate them to particular sites or places. Arguably, traditional zoning already does this because, whilst the functional categories and their qualities are fixed at a generic level, they are applied via the zoning plan to actual sites or localities. However, the coarse nature of traditional zoning has often left it open to the charge laid by Emily Talen (2011) that its legacy has been "homogeneous, simplistic, monotonous forms of order . . . [with] . . . negative effect on housing costs, market readjustments, spillovers, segregation, environmental quality and other social and quality of life issues".

More sophisticated forms of zoning, including custom zoning (planned unit development[8]), performance zoning, and incentive zoning (see later), all represent attempts to better tailor zoning to particular circumstances, and to allow greater sensitivity and discretion in how its provisions are applied. The instigation of form-based codes also attempts to move the focus of zoning, this time away from land use and density towards building form and typology as the basis for regulation, in the process allowing a much greater sensitivity to the nature of the individual locations being zoned. In the case of SmartCode (developed and heavily marketed in the United States by Duany Plater-Zyberk), codes are applied to zones ranging along a notional transect from rural to urban, whilst the codes themselves can be adapted for local traditions and preferred morphological patterns as desired. For John Punter, the danger of such approaches is one of over-prescription and obsessing about architecture at the expense of broader social and ecological design issues (2007: 180), whilst Jonathan Barnett has warned of the danger of divorcing the sweeping aspirational prescriptions of such codes from the urban geography and real estate markets of contemporary cities; in other words, a step away, rather than a step towards, locational prescription (2011: 218). Talen, however, argues that "One might as well leverage the legal authority of codes and put them to good use rather than allow urban form to evolve by default, subject to the narrow interests of fire marshals, transportation engineers, parking regulations, or land use attorneys," all of whom would impose generic rules based on their own narrow pursuits rather than what is in the best interests of high-quality, place-based design (2011: 532).

In Europe, the use of typomophological approaches to regulation represents a well-established tradition best seen in French Plan Local d'Urbanisme, in which detailed codes based on street and plot patterns are laid out covering factors such as size, proportion, access, buildable area, and position relative to front and side boundaries for each zone or plot (Kropf 2011). In the United Kingdom, the pursuit of site-specific design codes has more recently come back onto the agenda, although arguably reflecting traditions that go back centuries. Faced with the increasingly urgent need to deliver more housing whilst preserving environmental quality and retaining community support, in 2004, the then government launched an extensive pilot programme in England aimed at assessing the potential of design coding to deliver better-quality development more rapidly (see Chapter 4).

The research defined design codes as "a distinct form of detailed guidance that prescribes the three dimensional components of a development and how these relate to one another but do not prescribe the overall outcome . . . Design codes usually build upon the design vision contained in a masterplan or development framework and provide a set of requirements (the codes themselves) to achieve the vision" (Carmona & Dann 2006: 7). The codes consequently focus on urban design principles aimed at delivering better-quality places (2.5). Following up on the original research six years on, Matthew Carmona and Valentina Giordano (2013) identified that design codes had become mainstream practice in the United Kingdom. Their success, it seems, was founded on the creation of collaboratively produced design codes aimed at guiding the 'essential' non-negotiable parameters of particular places. As Carmona (2014f) concluded, "Ultimately, despite their perceived benefits, the effectiveness of codes will depend on whether those responsible for their production consider their preparation to be a worthwhile investment"; an upfront investment that, because of their site- or area-specific focus, can be significant.

Design Policy

The category of design policy includes a range of potential tools from policy in development plans, to generic design guides produced by city or local governments in order to encourage particular sorts of design behaviours, to policy and guidance produced at the regional/state/national governmental levels, and even performance zoning; a much more flexible form of zoning that has recently gained traction in the United States and that dispenses with functional categories in favour of flexible performance criteria (Flint 2014). Whilst design policies can be locationally specific, for example relating to a particular development opportunity, their lack of prescription makes them less meaningful at that level unless related directly to a particular design proposition.

In England, for example, design policies in local plans set out the parameters by which development

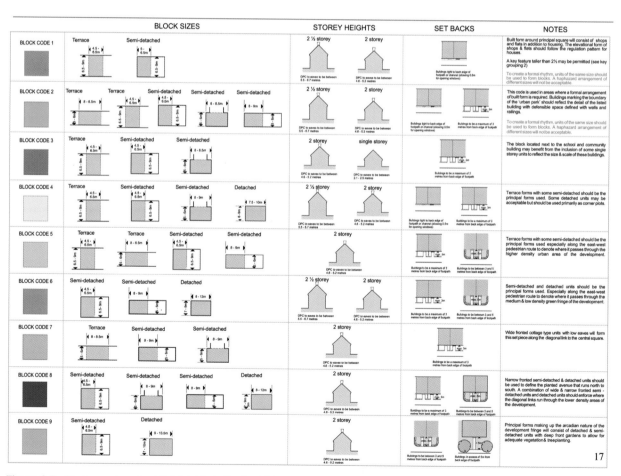

Figure 2.5 Design code extract Fairfield Park, Bedfordshire

Source: Thrive Architects

will be negotiated and assessed (2.6), under statutory (enforceable) powers (see later), and these are in turn subject to a further set of performance guidelines on the national scale as set out in the National Planning Policy Framework (NPPF—see Chapter 5) and its more detailed explanatory Planning Practice Guidance (PPG). In addition, many local planning authorities will possess various Supplementary Planning Guides (SPGs) dealing with different types of development that will typically contain a wealth of further advisory guidance for interpretation by planners and anyone seeking to develop.

Perhaps the most comprehensive study of design policy was undertaken of English design policies in development plans of the 1990s. Following the study, John Punter and Matthew Carmona (1997) argued

first, for the central role of design within the planning system, and second, that this should begin with the comprehensive treatment of design within local authority development plans. More specifically, they argued that this would be the first step on the road to delivering a more positive, enabling, and even visionary planning process.

The experience in the twenty years since has shown that whilst such policies may be a valuable step on the road to shaping the design decision-making environment, and are certainly an important fall-back in the absence of anything better, because of their lack of locational specificity and their essential flexibility, they are not very effective instruments through which to drive local design governance. As Tony Hall concluded: "Not only do the physical consequences of

---

Policy 10: DESIGN AND ENHANCING LOCAL IDENTITY

All new development should be designed to:
a. make a positive contribution to the public realm and sense of place;
b. create an attractive, safe, inclusive and healthy environment;
c. reinforce valued local characteristics;
d. be adaptable to meet evolving demands and the effects of climate change; and
e. reflect the need to reduce the dominance of motor vehicles.

Development will be assessed in terms of its treatment of the following elements:
a. structure, texture and grain, including street patterns, plot sizes, orientation and positioning of buildings and the layout of spaces;
b. permeability and legibility to provide for clear and easy movement through and within new development areas;
c. density and mix;
d. massing, scale and proportion;
e. materials, architectural style and detailing;
f. impact on the amenity of nearby residents or occupiers;
g. incorporation of features to reduce opportunities for crime and the fear of crime, disorder and anti-social behaviour, and promotion of safer living environments;
h. the potential impact on important views and vistas, including of townscape, landscape, and other individual landmarks, and the potential to create new views; and
i. setting of heritage assets.

All development proposals, and in particular proposals of 10 or more homes, will be expected to perform highly when assessed against best practice guidance and standards for design, sustainability, and place making, as set out in Local Development Documents.

Development must have regard to the local context including valued landscape/townscape characteristics, and be designed in a way that conserves locally and nationally important heritage assets and preserves or enhances their settings.

Outside of settlements, new development should protect, conserve or where appropriate, enhance landscape character. Proposals will be assessed with reference to the Greater Nottingham Landscape Character Assessment

---

Figure 2.6 Example of a design policy from a 2014 English local plan, in this case relating to the entire plan areas of three Nottinghamshire planning authorities

the pursuit of more strategic spatial objectives need to be spelt out, but an understanding of urban design principles needs to be fed into the preparation of these spatial policies" (2007: 23). The need, arguably, is for interventions in the design and development processes that reflect the potentially proactive role of the public sector in shaping places, and this requires a greater degree of locational place-specific 'vision' (and perhaps prescription) than is possible in generic policy, no matter how comprehensive or well intentioned.

Design Frameworks

The final category is different from the earlier categories because, unlike other forms of design guidance, design frameworks are concerned with making spatial design propositions for particular sites or places, and not with establishing abstract rules. Design frameworks come in many different guises and are subject to a confusing, poorly defined, and overlapping nomenclature. In the United Kingdom, for example, such tools are known as masterplans, urban design frameworks, development frameworks, development briefs, design briefs, design strategies, area action plans, and so on. Whilst the level of detail and prescription may vary (masterplans are likely to include a greater level of local fixity whilst urban design frameworks will be more conceptual and strategic in nature), ultimately, when used by the public sector, such tools are designed to 'positively' shape development in the public interest and in a more directive manner through specific visions for change. In this regard they are locationally specific, but they are also, typically, highly flexible and open to significant interpretation. If used in this way, they guide rather than dictate the final form of development in a manner that remains sensitive to changing market and political/policy circumstances over time. Like design policy, they specify expected performance (in this case spatially) without defining exactly how that will be achieved. This fits in with Carmona's assertion that guidance tools do not include fixed 'blueprints' because the term 'guidance' "suggests a sense of direction for, but not an end solution to, a design problem" (2011a: 289).

John Punter (2010: 338) observes that the report of the Urban Task Force (1999) in the United Kingdom played a very significant role in reviving master planning as a governance tool, with CABE (2004e) subsequently turning the recommendation into a set of influential best practice principles through its research and advice (see Chapter 4). In this, the 'spatial master-plan' was seen as a detailed and three-dimensional vision-making and coordinating tool, the product of a multi-professional team and of public engagement in its creation, all fully tested in the market for feasibility. To this, Husam Al Waer adds, the master-planning process envisaged for the twenty-first century needs to be seen as a "framework for managing change ... rather than just the spatial rendering of a property development on a site". It should involve a continuous process of decision-making that is both long term and flexible and fully embedded in local governance arrangements "without which the physical strategy has no legitimacy" (2013: 28).

For Punter, contemporary master-planning processes frequently fail to match up to the optimal process that CABE set out, although he recognises that developments such as Kings Cross in London (2.7), Walker and Scotswood in Newcastle upon Tyne, and the Western Harbour in Edinburgh have all benefitted from successful master-planning processes that balance flexibility with certainty (2010: 338). During the 2000s, also, city centre urban design strategies in cities such as Bristol and Nottingham successfully guided ambitious public realm proposals and private sector investments, helping to reinvigorate those city centres.

Despite their frequent use, the terms *masterplan* and *master planning* remain problematic when used in association with design governance because of their association with what Nicholas Falk refers to as 'big architecture' projects through which designers incorrectly assume that "if you can visualise everything, you have solved the main problems of development" (2011: 37). He quotes Joel Garreau, who defines master planning as "that attribute of a development in which so many rigid controls are put in place, to defeat every imaginable future problem, that any possibility of life, spontaneity, or flexible response to unanticipated events is eliminated" (Garreau 1991: 435). Instead, Falk argues, a 'trellis' is required, rather than a blueprint with which to guide community growth. Whether in the form of standards, coding, policy, or frameworks, viewing guidance tools as a trellis up which public design

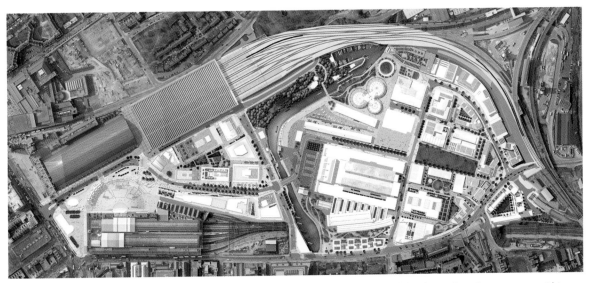

Figure 2.7 In Kings Cross, a flexible urban design framework was agreed through which land use allocations can vary within a defined building envelope whilst guaranteeing an extensive catalogue of community and public realm goods, all shaped through community engagement

Source: Allies and Morrison

aspirations can grow seems like a helpful metaphor for design governance more widely.

Mixing the Tools

In reality, the divisions between guidance tools is not nearly so clear-cut as the discussion so far suggests. Design frameworks, for example, will often include design standards, policy, and coding embedded within them in support of the design proposition. In the United States, the extensive use of regulating plans might be seen as a halfway house between locational design coding and design frameworks through the auspices of a two-dimensional plan locating and setting out the coded development parameters of a site: building lines, frontage widths, block and street dimensions, active frontages, and so forth. In effect, they relate codes to particular sites through a plan and are reminiscent of the Bebauungspläne used in Germany to designate urban development, acceptable land uses and development forms, and to make provision for infrastructure in areas of rapid change. These 'B-Plans' are legally binding documents local authorities prepare in partnership with developers to control urban form through site coverage, maximum building height, and the 'Baufenster'. The 'Baufenster' sets out the area within which any development has

to be located as defined by two different boundary conditions: 'Baulinie' (build-to line) and 'Baugrenze' (building boundary). The former describes the line on which a building has to be located and the latter the maximum 'footprint' it may occupy; all accompanied with a textual justification that can be downplayed or emphasised (replacing aspects of the urban form controls) to give an element of flexibility to the plan. Regulating plans and B-Plans demonstrate the strong locational specificity and propositional nature of performance frameworks, but are typically highly prescriptive and subject to little flexibility in their interpretation.

Ultimately, whichever tool is used, the outcomes will be only as good as the thinking that goes into their preparation and subsequent application. In this respect, B-Plans, just like other mechanisms, can and do contribute to high-quality design—Vauban in Freiburg (2.8), for example—but just as easily can and do lead to "monotonous, land hungry developments of single-family homes that are unsustainable in terms of access, mix of tenure and use" (Stille 2007: 26). The danger with setting design requirements in stone for very large developments may be that the certainty this provides comes at the expense of the flexibility required when market or other circumstances change—an issue that returns the discussion once again to the design

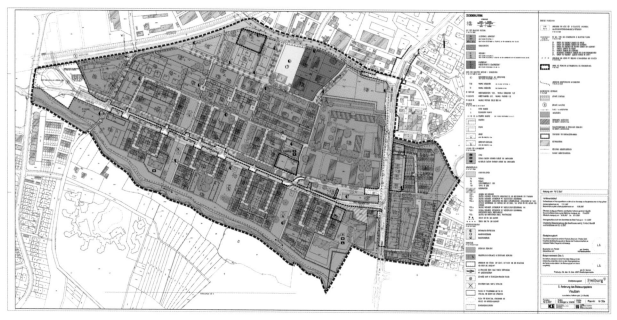

Figure 2.8   B-Plan extract and key, Vauban Freiburg

Source: Stadt Freiburg, Stadtplanungsamt

governance problematics discussed in Chapter 1: how much intervention is required and what is the legitimate role of the state?

Incentive

The preparation of guidance of various types is a proactive but often less directly interventionalist form of governmental activity than incentive and control because, whilst it is a positive response to shaping the decision-making environment, in the large majority of cases, public authorities will still depend on private actors interpreting the guidance and coming forward with development proposals. Clearly, as guidance becomes more locationally specific and/or less flexible in the degree to which it enables interpretation, its relative power to shape outcomes will increase. Forms of incentive are likewise more or less interventionalist depending on whether they involve the state directly putting in public resources in order to encourage certain outcomes, or whether they are indirect and focussed on rewarding defined 'good behaviour' with enhanced development rights.

In this regard, Jon Lang identifies two ways of incentivising developers to produce particular design/development outcomes, first, through direct financial incentives, and second, through what he calls trade-offs: "Financial incentives reduce the monetary risk to developers of making specific types of development. . . . Trade-offs tie developments which are uneconomic in the market place to highly lucrative development" (1996: 17). In both, the fundamental objective is an economic one, namely to stack the scales so that a particular development proposition swings from being uneconomic to economic, making development more likely, or, in terms of Christopher Hood's (1983) classification of governmental tools, the application of state 'treasure' to the problem.

Seen in such terms, if enough non-refundable state treasure is applied to any private development proposition, then eventually it will become viable, although this will not necessarily guarantee good design and may be deemed illegal state aid. The critical task is not simply to incentivise development, but to incentivise high-quality development. Moreover, in a neoliberal environment where increasingly the private sector is being looked to in order to provide a wide range of public goods and where state resources are often limited, means of incentivisation based on encouragement rather than state expenditure are all the more important.

The state aided/state encouraged nexus provides a first means to classify incentivisation processes as they

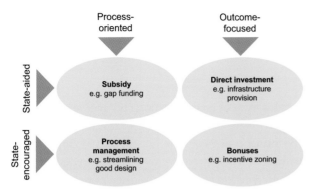

Figure 2.9 Typology of design incentive

relate to design. Processes of incentivisation can also be distinguished in terms of what they relate to and in particular whether they focus on facilitating the process of design/development or whether they directly focus on outcomes. Together, these two fundamental qualities underpin a four-part typology of design incentive as expressed in 2.9.

Subsidy

Crudely, the first incentive tool is the most straightforward, involving, in one form or another, the granting of state aid (treasure) to projects. Under the meta-category of stimulus instruments, David Adams and Steve Tiesdell identify price-adjusting and capital-raising instruments (2013: 134). The first act through offering direct grants to projects, perhaps to fill a gap in funding and make a particular scheme more likely, or through the granting of tax incentives to encourage certain sorts of development or development in particular locations. The second oil the wheels of development through using the financial weight and security of the state to guarantee investments, to loan funds at favourable rates, or to support projects directly through public-private partnerships.

Whilst these sorts of instruments are typically focussed on ensuring development happens/happens sooner/happens in a particular locality, rather than with guaranteeing levels of quality, "development stimulus instruments can be changed into development + design stimulus instruments by adding 'design strings' to the basic development stimulus instruments" (Tiesdell & Adams 2011: 25). In the United Kingdom, the instigation of a first wave of Enterprise Zones in the 1980s,

most notably in London Docklands, included a significant package of tax advantages such as business rates relief and capital allowances (tax relief) to businesses investing in these areas, and this went hand in hand with a simplified planning regime with almost no control on design. The very poor quality of design that resulted in the first phase of development led to the developers of Canary Wharf (in the second wave) imposing their own private design governance regime on their huge project, with a flexible design framework and design codes ensuring that the creation of place quality sat at the heart of the development (Carmona 2009a: 142). The lessons have been learned and the recent designation of the Royal Docks Enterprise Zone (designated in 2012) combines similar tax incentives (in effect, subsidies to development) with a flexible design framework and set of design policies contained within *Royal Docks Spatial Principles* (Mayor of London & Newham London 2011). In other words, developers will not benefit from the subsidies unless they also deliver on the design aspirations.

Direct Investment

If subsidies represent direct financial means to oil the wheels of the development process in order to incentivise particular actions, then nonfinancial means can also be used as a form of indirect subsidy. Because of their more tangible nature—land acquisition, assembly and remediation, provision of an enhanced public realm, provision of infrastructure or public amenities, and so forth—these might be referred to as direct public investments. Like subsidies, they can be used to stimulate development by closing the gap between viable and unviable propositions (e.g. improving the accessibility of sites through roads and public transport provision) or by reducing the risk private actors are taking (e.g. through compiling and cleaning land ready for redevelopment). They can also be used to establish a 'level of quality' in order to set the threshold for subsequent interventions, for example through the direct public provision of a high-quality public realm, parks, and public amenities such as schools and community facilities built to a high standard.

Peter Hall, for example, in his final book, *Good Cities, Better Lives*, made a passionate case for the public provision of high-quality connecting

Figure 2.10   In Hammerby Sjöstad in Stockholm, the state-provided infrastructure ranges from the tram system, to roads, bridges, and a coherent public and open space network, to integrated energy and recycling infrastructure, and a choice of schools

Source: Matthew Carmona

infrastructure prior to development. Based on his analysis of exemplar development projects across Europe, in the Netherlands, Germany, Scandinavia, and France, Hall argued that these investments not only connect up cities, but are typically accompanied by generous treatment of public space that together provide significant place marketing potential for the cities concerned (2014: 282) (2.10). In continental Europe, this up-front provision of infrastructure is often accompanied by mechanisms to reclaim value for the state through the development process, for example via public landownership, but in essence the public investments incentivise developers to participate in certain locations, help to establish quality thresholds, ensure that from day one developments are properly served by all necessary infrastructure, and offer a more certain environment in which to invest for both developers and eventual homeowners alike. Falk (2011) concludes that such advance investment "incentivises developers to (a) take part and (b) take part now"; in the process helping to overcome known problems with other tools such as the tendency for the public sector to endlessly commission masterplans for the same difficult sites with little tangible change on the ground.[9] Direct state investments, from major infrastructure provision to land remediation, have the potential to stimulate change in a very proactive manner, albeit a potentially costly one if no mechanisms

(either through the market or taxation) are put in place to recoup the outlay.

Process Management

A third form of incentivisation concerns nonmonetary means to encourage particular outcomes that precede the formal control process yet still help to shape it, thus making it more attractive to users and reducing their risk. Regulation of all forms is often criticised for adding burdens on the development process, and most notably for slowing down development with knock-on impacts on economic performance and project viability. The time taken to consider and influence design, particularly when involving discretionary processes (as discussed later), often falls foul of such critique with concerns that such processes are "time-consuming and expensive", leading to delay (Brenda Case Scheer 1994: 3). If this is the case, then processes that streamline the formal systems of control, or that otherwise manage the process in order to assist applicants to get successfully to the regulatory starting line, can also incentivise good design.

Alongside fiscal incentives, the Enterprise Zones used from the 1980s onwards in the United Kingdom also included provisions for a streamlined planning process as part of the package to attract developers to particular localities. Whilst these simplified processes were subsequently criticised as deregulation at the expense of quality, the research on design coding referred to earlier (Carmona et al. 2006: 281) argued that if such mechanisms were used in conjunction with a design code, they had the potential to streamline planning although on the basis of clear pre-agreed design parameters.[10] In exploring other approaches to streamlining the mainstream British planning process, Carmona and colleagues identified four critical means to encourage swifter decision-making with more certain outcomes (2003: 191–194). Adapted to relate more closely to design, these are:

- Fast-tracking processes, including explicitly fast-tracking proposals made by architects, or that are deemed to represent high-quality design.
- Developer subsidies, looking to developers to fund the preparation of design frameworks and codes or to fund dedicated design expertise within the

municipality in order to more effectively manage their project.

- Pre-application discussions, to provide early design advice in order to agree on key design principles before projects are formally submitted for consideration through the statutory process of development management.
- Protocols and timetables, to agree in advance the timetable for complex planning applications and how they will be considered, including when and in what detail and formats design information should be supplied.

Each of these could help to overcome concerns around the time taken for design to be adequately addressed by explicitly making high-quality design the key to unlocking a streamlined process.

Figure 2.11 New York 'bonus' plaza. The small wall-mounted plaque in the middle of the picture reads, "Plaza rules of conduct: No smoking, No pigeon feeding, No rollerblading, No skateboarding, No loitering"

Source: Matthew Carmona

Bonuses

Systems of development bonuses (incentive zoning) are widespread in the United States, where, in exchange for extra floor space, developers can provide public amenities such as better design features, landscaping, or public spaces. In New York, for example, Jerold Kayden (2000) describes how between 1961 and 2000, 503 new public spaces had been obtained through this route. Most of these were attached to office, residential, and institutional buildings and, in exchange for the new pseudo-public spaces, these had been built higher or larger than otherwise would have been possible (typically with a 20 per cent increase in floor space).

Although effective at delivering public amenities, the limitations and abuses of such bonus systems have sometimes discredited them as means to achieve better design (Cullingworth 1997: 94–99). These problems include the tendency for developers to see bonuses as 'as-of-right' entitlements; the tendency to increase floor space (and building heights and volumes) regardless of impact; failure to deliver the public amenities after bonuses had been taken; the inequitable and time-consuming nature of a system lacking clear ground rules; and the poor quality of many of the 'public' amenities provided (Loukaitou-Sideris & Banerjee 1998: 84–99). In New York, for example, despite the impressive quantity of new public spaces and some exemplars of quality, new public spaces were often

barren, hostile, and highly controlled, and too often resulted in the separation of buildings at ground level— "towers that stand in their individual pools of plaza space" (Barnett 1974: 41) rather than the creation of unified built frontages (2.11). Moreover, it follows that bonuses and their associated 'public goods' will only be provided where developers want to build rather than where new public spaces are needed. Bonuses, like subsidies and process management, will typically be relatively blunt tools with which to influence particular design behaviours, and, in contrast to direct investment, will ultimately depend on how private actors interpret and react to such incentives, rather than on the ability of the public sector to lead the way.

Control

The prospect of achieving the variety of permissions necessary for development to proceed is, of course, a major incentive in its own right for development actors and, like other tools, control processes can be shaped in a manner that facilitates or hinders better design. Equally, if incentives are viewed as the 'carrots' for good behaviour, then control might be seen as the 'stick', and as a disincentive to certain behaviours. The key challenge in designing regulatory systems for design is to make the 'good' easy and the 'bad' arduous, although this presupposes being able to distinguish good from bad (the role of design guidance) and having a system of sanctions (and incentives) in place to encourage it. As the ultimate sanction of regulatory processes is to deny permission to do something (to develop, in the case of urban design), the prime incentive will be to achieve consent for a proposal while the main sanction will be to withhold it.

Control processes themselves reflect one of two major types. They are based on fixed legal frameworks with unquestioning administrative decision-making as typified by American and European zoning systems. Alternatively, they are discretionary with a distinction drawn between law and policy, as is the case in British town and country planning; the latter enacted through 'guiding' policy and plans, skilled professional interpretation in the light of local circumstances, and political decision-making (Reade 1987: 11). Beyond arguments over the inherent pros and cons of discretionary versus fixed legal systems (2.12), the diversity of control process and systems, and their often disjointed, uncoordinated, and even contradictory nature is sometimes a cause of complaint, and adds to a perception held by some that "a marathon of red tape needs to be run" (Imrie & Street 2006: 7). Reflecting their relative strengths and weaknesses, many administrations adopt a mix of the two basic forms of regulation for different purposes. In the United Kingdom, for example,

planning, conservation, and environmental protection are discretionary, although a shortage of key skills amongst the professionals charged with their interpretation can lead authorities back in the direction of adopting fixed standards (Carmona 2001: 225–227). By contrast, building control and highways adoption processes (see later) are fixed technical processes, open to little interpretation, and have no recourse to appeal (apart from in the courts) if decisions go against the applicant.

Both forms of decision-making retain the potential to contribute towards the regulatory tyranny described in Chapter 1; the first because of its perceived arbitrary, inconsistent, and subjective nature, and the second because of its lack of flexibility or inability to consider nonstandard approaches. Perhaps because of this, in recent years, the two systems have converged,[11] although even where this has happened, the two forms of regulation remain distinct because of the very different legal and administrative systems with which they are underpinned. Nevertheless, the overlay of design review procedures onto fixed legal zoning systems to give more flexibility on design, or the addition of more detailed and authoritative guidance to increase certainty in discretionary systems, are clearly examples of convergence.

The move in the United Kingdom to a 'plan-led' system of planning in the early 1990s is an example of

	Pros	Cons
Discretionary systems	Flexible decision-making Speedier plan-making Responsive to individual circumstances Responsive to community representations Potential for negotiation	Uncertain decision-making Slower planning applications Inconsistent decision-making Arbitrary decision-making Potential for conflict in decision-making
Fixed legal systems	Certain decision-making Faster planning applications Consistent decision-making Objective decision-making Avoidance of conflict in decision-making	Inflexible decision-making Slower plan-making Unresponsive to individual circumstances Unresponsive to community representations Little potential for negotiation
Crossover systems	Some flexibility Reasonably certain decision-making Responsive to individual circumstances Responsive to community representations Some potential for negotiation More consistent decision-making More objective decision-making	Some inflexibility Some uncertainty Slower planning applications Slower plan-making Potential for conflict in decision-making Some inconsistency Some arbitrariness

Figure 2.12   The pros and cons of discretionary, fixed-legal, and crossover regulatory systems (adapted from Carmona et al. 2003: Table 7.1)

the latter, and whilst this system has many of the advantages of both discretionary and fixed legal systems, it also (to some degree) has many of the disadvantages. In particular, although the system offers a greater degree of certainty and consistency in decision-making (whilst retaining a degree of flexibility), it also retains a degree of inconsistency, uncertainty, and arbitrariness, because discretion in any form invites these qualities. The system also possesses the potential for conflict and delay in the making of decisions on planning applications and has greatly increased the delays associated with plan-making, as the status of development plans—and therefore attempts by developers and others to influence what goes in them—has increased (Carmona et al. 2003: 108).

Looking beyond the two fundamental types of control, it is possible to distinguish a four-part typology of control tools (2.13) based, first, on whether they are primarily development or construction related, a factor that also reflects when in the larger place-shaping process the permission is given: pre- or post-development. It also reflects, second, to whom the benefit of the decision primarily accrues; whether a contribution from the developer to the state (the public gets something), or an authorisation given from the state to the applicant (who is allowed to proceed with, or successfully complete, a development). Each of these categories has potential for both discretionary and nondiscretionary regulatory systems to hold sway, although typically the more technical processes concerned with construction are more likely to be nondiscretionary than those associated with less certain development processes.

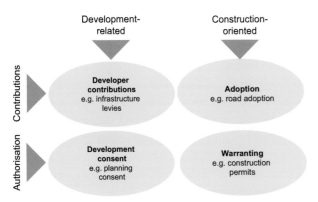

Figure 2.13 Typology of design control

Developer Contributions

At first sight, developer contributions might be deemed similar in their essentials to the previous category of bonuses: 'I will give you this if you give me that.' In fact, they are quite different. Whilst bonuses are an optional benefit granted for (and to encourage) good behaviour, developer contributions are the societal price paid for development to proceed. They might even be characterised as reverse incentives—from the developer to the state—in order to incentivise the grant of the necessary authorisations. Development contributions might be levied or negotiated for a number of reasons:

• First, and most crudely, as a simple price to be paid for permission ('you can build your shopping centre if you pay for our school').
• Second, to rectify any negative externalities from a development ('your development will increase congestion, and therefore you need to build a new road').
• Third and finally, to ensure that society gets a fair slice of any uplift in value (planning gain) from changes to development rights on a piece of land ('with this consent, your land will increase in value X times and a proportion of that will be levied to the public purse in recognition of that').

Syms argues, "Ideally planning obligations should enhance the quality of the development and the wider environment" (2002: 315). In fact, the pursuit of design quality is not the primary purpose of developer contributions (nor indeed of the other control tools). Nevertheless, it can be a key beneficiary if factored into relevant negotiations, for example through directly funding or cross-subsidising the necessary infrastructure and amenities to shape places of lasting quality, or through using the income to fund a higher standard of design and/or management of the public realm or affordable housing. Contributions can also be used as an effective tax on certain sorts of undesirable design outcomes. Some municipalities in Canada use their powers to levy Development Charges which penalise developments that sprawl (Baumeister 2012), justified on the basis that sprawl gives rise to higher infrastructure costs.

In England, developer contributions can be levied in three key ways: as a 'condition' to the planning permission, as a separately negotiated 'obligation' as part of a planning agreement, or, since 2010, by way of a Community Infrastructure Levy (CIL); in effect, a standard charge set according to the types and extent of development. Whilst the first two are discretionary and negotiated on a case-by-case basis, the third is fixed by a local authority and is thereafter non-negotiable except in exceptional circumstances. However raised, developer contributions represent a key benefit to society and an important opportunity to push for design quality as an integral part of the larger control process.

Adoption

In some countries, local infrastructure such as roads and public space is primarily built by the state. In others, it is built first by a private developer and then transferred into state ownership. In the United Kingdom, whether through a defined developer contribution or simply in the process of building out an approved masterplan, this process is known as adoption. Elsewhere, it is known by many names, including gazetting, dedicating, addition, and expropriation. Whatever it is called, the process represents, on one hand, a public benefit in the form of a gift of completed infrastructure (or at least the land on which to build it), and, on the other, a liability in the form of infrastructure that needs to be managed and maintained at state expense, ad infinitum. Whilst developer/investors (particularly of commercial development) may wish to keep this infrastructure in private hands (for instance the sorts of bonus spaces already referred to) as an integral and 'value-adding' part of their investment, residential developers in particular will see such infrastructure as an on-going liability that they will typically be keen to divest themselves of as quickly as possible.

The state taking on such liabilities has an incentive to ensure that local infrastructure is constructed in such a way that it will last and can be easily managed and maintained without exorbitant expense. Because local government (who typically takes on these assets) will not agree to adopt them until they are satisfied that the infrastructure meets its standards for adoption, this puts the state in a very strong position to demand high-quality design. Equally, local authorities will often be reluctant to take on high-specification materials, bespoke street furniture, or public realm elements representing potentially expensive on-going liabilities such as planting, grass verges, public art, amenity lighting, play areas, and so forth because of the financial commitment and management responsibility they represent. The tendency, therefore, can be to dumb down design and insist on low-management, low-maintenance outcomes, without due regard to the quality of place. In the United Kingdom, for example, stories of street trees being planted in new residential developments, then being removed prior to adoption, are not uncommon.

In this regard, Roger Evans Associates has argued that "where existing standards cannot deliver the quality required, designers and scheme promoters should work with local authorities to develop and adopt new standards" (2007: 158). This may be easier said than done, particularly given the range of local infrastructure that in large schemes is subject to adoption, ranging from the public highway to cycle ways, footpaths, public spaces, street lighting, street furniture, public art, verges, play areas, open space and sports facilities, allotments, parking areas, community buildings, schools and health facilities, SUDs and other water features, sewerage, recycling and waste facilities, local energy generation infrastructure, and so on. Whilst the exact package of local infrastructure to be adopted will vary from place to place, if used well, these tools can be amongst the most powerful (and also destructive) in the design governance armoury and deserve careful consideration early in the development process.

Development Consents

Processes of gaining the necessary consents for development to commence typically relate to a diverse range of regulatory regimes that variously include: planning, zoning, subdivision, heritage/conservation controls, and design review. These may be integrated with each other in various combinations or separated. Carmona and colleagues, for example, discuss integrated and separated models for evaluating design quality (2010: 322). In 'integrated' models (2.14i), design is treated as an integral part of wider planning and/or zoning processes, and connections between design and other planning issues—economic development, land uses, social infrastructure, and so forth—can be made, understood, and weighed one against the other, with

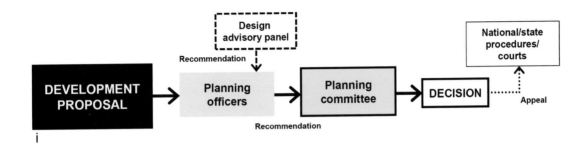

Figure 2.14 (i) integrated consideration of planning and design (ii) separated planning/zoning and design review (adapted from Carmona et al. 2010)

informed and balanced judgements made. The danger, however, is that design objectives can be and often are sacrificed in the pursuit of other economic or social objectives. The United Kingdom's planning process provides an example of an integrated approach in which judgements about the acceptability of design are ultimately made by local planning authorities, although authorities may seek advice on design matters from national or local design review bodies who sit outside of the statutory regulatory processes and whose deliberations have no formal status.

In separated models (2.14ii), decisions on design are deliberately split from other planning/development concerns, with a separate body responsible for reviewing design (a design review board or commission) which either makes a recommendation to the zoning board or grants a separate design consent itself. This arrangement is prominent in the United States, where a process of design review often sits alongside but separate from zoning. Under such circumstances, the promoters of projects are compelled to undergo design review and, arguably, design issues will consistently receive an appropriate weighting

before development approval is given or refused. This will be undertaken by staff or advisors with a well-developed design awareness, something that may not be the case in integrated models. A shortcoming, however, is the difficulty in making the necessary connections between design and other development issues, some of which—such as decisions on land use zoning, density, and transport/infrastructure provision—will have a major impact on design outcomes. In these circumstances, the danger is that consideration of design is reduced to 'mere' aesthetics, throwing the legitimacy of such processes into question (Case Scheer 1994: 7–9).

Whether separated or integrated, a number of characteristics distinguish design consent processes. They are:

- Development-related, in other words, concerned with the principle of development, and determined on the basis of pre-construction plans and proposals.
- Reactive, involving responding to the proposals of others (usually by the private sector, but sometimes by public agencies).

- Evaluative, because they require that an assessment (however simple) be made against whichever criteria (formal or informal) have been established to evaluate proposals (in some form of design guidance).
- Bureaucratic, in the sense that they rely on a bureaucracy to administer the process in (hopefully) a fair, consistent, and effective manner.

Within these broad characteristics there is nevertheless a huge variation in practice defined first and foremost by the nature of the regulatory process, whether discretionary or not. To obtain planning permission in the United Kingdom, for example, involves considerable discretion which plays itself out in consent processes (across different spatial scales) involving assessing private (and public) development proposals against policy and other guidance and involving advocacy, negotiation, persuasion, and even brinkmanship and bluff (threatening to deny planning permission when necessary). It is a complex (2.15) and highly skilled process

that necessitates the weighing and balancing of public aspirations against private needs, and the separation out of public sector proposals for the public realm into their own control regime. It can also lead to the squeezing out of design altogether in the face of other more pressing 'material considerations' (Paterson 2012: 152).

For their part, fixed legal systems have a tendency to become increasingly complex over time in an attempt to be more responsive to local peculiarities. In New York, for example, the Uniform Land Use Review Procedure (ULURP) through which development consent is granted evaluates proposals in the context of three basic zoning categories—residential, commercial, and manufacturing districts—but these are now subdivided into 114 subcategories, on top of which there are fifty-seven Special Purpose Districts (each with its own zoning regulations because standard zoning practice is considered too blunt an instrument for their special character); forty-one Contextual Zoning Districts where new buildings in an established area of character are required to conform to the existing

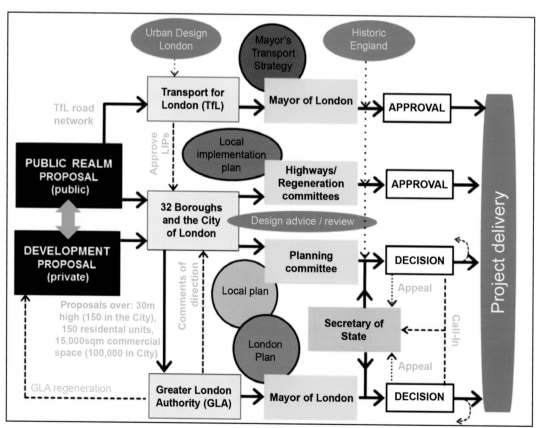

Figure 2.15   The complex process of controlling design quality in London

characteristics of the neighbourhood; and thirty-eight Overlay Districts where one zone overlays another to achieve hybrid outcomes. Very large new developments (more than 1.5 acres) can even, at the discretion of the City Planning Commission, break away from key aspects of the zoning ordinance altogether in order to achieve a better arrangement of bulk and open space on the site.

With all this complexity, it should be no surprise that New York's zoning ordinance has grown from thirty-five pages when originally devised (in 1916) to 900 pages today and has become a significant challenge to interpret, whilst circumstances still increasingly conspire to require departures from the zoning ordinance altogether. In such cases, a Zoning Amendment, Special Permit, Authorization, or Variance can be applied for, each of which requires that either the City Planning Commission or the Board of Standards and Appeals meet and agree to the proposed change, in the process introducing an element of discretion (and also uncertainly) not dissimilar to discretionary systems. There also remains the ability to move development rights in their entirety from one site to another in specified circumstances. These Transfers of Development Rights (TDRs) typically occur when unused development rights associated with, for example, a landmark building are sold to a developer on a neighbouring site to allow a higher building to be built, a process requiring a special permit. Other lots can be entirely merged and development rights shifted around the now enlarged site in order to optimise development outcomes. These process have significant design implications, for example encouraging the construction of larger towers than would be possible on smaller sites.

Like systems of control elsewhere, it is clear that planners and politicians in New York have increasingly been looking to their system to deliver much more than was originally envisaged of it, and to secure a consents process that is far more responsive to the city's multifarious complexities. To achieve this, layer upon layer of additional regulatory complexity has been added, all interpreted, argued over, and challenged by legions of zoning lawyers ranged against the planners who created and now maintain the system (Carmona 2012).

Staying in the United States, this critical relationship between discretion and fixed certainty is represented very well in the stark differences between the regulation of subdivisions and processes associated with design review. Subdivision is the division of land into lots and has a long history in America stemming back to the surveying and opening up of the land to settlers. Today subdivision is a process separate to zoning, planning, and design review, guided by its own processes of pre-application, preliminary plat, and final plat which were established nationally in the 1930s and 1940s and underpinned by standards laid down quickly after. These processes and standards have since been overlaid, according to Eran Ben-Joseph, by a "jumble of codes, regulations and design requirements", and by "multiple agencies and committees involved in the process" (2005a: 179, 181–182). Such complexity, he contends, is poorly handled by an essentially rigid process in which negotiation and revision is difficult to achieve and in which design quality is often sacrificed on the altar of early twentieth-century objectives for health and safety that "have hardly any bearing on present-day reality". Through such means, it is not uncommon for paved roads and other space to reach 50 per cent of the total land take of new developments (Ben-Joseph 2005a: 179).

Formal processes of design review, by contrast, are a relatively recent phenomena in the United States, originating in the 1950s, but not gaining traction until the 1980s, when practices spread so rapidly that by 1994 Brenda Case Scheer was able to report that 83 per cent of towns had some form of review, although with wildly varying practice and little national coordination. Case Scheer defines design review as: "the process by which private and public development proposals receive independent criticism under the sponsorship of the local government unit" with a focus on urban design, architecture, and visual impact (1994: 2). At that time, 82 per cent of design review processes were mandatory and legislated (as opposed to advisory), but only 40 per cent of review processes were founded on design "guidelines with 'teeth', that is, guidelines that are legally binding", and there was no model code of any form to shape these tools. This gave rise to a withering set of critiques around the potential for design review to be arbitrary, inconsistent, expensive, easily manipulated, under-skilled, subjective, vague, unfair, uncreative, and superficial—critiques that twenty years on find echo in Willow Lung-Amam's (2013) study of the social, cultural and political tensions underpinning the control of McMansions in the United States through design review (see Chapter 1).

For John Punter (2007), however, the critiques of design review from the 1980s and 1990s have been answered by the flowering of design review practice from which he has been able to draw a set of best practice principles (2.16). Typically this involves extending the remit of review beyond a narrow regulatory function. Auckland in New Zealand and Vancouver in Canada, for example, have both utilised urban design panels to deliver a design review service, but with the multiple aims of giving early and constructive advice to developers on specific development proposals; advising their respective cities on policy and guidance frameworks; and generally championing good design across the professional establishment and community at large (Punter 2003; Wood 2014).

Ultimately, many of Punter's prescriptions relate to the formal processes of design review, and in particular to the need to situate processes of control within a context in which key aspirations for design have already been established (in design guidance and other tools); stakeholders have engaged in a range of pre-application processes; and control can then be conducted in a constructive and non-confrontational setting. As Elizabeth Plater-Zyberk, the *bête-noire* of many architects and academic commentators worldwide, has claimed:

> [C]ontrol and freedom can co-exist most effectively when incorporated in regulations that precede the act of design, framing parameters of a given programme, rather than conflicting in judgement exerted on the completed design. Review without regulations, or some clearly articulated intention, is nonsensical.
>
> (1994: vii)

Warranting

Whilst development consents give approval for developments in prospect and establish the principle of a particular sort of development happening in a particular location, they do not guarantee the outcome. This is inevitable because consents occur prior to development

---

Community Vision
1. Committing to a comprehensive and coordinated vision of environmental beauty and design
2. Developing and monitoring an urban design plan with community and development industry support and periodic review

Design, Planning and Zoning
3. Harnessing the broadest range of actors and instruments (tax, subsidy, land acquisition) to promote better design
4. Mitigating the exclusionary effects of control strategies and urban design regulation
5. Integrating zoning into planning and addressing the limitations of zoning

Broad, Substantive Design Principles
6. Maintaining a commitment to urban design that goes well beyond elevations and aesthetics to embrace amenity, accessibility, community, vitality and sustainability
7. Basing guidelines on generic design principles and contextual analysis and articulating desired and mandatory outcomes
8. Not attempting to control all aspects of community design but accommodating organic spontaneity, vitality, innovation, pluralism: not over-prescriptive

Due Process
9. Identifying clear a priori roles for urban design intervention
10. Establishing proper administrative procedures with written opinions to manage administrative discretion, and with appropriate appeal mechanisms
11. Implementing an efficient, constructive and effective permitting process
12. Providing appropriate design skills and expertise to support the review process

Figure 2.16   Best practice principles for the development of design review (adapted from Punter 2007)

which, thereafter, may or may not happen, or may happen in a different form, requiring a fresh consent. They almost certainly (except in the case of heritage schemes) will avoid considering the detailed design of the proposition, and this will then need interpreting on the journey from design to construction. By contrast, building or construction permits will largely focus on the detailed design and construction of a development against a published construction code or set of regulations (e.g. building regulations in the United Kingdom). This will typically include pre-construction appraisal of construction plans, leading to a post-construction inspection of actual works (largely stage by stage following construction). Whilst much of this will focus on a range of technical concerns such as: structural stability, heating and utilities, lighting, ventilation, sound insulation, and drainage and waste (largely hidden from sight following construction), it will also cover dimensions with a more profound impact on external aesthetics, including external heat loss/insulation and fire transmission, and on issues with a profound impact on layout, such as accessibility and the use of renewable technologies.

In effect, once the notice, certificate, or permit has been issued, this provides a 'warrant' that the works are legal and up to standard, and, particularly, that they are safe and secure. The process is thereby quite different to processes of development consent that rarely include post-development inspections for compliance and that instead represent a consent to proceed rather than a warrant of standards achieved. As a result, the regulations setting out construction requirements will tend to be technical in nature, although they are likely to combine both prescriptive requirements (open to only limited interpretation) alongside broader performance objectives (open to negotiation).

Few academic studies have examined these sorts of tools, although those that have tend to identify the exponential expansion and increasing complexity of the matters addressed by warranting in recent decades, extending coverage from an early concern around issues of health and safety onto a larger 'quality' remit, most notably around climate change (Fischer & Guy 2009). From the standpoint of architectural regulation in the United Kingdom, Rob Imrie and Emma Street argue this "reorientation of regulation towards new regulatory objects" raises questions around the legitimacy of such control and ultimately over "what the

appropriate level of state direction is or ought to be to ensure the (re)production of good quality design" (2011: 280). These questions flow through all the formal tools of design governance and throughout this book.

Informal Tools, or Tools without Teeth

Indirect Design Governance

If the reality of design governance across the world is defined by processes that remain strongly wedded to tools of control, supported by allied guidance and incentive processes that are focussed almost entirely on underpinning the control function, then design governance will remain a largely technocratic and reactive process. Many have argued, for example, that this has too often been the dominant practice in the United Kingdom, where proactive guidance tools have been usurped by generic policy and crude standards applied in a reactive manner (Farrell 2014: 83). Because formal processes will always be defined within and limited by the legislative frameworks within which they are created (and by the minds of the politicians and technocrats who draft them), it may be that informal, non-statutory means are ultimately required to break through the tried and tested, but all too often unsatisfactory ways of doing things.

Returning to Lester Salamon's view that the neoliberal era has brought with it a proliferation in the tools available to government, he also argues that many of these 'new' tools share an important characteristic in common: "They are highly indirect. They rely heavily on a wide assortment of third parties—commercial banks, private hospitals, social service agencies, corporations, universities, day-care centres, other levels of government, financiers, and construction firms—to deliver publicly financed services and pursue publicly authorized purposes." For him, "the upshot is an elaborate system of third-party government in which crucial elements of public authority are shared with a host of non-governmental or other-governmental actors." Consequently, they also involve sharing with third-party actors a key governmental function: "the exercise of discretion over the use of public authority and the spending of public funds" (Salamon 2002: 2). Returning also to the distinction made in Chapter 1 between tools and administration, administration represents the other side of the tools coin in that an administrative infrastructure, appropriate procedures, and the full range of human, financial, and skills resources are required to operationalise any sort of tool. In this respect, it is not just the tools that are increasingly indirect, but also their administration.

John Delafons identifies a typology of 'aesthetic control' (1994: 14–17).[12] Whilst this mixes tools with administration, by stripping out the tools-only categories,[13] a three-part typology of design administration remains:

- The Regulatory Mode (the traditional municipal control of design through regulatory means).
- The Authoritative Intervention (appointing an 'independent' or at least arm's-length and apolitical body to take on the 'design' function).
- The Proprietorial Injunction (involving the complete abstinence from public design governance in favour of private landowners and developers controlling themselves).

More simply, these three systems might be characterised as 'traditional', 'indirect', and the 'private' administration of design. Whilst completely private processes fall outside of the scope of the definition of design governance established in Chapter 1 (and thereby outside the scope of this book), the application of indirect modes of governance and the sorts of tools this gives rise to offer a potentially rich source of innovation and a means to move beyond the traditional forms of design governance that have so often given rise to substandard outcomes. The work and experience of the Commission for Architecture and the Built Environment (CABE) in England from 1999 to 2011 represents perhaps the most important experiment (globally) within this mode of working.

The CABE Experiment, Rethinking Design Governance

Whilst CABE clearly operated within and was wholly funded by the public sector, it was detached from national and local government and from 1999 operated as a company limited by guarantee, only attaining a statutory status in 2006 as a non-departmental public body (NDPB). Yet, despite its status and the various provisions included in legislation and incrementally in policy about its role (see Chapter 4), CABE operated throughout its existence in the absence of any regulatory framework through which to achieve its ends, and from 2006 with only the most general statutory powers giving it the right to exist and to conduct operations. It never possessed the right to make decisions that would be binding on others.

Despite this, CABE can be viewed as part of an attempt, through active government, to improve design quality in the built environment, thereby addressing the need stemming from the perceived failure of both market and state to fully recognise the importance of good design. Although the legal successor to the Royal Fine Art Commission (RFAC) established in 1924 by a Conservative administration (Chapter 3), CABE represented a perfect example of Tony Blair's New Labour government at work, namely a combination of "economic neo-liberalism with a commitment to active government" (Hall 2003). CABE spent, for example, considerable time and resources placing its arguments in the context of the market-of creating economic value-although, given the absence of any statutory powers or regulatory framework with which to achieve its ends, the organisation might be seen as the 'David' of design against the 'Goliath' of the market.

Indirect Administration to Informal Tools

Seen in this light, CABE was clearly in what Hall (2003) classified as a subordinate role to the market, an influencer rather than a regulator, and reliant on developing, refining, and deploying a range of pre-existing and newly developed informal tools to achieve its ends of improving design. Commenting more broadly on the new forms and tools of public administration, Salamon argues that the proliferation of new tools has created new opportunities to tailor public action to a much wider range of public problems, and in the process to enlist a diverse assortment of governmental and non-governmental actors to meet those needs (2002: 6). At the same time, he suggests, this development has vastly complicated the task of public management: "Instead of a single form of action, public managers must master a host of different 'technologies' of public action, each with its own decision rules, rhythms, agents, and challenges. Policymakers must likewise weigh a far more elaborate set of considerations in deciding not just 'whether', but also 'how' to act, and then how to achieve some accountability for the results. And the public at large must somehow find ways to make sense of the disparate actions that are then taken on their behalf by complex networks of public and private actors."

Whilst CABE was not the first national body in England to have responsibility for design in the built environment, building as it did on three quarters of a century of RFAC experience, in reality that experience had been extremely narrow and largely focussed on design review of an informal and purely advisory kind. Consequently, although the mission of the RFAC extended into the neoliberal era with its proliferation of governance tools and approaches, cossetted in its headquarters in St James's Square, those trends largely passed the old Commission by. As a consequence, CABE represented the first UK-based organisation of its type to fully embrace the new governance landscape, and a willingness to experiment with the range of new informal tools available to it became one of its defining features.

In the terms Schuster and colleagues (1997) set out to classify the generic tools of government, CABE was denied access to: ownership and operation; regulation; and establishment, allocation, and operation tools and the use of incentives (and disincentives) was severely limited by CABE's relatively modest core funding (despite 'financial assistance' being listed as one of its legitimate roles in the 2005 Clean Neighbourhoods and Environment Act[14]). For the most part, CABE operated within the final category of tools—'information'—which Mark Schuster (2005) defines very broadly using the contrasting examples of 'listing' historic assets and informal design review, both of which operate through singling out an asset or project and publicising its strengths and weaknesses in an authoritative manner in order to inform subsequent decision-making. Within their meta-category of shaping instruments, Steve Tiesdell and Phil Allmendinger (2005) include 'generating information or promoting coordination' alongside 'capacity-building', the latter encompassing education and training, exchanging information, and building networks of support and expertise. All can be encompassed within the informal group of tools.

The Australian Public Service Commission brings these types together into a category it calls 'Education and information instruments', and whilst its analysis does not relate specifically to design, its conclusions are insightful: "This category of instruments cannot usually be relied upon in isolation, particularly where there is a substantial tension between public and private interests," as there often is in urban development (2009: 9). Instead, "A key function of these types of instruments is to internalise the desired behaviour into corporate and individual decision-making." This, they argue, is especially important in order for governments to successfully address some of the most complex policy problems such as climate change or obesity. The pursuit of design quality certainly falls into this category.

A Typology of Informal Design Governance Tools

Reflecting the limitations enshrined in its foundation, which in effect largely restricted its operations to the education and information field, CABE worked hard to expand the scope and effectiveness of the tools available to it. Consequently, rather than adopting any pre-existing tools frameworks, it makes sense to simply categorise the activities of CABE in order to conceptually organise the various tools of informal design governance. Few attempts have anyway been made to systematically classify tools of the urban design process, and typically when this has been done discussion of informal tools has been omitted altogether or treated in isolation.[15]

In large part, CABE focussed its efforts on advising others, generating advice, disseminating it, using it to argue for particular outcomes, or offering it directly to project teams. The analytical framework in 2.17 was

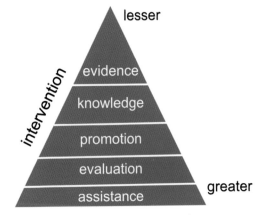

Figure 2.17 The informal tools, by level of intervention

produced by applying an expanded version of these roles to a continuum of intervention, from lesser to greater (hands-off to increasingly hands-on), or what Bruce Doern and Richard Phidd (1983) rather pejoratively refer to as the 'degree of intrusiveness' of instruments. In this framework, interventions range from: the gathering of evidence to the dissemination of knowledge, through the active promotion of design as a cause to the 'detached' evaluation of design quality, and finally to direct assistance with projects (at the coalface) and/or with processes of design. Through the lens of CABE's work, these categories are discussed extensively over the next few chapters, so here they are only very briefly introduced by means of unpacking each category to reveal the sorts of tools it contains.

Evidence

The informal tools start with gathering an evidence base about design and design process as a means to: support arguments about the importance of design, underpin advice about what works and what does not, and monitor progress towards particular policy objectives or to gauge the state of the built environment. The search for evidence to underpin policy represented a cornerstone of the New Labour project, with the 'third-way' politics of the time reinforced by a determination to move away from ideology as the driving force for governmental action and instead to support 'what works', preferably on the basis of evidence (Solesbury 2001: 2). Thus the Cabinet Office argued that government "must produce policies that really deal with problems, [and] that are forward-looking and shaped by evidence rather than a response to short-term pressures" (1999: 15). At the heart of this policy turn was research, but in design terms evidence also extends to audit.

Research

From fundamental questions around the nature of design or place quality, to pragmatic issues concerning the design and/or development process, research as a tool of design governance is potentially powerful because our understanding of the designed built environment and the processes that shape it is often crude

and/or incomplete whilst the processes that shape it are complex and profound in their impact. As Matthew Carmona has argued, policy makers, both professional and political, and the interest groups who influence them will be amongst the key audiences for (and commissioners of) urban design research (2014a: 8). Therefore, whilst "by its very nature research should be 'cutting edge', in the sense that it is generating new knowledge or information about a subject", this "does not imply that every piece of research will be paradigm changing". It is equally likely to "reflect on particular dimensions of professional practice, policy or design, with a view to incrementally improving them".

Audits

Audits might also be known as appraisal, diagnosis, analysis, or by a range of other names and are fundamentally about understanding the character and/or qualities of place. Typically this would apply to local areas at the scale of an urban quarter/district/neighbourhood or alternatively at the site-specific scale in relation to a particular development. Sometimes it extends up from there to the scale of the municipality at the city/regional scale, and exceptionally even countrywide (Carmona et al. 2010: 302–306). Methods will also vary, from those primarily focussed on the physical built environment or aspects of it (such as heritage assets), to those concerned with natural form and landscape, to issues of the social public realm and/or perceptions about place incorporating community engagement. And, of course, mixes of all of these. Audit might precede development in order to understand the qualities of place for which development needs to have regard, or may be concerned with taking the 'state of the nation' at any point in time in relation to particular design/development practices (such as those concerning the quality of housing design), or simply as regards the overall quality of the built environment.

Knowledge

Whilst evidence, including through research or audit, forms the basis of knowledge, and is intrinsically of value in itself to inform practice and debate, its proactive use will depend on how it is utilised in combination with the other tools in the remaining informal categories and in relation to the formal tools already discussed. It should, for example, underpin the range of knowledge tools, the main purpose of which is to spread knowledge about the nature of good design, good and poor practice, and why it matters. In so doing, these tools can help to deal with a deficit in design awareness that, in the United Kingdom, the Urban Design Skills Working Group argued extends across the demand and supply sides:

> First, on the demand side we must reawaken the public's interest in the quality of the spaces outside their own front doors, on the journey to work and in the places they visit. Adequate community participation and the stimulation of grassroots involvement in the development process are essential. Second, on the supply side, we must increase the skills base available to design and produce better places. Third, we must reach a position where local authorities make use of those skills in administering the planning process and other statutory functions. Fourth, we must bridge the divide between different disciplines concerned with the built environment.
>
> (2001: 7; see Chapter 4)

These are all essentially knowledge issues in relation to which a number of key tools exist.

Practice Guides

The term *guidance* has already been used to refer to the sorts of design guidance produced as part of formal design governance processes and which is used to guide the design of development in particular areas or in relation to defined development projects. Here the term *practice guide* refers to informal guidance on generic aspects of practice with the intention of sharing best practice, either in process or outcomes. Such guides can be produced by a range of organisations—public, professional, charitable, or private—at the national or local level, and are typically produced in order to disseminate the accumulated wisdom of particular groups or the insights garnered from research. In the United Kingdom, the most influential practice guide of this type was *By Design*, published in 2000 by the government[16] as a guide to the treatment of design within the planning system (see Chapter 4). The seven objectives

of urban design—character, continuity and enclosure, quality of the public realm, ease of movement, legibility, adaptability, and diversity—were very widely adopted in local policy, and in the guide, they sat alongside advice on their implementation through planning DETR & CABE.

Case Studies

Whilst practice guides act to distil desired practice and to present it in a digestible form for others to follow, a rawer form of knowledge and yet, arguably, a more directive one is the published case study, or compilation of case studies. These are designed to identify and share best practice in order to inspire others to follow the examples given and are more directive in the sense that they move beyond generic principles to advancing actual models of 'best practice'. Whilst such (typically online) resources of case studies are often written against a common structure to allow cross-comparison, and more often than not are written with a particular spin to bring out key arguments, it is left to readers to digest them and to interpret the relevance to their own given situation. Examples include *Design Case Studies* for residential development maintained by the State Government of Victoria in Australia[17] (2.18) or *Great Place Archive* of the Academy of Urbanism in the United Kingdom.[18]

Education/Training

Even more directive again are face-to-face educational or training programmes for professionals and politicians in order to educate key decision-makers about the importance of design and to up-skill those involved in delivery. This category encompasses both formal educational programmes (from school to university) and post-professional training as part of continuing professional development, and is provided by schools, universities, professional institutes, private, and non-for-profit providers. In the United States, for example, New York's Project for Public Spaces offers an ongoing training programme directed in large part at key decision-makers across North America,[19] whilst in the United Kingdom, since 2000, Open-City has developed a range of resources for use in schools to engage children with the built environment and to raise

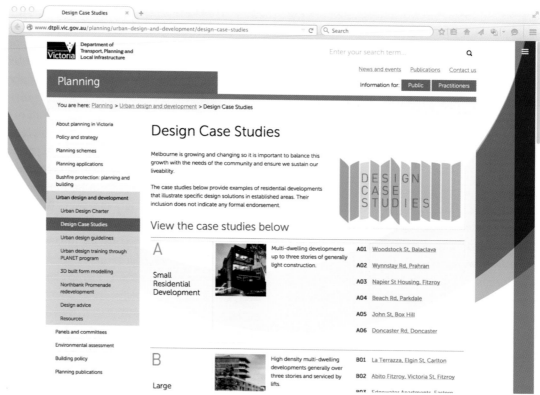

Figure 2.18   *Design Case Studies* for residential development, State Government of Victoria

Source: Department of Environment, Land, Water & Planning—Victoria State Government

awareness about design quality.[20] Ultimately education and training is about raising awareness and ambitions, but also about increasing capacity within the formal processes of design governance in order to better inform and shape the decision-making environment.

Promotion

Knowledge tools by their nature will have an advocacy role, helping to advance particular normative aspirations for outcomes and/or processes based on evidence or practical experience, including the accumulated wisdom from the sorts of evaluation or assistance processes still to be discussed. Promotion tools will also rely on these same sources of information to make the case for design quality in a more proactive manner. Instead of waiting for organisations and individuals to seek out knowledge, these tools take the knowledge to them, seeking to package key messages in a manner that engages attention and wins over hearts and minds to the importance of good design. Another means to

describe these processes might be proactive communication (as opposed to passive communication through means such as on-line case studies). Evert Vedung and Frans van der Doelen (1998) call these 'sermons', or "Efforts to use the knowledge and data available to governments to influence consumer and producer behaviour in a direction consistent with government aims and wishes" and/or to "gather information in order to further their aims and ambitions". In the case of design, they are about persuading and exhorting particular behaviours that benefit good design, sometimes face to face and sometimes not. The category encompasses four key tools:

Awards

The least interventionist form of promotion is the design award. Architectural design awards come in many varieties, from high-profile international prizes such as the Pritzker Architecture Prize, to national awards such as the Prime Minister's Better Public

Building Award in the United Kingdom,[21] to awards given by local governments where categories tend to distinguish projects typologically, for example: urban design, landscape, new building, conservation, minor development. At this spatial scale, the awards are explicitly design governance tools in the sense that they help to set aspirational design standards and identify exemplar schemes in particular localities. They also generate local publicity for good design, help to critically reflect on regulatory processes, and offer encouragement to those who have achieved high standards of design (Biddulph et al. 2006). At the same time, they are retrospective, looking back at projects after they are completed, and have no actual direct bearing on how projects are conceived. Whilst there has been little research on design awards to determine whether they actually have an impact in driving up design standards, and almost none on local design awards, the limited available research indicates (perhaps unsurprisingly) that assessment of outcomes depends on who you ask, with, for example, designers prioritising appearance whilst users are more concerned with functionality (Vischer & Cooper Marcus 1986: 81). Furthermore, the criteria adopted for award schemes will typically be in line with the concerns of the professional groups to which an award is targeted. "Giving awards is not, therefore, an unbiased and value-free process" (Biddulph et al. 2006: 60).

Figure 2.19 Early 'Keep Britain Tidy' poster (used with the kind permission of charity Keep Britain Tidy)

Campaigns

This tool represents the very essence of promotion in the form of the active marketing of particular ideas or issues to selected groups. Government has long used campaigns to impart key messages such as the 'Your Country Needs You' or 'Keep Calm and Carry On' campaigns of the British government during the First and Second World Wars. Today, governments use campaigns to influence behaviour on everything from drink driving, to entitlement to benefits, to health issues, and across an increasing range of media: poster, broadcast, print, virtual, and social. Whilst many government campaigns are aimed at a general audience, such as the long-running 'Keep Britain Tidy' campaign to discourage littering in public spaces (2.19), others are more specialist and aimed at particular decision-makers, influencers, or consumers. The latter include

the extensive use of place marketing by government regeneration agencies (and others) to encourage inward investment into, or to change attitudes about, particular localities. As these later examples show, over the years a subset of such campaigns has a clear built environment focus.

Advocacy

Even the best campaigns are likely to be hit and miss in their impact. More direct will be forms of advocacy that attempt to seek out and convince key individuals and/or audiences about the value of a particular approach or set of objectives. Processes of the private sector lobbying government and its various agencies are already part of the modern political landscape. Equally, different arms/agencies of government are not immune to lobbying other parts, whilst politicians and officials are active in advocating for particular policy positions amongst a wide range of private, professional, and not-for-profit groups. This occurs both publicly, for example through events and conferences, and privately behind closed doors. Organisations can even establish internal advocacy roles within existing structures as permanent advocates for particular issues. In the United Kingdom between 1997 and 2013, both the New Labour and subsequent coalition governments were particularly keen on such mechanisms, creating more than 300 'Tsars' for everything from fuel poverty to children (Levitt 2013). At the local level, the tenure of Sir Terry Farrell as the Design Champion for Edinburgh from 2004 to 2009 represented a design-focussed advocacy role; in that case, an unpaid advisory appointment designed to "shift the city from planning being driven by reactive development control to proactive and creative city making" (Farrell 2008: 3).

Partnerships

Like marketing, advocacy may or may not find a receptive audience. An alternative is to seek to establish a formal or informal partnership with allied organisations who can become partners in helping to deliver a particular agenda, the eventual aim being to construct a wider coalition of interests that both brings together key stakeholders involved in delivery and extends responsibility. In the United Kingdom, a classic example is the typical separation of planning and highways functions in local government, sometimes into different departments of the same authority and sometimes across different tiers of local government (e.g. district and county), despite both being collectively responsible for key elements of local place, notably streets. In such circumstances, a partnership around common agendas, including design quality, could help to deliver more effective and more efficient services, and better outcomes for both parties. It would be one step on the road to organising the functions of local government "around issues and objectives, rather than on the basis of organisational convenience, traditional sectors or professional loyalties" (Carmona et al. 2003: 163). Other sorts of partnership might occur between government departments or agencies, or between government and private or third sector service providers, for example, between government and the Tidy Britain

Group who, since the 1950s, has run the Keep Britain Tidy campaign already referred to.

Evaluation

The final two categories move from a more general focus on issues to the evaluation of particular projects or places. Reflecting this, the degree of intervention steps up as, whilst still informal, these tools have the potential to shape particular outcomes rather than just the decision-making environment.

The penultimate category—evaluation—contains a series of tools through which judgements are made about the quality of design by a party external to and therefore detached from the design process. This brings us up against a key problematic, the extent to which it is possible to systemise such evaluation. Commenting on the problem of 'measuring quality' across governmental services, John Beckford asserts: "Not everything can be proceduralized, in the service sector" (2002: 278). Instead, he argues, "The only way to solve the problem of quality in the service sector is to employ trained, educated staff, and grant them the freedom necessary to do the job." Applying this logic to the challenges of measuring quality in planning, Matthew Carmona and Louie Sieh make the important distinction between, on one hand, the need to be selective in what is being measured during complex processes such as design in order to make such tasks manageable and the resulting assessments useful, whilst on the other, avoiding the trap of being reductionist (2004: 300). For them, the key means to balance easily measurable (simple or objective) and less measurable (complex or subjective) dimensions of design was 'expert judgement', and in one way or another even the most systemised tools in this section rely on that.

Indicators

Indicators seek to measure and represent aspects of performance in a manner that can be easily understood and used. There are many types of indicators, but typically they seek to simplify complex phenomena to a range of easily and concisely communicable measures. Whilst this is their key strength, it is also a major weakness: "because complex situations are poorly described by simple means", leading potentially to distortion, to misrepresentation, and to the danger of measuring only that which can be easily measured (Carmona & Sieh 2004: 81). This has certainly been the case in British planning for decades, where highly reductionist performance indicators for the speed of processing planning applications have often been used as the sole indicator of 'planning quality' instead of any measure of the quality of outcomes. Yet indicators in a wider sense need not be simple quantitative tools; they can also be conceived as developmental tools, designed to diagnose qualities, rather than simply to represent them. *Placecheck,* devised and developed in 1998 by the short-lived Urban Design Alliance (UDAL) (see Chapters 3 and 4), represents a case in point. In essence, the tool is an evaluative framework for local place quality that begins with three simple questions and then spirals up to a range of more detailed and penetrating questions that communities and others may ask in order to appraise the quality of their local environment. *Placecheck* is therefore a structured thinking and appraisal tool, one that indicates both qualities of place and suggested actions for improvement.[22]

Design Review (Informal)

The practice of design review has already been discussed in connection with formal processes of development consent. In addition to these formal processes, design review has developed as a practice outside of statutory regulatory frameworks as a means of evaluating projects through impartial expert opinion in order to offer critique and (preferably) constructive advice to development teams. Used in this manner, informal design review should be an improvement tool, focussed on adding value to developments prior to being submitted for regulatory consents. Reflecting on the work of the Boston Civic Design Commission, which "was created to be advisory and was given no direct decision-making power of its own", Mark Schuster asks how more subtle forms of influence can be wielded through such informal panels:

> Does a design review board function like a jury, hearing the various sides of a story and then deciding on the appropriate outcome? Or does it function more like a peer panel review, in which people with

specialized knowledge recognize and encourage quality in others' work? . . . Or does it function like a building inspector, checking adherence to a set of rules? Is it a mediator arbitrating between other people's knowledge, or is it an expert decision maker, deciding an issue based on its own knowledge? Or perhaps it acts as a facilitator, with an emphasis on inclusion and equity-related issues through public participation . . . [or] as a professional support group . . . for the designer, providing leverage against the developer. . . . Viewing a design review board as a planning consultant may also be appropriate in getting a project through the political process and mitigating concern from the community. . . . Along the same lines, in an ironic way, a design review board may also be an expediter, . . . to help get through the permitting and political process as quickly as possible. [And] . . . perhaps design review functions as an educator . . . to sensitize those engaged in the development process as well as the public more generally to the needs of the public realm and the importance of good design.

(2005: 352–353)

For Schuster, it is not unreasonable to understand such tools as operating in many different ways, often simultaneously, and that the informal processes of bringing the project into dialogue with the community are more important than that of imposing any particular criteria on a scheme (2005: 353). The nature of the community, in this regard, will vary depending on the process, but as likely as not will be the narrow professional one involved in a scheme, rather than the community at large.

Certification

Whilst informal design review will typically result in oral and/or written advice, going a stage further are tools that provide certification of some sort for schemes on the basis of review. Such tools do not (typically) proffer any formal consent or warrant, and instead offer projects the status of having reached a defined and verified benchmark of quality, for example for energy efficiency, sustainability, accessibility, and so forth. Biddulph and colleagues (2006) include such tools in their analysis of awards (see earlier), classifying them as, 'Bench mark awards' or 'Category awards' on the

Figure 2.20 In 2011, the new UNISON headquarters on Euston Road, London, achieved a BREEAM 'Excellent' rating

Source: UNISON

basis that a stamp or kite mark is 'awarded' for the achievement of a defined standard, whilst pointing out that this form of award (if award it is) is the easiest to obtain as judgement is against the standard and not on the basis of choosing the best amongst a peer group of projects. This very distinction, however, justifies separation of certification into a separate category as a more proactive form of evaluative tool with a more extensive outreach beyond the exceptional schemes granted awards. In fact, certification schemes such as BREEAM in the United Kingdom (2.20) or LEED in the United States constitute highly sophisticated toolkits of: criteria, evaluation frameworks, assessment panels, and certification processes. Developers and others actively use them to market their projects, and local authorities and others employ them to define aspirational targets that developers are encouraged to reach.

Competitions

The final evaluation tool is the design competition. These come in many shapes (open, limited, invited) and sizes (local, national, international) across two fundamental types: conceptual (ideas only) and project (relating to a tangible building project) (Lehrer 2011: 305–307). They are informal tools because, whilst they may inform or even be part of a formal design governance process (for example leading to a development consent), a requirement to conduct competitions is rarely mandated by the state.[23] Commentators generally view the competition as an effective means of driving better design outcomes, not least because they start from the fundamental recognition that for any design problem, "there is not just one but a number of approaches with different merits and drawbacks" (Lehrer 2011: 316). Jack Nasar even goes so far as to argue that countries with the highest quantity of architectural competitions also exhibit the greatest quality of architectural design (1999: 6). Steven Tolson, by contrast, recognises that competitions mean different things to different stakeholders and are not simply design tools: to the designer, competitions are about identifying the best most creative design solutions, for the estates surveyor, they are about attracting the best offer price for land, and for the politician, they may be about identifying the most equitable and democratic process (2011: 159). They might also be about raising the profile of a development, choosing a developer (as well as a designer), encouraging public engagement (in judging), or about simply stimulating ideas and debate. As a design governance tool, competitions can involve the public sector in a hands-on or hands-off manner, although, as Tolson counsels, "to achieve a good competition there needs to be a clear understanding of more than just matters of design, otherwise the developers will not be interested and will not engage" (2011: 160). Ultimately the most creative proposal may also be the most expensive and unviable, revealing a key conundrum when working with this tool.[24]

Assistance

The final category is also the most hands-on and proactive because, effectively, it engages the public sector directly in the process of design. This may, and often does, happen as part of the sorts of semi-formal pre-application consultations that precede the depositing of a formal proposal for development consent, for example when a public official (planner, or specialist urban design, heritage, highways, or landscape professional) gets his or her pens out and begins to work with the applicant to shape a scheme into a more acceptable form. The relevant authorities often encourage such processes in order to try and ensure first, a better outcome, second, a more efficient processing of the formal application for consent once it is made, and, third, to help develop a more trusting and collaborative relationship between applicant and authority (Carmona et al 2003: 192–193). Beyond these ad hoc and essentially reactive processes, however, are more proactive opportunities to engage directly in projects or in otherwise shaping the decision-making environment within which design occurs. Two tools feature here.

Financial Assistance

Providing direct financial assistance to private or third sector projects is perhaps the most significant form of intervention short of the public sector actually designing and developing projects itself, and typically this will occur through formal incentivisation processes as already discussed. Resources can also be transferred via less direct means, in the process helping to buy an influential seat at the table of whichever organisation or initiative is being assisted. In the United Kingdom, for example, for many years large numbers of conservation officer posts in local authorities (particularly in London following the abolition of the Greater London Council in 1986) were directly funded by English Heritage (now Historic England), the national heritage agency (Grover 2003: 52). The posts not only increased local capacity to deal with heritage matters, but also helped to spread the ethos and practices of the funding organisation to the local authorities involved. Resourcing of this nature is most likely to be used to fund specialist staffing capacity (as in the example), although it might also be used to fund a wide range of other organisational and/or project needs. For example, local government in England has a wide range of so-called General Powers of Competence to proactively protect and enhance locally important place-based assets, facilities, and qualities, such as pubs, post offices, and green spaces, or to support relevant local organisations to do this work for them.[25]

Enabling

The final informal tool is enabling, or direct targeted expert assistance on projects. In this regard, there has long been a tradition of national groups, agencies, and institutes offering advice and expertise to localities, in the United Kingdom dating at least back to the Architectural Advisory Panels that the Royal Institute of British Architects (RIBA) established from the 1920s onwards. These were formed in local authorities across the country and eventually covered a fifth of councils (Punter 2011: 183). More recently (since 1987), the Princes' Foundation for Building Community has used its Enquiry by Design method to fill gaps in knowledge locally and to enable local authorities, communities, and others (internationally) to understand the nature of places and their development opportunities.[26] Today, when local governments or other public organisations require expert assistance that they don't already possess, they will tend to commission it through the market, or, given the likely costs of such consultancy, may decide to go without. An alternative is a collaborative model where shared resources are pooled to deliver expertise where it is not needed or not affordable on a permanent basis. This was the case in the English

County of Essex where, for forty years,[27] the County Council offered the services of its highly regarded design team to its fifteen constituent district councils for urban, architectural, and highways design (although not all of them used it—Hall 2007: 86). Whilst design advice is sought and obtained through all these means, arguably the most effective forms of enabling will have an educational as well as a project delivery purpose. They will avoid parachuting in of expertise to address a defined and limited problem such as a particular masterplan, policy framework, or community engagement exercise, and will instead engage local professional staff, politicians, and others in a manner that leaves a lasting legacy of improved skills and expertise to address the problem next time.

Community Participation (as Symptomatic of a Larger Problem)

Before closing this discussion of informal tools, it is important to deal with the issue of community participation as it relates to the governance of design. Whilst the act of community participation in the process of shaping places could be viewed as a separate 'tool' of government, in fact, forms of engagement feature in connection with a range of the formal and informal design governance tools already discussed. For this reason, participation is not singled out as a tool in its own right, but is instead treated as an activity underpinning others, most notably:

- Guidance—by way of direct participation in the production of design guidance in order to improve its content, encourage unanimity of vision, avoid discord, and ultimately improve outcomes.
- Control—through interested parties making inputs into concrete development proposals as they come forward through regulatory regimes, either through tokenistic processes of consultation or more positively and influentially through the sorts of deeper engagement with communities that are possible in the pre-consenting phases of the development process, for example through charrettes and other participatory mechanisms.
- Evidence—as part of processes of understanding places through revealing the aspirations and preoccupations of communities either in isolation

(focussing on particular communities and/or places) or as part of larger audit processes in order to help to shape public policy responses to questions of place quality.
- Knowledge—through targeted education/training for communities directly engaged in the development of design/development/planning propositions, for example the sorts of community-led neighbourhood planning processes that are now a feature of British planning and that are supported (in some cases) by a limited package of centrally funded technical assistance.
- Assistance—in order to raise aspirations for design amongst local communities and stakeholders as part of long-term efforts to reshape the decision-making environment, including through local enabling activities.

The first and second are pragmatic and (if done well) inherently democratic responses to encourage citizen involvement in the design of projects and/or places as part of formal urban governance processes. Typically their use is prescribed in legislation linked to planning or urban regeneration, although the reality may amount to little more than tokenistic gestures towards involvement. The remainder sit within the informal sphere of design governance and are therefore, usually, discretionary.

Whether formal or informal, most commentators argue that participation is inherently desirable, and a wide range of tried and tested methods are now available to conduct it (Hou 2011; Wates 2014). This, however, should not imply that participation is always desirable in relation to design governance tools, or necessarily that deeper and more immersive forms are always superior to those less so (Biddulph 1998: 45). In the case of design guidance, for example, whilst the explicit focus on physical design offers something tangible for communities to engage with (far more so than some other seemingly intangible planning concerns[28]), research into the use and utility of design codes has revealed that non-professional audiences struggle to understand and engage with the more technical types of guidance. As a consequence, Matthew Carmona and Jane Dann argue "the masterplan provides the correct vehicle for community engagement, a process in which codes and other forms of detailed design guidance can play only a supportive role" (2006: 43). This is because whilst design standards, policy, and coding are likely to have significant impacts on how places are shaped, it is only the various types of design frameworks which set out graphically and spatially a future vision for particular places, that move beyond the abstract to the tangible.

The low levels of public engagement with many place-focussed regulatory processes is in part explained by this communications gap.[29] So is the potential and power of design frameworks to bridge the gap if shaped by or at least subjected to early, meaningful, and fundamental community participation through charrettes and other locationally specific engagement exercises (Walters 2007: 163–181). Unfortunately, the lack of positive engagement of communities across the formal tools spectrum is symptomatic of the larger problem, already discussed, concerning the overreliance on standards and/or policy, and subsequently on processes of control, as well as to a general failure to positively shape the decision-making environment by other formal and informal means that precede the act of control.

Conclusion

In this chapter, the nature of tools in government has been explored and related to the particularities of design. The dominant 'formal' tools of design governance have been set out in some detail, followed by a shorter introduction to the 'informal' tools of design governance which constituted the armoury of CABE in its role as English national champion for design quality in the built environment.

Whilst CABE was clearly influential, its powers were actually severely limited and the organisation never had access to some of the most powerful design governance tools in the box. Instead, CABE represented a unique experiment exploring the use of informal 'tools without teeth' to advance its design agenda. As much has already been written (outside of this book) about the use of formal tools of design governance, Part III of this book examines, in depth, the softer forms of informal or non-statutory tools that CABE adopted or developed during its eleven years, utilising the 'why', 'how', and 'when' of 'process quality' from Chapter 1 to unpack them.

Within the tools of government literature, most studies still focus on the utility of single tools and their use in particular circumstances, rather than on the interrelationships between tools and on the decision-making processes used to distinguish when to use one tool over another (Linder & Peters 1989: 55–56). In the field of design governance, and specifically with regard to the informal tools, the research underpinning this book aimed to address this deficit by exploring the tools used by CABE and their interrelationships.

The demise of CABE represented an important moment and an opportune window through which to take a fundamental look at design governance in England. As has been argued, CABE was a unique experiment of international significance, and to understand the experience, it is necessary to place the story within its wider context: first of the political economy for design policy; second, of the transforming policy landscape within which a concern for design in the built environment fits; and third of the pragmatics and problematics of engaging with this agenda. These dimensions are now explored in Parts II and III of this book.

Notes

1. In reality, urban design is not a linear process at all, but instead a continuum in which stages in the process come around and around again and the shaping of place, knowingly or otherwise, never actually ends (see 1.2).
2. www.planningportal.gov.uk/planning/planningpolicy-andlegislation/currentlegislation/acts; www.pps.org/training/
3. http://planningjungle.com/consolidated-versions-of-legislation/
4. www.gov.uk/government/uploads/system/uploads/attachment_data/file/39821/taylor_review.pdf
5. As preferred by John Delafons because it implies less rigidity (1994: 17).
6. A quality determined by an amalgam of the other factors, including the degree of prescription, governance level, and ambition.
7. Drawing from Lang (1996: 9) and Hall (1996: 8–40).
8. These zones are now added to many ordinances in the United States to allow for the custom zoning and subdivision of property in single ownerships, typically based on a good degree of discretion and much greater flexibility than traditional zoning (Barnett 2011: 215).
9. He suggests, for example, that more than seventy masterplans have been produced for London's Royal Docks.
10. In this case, a new mechanism, a Local Development Order (LDO) (introduced by the 2004 Planning and Compulsory Purchase Act in England), was proposed to

operate alongside design codes. LDOs allow local authorities to extend 'permitted development rights' in designated areas to the sorts of development listed in the Order. In other words, if they comply, then planning permission is automatic.

11. Philip Booth, for example, has argued that studies of zoning in the United States and Europe have revealed that decision-makers are "constantly kicking at the limits that the systems themselves impose" (1999: 43). Thus decision-makers regularly find means and mechanisms to circumvent the constraints of such systems and to give themselves an element of discretion (see the discussion of the New York case later).

12. *Aesthetic control* was a term used in the United Kingdom up until the early 1990s, and reflected (at the time) policy makers' very narrow perspective on the governance of design, namely, one primarily concerned with aesthetics (see Chapter 3).

13. 'The stylistic imperative' (strict style-based zoning/ design review), 'the competitive alternative' (the use of design competitions), and 'the design guidance' (design guidance of various types and levels of sophistication).

14. CABE did give grants to the network of Architecture and Built Environment Centres (ABECs) that emerged in the 2000s and administered the £45 million Sea Change programme in its final years (see Chapter 3). Both of these represented dedicated programmes with ring-fenced resources from government, although CABE was in a powerful position to set the terms of the grant-giving and thereby incentivise particular practices.

15. Carmona and colleagues' framework for public sector urban design (already discussed) goes some way to addressing these concerns, with its category of education and participation, alongside the more formal categories of policy, regulation, and management, and the cross-over categories of diagnosis and design (2010: 297). Another can be found in the five meta-categories of the New Zealand Urban Design Toolkit: research and analysis, community participation, raising awareness, planning and design, and implementation; although there the intention was to identify the full range of urban design tools rather than those relating to design governance. In common with much analysis of urban design, this mixes formal with informal tools (Ministry for the Environment 2006).

16. Jointly badged by CABE.

17. www.dtpli.vic.gov.au/planning/urban-design-and-development/design-case-studies

18. www.academyofurbanism.org.uk/awards/great-places/

19. www.pps.org/training/

20. www.open-city.org.uk/education/index.html

21. Covering everything from individual buildings to large infrastructure projects.

22. www.placecheck.info

23. There are a few exceptions to this, for example the French state mandates a design competition for public buildings over a specified cost. In so doing, it builds on the Beaux Arts tradition of competitions that France has exported around the world.

24. A classic example was The Cloud project of Will Alsop (see Chapter 4), which won the completion for the Fourth Grace site on Liverpool's historic Pier Head in 2002, but was abandoned in 2004 in the face of spiralling costs and technical uncertainties.

25. www.parliament.uk/business/publications/research/briefing-papers/SN05687/local-authorities-the-general-power-of-competence

26. www.princes-foundation.org/content/enquiry-design-neighbourhood-planning

27. In 2013, the design service was reorganised along with other specialist services into Place Services, a self-financing company owned by Essex County Council and able to trade its services beyond the county. Its urban design staffing is now much reduced.

28. See, for example, Natarajan (2015: 7).

29. Until and unless individuals perceive themselves as directly affected by them (Hester 1999).

PART II

Design Governance in England

CHAPTER 3

The RFAC and Seventy-Five Years of English Design Review, 1924–1999

In Part II of this book, the focus moves from theory to the actual experience of delivering design governance in England over the past ninety or so years. Whilst the recent history of design governance in England has been dominated by the practice, impact, and now legacy of the Commission for Architecture and the Built Environment, CABE built on a much longer legacy of design governance at both local and national scales dating back at least to the evolution of a national planning system from 1909 onwards. A key milestone along this journey was the establishment of the Royal Fine Art Commission (RFAC) in 1924, an organisation that held the mantel of government advisor on design in the built environment for three quarters of a century, compared with the eleven years of its successor organisation, CABE. As the instigator of a national design review service for England and Wales, this chapter draws on archival and documentary evidence to explore the important work and concerns of the RFAC across three broad phases of its history covering its early years, the post-war construction boom, and its final decade and demise in 1999. Analysis of the archives was supplemented by what the limited available literature tells us about the RFAC and by a small number of interviews with key stakeholders with first-hand experience of the operation of the RFAC—those who either worked for it or were reviewed by it. The RFAC forms an important context for understanding

the later approaches and experiences CABE adopted. It also provides valuable insights into the practices of design governance in its own right.

The Early Years—1924–1939

In the Beginning

CABE was established by the Labour government of Tony Blair and wound down by the Conservative-led coalition of David Cameron, and will therefore always be associated with the New Labour political project of the left. However, as argued in Chapter 1, design governance per se is inherently apolitical and it was the Conservative government of Stanley Baldwin that set up CABE's predecessor, the RFAC.[1] The new organisation was chaired by the Conservative peer and politician the 27th Earl of Crawford and Balcarres, under whose leadership the process of reviewing design was first developed and refined.[2]

Whilst, prior to the RFAC, local governments had dabbled in a rather patchy and inconsistent manner with controlling various aspects of design, most notably through the auspices of the Town Planning Schemes enabled by the 1909 Housing and Town Planning Act, and later by a series of city acts such as the 1921 City of Liverpool Corporation Act (Punter 1986: 352–353), the instigation of the RFAC brought with it a new mode of design governance that John Delafons later christened 'The Authoritative Intervention' (see Chapter 2), in other words, seeking external, dispassionate advice from outside experts (1994: 16).

In the aftermath of the First World War, the Permanent Secretary to the Office of Works, Sir Lionel Earle (1912 to 1933), had been charged with responsibility to approve and site numerous war memorials across London. To help him in the task, he set up an unofficial advisory committee. The committee worked well at first, but soon ran into difficulties relating to the depiction of nudity in sculptures commissioned for The Strand and Hyde Park. The hubbub quickly confirmed in Earle's mind the need for a more independent and authoritative source of advice (Youngson 1990: 18–19). The idea was taken up and put to the Cabinet in 1923 with the new body announced in January 1924 covering England and Wales.

The new commission was based in London and had absolutely no powers to either insist that projects were referred to it or to demand that its recommendations were followed, or even that its deliberations were given due consideration; although Lord Crawford expected that statutory powers might eventually be granted (Youngson 1990: 38). Initially its membership encompassed eight (all male) establishment figures, including four architects, one planner, two non-professionals, and an artist, who met under the rather obscure title of the Royal Fine Art Commission.

The Rules of Engagement

The Commission met for the first time on 8 February 1924, after receiving a government grant of £2,000 and amid what appeared to be confusion among the commissioners about the nature of their role. The Commission had to interpret both what the press felt was its duty and what the government had in mind. According to the press (as quoted in RFAC minutes), "the duty of the Commission is not only to prevent blunders but to 'beautify England'" (RFAC 1924b: 2), suggesting a dual mandate to be both active and reactive. But according to its establishing communiqué, the Commission's ability to do this was extremely limited, as it was "purely advisory" and only able to "intervene when invited by some responsible body" (RFAC 1924b: 2).

In order to establish the boundaries of the Commission's involvement with schemes, commissioners elected to establish two guiding principles. First, the RFAC ought be involved 'prima facie' in projects, in other words, from the earliest stages of a design, in order, as they saw it, "to avoid blunder". Second, their role should be limited to critique, in other words, they would not take part in any drafting, instead favouring critical examination and suggestion (RFAC 1924b: 3). Precedence, as with any government institution, became an important determinant of future behaviour, and these principles remained intact throughout the life of the RFAC.

Another early preoccupation related to the professional conduct of commissioners. On this issue, there was an identified tension between the dual role of commissioners as simultaneously professionals in their 'day jobs' and public servants working for gratis for the Commission. Taking the stance that the commissioners should not gain (directly) from their position, the Commission determined it would not get involved in recommending specific professionals to those in need of advice beyond that which the Commission itself could give (RFAC 1924a: 2). Whilst this need to avoid conflicts of interest by clearly separating professional commitments from the work of the Commission survived through to the end of the RFAC, the issue came back to haunt its successor, CABE (see Chapter 4), indicating how precepts based on gentlemanly conduct and precedent that might have been fit for the 1920s increasingly became outmoded as the larger governance context within which the RFAC operated modernised. Despite this, little evidence can be found that the RFAC was ever significantly compromised, and commentators are often at pains to point out how commissioners themselves (despite their eminence as practitioners) frequently fell fowl of Commission judgements (Stamp 1982: 29).

Amenity and Artistic Merit

In the rush to establish the Commission, it had been set up without agreed terms of reference, and it wasn't until April 1924 that an amended Royal Fine Art Commission directive set out its duties:

> To enquire into such questions of:
> Public amenity or of artistic importance, as may be referred to them by H.M. Government, and to report thereon.

Furthermore, to give advice on similar questions when so requested by public or quasi-public bodies where it appears to the Royal Commission that their assistance would be advantageous.

(RFAC 1924c)

This (which also formed the basis for its royal warrant granted in May 1924) inevitably raised issues about how to interpret the key concepts of 'artistic importance' and 'public amenity' that defined the limits of their remit. Whilst there was never a public record of the interpretation of these concepts, early minutes reveal that the commissioners did discuss such matters and quickly agreed not to agree on a defined 'official' interpretation. For example, according to the minutes of its second meeting, discussion took place about the nature of design and about whether any pre-agreed principles should be adopted as approved 'good design'. On this front, it was decided that designs should be critiqued on a case-by-case basis and that no architectural styles or principles would receive special treatment (RFAC 1924a: 2). Again this early precedent informed the work of the Commission for many decades, although the RFAC did, in its later years, become more willing to set out the principles of good design that it expected others to follow. There was also discussion about the extent to which the Commission should concern itself with the viability of schemes; economically and in terms of their engineering. On this the commissioners resolved that as these were not matters of artistic expression, they would not form part of the Commission's recommendations.

Working without Power

The informal status of the RFAC as an organisation without power of intervention left it relatively impotent to deliver on some of the early aspirations. The only patrons of the Commission in its early days were public entities, and when affected by its deliberations private interests could easily ignore its recommendations. In fact, Commission minutes show that no private builders came to the Commission in its first year, and rarely did any seek the Commission's advice in its first decade. This was as intended given the reference to public and quasi-public bodies in the directive

setting up the RFAC, although at the same time it greatly limited its potential impact. Further, although public authorities engaged in development were much more inclined to appear before the Commission than their private counterparts, even public projects could be out of the Commission's reach if project champions did not request advice.

In its early work the Commission might have been accused of being a little timid. Certainly many of its recommendations related to minor changes to public realm proposals, such as its recommendation that the Royal Artillery Memorial be turned to face Grosvenor Place—a proposition accepted without opposition (RFAC 1924d). On another occasion, the RFAC helped advise on the layout of a cemetery and on how University College London's (UCL) Gower Street buildings could best articulate with the surrounding area: UCL's architects preferred a colonnade while the RFAC suggested a walled façade, leaving the Portico as the only columned section. This idea was embraced and is manifest at UCL today (3.1).

Another project was a commission by the Postmaster General for the RFAC to oversee a design process for the country's phone boxes (RFAC 1924e). The existing design (K1) was considered unsatisfactory, and so the Commission organised a competition, collected the designs, and ruled on the winning proposal by Sir Giles Gilbert Scott. This became K2 (3.2), the iconic British red phone box, which set the standard for British phone boxes—K2 to K6—for many years to come.

The issue of bridges was a recurring theme for the Commission in its first few years, and the commissioners' reviews showed a clear and early penchant for venturing outside of their self-imposed boundaries, from architecture to engineering. Their Third Report (RFAC 1928) was dominated by the issue and demonstrated two early concerns that remained with the organisation throughout its existence. The first was with the impact of traffic on towns and the second was the importance of design honesty. The critique echoed a larger concern first raised in the Commission's Second Report to Parliament (RFAC 1926), namely that whilst the Commission strongly favoured the conservation of important townscape qualities (at a time when conservation was still a minority concern) and often argued vociferously for it, it did not favour

Figure 3.1   UCL from Gower Street following the RFAC's recommendations

Source: Matthew Carmona

pastiche and was at pains to point out that no architect should feel obligated to copy the design of buildings they were extending. Instead, they should feel free to explore the latest thinking on design whilst respecting the context within which they were intervening.

Alexander Youngson argues that the Commission was generally successful in its early years, and that this reflected two factors (1990: 36–37). First, its work was almost entirely focussed on a radius of thirty miles from London; a London-centric view that arguably

Figure 3.2   The K2 telephone box, the winning proposal from an RFAC design competition, organised during the RFAC's first year

Source: Matthew Carmona

remained with the organisation throughout its existence. Second, and helping to explain its focus, in these years, it was largely reporting to Sir Lionel Earle, who set it up, and who mainly wanted advice relating to London. Indeed, when advising others, it was arguably less successful, for example when called upon to review a design for South Africa's new embassy on Trafalgar Square which the Commission argued was too dominant and should be subservient to the adjacent National Portrait Gallery. The architect disagreed and effectively ignored the advice.

A Polite Institution

Reflecting generally on the work of the RFAC, John Delafons argues: "For many years the Commission pursued a policy of discretion to the point of virtually abstaining from public comment" (1994: 16). This was certainly very clear in the early years. For John Punter, this tradition continued at least to the 1960s, with the Commission hardly making any impact on wider debates over the merits and purpose of 'aesthetic control', as the governance of design came to be known in the United Kingdom (in part no doubt because of the explicitly aesthetic remit of the RFAC). Instead, he argues, the work of the Commission was "unobtrusive and discreet and generally typical of English polite institutions" (Punter 1986: 354), working inside the system in a quiet and determined way, but not making too much fuss.

Nevertheless, reflecting a growing confidence in its role, in 1933 (just as Sir Lionel Earle was retiring), the royal warrant of the RFAC was extended by adding the significant power to:

> Call the attention of the Government and public authorities to any project or development which may appear to the Commission to threaten amenities of national or public character.

This represented an important innovation as, whilst still working within the system, the revision charged the Commission to become more proactive, giving it the power to initiate enquiries rather than just waiting for matters to be referred to it. The RFAC certainly became increasingly established in the run-up to the Second World War with a wider range of government departments and increasingly local authorities (county, borough, town, and urban) seeking its advice. The result was that between 1935 and 1936, more than 100 enquiries were in progress,[3] but it was in the post-war period and in the context of a more active and interventionalist, if not always very design-sensitive state, that the work of the Commission was to significantly escalate.

The Post-war Commission—1940–1984

Changes in the Commission

As the focus of the nation turned from fighting to rebuilding following the Second World War, and as the state took a new, more active role in everything from planning to building, the scope of the Royal Fine Art Commission's workload expanded greatly, in both its breadth and depth. In terms of breadth the Commission was now reviewing numerous proposals for public realm elements, most notably street lighting and furniture in towns across England. There were also more *art-qua-art* projects, including reviewing centenary stamp options for the postal service, although reviews of actual 'fine art' were relatively rare, for example just four pieces between 1968 and 1971 (RFAC 1971).

At the other end of the scale, planning cities had become a primary concern through the review of detailed masterplans for large areas of towns and cities. This continued until the 1970s when these sorts of grand plans became increasingly rare and non-existent in the 1980s. This emphasis was, to some degree, reflected in the membership of the Commission, with Patrick Abercrombie, William Holford, and Charles Holden all appointed under (from 1943) the chairmanship of the 28th Earl of Crawford, who stepped into his father's footsteps (*The Herald* 1949). Whilst post-war planning was still predominantly a physical planning activity undertaken by architects, the Commission was no longer a purified aesthetics review board.

The Commission was also spurred on by the addition of ancillary powers in 1946 that gave it access to documents, places, and people in the public sector of relevance to its enquiries. As its Twenty-Second Report later proclaimed, the Commission may even "demand entry into a building or onto a site" in pursuit of evidence to carry out its work (RFAC 1985: 12). Although no proof exists that this ever actually occurred, in direct contradiction with its earlier practices, the RFAC soon began to establish a more proactive side to its operations. By the mid-1950s, for example, it was regularly broaching concerns with departments of government or local authorities if it saw a threat to public amenity.

Under this concern for 'public amenity', it set itself against some of the key post-war design and building trends, including what it saw as the misplaced monumentality of many of the new buildings, particularly office blocks, that were being proposed across the country. These, commissioners argued, were usurping the position usually reserved for key civic or religious buildings (RFAC 1952: 4). Certainly this was a period that saw no shortage of monumental thinking, either in architecture or planning.

The Commission and Post-war Planning

Some of the premier planning challenges were faced in London, which had been so heavily bombed during the war. Thus even whilst the war still raged, the City of London requested assistance from the Commission to review its emerging plan. The plan included maps for "traffic flow, land utilisation, war damage, pre-war redevelopment" and "a new traffic scheme", as well as a "draft plan for reconstruction" (RFAC 1943a)—all previously issues that would have been regarded *ultra vires*. The RFAC agreed to review the plan, although it quickly presented something of an existential crisis for the organisation because of the complex interrelationships between the physical city and the innumerable other processes of urban functionality that planning encompassed. In May 1943, the RFAC initially focussed its attention on height and zoning concerns because of their public amenity implications, but in August, commissioners attempted to reduce their consideration to the aesthetic implications of the plan (RFAC 1943b) before, in September, accepting that was impossible and requesting information on traffic and congestion (RFAC 1943c). In fact, the Commission (along with many others) was highly critical of the proposed City plan for focussing too much on traffic at the expense of other layout and architectural concerns (RFAC 1945: 198–199).

By 1950, the Commission was increasingly acting as a champion for planners against projects that seemed incongruous with their plans, most notably (and perhaps unsurprisingly given Patrick Abercrombie's position on the Commission) those that seemed to undermine the *County of London Plan* (3.3) (RFAC 1950: 9). So whilst the Commission set itself clearly in opposition to some of the key precepts of Modernist planning—high buildings and planning for the car—when these seemed to conflict with local contextual factors, this did not extend to all such precepts, and a penchant for clear bold physical planning was amongst the qualities the Commission favoured.

This marked an on-going preference held by the Commission, and as the century wore on and physical planning went out of style, the RFAC increasingly bemoaned the absence of proactivity and vision in modern planning (Punter 1987: 32).[4] Thus as early as 1958, commissioners wrote: "it is not enough to invite private developers to submit their own schemes with little guidance from the Planning Authority, and then to accept the highest bid whatever architecture may happen to have been included" (RFAC 1958: 8). Later they also directed a similar attack at municipal engineers and their highways schemes, arguing that engineers must compromise somewhere between the most economic road placement and the least aesthetically

destructive one (RFAC 1962a: 8). In short, the Commission increasingly abhorred the divorce, as it saw it, of design from the practices of modern planning and highways engineering and was one of the first public agencies in the United Kingdom to recognise the dangers this separation would cause.

Designing the Post-war Architecture

Because of the sheer scale of the Commission's involvement in post-war reconstruction, many details from this period are unclear or lost from the documentary record. For example its reports to Parliament became more and more irregular and included a gap of thirteen years—1971 to 1984—between its Twenty-First and Twenty-Second Reports. As previously, the majority of the Commission's work related to architectural design, and initially to the reconstruction of war-damaged buildings about which the Commission was able to limit itself to aesthetics.

The balance between conservation and the new became a recurring theme of RFAC deliberations, which argued that where restoration of significant buildings was not possible, reconstruction should avoid mimicry and ought instead to follow a comparable style along with the same height and massing (RFAC 1962a: 8). Also, whilst the Commission did not support building in the local vernacular merely to acquire planning permission and believed imitation was generally unacceptable, new buildings should adhere to the qualities of any dominant streetscape (RFAC 1985: 8). By contrast, new landmark buildings were given special attention and much greater latitude as shown in its support for the proposed National Theatre, which the Commission successfully argued should be placed close to the River Thames in order to address the waterfront and maximise public amenity through new riverside public space (RFAC 1951).

At the significant risk of being criticised for being out of step with the times, the Commission continued to demonstrate a strong preference for contextually sensitive design. Famously, plans in the early 1960s to redevelop Euston Station led to a decision to demolish a hugely imposing Doric archway on Euston Road. Although the Commission strongly supported the new station design, an uncompromisingly modern aesthetic, it explained that the arch was critical to the character of the area and contributed greatly to the beauty of the

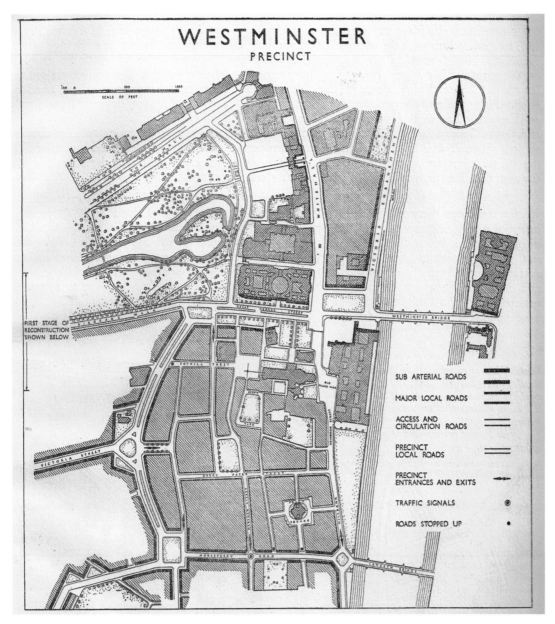

WESTMINSTER
PRECINCT

Figure 3.3 The Commission opposed proposals that undermined the Westminster precinct envisaged in the *County of London Plan*

original station (RFAC 1962b). Whilst the public was on the side of the RFAC and the episode strengthened the burgeoning conservation movement, nationally, British Rail remained unmoved and persuaded Prime Minister Harold Macmillan to sanction the demolition.

The example reflected an on-going battle in which the RFAC was fully engaged, fought between proponents of the most dramatic forms of scorched earth Modernist redevelopment and a desire amongst many

to see a more sensitive response to urban development (RFAC 1962c). As part of a much larger coalition, it won some of these fights, such as the series of proposals to redevelop Piccadilly Circus throughout the 1960s, whilst others were lost. Looking back on this post-war period with the characteristic understatement of the time, the Commission observed: "fundamental improvements to the planning and design of buildings, following the Commission's criticisms, are not uncommon" (RFAC 1985: 25).

Building High

A major dimension of this concern was the issue of building high, which became a dominant theme of the Commission's work from the early 1960s onwards. The Commission was not opposed to tall buildings per se, neither was it opposed to all buildings that deviated from the historic contextual norms; whilst, for example, initially hesitant about plans for Richard Seifert's 1966 Centre Point tower on Oxford Street, commissioners later described it as "having an elegance worthy of a Wren steeple".[5] By contrast, commissioners vehemently opposed a new barracks for the Household Calvary on Hyde Park (later built), about which they wrote to *The Times*: "I hope it will be understood that this letter is not about architectural design. It is about something that matters even more—the basic sizes and shapes of buildings in relation to the places where they are to be built" (reproduced in RFAC 1971: 26).

Out of London a good example of commissioners' approach included opposition to a proposed fourteen-storey hotel on the Eastbourne seafront that threatened to dominate the seafront and block views from many other buildings. To address the problem the RFAC recommended height zones with the intention of staggering building heights from two storeys upwards towards the town centre, immediately behind, thus preventing what they termed 'aberrations' (RFAC 1968). For the Commission, the question of height was a matter of transition and coherence, as well as of the sorts of spaces that high buildings tended to give rise to at their base that: "suffer the whistling drafts set up by the towers above and around them" (RFAC 1971: 13). But as the Eastbourne example demonstrates, they were prepared to engage with the problem of building high in a constructive manner as long as tall buildings were well designed. On that front, they continued to evaluate design proposals on a case-by-case basis, and in so doing, fitted in squarely with the British discretionary tradition with its avoidance of fixed legal entitlements (see Chapter 2).

Taking Sides

On one area the Commission attempted to be strictly dispassionate, that of style. Thus in the Commission's Twenty-Second Report, it pointed out why it always evaluated proposals on a case-by-case basis: "Today there is no consensus about style and there are almost as many styles as there are architects" (RFAC 1985: 25). In this report, the Commission contrasted Quinlan Terry's eighteenth century-inspired Richmond Riverside with the uncompromisingly modern designs for the Lloyds Building in The City, both of which the Commission endorsed, refusing to "take sides" (RFAC 1985: 26) on the matter of style, except where that

Figure 3.4   (i) Richmond Riverside (1984) and (ii) the Lloyds Building (1979), starkly contrasting architecture, both lauded by the Royal Fine Art Commission because of their quality rather than their style

Source: Matthew Carmona

stance compromised its larger concerns around context (3.4). On this issue, and on principle, the Commission did not approve of glass curtain buildings, arguing that "while there may be special situations where the scale-less and dissolving nature of such buildings is an advantage, in the majority of cases it is no help at all" (RFAC 1985: 26).

Yet the slight whiff that the Commission in fact favoured more modern styles never entirely vanished and was probably inevitable given its choice of commissioners, the architects amongst whom were invariably within the orthodox Modernist canon. In 1982, in an interview with the eminent architectural historian Gavin Stamp, the long-standing secretary to the Commission, Sherban Cantacuzino (1979–1994), seemed to confirm this. Stamp (1982) writes: "in a time of cultural anarchy with no generally accepted style the Commission must be democratic to a degree and reflect public attitudes, otherwise it will not command respect. On the other hand, Mr Cantacuzino is certain that 'there are standards of design' and that the Commission should encourage good modern design and reject what is pejoratively dismissed as pastiche—even if it is wanted by the public." For Stamp, there was undoubtedly a paradox there, although for the RFAC, it was simply a matter of supporting what it saw as excellence in style.

Steady as She Goes

In the forty or so years following the war to the end of its report covering the period 1971–1984, the work of the Commission continued to develop and grow, with the RFAC itself reporting that by the end of the era, it was not only advising government departments and local authorities, but also nationalised industries, private companies, developers, and amenity societies throughout England and Wales (RFAC 1985: 13). In today's terms, much of the Commission's work might be described as 'urban design', although the term and the ideas surrounding that discipline had not yet caught up with the Commission, and, perhaps portraying an increasing inability to evolve, never really did.

Instead, as the twentieth century wore on, the RFAC might charitably have been said to have adopted a 'steady as she goes' approach under a series of 'establishment' chairmen such as the career civil servant

Lord Bridges and later the eminent professor of engineering, Sir Derman Christopherson, none of whom believed in rocking the boat. In his memoirs, the architectural writer J.M. Richards, who served as a commissioner (1958–1972), went so far as to argue that the Commission suffered from "an habitual reluctance to come out into the open, to announce its disquiet about any proposal at an early enough stage for public opinion to be effective" (1980: 24).

This along with its now much heavier workload meant that more often than not the Commission tended to work under the radar rather than trying to make a public splash. Others were less kind, with *The Telegraph* describing the RFAC in this period as "a dozy quango[6] which, for many years, could hardly even be bothered to produce an annual report".[7] So whilst in its Twelfth Report of 1954, the Commission complained that it was too often either not consulted at all or only consulted when it was already too late for its advice to be fully considered, by 1971 it was sanguine, arguing that "Sometimes its advice is ignored or overruled, even, perhaps predominantly, by government departments," yet "It should be noted that failures of this sort by the Commission are more newsworthy than its successes." These, it suggested, were by contrast "rarely noticed because the greatest part of its work is done unobtrusively, and more effectively, by reasoning and persuasion" (RFAC 1971: 9). Writing in *The Spectator*, and looking back on the work of the RFAC over its first sixty years, Gavin Stamp agreed: "When I began the research for this article, I was rather minded to see the RFAC as an effete quango, but I now have no doubt that over the years it was usually on the side of the angels and that, had its advice been taken more often, London and England would be the better for it" (1982: 29).

The Later Years—1985–1999

Watchdog or Guard Dog, a New Broom

By the 1980s, after decades of earnest, important, but often invisible work, a gear-change in the role of the RFAC was arguably long overdue. The move was presaged by the appointment as chairman of Norman St John-Stevas MP (later Lord St John of Fawsley), the charismatic Conservative politician and former Leader

of the House of Commons and simultaneously Minister of State for the Arts under Margaret Thatcher (Kavanagh 2012). On awarding him the role, the then Secretary of State for the Environment, Patrick Jenkin, gave him the explicit remit of boosting the profile of the Commission and bringing a greater influence to bear on the patrons of architecture (Chipperfield 1994: 26). St John-Stevas certainly raised the profile of the Commission, although his tenure as chair was not entirely uncontroversial. As reported in his obituary: "It was hoped that his appointment would inject a bit of panache and excitement. It did. . . . But critics accused him of turning it into a personal publicity vehicle (one annual report featured no fewer than six full-colour photographs showing the chairman striking one pose after another in the company of the great and good), and of allowing his own wayward preferences to take precedence over the views of the experts."[8]

Yet despite his style, in the second half of the 1980s, the Commission did begin to significantly influence the course of the country's governance of design through its pronouncements and lobbying (Punter & Carmona 1997: 16). To some degree, given the times, this was remarkable. Thus in 1980, the new Conservative government committed to unfettering private enterprise had issued Circular 22/80 (*Development control*), which set the pattern for governmental views on design until the early 1990s. The overriding emphasis was on restricting any control of design to environmentally sensitive areas based on the argument that design was essentially subjective (Carmona 2001: 28). Given the context, the instruction to the RFAC to 'raise its game' clearly ran against the prevailing political environment.

The RFAC itself had criticised this turn in government policy in its long-delayed Twenty-Second Report, in doing so taking issue with the government's characterisation of design as subjective and its control as interference. For the RFAC, each building ought to be considered in relation to its context and none should be above planning considerations that, on the whole, had "raise[d] the general standard both of layout and design" (RFAC 1985: 21). This critique of government policy continued in its next report (the first under St John-Stevas), in which it argued that public intervention was no substitute for good architects and good patronage, but, when required, assessments of design could "be quite coherently expressed in terms of urban pattern, building height and scale" (RFAC 1986: 12), in other words, objectively.

It is difficult to explain this contradiction in government policy, supporting on one hand the work of the RFAC whilst on the other discouraging aesthetic control. Most likely it stemmed from an association of the Commission's work with the limited remit of one-off exceptional schemes and with safeguarding design quality in historic areas. This assessment seems to be supported by the further codification of a national role for the RFAC in the government Circular 8/87 (*Historic buildings and conservation areas*), which gave special mention to the role of the Commission in providing advice on design in historically sensitive areas (DoE 1987: para 26), advice reinforced in 1994 in the circular's sequel—PPG15 (*Planning and the historic environment*). For its part, the RFAC was clear that its advice should no longer be confined to London and the "finest historic towns", but should also extend to key sites in the "ordinary towns of England and Wales" (RFAC 1985: 21).

A More Assertive Commission

Whilst policy was slow to change, and didn't begin to until 1991, and not substantially until 1997, by the 1990s, the RFAC had begun to be more assertive as regards its views on design. It did this largely through a programme of publications. Some of these were commissioned pieces, some were the result of seminars or exhibitions held at the RFAC, and others were generated internally, drawing on the experience of commissioners reviewing schemes.

Between 1980 and 1999, sixteen titles were published, and whilst some of these dealt with specialist topics that the RFAC saw as significant challenges, for example the state of design under the Private Finance Initiative or the design of light rail systems, others fell into three main categories: the management and regeneration of urban areas and their streets; design in the historic built environment; and principles for effectively and objectively evaluating aesthetic quality. It is difficult to gauge the impact of these reports, although Sir Geoffrey Chipperfield, in his review of the work of the RFAC (see later), was less than impressed. He argued, "It is not clear to me how the papers relate to the Commission's detailed work, nor that practitioners

and planning authorities have found them of value in considering individual schemes" (1994: 5). Certainly many of the reports sank without trace, but others, particularly those dealing with issues of urban management and regeneration as they relate to design, were widely read and represented key statements on these issues before the association between design and regeneration became more mainstream in the 2000s.

Likewise, the Commission's statements on aesthetics were the only positive 'official' statements on the subject during the 1980s and 1990s and unashamedly argued the case for the importance of beauty in the built environment and for a public sector role in helping to guarantee it (e.g. RFAC 1980, 1990). In doing so, they echoed and amplified a wider groundswell of concern towards the end of the 1980s (cheer led by the Prince of Wales) about the poor state of the built environment in the United Kingdom and the highly constrained role of planning in tackling it (Punter & Carmona 1997: 30). In response, the then Secretary of State for the Environment, Chris Patten, in a groundbreaking speech to the RFAC, accepted the need to redefine government guidance on design and that local authorities should have a role in providing guidance to architects and developers. The result of the speech was a joint statement by the Royal Town Planning Institute (RTPI) and Royal Institute of British Architects (RIBA) that aimed to replace, as the official government statement on design, the advice in Circular 22/80 (that had been restated in 1985 and again in 1988 in PPG1 *General Policy and Principles*) (Tibbalds 1991: 72). After minor amendments by the Department of the Environment (DoE), the statement was incorporated into government guidance as Annex A to a revised PPG1. It was released in 1992.

No mention was made of the role of the RFAC, but the Commission had played an important part in bringing the new guidance about, and in 1994 went on to issue its own most authoritative report, *What Makes a Good Building* (RFAC 1994a). The report remains one of the clearest articulations of architectural design criteria for making impartial aesthetic judgements, structured around six criteria: order and unity, expression, integrity, plan and section, detail, and integration (the last further distinguished by: siting, massing, scale, proportion, rhythm, and materials). Recognising the need to avoid turning generally desirable principles

into dogmatic imperatives, the report stressed that a building could embody every criterion and still not be a 'good building', and, conversely, could be a good building without complying with any of the criteria. In essence, it reinforced the need and value of 'expert judgements' on design quality made on a case-by-case basis, just as the RFAC had been doing since 1924.

Reviewing Projects

In the midst of all the publishing, the Commission was examining less than half of the designs submitted for review—139 out of 331 in 1994—roughly two thirds of which were located in London (RFAC 1994b: 12). Whilst the Commission still advised "on all matters affecting the visual environment, particularly art in public places and architecture" (RFAC 1994b: 43), in reality schemes had to satisfy at least one of four key criteria:

- Is this proposal of national importance?
- Is this site of national importance?
- Will this proposal have a substantial impact on a sensitive environment?
- Does this site provide an opportunity to upgrade the quality of the surrounding environment?

By this time, the Commission had more than doubled in size from its original eight commissioners in 1924 to eighteen in the 1990s. As before, half of these were architects with, typically, one civil engineer included on enquiries that involved engineering matters. The group remained dominated by white male establishment figures, although women were now represented, largely in the non-architect category.[9] To handle the workload, schemes that were received were first reduced in number (typically by half) by the secretary to the Commission (Chipperfield 1994: 5), before being presented to a 'Preparatory Committee' of three or four commissioners that would meet once a month to review and prioritise submissions. The secretary or deputy secretary and representative commissioners would then visit the site with the full Commission meeting occurring ten days later.

Typically, projects were presented to committees by their architects in the presence of the relevant authorities. This included the planning officer (who was always asked to give a view) and the client. A letter with the views of the Commission (including identification of any design deficiencies and, if appropriate, remedies for action) was then sent as soon as possible after the meeting to all interested parties who had been present. These letters remained private except when the Commission felt that a public airing of its views was necessary. Letters were divided into four types (RFAC 1985: 11):

- Projects immediately and enthusiastically approved.
- Acceptable projects which did not call for any special commendation.
- Projects which might be acceptable if deficiencies were made good.
- Projects which were unacceptable.

In its Thirty-Second Report (RFAC 1994b: 13), the RFAC noted that the vast majority of proposals were amended in some form at the behest of the Commission (78 per cent)—which the chairman called "heartening in view of the Commission's lack of any formal powers of compliance" (RFAC 1994b: 13). For those projects that fell into the fourth category, however, after 1985 the Commission was increasingly less inclined to pull its punches, with letters often penned by the chairman himself, who, for example, denounced one scheme as "a blot on the landscape" and an "architectural disaster" (Lord St John of Fawsley quoted in Fisher 1998). Writing in *The Independent*, architecture critic Amanda Ballieu (1993) agreed with the RFAC's approach, arguing that "On the whole", the Commission's "decisions help to improve the quality of British public design and buildings", and citing the RFAC's role in "stopping the Government from building a banal new headquarters for the Inland Revenue in the shadow of Nottingham Castle".

The Projects

During this period, projects seen by the RFAC remained diverse, including public art, public space, lighting, and major infrastructure, alongside site-based master planning and architecture. Notably, however, the Commission's involvement in planning ceased. Some of the larger projects in which the Commission was involved related to London's transport infrastructure, including early plans for what became Crossrail.

With respect to public works such as this, the RFAC was always critical of visible attempts to cut costs resulting in "crude structures" (RFAC 1994b: 37). Regarding street spaces, it continued a long-term critique dating at least back to the 1950s against the proliferation of what it regarded as street 'clutter'. On these grounds, in the early 1990s, it criticised plans for Victoria Square in Birmingham, a scheme that (despite its many bollards) quickly became a national icon of the reviving interest in British urban design. Here, and elsewhere, the Commission was always prepared to admit its mistakes and declared Victoria Square a great success upon visiting the finished scheme (RFAC 1994b: 28; see Figure 3.5).

Cost cutting by the public sector was at the forefront of the RFAC's concerns during the 1990s when the Private Finance Initiative (PFI) was launched in the United Kingdom.[10] While the Commission avoided commenting on the political and economic rationalities underpinning PFI, its far-reaching architectural implications became a major worry when good architecture was seen as 'expendable' if costs needed to be pared down, or when to maximise their profits developers "crammed commercial uses into every spare cranny" (RFAC 1995: 8).

The City of London remained a concern for the Commission in its later years, as the spread of "Monolithic office buildings" contributed "little or nothing to the streetscape and townscape" (RFAC

Figure 3.5 Victoria Square Birmingham, criticised by the Commission at the design stage, but later lauded as a great success

Source: Matthew Carmona

1995: 15), the key issue being how the bulk of buildings was distributed within the form. Here, as elsewhere, height remained an on-going concern for the Commission, although its response was more relaxed than in earlier years, perhaps accepting that London was now a far more diverse city, height-wise. From time to time, commissioners even recommended building higher if the result was a more slender and attractive form (RFAC 1995: 16). By contrast, when it came to Norman Foster's proposal for a 386-metre-tall Millennium Tower in the City on the site now occupied by Foster's 'Gherkin', "The Commission had no doubts about the brilliance of the design", but nevertheless argued that sheer quality of architectural design alone was not enough, as it was "simply out of scale, not only with the City, but with London as a whole" (RFAC 1996: 14).

As for historic buildings, the Commission maintained its support for adaptive reuse so long as it maintained the character of the original structure. When, for example, Herzog de Meuron was chosen for its

design for Tate Modern at Bankside Power Station in Southwark, the Commission gave its support, although it did find issue with the holes the design called for in the chimney in order to make it a viewing tower, and this element was dropped from the scheme (RFAC 1995: 21). At the same time, Foster and Partners proposals to redesign the British Museum's interior courtyard and reading room were under scrutiny. In this case, the Commission disapproved of the various bridges proposed to connect the new central drum surrounding the historic reading room with the existing gallery spaces. Further, it asked the architects to reconsider the rectangular ribbing suggested for the dramatic new glass dome. The amended design "satisfied every detail" (RFAC 1995: 25), leading to the presence of only one bridge from a new much reduced upper level and to the iconic triangular pattern in the glazing of the dome (3.6). Such interventions, some small and others large, were the bread and butter of the RFAC and the archive is replete with case upon case upon case.

Policy Turns and Problems Mount

Whilst the everyday work of the RFAC continued throughout the 1990s, a momentous change was under way that would ultimately lead to the demise of the RFAC as well as to the sort of political environment for better design that the RFAC had long hankered after. In particular the arrival of John Gummer as Secretary of State for the Environment in 1993 with a personal interest in conservation and the environment greatly hastened the policy turn in favour of design that had already begun under Chris Patten.

In 1994, he launched his Quality in Town & Country initiative, setting out the government's changing thinking on issues of design and the local environment, and moving away from a focus on aesthetics to one on urban design. On launching the initiative, Gummer railed against: "the relentless homogenisation which has eroded so much local colour", against "monotonous building which is designed for nowhere in particular" and against the nature of urban design as "a neglected profession, cast into the wilderness by a reaction against the abuses of the 1960s" (Gummer 1994: 8, 13). This was the first time that ministers had directly addressed 'urban design', and in time the new thinking flowed through into policy with a revised

Figure 3.6 The British Museum Great Court with its iconic dome on a triangular grid, a direct consequence of RFAC intervention

Source: Matthew Carmona

PPG1 (*General Policy and Principles*) issued in 1997. The revised policy was certainly mould-breaking (Carmona 2001: 72), unequivocally stating that "Good design should be the aim of all those involved in the development process and should be encouraged everywhere" (DoE 1997: para 3, 15).

The policy statement lasted until 2005, but the Conservative administration fell later in 1997 to be replaced by New Labour with a strong reforming agenda, and with John Prescott as Secretary of State for the large new Department for the Environment, Transport and the Regions (DETR). New Labour was a pragmatic force and Prescott was a savvy politician who could immediately see the success of Gummer's initiatives on design. Consequently he quickly adopted and escalated the pursuit of good design as one of his key means to drive a larger ambition around the 'renaissance' of English cities. So where was the RFAC in all this? The answer, too often, seemed to be nowhere to be seen.

The Commission under Fire

Problems began to mount for the Commission after Lord St John was elected Master of Emmanuel College, Cambridge, in 1991. Whilst his position at the RFAC was unpaid, it was also central to steering the organisation's work and priorities, and so when academic politics began to prove highly diverting, "his frequent absences from the Commission's offices in London raised eyebrows."[11] Making matters worse, this happened at a time when the Commission's role had been widening, at least in part due to Lord St John's earlier commitment. The expectation now was of "the need to exercise some 'general influence' on aesthetic design and architectural standards" (Youngson 1990: 113), for example through its various seminars and publications, but also through links to other important bodies, visits to local authorities around the country, and a new role advising on the design of foreign embassies in London and British embassies abroad.

With a greater role and a higher profile also came greater public scrutiny of the RFAC's work, and this "caused the RFAC to make real enemies for the first time" (Ballieu 1993), including over plans for the redevelopment of Paternoster Square in the City. In the

1980s, a broadly Modernist scheme designed by Arup Associates had won the international design competition for this important development in the shadows of St Paul's Cathedral before an intervention by the traditionally minded Prince of Wales ensured that the scheme was abandoned. The RFAC set itself against the classically inspired scheme that came in its wake, master planned by Sir Terry Farrell, raising considerable disquiet that the RFAC had become too wedded to Modernist ways of thinking (Ballieu 1993). Despite the Commission's concerns, the Farrell scheme eventually obtained planning permission before being killed off by the recession of the early 1990s. When the economy recovered, the next scheme was arguably something of a compromise[12] in order to avoid controversy and guarantee that a development happened (Carmona & Wunderlich 2012: 99). This project also obtained planning permission (in the RFAC's final year), and in the process secured the RFAC's support, if not its enthusiasm (3.7). The experience illustrates the dangers of too many hands in the design process, and plays into a long-term critique of design governance (see Chapter 1) that such processes can unintentionally lead to 'design by committee'.

The undue influence of the chairman on Commission business was also raised and in particular what was seen as his own particular architectural prejudice, not least against international architects (Ballieu 1993). Reacting to the anxiety, in 1994, the government called in retired civil servant Sir Geoffrey

Figure 3.7 Paternoster Square, the final scheme, more compromise than conviction

Source: Matthew Carmona

Chipperfield to examine the Commission. The inquiry did not get off to a good start, and in the final report he alludes to what he saw as a general ambiguity in the Commission's mission. He concluded that while a wide body of opinion believes the work of the Commission adds value, and importantly that the government itself valued the role as an independent evaluator of the design of major developments, "there are also those who say the Commission acts in an arbitrary inconsistent manner and is not respected," including being too divorced from the economic realities of development (Chipperfield 1994: 6).

Chipperfield's own views were hardly glowing, but were couched in the terms of an experienced civil servant merely putting options to the minister, whilst gently steering the minister's hand. Thus Chipperfield (1994: 23) recommended a scaling back of activities not explicitly linked to the task of reviewing schemes (such as research, publications, and publicity relating to the work of the Commission) whilst there should be a strengthening of the links between the Commission's core reviewing activities and that of the statutory planning process. On the latter, he recommended strengthening guidance on when the Commission should consider schemes, and what the consequences of failing to refer an appropriate scheme or otherwise failing to take the advice of the Commission into account would be. Running through the report was a sense that Chipperfield regarded the Commission as having grown beyond its remit as established in its royal warrants and as increasingly profligate.

The response of the Department of National Heritage (DNH 1996), under whose ambit the RFAC now fell,[13] was somewhat dismissive of Chipperfield's report. It strongly supported the chairman and argued that "the wider projection of the Commission [through its public relations and publications] is an important element of its overall impact." On that basis, Lord St John was appointed for a third time in 1995, although some of the mud Chipperfield raked up clearly stuck and played into the narrative around the RFAC when just three years later its role was again called into question, this time more seriously. In hindsight, also, the chairman did not seem to register the Chipperfield report as a serious shot across the bows of the organisation, and with DNH acquiescence seemed more than a little complacent about its findings. Nowhere was

this more apparent than in the near invisibility of the RFAC in the various activities of John Gummer's Quality in Town & Country initiative, which arguably represented a once-in-a-generation opportunity to raise the importance and profile of design within government. Consequently, the Commission might have been expected to play a key role in driving the initiative forward as a means to both advance the design agenda and to re-stake its claim to be the national voice on such matters; as the press had put it seventy years before: to be active in the beautification of England (RFAC 1924b: 2).

Whether through lack of capacity, because Quality in Town & Country was being led by a different government department to that which sponsored the Commission, or because the chair was simply distracted by other matters, this did not happen, and instead increasingly the RFAC came under attack as elitist, secretive, reactive, and susceptible to cronyism (Ballieu 1993; Fairs 1998; Fisher 1998). Thus even before the Labour Party came to power in 1997, the RFAC was in its sights: "an easy target: an undemocratic, elitist, pompously titled quango, run out of stuffy St James's Square by a Tory peer who served as a minister under Mrs Thatcher" (Fisher 1998).

The Downfall

At the turn of the twenty-first century there was a zeitgeist of change, and the 1997 elections brought an end to eighteen years of Conservative rule. Like all new governments this one began with a fundamental review of public expenditure, and in the process the RFAC came under scrutiny (Simmons 2015: 408).

The emergence of CABE was undoubtedly part of a watershed in the history of support for design in government policy in the United Kingdom, but it built on changes already under way. Urban issues and design were on a journey to the forefront of political thinking and in the words of a commissioner from the first days of CABE, "when the Labour party was elected in '97, there were an awful lot of people who were in the cabinet or in positions of power who'd got the design message." Tony Blair was open to this new urban agenda, and his deputy John Prescott actively sought it out whilst other key figures such as Mark Fisher followed by Alan Howarth as ministers of state in the sponsoring department (now the Department for Culture, Media and Sport—DCMS) were highly influential. This interest was received with enormous enthusiasm by the professional world, and in the words of one urban designer: "we were all very encouraged by the energy and the change that they wanted to bring about."

The first sign of real change came with the publication by the new Secretary of State for Culture, Media and Sport, Chris Smith, of a consultation paper on the arts in 1998 in which he announced a review of the RFAC with views sought on several scenarios, including complete abolition. At this stage, the Commission remained optimistic about outcomes, with the final secretary to the RFAC, Francis Golding, commenting, "We can't see that they can come up with anything other than the option we want" (quoted in Fisher 1998), namely the retention of a strong independent body but with the new power to call in planning applications that raise design issues of national significance (Lewis & Blackman 1998). But whilst few were prepared to speak up against the RFAC on record (for fear no doubt of their work being less favourably reviewed by it), behind the scenes the knives were being dug in.

The proposals for a more radical solution received particularly enthusiastic support from two key organisations, the first discreetly, the second, less so. In the United Kingdom, a patchwork of urban design-related bodies had long existed with various levels of influence. Whilst individually they constituted an important force within the design governance landscape, it wasn't until, seizing the moment created by Quality in Town & Country, that they came together to form the Urban Design Alliance (UDAL)[14], a body capable of a sustained dialogue with government. Through UDAL, the professional institutes had finally woken up from a deep sleep to recognise their joint responsibility for the thing that united (and too often divided) them, urban design. Whilst this shared commitment lasted less than a decade, it was UDAL that persuaded Chris Smith that a rarefied view of design based foremost on aesthetics was no longer appropriate.[15]

More significant, this cross-disciplinary urban agenda was supported and further articulated through the work of the Urban Task Force led by Lord Rogers of Riverside, which from 1998 John Prescott had constituted to identify the causes of urban decline and to suggest ways forward. The resulting report, *Towards an Urban Renaissance*, concluded that the quality of urban design and strategic planning in England lagged twenty years behind practice elsewhere in Europe, and advanced a wide range of recommendations based on two central convictions: that "regeneration has to be design led" (Urban Task Force 1999: 7); and that government leadership was needed. Whilst the report itself was not published until 1999, the Urban Task Force had previously submitted its views on the RFAC to DCMS, and in a letter to Chris Smith, Richard Rogers wrote: "We explicitly do not support simply tinkering with the architectural functions of the RFAC which has proven to be reactive and remote in dealing with the advisory needs of local authorities, developers and others" (quoted in Fairs 1998). A clean start was required.

In December 1998, Chris Smith announced that from autumn the following year the RFAC would cease to operate, with its functions inherited by a new organisation with a broader and more proactive remit. His consultation paper had revealed a strong preference for a new architecture champion (60 per cent), that three quarters of respondents felt such a champion should remain independent, and near unanimity (95 per cent) that it should have a strong regional presence (Lewis & Fairs 1998).

The details of the new body were somewhat sketchy at first, prompting Lord St John of Fawsley to express "deep regret" at the announcement, which he described as "rash and ill thought out" (quoted in Lewis & Fairs 1998: 1). However, the general direction was clear, with Smith arguing that the new body should be "a real voice not just for architecture, but urban design generally" (quoted in Lewis & Blackman 1998), whilst Minister for the Arts Alan Howarth argued that the body needed "to spread the promotion of good architecture to a wider constituency" (quoted in Baldock 1998), with an educational role stretching beyond the hallowed halls of London aesthetes. The new body would absorb the annual RFAC grant of £705,000, as well as the Arts Council's architecture grant programme (£220,000) and Royal Society for Arts funding for Art and Architecture (£105,000), and was promised a £300,000 uplift in funding from the following year. Like the RFAC, it would not be led by an architect to avoid the charge of the new body associating with a particular architectural style (Lewis & Fairs 1998).

As for its name, that had to wait until the following year when lobbying, in particular from UDAL under the chairmanship of Terry Farrell, convinced ministers to add '& the Built Environment' to the 'Commission for Architecture', which until then had been favoured by the DCMS. The RFAC ceased to exist on 31 July 1999, with CABE immediately taking on its staff and premises and continuing seamlessly its programme of design reviews.

Conclusion

Over the seventy-five years of its existence, the RFAC made a significant mark on the built fabric of England and Wales, both on what was built and on what was not. It is difficult to quantify that impact because much of it went unremarked and uncelebrated in the day-to-day work of the organisation commenting on projects, encouraging those who came before it to rethink when required, and unambiguously supporting good design when they saw it. As Gavin Stamp argued long before its abolition was on the cards: "I would certainly not have the Commission abolished or reformed out of existence, we need every body that is a barrier to architectural barbarism. On the other hand, paradoxically, it could not possibly have the power to enforce its advice; if it did, the Commission would probably cease to command respect and possibly become open to corruption. Committees of taste can be dangerous things. The Fine Art Commission tries to strike a civilised balance; John Summerson [the architectural historian and commissioner] considers that as a whole it did a good job in a funny inarticulate sort of way. . . . I am now rather inclined to agree" (1982: 30).

For Alexander Youngson, whilst the Commission's judgements were never infallible, as indeed they could not be for questions concerning design about which there was typically no right or wrong answers, "an experienced and not entirely professional body with no axe to grind is in a very strong and quite exceptional position" to help resolve such matters, even if only by preventing the worst forms of design illiteracy (Youngson 1990: 109, 115). This role, he argued, was facilitated by two key qualities of the Commission, its unique role, stretching across the design dimensions of professional remits—architecture, planning, and engineering—that have a tendency to see things in narrower terms than

the required holistic view of design; and its independence: "Pressure can be put on local politicians or officials, sometimes even on national politicians and officials, but not [he believed] on Royal Commissions."

Geoffrey Chipperfield, author of the 1994 inquiry, disagreed, and in hindsight correctly argued that "The Commission does not, and cannot, stand wholly apart from the government of the day." In such a context, frustrating or otherwise embarrassing a government can be a dangerous occupation when, ultimately, the very existence of the organisation is in the hands of ministers. This was certainly the case when the RFAC was highly critical of the new City Hall building planned for London in the run-up to the election of its first mayor in 2000. As Minister for Housing, Planning and Construction Nick Raynsford recalled: "they were solely interested in the potential adverse impact on the Tower of London, the other side of the river. There was no interest whatsoever in the new building" (3.8). For him, "that made a very important

Figure 3.8 City Hall, London, home of the Greater London Authority, designed by Norman Foster but opposed by the RFAC and since derided by many as reminiscent of, among other things, Darth Vader's helmet, a woodlouse, an onion, and a glass gonad

Source: Matthew Carmona

point that the one body that was then supposedly acting as the watchdog for architectural design was interested in heritage preservation, but actually had no real interest in promoting good, modern architecture." The impression may have been misconceived when seen in the light of the full body of work the Commission was then engaged in, but the perception, at a time when the powerful new DETR was responding to the DCMS's consultation on the future of the RFAC, would not have helped its case.

The influence that it was able to exert was largely done without formal powers and instead: on the basis of the reputation collectively and individually of its commissioners; its authority as a royal commission; and through its unswaying belief that through its actions the design of the built environment would be improved. The calibre and experience of its commissioners was certainly very high. As one former employee commented, "The average age of the Royal Fine Art Commission was quite high, it was a bit of a gerontocracy, but not necessarily in a bad way. There was a huge amount of experience and authority there." During his tenure, Lord St John of Fawsley is reported to have calculated the service of the Commissioners to have been worth £500,000 a year (Youngson 1990: 115).

Over the years the Commission became increasingly bold, bolstered by slight tweaks to its warrant, and in later years was able to intervene more forcefully when required (Delafons 1994: 16). Ultimately, however, as the commissioners themselves admitted: "Control from without cannot turn bad architecture into good architecture, because it cannot turn bad architects into good architects; and good buildings need good architects" (RFAC 1971: 11). Consequently, their influence was always limited, not least because one review panel sitting in London could only ever scratch the surface of the work that needed to be done, and even where it did intervene it had no power to enforce its decisions and no resources to offer anything but advice.

Even the principles underpinning the advice were relatively fluid and the Commission's views on matters such as building height clearly evolved, along with its willingness to comment on the detail of designs. In general, the Commission's claim to be less concerned with ephemeral architectural styles and more concerned with enduring qualities like relative scale,

massing, architectural honesty, and articulation can be verified both through its own deliberations and in its staunch and repeated arguments to government in response to the limiting policy frameworks of the 1980s and 1990s.

Unlike its successor (CABE), the RFAC was never shy of setting out its arguments in aesthetic terms, and this contributed to an impression that the RFAC was first and foremost concerned with a rather narrow view of aesthetics; a perception that remained throughout its existence and eventually contributed towards its demise. To some degree the impression belies its post-war influence on the re-planning of a war-torn England (particularly London) and its influence over three quarters of a century on the design of the public realm, key public spaces, and infrastructure, which should not be underestimated. Despite this, it was primarily an aesthetic view that the Commission brought to its deliberations, and this was apparent across the scale of its work, from advice on city plans to critiques of public art.

For much of that time the Commission often seemed to row against the general zeitgeist in the architectural world, not least in its support for conserving important historical landmarks and townscapes and generally for supporting the careful fitting-in of development. Yet because its work was often discreet and behind the scenes, the organisation largely went about it without comment or criticism, at least until the 1980s. In the 1980s, the RFAC was again rowing against the zeitgeist, but this time against the government's attitudes to design, rather than any particular architectural movement. At this time, the Commission played a valuable part in raising design up the agenda and generally in pushing back against a state bent on the primacy of the free market. But in raising its head above the parapet, it also became the target of more regular criticism whilst the undue influence of its charismatic chairman left it looking both out of touch when a sudden turn in public policy, towards design, finally came in the mid-1990s, and somewhat elitist and divorced from the realities of a now less deferential country about to move into the twenty-first century. It was an easy target when the axe came and, despite its immense contribution to the nation, was swept away (or more accurately consumed by CABE) with few mourners to grieve its passing.

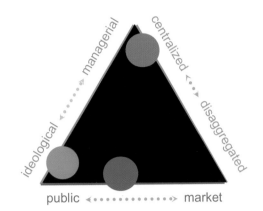

Figure 3.9 The RFAC design governance model

Relating the work of the RFAC to the triad of fundamental urban governance characteristics—operation, authority, power—from Chapter 1 (3.9), the organisation can be represented as:

- Ideological—uncompromisingly focussed on a single core objective, the aesthetic improvement of the nation's built environment, and doggedly sticking to a very narrow range of informal tools to address it (design review and latterly practice guidance).
- Centralised—working as the single national voice on design, but, through the dogged pursuit of its independence, without the authority provided by strong governmental backing to deliver its aims.
- Publicly-oriented/passive—100 per cent state funded, but beyond its status and the credibility of its advice, ultimately weak and reliant on others, public and private, to deliver on its recommendations.

Notes

1. Although the RFAC didn't actually meet until February 1924, two weeks into the first ever Labour administration.
2. At the time, the Commission's work referred to processes of 'enquiry' into schemes. The term *design review* was not widely used in the United Kingdom until CABE adopted it to describe its own activities. RFAC enquiries nevertheless involved reviewing design proposals and passing judgement on their merits, and therefore the term *design review* is used in this chapter, as throughout this book, as the generic term for such activities.
3. http://hansard.millbanksystems.com/commons/1936/dec/08/royal-fine-art-commission
4. A critique of planning in the United Kingdom that continues to have strong resonance, as the recommendations of the 2014 Farrell Review testify (see Chapter 5).
5. http://londonist.com/2012/05/londons-top-brutalist-buildings - London's top Brutalist buildings
6. Quasi-autonomous non-governmental organisation.
7. www.telegraph.co.uk/news/obituaries/9124613/Lord-St-John-of-Fawsley.html
8. www.telegraph.co.uk/news/obituaries/9124613/Lord-St-John-of-Fawsley.html
9. For example four women were included in the 1985 Commission, one of whom was an architect (RFAC 1986).
10. PFI is a form of public-private partnership in which the private sector builds and manages key public assets which the public sector then pays for over the life of the contract.
11. www.telegraph.co.uk/news/obituaries/9124613/Lord-St-John-of-Fawsley.html
12. Master planned by Sir William Whitfield, a RFAC commissioner.
13. Responsibility for architecture policy was moved from the Department of the Environment to the Department of National Heritage when it was created from various other Departments in 1992 (later to become the Department for Culture, Media and Sport). This set in place a division between design and planning (the latter remaining with the Department of the Environment and its various reincarnations—DETR, DTLR, ODPM, DCLG) that lasted almost a quarter of a century until the two were brought together in the Department for Communities and Local Government just prior to the 2015 general election.
14. A loose federation spanning the Royal Town Planning Institute, Royal Institute of British Architects, Royal Institution of Chartered Surveyors, Institution of Civil Engineers, Urban Design Group, and the Civic Trust.
15. www.rudi.net/books/11431

CHAPTER 4

CABE, a Story of Innovation in the Governance of Design, 1999–2011

This chapter recounts the story of CABE from its beginnings to its demise. In doing so, it journeys through the three key phases of its development: first, Agile CABE, when, in its early years, CABE was seen as a dynamic and effective but unconventional newcomer; second, Growing CABE, when the organisation grew rapidly and sat at the core of a confident New Labour focus on delivering real change; and third, Mature CABE, when, as a well-established and trusted organisation, CABE found itself increasingly heavily relied on by government, but also more constrained in how it operated and therefore less able to independently shape its own core mission, the pursuit of better design. This history charts the people, programmes, and changing political and governance context within which CABE operated, as well as the changing priorities and problematics to which it addressed its energies, and ultimately the story of CABE's demise.

Agile CABE—1999–2002

A Dynamic New Body

On 20 August 1999, CABE was established as a national body, taking the form of a non-departmental public body (NDPB) or quango, but incorporated as a company limited by guarantee. There was a relatively smooth institutional transition from the Royal Fine Art Commission (RFAC), as CABE inherited the Department for Culture, Media and Sport (DCMS) as its sponsoring government department, the RFAC's budget and staff, and even the former RFAC secretary, Francis Golding, as CABE's first chief executive. This arrangement did not last long, however, as a clash of styles with the incoming chairman, Sir Stuart Lipton, led to Golding's early departure and to the appointment of Jon Rouse in the role. It was with the arrival of Rouse in the summer of 2000 that CABE quickly developed its own style of leadership and a decade of innovation in the governance of design began, facilitated by increased funding jointly from the DCMS and John Prescott's mega-ministry, the Department for the Environment, Transport and the Regions (DETR) (later DTLR, ODPM, and now DCLG[1]).

While there was a good amount of consensus around the need for new design governance infrastructure and a more cross-sectoral agenda, there was disagreement about the need for a single organisation. The Urban Task Force report had emphasised the need for design leadership at all levels of government and made the case for dispersing the governance function among the regions through multiple coordinated centres that could enhance local skills and engage in regeneration (1999: 41). By contrast, CABE initially maintained the RFAC's centralisation of the role of 'design champion' at the national level, although it began to reach out to the regions as early as its second year through (at first) small-scale grant funding to some of the architecture and built environment centres that already existed in England and that typically led a precarious hand-to-mouth existence. Regional representatives were also appointed across the country with the specific remit of representing CABE in the regions and extending its reach.

CABE, centrally, began life as a much better supported body than the RFAC had been (with almost double its budget—see Chapter 3), and lost little time establishing a dynamic decision-making structure, a reinvigorated group of staff, and, from 2000, a new headquarters away from the "stuffy" St James's Square to the far less impressive, but (important) far less exclusive environment of the Tower Building at Waterloo. In governance terms, the chairman headed the Commission and worked together with the commissioners to give strategic direction to CABE, although in reality the executive had considerable discretion to direct the new organisation on a day-to-day basis. When Jon Rouse took the helm, Lipton and Rouse quickly developed a new and different type of leadership that was less typical of a public body, and quite different from the RFAC that had preceded it. Rouse had been handpicked for the role following a recommendation by Richard Rogers, and was widely considered the ideal candidate, reflecting his reputation as a strategist, his knowledge of the workings of government, and his work with the Urban Task Force.[2] As a developer, Lipton was a more controversial appointment with a profile that departed quite significantly from the more rarefied appointments that had typified the RFAC. Like the RFAC, however, there was a strong sense (which persisted until its demise) that the new Commission should not be led by an architect, and Lipton's experience and standing as the developer of design-led schemes, including Broadgate in the City of London, cancelled out any concerns. Ultimately his appointment was a signal to the development industry that better design was on the agenda and was increasingly to be a policy priority.

In the words of a long-standing staff member, "you stand on your reputation and if people think you're not making valuable comments, then they won't come and it won't work." In fact, through its growing in-house team,

its commissioners (who had to be formally appointed by DCMS[3]), and, most significantly, the exhaustive work of its chairman and chief executive, CABE very quickly established its credentials as 'the' national voice on design in the built environment and as a trusted authority in the field. The commissioners were carefully selected to span the range of architecture and built environment fields, and following the long-established precedent of the RFAC, just half were architects with others drawn from the fields of planning, engineering, education, heritage, and media. This diversity was maintained throughout CABE's existence.

From the start commissioners were encouraged to be proactive in their representation of CABE, something which, at the time, was unusual for such roles. In addition to speaking independently about their own areas of expertise, they were actively involved in delivery of the organisation's undertakings through being given direct responsibility for different aspects of CABE's programme. Paul Finch, for example, chaired the design review panel, Sunand Prasad launched the programme of enabling, and Les Sparks took the regional agenda. As one founding commissioner recalled, in the initial appointments the chair "was looking for pro-active people who actually wanted to be engaged, . . . actively engaged, with the programmes, helping to set priorities and being involved in their running".

Looking back, some commentators reflected a feeling that the new group was to some extent an inevitable regrouping of "the great and the good", although only the chairman himself, the architect Ian Richie, and the conservationist Sophie Andreae continued over from the RFAC.[4] The new executive was also markedly different to the RFAC, and developed a reputation for being amenable to suggestions, as well as having a robust style in communicating with external parties. Thus strategy drew on internal conversation between the executive and staff or commissioners, and key decisions were made through open and sometimes challenging debate between the executive and the chair.

Resourcing the Organisation

From its inception CABE received funding from central government, and its income grew rapidly both in terms of volume and type (4.1). Its initial 'grant in

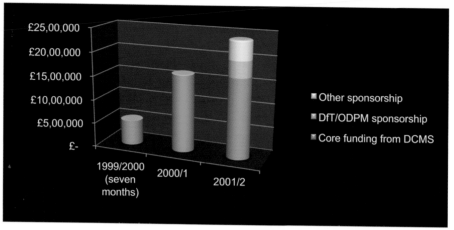

Figure 4.1   CABE's income in its first three accounting years (data extracted from CABE annual reports)

aid' amounted to just more than £500,000[5] and tripled in the following years. From 2001 onwards, CABE was also in receipt of significant direct sponsorship from the Office of the Deputy Prime Minister (ODPM) which continued over the lifetime of CABE and by 2003 outstripped the core funding of the DCMS. By its third operating year, CABE was also earning around one sixth of its total income from other sources, most significantly from the Arts Council for England.

At its launch, CABE had only a very small staff of ten (equivalent to only five full-time posts), including its head of design review, Peter Stewart, who had come over from the RFAC and remained until 2005 when he was the last man standing. There was a small secretariat providing communications and administrative support, and directorates were established for core activities covering design review, enabling, the regions, public affairs, policy and research, and communications, each with a named commissioner. From its earliest days, the model adopted in order to spread CABE's influence and overcome its diminutive size was to involve as many able and willing volunteers as possible. This 'CABE family', as it came to be known, was a network of largely professional collaborators who undertook considerable work on behalf of CABE, typically for no or nominal pay. The relations did indeed appear familial in as much as they were based on goodwill, commitment, and the voluntary devotion of time. At this stage, when the executive was so small, the family was a critical resource, but as the organisation grew, the family grew with it and in effect became

the flexible and nimble means by which CABE services were delivered.

As a DCMS minister of the time explained, "there were worries in the beginning that there might not be money to support design review in some parts of the country and CABE would only do relatively large projects"; instead, CABE tapped into "the goodwill of large numbers of people, many of whom were very respected professionals . . . for just a modest honorarium if not pro-bono". Regional representatives, for instance, were paid a set amount of days each month, but would typically spend significantly more time than had been budgeted in attending events on behalf of CABE. In the words of a senior professional, "the CABE family was a very clever way of deploying resources because normally what you do is have regional offices with all the stuff that comes with that, the rents and all the rest of it, but CABE didn't do that so the deployment of money around the country was very, very good—and kept all the fixed costs right down." In effect CABE was able to leverage its position and drive down its operating costs. Senior staff, commissioners, and ex-ministers consistently recall how CABE relied on a shared sense of purpose, and as one CABE employee recounted, "I very rarely got the sense that anybody was doing it begrudgingly; quite the reverse, it was that they felt incredibly galvanised by the focus that CABE had given to [design quality], which had been a passion for all of them."

There is no doubt that throughout the life of CABE this wider group of professionals helped CABE to punch well above its weight in terms of skills, reach, and funding, and to spread the key messages of the organisation far beyond what would have been possible through more traditional means. Even this, however, did not allow CABE to do all it wished to, with demand for its services, such as design review, far outstripping its capacity to deliver. This did not change throughout CABE's life, but was particularly acute in the early years.

A Dose of Urbanism

In these first years, CABE was a high-energy, relatively free agent, whose leadership had a clear vision: "to inject architecture into the bloodstream of the nation,"[6] where architecture would respond to the calls for interdisciplinarity and help to address the urban issues of the day. This in turn was part of the larger mission established by the Urban Task Force (1999) to drive an urban renaissance in English cities via a new emphasis on urban design, hand in hand with a widespread reinvestment in urban areas. It was conceived as remedial work in the public interest, where "social dysfunction so often has its roots in bad buildings and poorly designed places and spaces—and, conversely, that buildings which raise the spirits and respond intelligently to their surroundings so often have a positive impact beyond their own four walls" (CABE 2000a: 4). In pursuit of these aims, CABE recognised that design review, by itself, could have only a limited impact and that a more proactive set of tools was required. Design review was almost immediately (and before the arrival of Jon Rouse) joined by a research dimension, by practice guidance, and by Stuart Lipton reaching out across Whitehall to government departments that were less amenable to the CABE message. Work with regional partner bodies, a programme of project enabling in local government, and a focus on skills and education quickly followed. These activities were intended to have a short, sharp impact and to give the nation a dose of urbanism.

A central pillar of CABE's strategy was to address professional 'silo' cultures. Deep divisions had long been a feature of relationships between the different professional specialisms in the United Kingdom, with each group failing to fully appreciate the role and significance of the others. For some time, urban design

practitioners had been trying to address the problem through the auspices of the Urban Design Group, and later the Urban Design Alliance (UDAL), as well as seeking to resolve a general lack of understanding about urban design in the professional world. For example design literacy in planning was said to be at an all-time low following the disengagement of planning from design in the 1960s and 1970s and of government policy from design in the 1980s (see Chapter 3). CABE therefore faced the somewhat daunting task of promoting a broader culture change, both in the professions and amongst politicians and in the population at large. To do this, it needed to avoid the risk of becoming too dominated by architects or too focussed on the architectural profession, although this was not something about which there was unanimity in the Commission. Internally, one commissioner (an architect) was cited as saying: "CABE can't promote something that doesn't have the word 'architecture' in it." Conversely, a key figure within planning explained, "I always felt that the broader civic design, built environment design agenda, was subservient to an architecturally dominated dialogue."

Despite the scepticism, CABE was positively engaging with a broad urban agenda from the start, and not least with the question of how to raise the profile of urban design. For example, soon after Jon Rouse arrived, CABE managed to persuade Lord Falconer, minister at the Department for Transport, Local Government and the Regions (DTLR), to commission an enquiry into urban design skills in England. Surveys were commissioned, preparatory papers were written, and an Urban Design Skills Working Group was established under the aegis of CABE and chaired by Stuart Lipton to enquire into the subject. In 2001, it published its report that concluded, "urban design, as an activity which to some degree touches on the work of all built environment disciplines, is well-placed to serve as an agent of rapprochement" between the silos. Given that CABE facilitated the Working Group and Jon Rouse largely wrote the report, it is perhaps unsurprising that this statement also summarises a good part of CABE's own agenda over the decade that followed, in which urban design (rather than architecture) loomed large. The report launched education and skills as one of CABE's key missions thereon in.

In Pursuit of Culture Change

This pioneer stage of CABE's evolution was very much about making a splash. Although CABE was still small in size, it was extremely driven and political. As a prominent commissioner described, "they weren't elected politicians, but their remit was to be political; they were political with a massive, massive P and the whole thing was about 'let's attack.'" CABE intended to have a significant impact on public perceptions and, as the 2001 annual report revealed, it was looking to champion "buildings, spaces and places that lift the spirits and speak of civic pride" (CABE 2001a: 3). In particular CABE intended to change perspectives on urban design, moving away from the lowest-cost mentality that had dominated in the 1980s and 1990s, and towards a 'best value' one, as earlier articulated by the influential report *Rethinking Construction* by Sir John Egan (Construction Task Force 1998). Gradually CABE became the central point in what one commentator described as "a fairly well joined up government push for high quality in development".

Influencing central government became a top priority for CABE, and in the words of a commissioner, "it was clear that one of the key things we should be doing was getting the Government to produce better buildings … to actually set an example." This new role as 'design champion' within government began with CABE intentionally needling ministries, "acting as a terrorist against Government, in a positive sense, trying to persuade Government that good design was good business and good for the nation". In the initial period there was a very good take up, albeit patchy, with some ministries (notably education[7]), immediately getting the agenda, whilst others, such as health, remained less engaged. This fed through into local government as well, where CABE enablers were working directly with authorities, particularly around schools. From a local government perspective, the fact that CABE and the design agenda was sanctioned by government gave the organisation tremendous weight and made others sit up and take notice.

Design review was central to CABE's strategy to quickly establish itself as the national voice on design. The outcomes of its reviews were made public and the architectural media frequently carried reports about the high-profile developments under review, such as the new Selfridges in Birmingham (4.2), the Oxford Castle redevelopment, or schemes for tall buildings in London, including The Shard, Shell Centre redevelopment, and Heron Tower (4.3). CABE used print and TV media to challenge and confront developers, and, as one insider commented, "there was a genuine fear; for the first time ever I saw developers thinking, 'well, we had better think about this, because if we don't, there's a watchdog on top of us' and there hadn't been a watchdog before"; at least not one with the profile of CABE and the ability, in its honeymoon years, to steer the media towards its ends.

But the honeymoon didn't last long, and CABE quickly found that its higher profile could be something of a double-edged sword with the media only too quick to exploit any discord for a headline (4.4). Rouse and Lipton took the brunt of the negative reactions, and, as one affected party commented, "They weren't loved by many in the private sector; people found them quite challenging. Some of that was really good because they were pushing the boundaries of design, although sometimes they were a little bit preachy and a bit high and mighty." Many of the buildings they saw became extremely controversial in their own right, but the media fanned the flames whilst CABE, and in particular the chair of its design review panel, Paul Finch, was not afraid to be outspoken and forthright, which inevitably brought criticism onto him too.

In some circles, these high-profile reviews began to feed an early dislike of CABE. For some outside of London, the headlines created the impression that CABE was mostly interested in prestige projects in the capital. As a planner with a practice in the Midlands put it, "Urban England was going on all around them, fast expansions of cities, creation of new villages, sprawling suburbs … the rest of England was completely reshaping itself and they really weren't interested. That really wasn't what they were turned on by and yet that was the front line." There was some truth in the accusation as, like its predecessor, a large proportion of CABE's London-based design review activities focussed on the capital: initially 70 per cent, reducing quickly to 50 per cent by 2001 (CABE 2001e), and later settling at around 45 per cent (Bishop 2011: 13). Over time, design review also became a progressively smaller part of CABE's total workload, with just 20 per cent of CABE's staff focussed on these activities over its lifetime.

Figures 4.2 and 4.3 Selfridges in Birmingham (4.2 - top) and Heron Tower, London (4.3 - bottom), both the subject of early high-profile design reviews by CABE

Source: Matthew Carmona

Quangos set to clash over City skyscraper bid

By Ben Willis 3072

The Government's two built environment advisors look to be on a collision course over the controversial Heron Tower building in the City of London.

The Commission for Architecture and the Built Environment (Cabe) last week announced it will give evidence in favour of the proposed 222-metre high skyscraper at a forthcoming inquiry into the scheme.

The decision will bring Cabe into conflict with English Heritage, whose claims that the tower would have a negative impact on London's skyline were partly responsible for the scheme being called in by the secretary of state.

Cabe chairman Sir Stuart Lipton said that the commission's limited resources only allowed it to present evidence at a small number of inquiries. But he added that Cabe considered the issues at stake in the Heron Tower situation to be of such "fundamental importance" to the future development of the capital that it felt it had to intervene.

"While Cabe had hoped this matter could have been resolved without the delay and public

Lipton: believes Heron Tower is crucial to the City of London

expense of an inquiry, it seems that opponents of the scheme are determined that the inquiry proceeds," he said. "Cabe must therefore speak out in favour of the right to develop a building that is well-designed and situated in a sensible and strategic location."

The difference of opinion between the two bodies casts a shadow over the joint policy statement they made in June that tall building proposals should only be considered if they were well-designed and complemented the surrounding environment (*Regeneration & Renewal*, 15 June, p8).

But a spokeswoman for English Heritage said: "The joint policy statement said that the views held by the two bodies wouldn't always coincide and this is one instance in which Cabe is clearly judging the scheme against its own criteria."

Cabe chief executive Jon Rouse said that Cabe was willing to go "head to head" with English Heritage over a scheme it believed to be suitable. "It's a bit like David against Goliath, but we have to stand up and be counted," he said.

The inquiry will be held in the autumn.

Figure 4.4 CABE quickly became a regular source of headlines in the built environment press "Quangos set to clash over City skyscraper bid"

Source: *Regeneration & Renewal*, 2001

Whilst design review got most of the headlines, leading to a misleading view about the preponderance of CABE's workload and of its geographic focus, the more complex design governance landscape in London actually counted against the city in CABE's other work programmes. At the Greater London Authority (GLA), Richard Rogers had become the advisor to the first mayor, Ken Livingstone,[8] and had set up the Architecture and Urbanism Unit (later Design for London). This provided an alternative forum for discussion of design in London and was centrally involved with schemes across the city through a process of embedded support (akin to enabling) rather than through design review. So while the other regions of England all had a member of CABE staff allocated to them, a regional representative, and later had regional design review panels, London had no such support. On the other hand, CABE and the GLA had relatively well-aligned messages on design. For instance, a prominent London design advisor explained, "The CABE/ English Heritage *Guidance on Tall Buildings* was basically the GLA's guidance . . . and the GLA's housing design standards are incredibly similar to nine of the Building for Life criteria" (see later). To some degree, therefore, the London focus was more a matter of perception than reality, but, just as it had been for the RFAC before it, this continued to be a concern for critics of CABE.

Finding Its Place

Despite its governmental backing, expert support, and high visibility, CABE still needed to position itself within the larger design governance landscape and in order to promote interdisciplinarity, it would have to interact well with the professional institutes and other organisations in the built environment. It therefore sought to work with the Royal Institute of British Architects (RIBA), the Royal Town Planning Institute (RTPI), and the Landscape Institute, both individually (for example working with the RTPI on local government urban design capacity) and collectively through the Urban Design Alliance (UDAL). Many involved at this level came to see CABE as "a really good space, which allowed people to debate the issues of the day around the built environment, all the urbanist people, from wherever they came", but establishing that forum was no easy matter. To varying degrees, long-established organisations already occupying the space tended to be fearful that CABE would undermine their own positions.

The RIBA felt particularly threatened by CABE muscling in on what it saw as 'its territory', and a frosty relationship at the start persisted with periodic rows between senior figures in the two organisations. In one meeting, the president of the RIBA "waived their Royal Charter at us [CABE's delegation] and said, 'it's our job to do what you do'". In practice, CABE's role was quite distinct. Whilst professional bodies had public interest aspirations as 'learned societies', first and foremost they served their members. CABE, by contrast, as an effective arm of government first and foremost served society at large. In the words of one commissioner, "We saw our community not as architects, but as the man in the street, general public, local

authorities, and everybody building things, from whatever profession they came."

Another body that CABE had periodic conflictual encounters with was English Heritage (now Historic England), over particular design reviews or the representations made by CABE to high-profile public inquiries into controversial building projects. Whilst the RFAC had always taken a broadly contextual stance in relation to new buildings, CABE seemed happier to support more dramatic contrast if it perceived projects as very high-quality contemporary designs. As English Heritage was the national guardian of the country's heritage, there was an obvious tension here, and as one of the first commissioners saw it, "CABE were the new kids on the block, but whereas CABE were very much the creation of an incoming government which was therefore committed to investing in its new baby and making sure that it succeeded, English Heritage had been around for a while and Tony Blair's new Britain wasn't about heritage." Indeed, at the time of the government's quinquennial review of English Heritage in 2002, Jon Rouse even wrote a contribution arguing that English Heritage should be split up as it was trying to do incompatible roles (act as regulator and as preserver of the built heritage[9]).

The view from within English Heritage tended to be that CABE was pretty unsympathetic to its mission, even though English Heritage itself was often very supportive of contemporary design, for example its support of Will Alsop's 2002 design—The Cloud—for Liverpool's Pierhead (also supported by CABE). Perhaps because of this flexibility, the two bodies managed to pull together on a number of projects, notably to produce the joint guide *Building in Context* (English Heritage & CABE 2002), the policy document *Guidance on Tall Buildings*, first published in 2003 and later revised (English Heritage & CABE 2007), the educational initiative Engaging Places (see later), and the Urban Panel. This final initiative under the chairmanship of Les Sparks (a commissioner in both organisations) was described by one member of the panel as "a very happy joint initiative" that involved sending a panel of 'the great and the good' around the country to engage with municipalities outside of London, to advise them on large-scale developments in historic areas, and to critique their approaches to design governance. By contrast, he observed, the "showtime of design review" often belied this range of very positive behind-the-scenes co-working as design review was "the moment when all had to be revealed" and when the discussion moved beyond "a quiet conversation with a nice learned English Heritage officer". This could, and often did, cause tensions.

Making the case for design was a constant priority for CABE and, as well as engaging directly with key decision-makers, it sought to do this through its research and publications. This created a lasting positive impression of the organisation and helped to fill a significant gap left by the retreat of the state from design in the 1980s, when very little (and almost no positive) guidance on design had been produced. The work started with the publication in 2000 of *By Design* (DETR & CABE 2000), the national guidance on design and the planning system. In fact, CABE had played very little part in the preparation of this guidance, which had been on the cards since John Gummer's Quality in Town & Country initiative (see Chapter 3), but which had been delayed and delayed, reflecting the hesitancy that government still felt over a more active pursuit of good design. CABE's role was to give the government some Dutch courage and insist that it be published. Eventually it was as a joint CABE/DETR publication and it remained the official government guidance on the subject until 2013. *By Design* was joined shortly afterwards by the publication of CABE's first research output, *The Value of Urban Design* (CABE 2001b). This inspired a raft of research around the value of design throughout CABE's life, regionally across England (funded, for example, by the Regional Development Agencies), and even internationally.[10] New Labour had pioneered 'evidence-based policy',[11] and in this new era even seemingly intangible 'public goods' or those understood previously as simply having intrinsic worth (such as good design) now needed to have proven value in order to convince the sceptics (the developers and politicians) of their worth.

At this point, research operations were bundled with policy, and, as a senior CABE researcher described, "it was very much about evidence gathering to shape ideas and persuade others." Whilst this part of CABE's work undoubtedly helped to spread its profile and ideas well beyond its own ability to deliver services on the ground, even here CABE had to find its place. In dealing with immediate policy issues, for example, some parts of the third sector felt CABE "didn't really provide the sort of intellectual / practical support that you would have hoped for". Others felt that CABE was not addressing wider strategic issues. Nevertheless, by the end of this period the organisation had become a prolific publisher of practical guidance on all aspects of design in the built environment, and had even joined the RIBA in funding and jointly managing its twenty-year horizon-scanning 'Building Futures' project. Some in the industry felt this explosion of design arguments and interests was insubstantial or unrelated to their work, and CABE soon came under fire for publishing too much. As one critic recounts, "CABE was a bit too airy fairy and a bit too effete from my particular perspective and it didn't do itself any favours . . . if you listen to some of the things that CABE were saying, or read the publications, then people would be a bit turned off by them." But in the early days such views were in a minority, and throughout this period CABE was clearly becoming increasingly influential within government, within the industry, and even, judging by the burgeoning column inches and exposure in the national press, in the larger civic society.

Growing CABE—2002–2006

The Delivery Agenda

In 2001, New Labour won a second term in office and moved up a gear in its programme, both releasing the shackles on public spending it had inherited from the previous Conservative administration and stressing the importance of 'delivery' across the public services. For CABE this meant two things, first, that government increasingly turned to its arm's-length agencies (and the private sector) to deliver the programmes of government, and second, with this came more funding for CABE to deliver government objectives and to pursue its larger mission.

In this second period, beginning with the start of the 2002/03 financial year and ending with a change of status in January 2006, there was a swift and significant expansion of CABE. The organisation's budget had already more or less doubled in each of the first three years of its existence, but in government terms, by April 2002, the organisation was still relatively small with a budget of around £2 million and a staff of just 31.7 full-time staff equivalent (4.5). In the two years that followed, CABE went up a league. First, in 2002/03, its core funding from DCMS doubled, and then from 2003/04 CABE began to receive very large grants from what had become the Office of the Deputy Prime Minister (ODPM), double what it was receiving from DCMS (4.6). The result was a rapid acceleration so that, by 2005/06, CABE was in receipt of in excess of £12 million of funding (a high water mark for the organisation) and had taken on whole new areas of work concerned with green space and skills. Staffing by this time had risen to 100,[12] and whilst still a minnow by government standards, CABE now had a critical mass to address the national design governance agenda in a far more comprehensive manner, and to attempt to do what the RFAC had never been able, to get high-quality design into the lifeblood of the nation (or at least the lifeblood of its governance).

In the words of a senior civil servant, CABE "went from being a small organisation that we got to do a couple of things, to something that was actually quite a big agent of government and was very much seen as part and parcel of the policy landscape, but a lot of that was to do with the government of the day and the policies of the day and was particularly to do with John Prescott's interest in the built environment". Through the auspices of his ministry, ever larger sums of public money were being invested in capital, skills, and liveability projects across England, and CABE was at the centre of this. However, the move this necessitated from a small, agile, and somewhat unconventional public organisation to a larger mainstream one with fingers in many pies proved a difficult transition. The sudden growth also led to greater scrutiny of CABE's work, and this ultimately necessitated a complete change in CABE's status and leadership, although from 2002 to the end of 2005, CABE continued to run itself in much the same way it had in the formative years, simply scaling its energy and initiative up to address the larger agenda.

A significant part of the new governmental concern for delivery followed from the ODPM 'Action Programme': *Sustainable Communities: Building for the Future* (ODPM 2003), which set out government goals around quality of life in local communities, and focussed on improving local economic, social, and environmental conditions, particularly by tackling the shortage and poor quality of social housing around the country. The plan was backed by an initial fund of £22 billion that eventually rose to £38 billion with CABE centrally involved in two of the key programmes. The first, 'Housing Market Renewal', launched in 2002 to actively (and controversially) renew areas where a viable market in housing had ceased to exist by improving "the quality of the physical infrastructure of the neighbourhoods concerned" (TSO 2008: 3). The second, 'Housing Growth Areas', aimed to build 200,000 new homes across the south-east of England by 2016.[13] CABE was heavily involved in both programmes across its range of directorates, but most notably through its enabling service, which had expanded greatly under its head, Joanna Averley, who fronted the positioning of targeted expert external assistance into

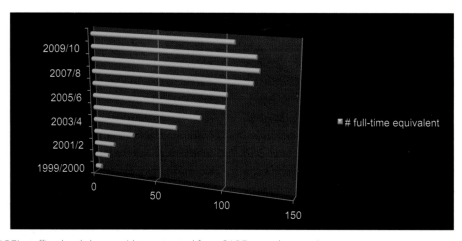

Figure 4.5 CABE's staffing levels by year (data extracted from CABE annual reports)

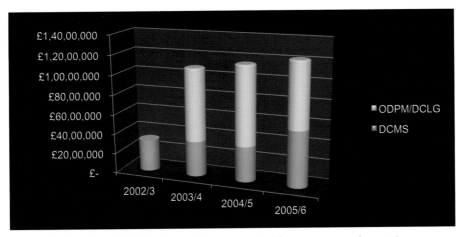

Figure 4.6 CABE's core funding from 2002/03 to 2005/06 (data extracted from CABE annual reports)

local authorities up and down the country where the scale of change required was beyond local skills and capacity to cope.

Along Came CABE Space

Another key focus of the second Blair government was 'liveability' following a high-profile speech by the prime minister in 2001 on the need for neighbourhood liveability and for high-quality, clean, and safe streets and public spaces. This agenda soon became known as the 'cleaner, safer, greener' agenda after the subtitle of the *Living Places* strategy of ODPM (2002), the strong 'green space' element coming on the heels of the report of the Urban Green Spaces Taskforce (2002). This had been set up by DTLR and earlier in 2002 had reported with an ambitious agenda to transform the nation's parks and green spaces. As a key figure from the Landscape Institute put it, "The Labour Government finally got round to looking at the importance of green space in the urban environment which had been pushed very, very hard over many years." The key concern was that the maintenance of parks had been suffering from years of neglect and underfunding, as recorded in the evidence to the 1999 Select Committee on Parks, and in the 1996 report from the Royal Parks Review Group. The report of the Urban Green Spaces Taskforce was very well received by the community of landscape professionals, who saw it as "not just hot air and general admonitions about what to do and what not to do, but actual clear ideas". As a result, ODPM folded green space concerns into the larger urban renaissance agenda

that the government had adopted and looked around for who might deliver it. Its gaze soon alighted on CABE.

While it was clear that a government body was called for, there were debates around whether a separate body dealing solely with parks and green space was required, or whether one organisation (namely CABE) could straddle both this and the remaining built environment. The arguments in favour of a single body won out, and 'CABE Space' was established in 2003 under its first director, Julia Thrift, who had moved from the Civic Trust. Initially, CABE Space was a distinct unit within the larger CABE body with its own commissioners,[14] a standing advisory group made up from individuals within the sector with policy and practice experience, and a separate funding regime. It was often described as a mini-CABE focussed on the design and management of parks and green spaces. It even had its own branding (4.7), enabling and research teams, events, training, and publications, although some of its staff had moved across from the parent organisation. In its first few years, it focussed almost entirely on green space, although its remit also extended to hard urban spaces (streets and squares), and it shifted further in that direction under its second director, Sarah Gaventa, from 2006.

The decision to collapse the green space remit into CABE was driven by ODPM, but initially was much criticised amongst green space professionals who were suspicious of CABE's ability to understand this sector. As a key parks professional stated, "I'm not sure that CABE itself was all that interested in CABE Space,

cabe
Commission for Architecture
& the Built Environment

cabe
space

Figure 4.7   CABE and CABE Space branding 2003
Source: CABE

but they wanted the money and it expanded their empire." In fact, there was some considerable reluctance from within CABE (particularly from Jon Rouse) to take on the new agenda, since it expanded the size and scope of the organisation beyond the original vision of a small body that was light on its feet. But, as a long-standing commissioner explained, "John Prescott was very insistent that we took on public space as a big pro-gramme, and he asked us a couple of times to do it, and we said, 'well, we can't because we don't have the resources,' but the third time he asked, he said, 'well, I'm giving you the resources,' and it wasn't really for us to say 'well, actually, you know what, we don't want to do it.'" Some within CABE Space suggested that these early difficulties were partly attributable to the subject matter which had long been a closed silo, but quickly CABE Space became a well-established part of CABE and was increasingly integrated into the whole, developing in the process a very positive reputation for its work.

Working with Government

Relationships with government always had to be care-fully managed. On one hand, CABE relied on govern-ment for its funding and government was its main

client. On the other, government was one of the key constituencies who needed to do better on design and needed to be regularly reminded of that. A minister from DCMS suggested: "CABE, in a sort of sense, was slightly un-British. We're quite unaccustomed to cul-tural dirigisme . . . the very active identification of the French state [for example] with questions of design and culture, is in striking contrast to the tradition in Britain." But initial hesitations from the Treasury to release new funding streams for CABE via DCMS were resolved, and ODPM negotiations were now complete. In just five years, CABE's resources were twenty-four times their original size and the balance of power had shifted. Both DCMS and ODPM were major investors in CABE from this point onwards.

Despite representing one government, CABE's two funders had very different ways of working. DCMS was a smaller, less well-funded department, acting through a large array of arm's-length quangos in the arts, culture, and sports. ODPM was much larger and better funded and generally more used to working 'on the ground', for example through directly funding programmes for physical and community regeneration. While DCMS had provided a logical starting point for CABE, having inherited the architecture brief from its predecessor, the Department of National Heritage (DNH), in some ways ODPM was a potentially more appropriate funder given its responsibilities for plan-ning, housing, regeneration, and local government policies, including parks.

The major funding streams from the ODPM enabled CABE to expand its activities, and particularly the more resource-intensive ones such as enabling. But more fundamentally, in the words of one commis-sioner, DCMS "were interested in architecture as an abstract, whereas [OPDM] were actually interested in architecture as something that delivered communities". Perhaps inevitably, two such distinctive departmental cultures and sets of objectives created tension at the management level for CABE. ODPM tended to 'micromanage' work and to get involved in the detail of operations (believing CABE needed its help to realise its goals), whereas DCMS took a light touch or a less directive approach. This also meant that ODPM tended to be less comfortable with the role of sponsor depart-ment for CABE, partly because it was less used to work-ing in this way and partly because the joint responsibilities did not allow it full control of its investment, for example with regard to the appointment of commissioners where ODPM had no influence outside of CABE Space.[15] Nonetheless, the two departments learned to work together, and, in the words of one government official, "it worked but it took a lot of work to make it work."

The different government departments were also attuned to CABE's priorities in different ways. ODPM was more interested in seeing actual impacts on the ground, whereas DCMS, having a laissez faire management style, could more easily support less tangible goals such as raising awareness about design. The arrangement also meant that some critical aspects of the developing design agenda were never really covered. The Department for Environment, Food and Rural Affairs (DEFRA) and ODPM had come to an agreement that DEFRA would do green space outside of cities and ODPM would do green space within cities. This meant that biodiversity, for example, became largely a DEFRA issue and was mostly ignored by CABE as DEFRA ministers and civil servants did not engage with CABE Space. Streets were a similar concern, with the Department for Transport having responsibility for roads, but little interest in design until much later in CABE's story.

The Hand That Feeds

For CABE, its relationship with DCMS had been relatively unproblematic and easy to manage, however, the new sponsor was more of a challenge and a double-edged sword. Having a strong relationship with ODPM allowed CABE to have a great influence over built environment policy. In the words of a commissioner, "we established a very strong role in sharpening government policy on design, which we couldn't have done from DCMS," a role born out by CABE officers' descriptions of regularly providing the actual wording for policy documents during this period. At the same time, ODPM's close monitoring of activities appeared to threaten CABE's independence.

As a non-departmental public body, CABE expected to operate at arm's length from ministerial influence with the freedom to propose and initiate activities. However, the department was very aligned with the sensibilities of ministers and at various times tried to limit CABE. This is well demonstrated, for

Figure 4.8   The Wasted Space campaign was conceived to draw attention to derelict spaces that blighted urban communities; its posters used high-profile personalities to highlight the potential of wasted urban land

Source: CABE Space

instance, by the reactions to CABE Space's first campaign, 'Wasted Space' (see Chapter 8). As one CABE employee recalled, "DCMS thought that pointing out that around the country there was some wasted spaces which were derelict and eyesores was fine, they had no problem with that. By contrast ODPM were absolutely furious, they were horrified that we were doing this," as if somehow it reflected directly on them (4.8). A little later, ministers were said to be angered when CABE's Housing Audits seemed to suggest that the quality of new housing in England remained very poor two terms into the New Labour government; although subsequently the data was used quite extensively in government publications, for example in *World Class Places* (see later).

In these years campaigning had become an increasingly prominent tool in CABE's arsenal, not least as a means to spread the design message beyond the captive professional audience, and the appointment of Matt Bell in late 2003 further bolstered this mission. Around the same time, however, funding ties were beginning to constrain the free hand that CABE had previously enjoyed and were even threatening to politicise the organisation, associating it too closely with New Labour. One such issue was the lack of investment in parks. As one prominent green spaces practitioner commented, "CABE Space found themselves in a really difficult position. Because they were sponsored by government they didn't want to go round banging the drum about neglect and were therefore always looking for design solutions to the problems in parks, but you couldn't design out a lack of funding." For him, "CABE Space did what they could do, and if they couldn't campaign about money, they campaigned about other things like skills—which had been destroyed."

In practice, both departments had to monitor the activities of CABE to ensure accountability, and with the funding came a set of annual performance targets, as was the norm for publicly funded bodies at the time.[16] To measure these, a range of performance indicators were used of tangible and intangible factors. Some of these quantified 'operational' delivery factors, such as the number of workshops held, and others allowed for complex 'outcomes' targets related to longer-term societal changes. Two problems arose from this. First, the operational objectives said little about the quality of CABE's services and tended to concentrate on counting things, for example numbers of seminars, research projects, website visits, guides published, network members, and so forth. Second, in the early years, the outcome targets often related to matters that CABE had little direct responsibility for and only very indirect impact on, such as (in 2002/03) the number of applicants to undergraduate built environment courses, public recognition of the contribution of architecture to quality of life, or the percentage of local authorities issuing design guidance (CABE 2003a: 34–35). In this respect, the input of ODPM and its more hands-on manner ensured that these performance measurement processes evolved to become more intense, and the targets themselves both more specific and more impactful on the conduct of CABE's day-to-day work. Such targets included the percentage of satisfaction with design reviews or training, public awareness of defined CABE activities, numbers of 'Green flags'[17] awarded to parks, and so on (CABE 2005c: 24–25).

The problems CABE faced with its targets were nothing new and reflected much wider critiques of the target-driven management approaches being used across government during the New Labour years. A typical critique, here expressed by a CABE commissioner, was that "It was corrosive because, in the end, you find all the organisations are merely making sure that they've met the numbers they're supposed to meet, rather than thinking, 'well, is this really what our principal task ought to be this month or next?'" This was

borne out in design review where, as a director described it, "We had to send feedback on how we were doing and how many reviews we had done.... It was onerous if we didn't keep up with it ... and if towards the end of the year you hadn't done enough reviews, then you had to quickly fetch more little ones in." CABE Space was under particular pressure. Its work programme was initially inspired by the Urban Green Spaces Taskforce, on which basis a large number of targets were set that allowed for little deviation from the government-dictated path.

Early on, CABE had scheduled quarterly meetings with its core funders to discuss quarterly reports, but the processes evolved to include more continuous interactions, and even, during some periods, day-to-day liaison. One example was the eighteen-month pilot programme for design coding (2004–2005) which ODPM funded but which CABE managed through its enabling directorate. As a civil servant recounted, "We were working very, very closely with CABE to do research jointly that helped influence, not only design coding policies in planning, but also some of the other wider policies." For CABE, the downside was that such close attention increasingly reined in the ability to both react to and shape events, a quality that many had seen as a key dimension of CABE's early effectiveness.

Other funders were also involved, and besides DCMS and ODPM, other government bodies and departments funded some of its activities through Service Level Agreements. From accounting years 2000/01 to 2005/06, the Arts Council for England funded CABE activities at just under £400,000, and the Housing Corporation, NHS Estates, and the Department for Education and Skills retained CABE's services at around £250,000 each. In addition, English Partnerships, English Heritage, Sport England, the Higher Education Funding Council, the Home Office, the National Audit Office, and the Corporation of London all funded activities at lower levels. CABE also had to deal with the Treasury to justify spending on design quality in the programmes it was involved with, and this form of auditing became a continuous distraction for CABE to justify the 'value for money' of its funding streams. A minister recalled the case being made "that the lifetime costs of a well-designed building were likely to be very appreciably less than the lifetime costs of a poorly designed building—not a complex proposition to grasp, you wouldn't think—but it was amazing how long it took to get the Treasury to take that on board and internalise it".

Developing the Offer

CABE's growth does not appear to have had a significant impact on its internal structure, although the directorates did grow and change. From the start, design review was the most prominent work stream, closely aligning with the architectural and cultural goals of DCMS. Reflecting its interest in 'everyday' places over one-off exceptional buildings, OPDM was more interested in enabling as a tool, and, as a source within the department suggested, "it was enabling that actually changed things on the ground and things with a physical outcome were DCLG's bigger interest." The demand for CABE enabling continuously outstripped the organisation's capacity to supply it (CABE 2001a: 3), and was kept in check only by CABE's ability to rapidly and continuously recruit an army of CABE enablers. By the mid-2000s, there were 250 of these across CABE and its CABE Space panels, and this rose to more than 300 by 2009.[18]

CABE also used this period to develop the reach of its enabling service from public building procurement to wider development processes, employing training and conference events around the country to reach out to those commissioning or otherwise involved in significant public projects. Through these means CABE was hand holding and advising on choices rather than reviewing schemes. With regard to public buildings, such as the hospitals being built under the Private Finance Initiative (PFI), there was frequently very low engagement with design (4.9). As a senior enabler recalled, "We took a load of hospital trusts away, and I remember standing around this model with a chairman of a major trust, and he said, 'why have you brought us here?'…And I said, 'well, you're building what's on this plan; you're building a bit of city,' and there was a kind of, 'oh God, yeah, I am, aren't I?'" The approach was felt to be particularly effective when used in relation to housing, and good parts of the housing sector were increasingly well attuned to design and welcomed the help, although others remained wholly unconvinced.

Across the directorates more time and resources were being spent on housing, which was an ODPM priority and with regard to which CABE had been criticised in its early years for not engaging with enough. Commissioners widely welcomed the change, because, as one commented, "Housing represents the vast majority of what gets built in this country, and it has been appalling since the war." The need for more affordable and better-quality housing had been articulated by the 'Barker Report',

Figure 4.9   Queen Elizabeth Hospital in Woolwich, the PFI hospital that first got CABE exercised about the very poor quality of design in the NHS estate

Source: Matthew Carmona

which called for a significant expansion in supply, whilst its author, the economist Kate Barker, recognised the challenge with regard to design. "The industry should work together with CABE to agree [on] a code of best practice in the external design of new houses, [and] where planners and housebuilders disagree on specific design issues, they should seek arbitration, possibly through CABE, to resolve these matters" (Barker 2004: 119). Volume housebuilders were also coming under strong criticism in the popular press with figures such as the fashion designer (and later chair of Building for Life), Wayne Hemmingway, helping to raise these issues in the national consciousness (Lonsdale 2004). In addition to CABE's enabling work in both the housing market renewal and growth areas, CABE was involved with three other important housing initiatives during this period:

- First, its programme of Housing Audits designed to systematically evaluate the quality of new housing design and development around the country[19] as a means to put pressure on the volume builders who were producing so much of the housing that many considered (and which the audits revealed to be) sub-standard. The audits received very significant press coverage and were used effectively to engage the housebuilders in debate (see Chapter 6).
- Second, a design coding pilot programme that CABE managed for the ODPM and that included a series of seven fully enabled pilot schemes around the country (4.10), a wider evaluation and research programme conducted by UCL covering nineteen cases, and the writing of design guidance that DCLG (successor to ODPM) later published alongside appropriate revisions in policy (DCLG 2006b). Despite initial reservations from CABE concerning the use and value of design codes as a tool, more than any other this episode demonstrated how a close working relationship between CABE and government could benefit both sides: CABE in helping to shape government ambitions and government in getting things done.
- Third, Building for Life (BfL), which began in 2001 following conversations between the Civic Trust and Home Builders Federation with CABE, shortly after, joining the partnership. This initiative quickly gained significant momentum and, from

2003, the Building for Life Awards were introduced and criteria in the form of twenty questions began to be used to assess the quality of new developments. Through the remainder of the 2000s, the tool increasingly gained traction, becoming the standard means by which assessments were made about residential design quality across a range of public sector programmes and initiatives (see Chapters 8 and 9).

As these initiatives demonstrate, CABE remained very active and engaged during this period of its development, innovating in important new areas of design governance, some of which it was solely responsible for, and others where it worked with partners, implementing and amplifying ideas that might otherwise have been far less impactful.

Another issue that was increasingly exercising CABE was the marginalisation of design through the PFI procurement model. This had been a major concern for the RFAC in the 1990s (see Chapter 3), but under Chancellor Gordon Brown government increasingly favoured PFI because of the way it shifted capital costs off the government books. One architect described his experience of working under this model. "It was never going to be about the quality of the design; it was actually going to be about the pounds, shillings and pence on the end of the quantity surveyor's bill of quantities, that was what would ultimately define whether it was value for money or not, which was sadly wrong." These issues led to a renewed focus on the public sector as client and to CABE attempting once again to convince the more sceptical government departments of its role in this regard. Drawing from its own now considerable experience enabling the public sector to take its role in commissioning projects more seriously, one of CABE's most important publications, *Creating Excellent Buildings, a Guide for Clients* (CABE 2003a), was produced, and remained a staple reference source for the organisation until its demise, followed a year later by *Creating Excellent Masterplans, A Guide for Clients* (CABE 2004a), which aimed to extend the lessons to the larger scale.[20]

Throughout this period, the design review directorate was also involved in reviewing a much larger range and quantity of developments. These included an array of transport, housing, hospitals, schools, mixed-use master-planning, cultural, and complex regeneration

Key

- ···· Coding Area (code 1/02)
- —— Character Area Boundary (code 1/03)
- —— Road Centre Line
- —— Adjustable Road Centre Line
- —— Active Occupied Frontage (code 1/F.01, 1/BL.01)
- ···· Semi-Active Occupied Frontage (code 1/F.03)
- – – Frontage Enclosure (code 1/F.05)
- Mews Frontage Reference Line (code 2/5.09.2a)
- ═══ Set-Back Frontage (code 1/F.02, 1/F.04)
- Possible Location of Additional Road Access
- Variable Building Line 100-75% (code 1/BL.02)
- Variable Building Line 74-50% (code 1/BL.03)
- Variable Building Line 49-30% (code 1/BL.04)
- Variable Building Line within Mews (code 1/BL.05)
- Maximum Variation in Building Line
- Plot series
- Vehicular / Cycle Zone (code 1/04.1) ⎫
- Shared Zone (code 1/04.1) ⎬ Public Highway (code /04)
- Pedestrian Zone (code 1/04.1) ⎭
- Possible Mews (code 2/5.09.2, 2/5.09.2a)
- Area of Specific Public Realm Design (code 3/PR.01)
- Existing Building
- River & Marina
- River Bank
- ✳ Landmark (code 3/B.01)
- ✳ Marker Building (code 3/B.02)
- ⟩ Corner Building (code 3/B.03)
- ⊲ Gateway (code 3/B.04)
- 1:30▷ Approximate Street Gradient
- ③ Shoulder/ Eaves Height

The Regulating Plan is also available at a scale of 1:500 (A0) by request from the Council

Figure 4.10   Design code pilot, Rotherham town centre river corridor regulating plan (unrealised)

Source: studio REAL

projects and numbers rose quickly from fewer than 100 per year when CABE was founded to an all-time high of 494 schemes reviewed in the 2004/05 accounting year (CABE 2005c: 24). These included both monthly full-panel review sessions and 'lighter-touch' internal and desktop reviews[21] (see Chapter 9), the latter of which later became the subject of heavy criticism by the Select Committee on the Office of the Deputy Prime Minister (2005) for being too cursory.

Despite the numbers, it remained more difficult to trace a clear-cut impact of design review than, for example, enabling, because of the more indirect and hands-off nature of the service. Real-world experience and local knowledge were needed in each instance in order to garner the respect of those being reviewed, and this was achieved with a 71 per cent satisfaction rating recorded for design review in the 2004/05 annual report (although the target had been 87 per cent—CABE 2005c: 24). Yet this could be quickly undermined if reviewers were not chosen well and did not understand critical aspects of a scheme. As one recipient of the service commented, "We did a complete urban design analysis as part of the justification for the tower, all of which was brushed to one side because they didn't like the way some of the bits of metal stuck out of the top of the building." Design review, throughout CABE's story, continued to be the most controversial of its services.

Tensions Mount

A particularly tricky issue for CABE was the question of designing for higher density, which, in the context of contemporaneous planning reforms that sought the reuse of previously developed land and higher built densities, was something that developers were exploiting. However, in the application of these principles, many felt that CABE was unduly influenced by a London mindset and by the narrative of urban renaissance that, some argued, was not appropriate everywhere. As one master planner from the Midlands described it: "the Lord Rogers agenda of town cramming, high density, mixed use, ban cars and all that sort of stuff, and packing people up in high rise blocks of apartments and the café culture". Like the RFAC before it, this perception of an out of touch (at least as regards the needs of the rest of the country) London

elite dictating to 'the provinces' was an easy criticism to make, and regardless of the truth, it was not easy to counter when so much of CABE's enabling and other work went largely unremarked in the press and therefore failed to have the same impact as a negative design review.

During this period, the tone of design review processes was nevertheless beginning to affect the reputation of CABE in some quarters. One reviewer noted, "if you get a few [architects] in a room that are complete buggers, it can go off, and did," and, as might be expected from such hard-hitting reviews, a criticism soon emerged that the confrontational nature of the process actively worked against its effectiveness. The criticism related to both what went on inside the room and outside of it. A planning consultant recalled, for example, that "a rather imperious letter would be sent to the council, and to us, saying, 'we have heard that you're doing something really important and vast in so and so, and we would like to take an interest in this; please attend at our office next Tuesday at 2 o'clock.'" Both the tone of CABE's decision letters (often described as fairly personal and rude) and the lack of access to the minutes of meetings added to impressions of an aloof process and poor accountability, although in reality letters varied as significantly as the schemes themselves (4.11).

While the advice itself was often seen as helpful in the planning process, changes to projects late in the day had huge knock-on financial impacts that fed into a widely held perception that CABE was uninterested and uninformed about financial viability concerns. This was particularly so for larger schemes where CABE was just one of a large number of voices, but, some argued, was not willing to acknowledge the value of others. As the director of a volume housebuilder commented, "If you were having disputes with the local authority, the developer, other landowners, English Heritage, the Environment Agency, and all these other groups that we have to talk to, they've probably all got an equal voice, whereas CABE had the view that it was the ultimate voice."

In this period, design review was the major cause of conflict with CABE, and it led to a degree of mistrust and to the use of the media (by some) to vent their concerns. An article in *The Telegraph*, for example, reported that Mr Wilkinson, secretary of the heritage

Thameslink 2000 - Blackfriars Station   i

City of London

Redevelopment of Blackfriars Railway Station in the City of London, including modifications to Blackfriars Bridge and new station on southern side. Designed by Pascall & Watson Architects.

6 November 2003
Tagged with: Design review | Design review panel | London | Transport and infrastructure

We regret to say that in our view these proposals fall far below the standard we would expect for such a prominent location in the heart of London. We believe there is a need to rethink the major elements of this scheme before the submission of the planning application in June if these proposals are to present a fresh and holistic approach to give London a station it deserves for the 21st century.

This in our view is a classic case of creating a design problem and then providing a solution that will simply lead to further problems. What is required is a real vision to make the most of this opportunity and develop something beyond what was highlighted in the inspectors report resulting from the TWA. We question this whole process which appears to us to result in mediocrity and muddle when it should be providing an example of best practice and embracing what is possible with the technology of today.

Centre for Contemporary Art   ii

Contemporary arts centre on a site in the Lace Market area of Nottingham. Designed by Caruso St John.

3 May 2005
Tagged with: Arts | Culture and leisure | Design review | Design review panel | East Midlands

This proposal strikes us as an elegant, high quality response to a challenging site and an exciting brief. In our view, the building forms a fine composition which responds purposefully to the topography of the site. Its form and appearance, and the way in which the internal spaces will be used, have clearly been thought about in a considered and sensitive way. We strongly support the scheme and offer the following thoughts and comments in that context.

Figure 4.11   Design review decision letters, introductory paragraphs to (i) Thameslink 2000 Blackfriars Station, London (2003) and (ii) Centre for Contemporary Art, Nottingham (2005)

Source: CABE

body SAVE, had written to DCMS to complain about CABE "not being 'properly informed' on heritage matters and questioned whether the quango was fully accountable" (Clover 2004). Tensions were also apparent within the organisation itself, for example stemming from the contrasting nature of the advice given by its enabling and design review divisions. As one insider commented, "There were particular cases where schemes came forward that got a hard time from the design review panel and a disgruntled client said, 'well, how could this possibly be because we've had CABE advice all along, from the enabling programme?'." In such circumstances, CABE enabling might have been "focussing on getting the right architect to meet a client's brief, or on getting the brief correct in the first place, and may not be dealing with the actual design, or only aspects of it". But these internal distinctions between design review, enabling, and other services within CABE weren't understood or even of much

interest to the outside world, and posed a risk to CABE when one sort of intervention was vaunted as a form of endorsement for another.

CABE also became a larger funder of other organisations and initiatives around the country. Whilst this acquired for the Commission the means to shape the broader environment for design governance, it also represented a challenge to some. Not only did the government funding to CABE draw on monies that arguably (and previously did) go directly to these organisations, but regional organisations quickly came to rely on CABE's funding, and therefore had to adjust to CABE and its priorities. This is often said to have impacted most directly the Civic Trust, set up in 1957 ostensibly to campaign for the improvement of new and historic buildings and spaces and to support the national network of civic societies. As a key figure from within that body put it, "The Civic Trust was very supportive of the foundation of CABE, nevertheless, from a business point of view it was to a certain extent stealing a bit of the Civic Trust thunder," ultimately contributing to its demise in 2009. The architecture and built environment centres that CABE funded in the regions also had to shape their work to attract the funding (see Chapter 8). This funding dramatically increased from 2003 onwards with both the number of centres and the extent of funding ramping up from that date on with the aim of establishing a complete national network of CABE-funded centres. This established the model on which design governance services at the regional level were (and largely still are, see Chapter 5) shaped, with a single dominant centre in each region providing design review and enabling. At the same time, CABE in London had no qualms about working in those same regions itself without any collaboration with the centres it was funding. Thus it acted both as funder and quasi-competitor, which one regional operator described as "a source of confusion and tension … if a request went through to CABE, there was nothing to stop CABE coming into the region and just doing stuff".

All Change

At this stage, CABE was still a bold and vocal campaigning organisation. It had a confident and energetic body of staff members who, from the outside, were seen as typically young and slightly pugnacious types with a idealistic mindset. CABE staff from the era describe the cohort in a similar way: "People were attracted to CABE because we were the new kids on the block, we were a bit … not punkish, but a bit young and stirring it up." There was some distrust of CABE related to its conduct of design review and around the establishment of CABE Space, but key people from CABE were making every effort to spread the message and to develop close relationships with important policy and practice stakeholders and organisations. Julia Thrift at CABE Space, for example, was particularly energetic in communicating and connecting with the green space sector, travelling around the country in order to mend fences and reach out and engage others in the first publications of CABE's green spaces arm. CABE also lent its growing expertise to others, such as the secondment during 2005 of Director of Learning and Development, Chris Murray, as interim chief executive of the new Academy for Sustainable Communities (ASC).[22] Whilst this new academy proved largely ineffectual and was quickly incorporated into the Homes and Communities Agency (becoming the HCA Academy), during its brief existence there was clearly some overlap between CABE's education mission and its own, and a sense that "it was a perfectly sensible thing for the academy to be working absolutely directly in harness with CABE". The two eventually ran a series of projects focussing on the design dimension of the sustainable communities agenda.

CABE was also continuing to deliver evidence to fill holes in knowledge around design, sometimes on quite specific concerns, for example on the low levels of minority ethnic representation within the professions, and sometimes as part of larger longer-term battles, including the fight to change perceptions about design being solely about aesthetics. This was an underpinning belief of CABE and reflected its move away from the preoccupations of earlier decades and that which the RFAC had so doggedly pursued through its seventy-five years. It was a steep mountain to climb, however, and the media did not help, for example characterising CABE's housing market renewal work as a "facelift for slums" (Sherman 2003). CABE nevertheless believed it necessary at the time in order to move policy makers' focus beyond appearance and to the wider and more fundamental impacts of design.

Helping in the task was the steady flow of research and guidance outputs that CABE produced, work that added strongly to CABE's authority and profile and that for many practitioners represented their only regular contact with CABE. Much of this material had its origins in the small research unit at CABE that Elanor Warwick headed from 2003.

However CABE was becoming somewhat unwieldy, and the extent of its work and the size of the directorates fuelled criticism of CABE as "not properly joined up". In some instances, connections were actively sought out, for example by sharing lessons across the organisation or occasionally cross-referring cases between directorates, but on the whole the directorates were becoming increasingly self-sufficient and disconnected so that the extent and configuration of work was no longer properly understood within the organisation itself. One director bemoaned this. "You would suddenly find that somebody was producing a document about supermarkets, when actually, you'd been doing all this work with supermarkets on the ground." The headline services of design review and enabling were often said to be particularly disconnected, and one commissioner noted, "You get instances where there'd be an enabling operation going on, and there'd be a design review operation going on in the same place, but no one was aware of the different roles the organisation was playing." At one stage, CABE even had to conduct a mapping exercise to scope for itself what it was doing and where.

Ultimately CABE was outgrowing its dynamic management style and the campaigning approach adopted to its activities was becoming harder to sustain. While the organisation continued on this trajectory for some time, it was an unfortunate debacle that finally destabilised it and through which it lost its leadership. Chairman Sir Stuart Lipton and other commissioners were accused of bias in relation to the design review of two schemes in South Kensington and Croydon Gateway, in which Lipton's property development company, Stanhope, had an interest (Blackler 2004). The episode led to a series of inquiries.

First, in 2004, the ODPM ordered an audit into conflicts of interest at CABE which was conducted by the accountancy firm AHL. Meanwhile, and before AHL could report, Jon Rouse was head hunted to lead the Housing Corporation and left CABE (conveniently dodging the bullets) in May of that year. Barely two weeks later, and forty-eight hours before AHL reported, Lipton also stepped down; ostensibly "to enable the organisation to respond freely to the report's recommendations" (Brown 2004), but in fact following a meeting with Heritage Minister, Lord McIntosh, at which Sir Stuart was given his marching orders. When AHL reported, it noted: "The potential impact of the cumulative effect of perceived conflicts of interest, on CABE and its reputation, is such that, in our opinion, it is now becoming untenable for this post to be held by an active property developer."[23]

Ultimately the allegations of cronyism at CABE did not stand up to public scrutiny. Critically it was acknowledged that "ten of the sixteen commissioners had professional interests directly related to the activities of CABE" and that this was inevitable given the government's initial decision to seek 'current' expertise in CABE's leadership rather than those who were no longer professionally active. The audit nevertheless made twenty-eight recommendations through which it was abundantly clear that commercial activities needed to be publicly declared by all involved in design review, and that the position of the chair of CABE should not be held by anyone with major commercial interests. These recommendations were subsequently accepted by the government (ODPM 2005).

There was certainly an intense media scrutiny of Lipton and extremely strong criticism of CABE during this time, but supporters and critics alike express the view that the chairman took the fall, although he could have avoided it. As one not untypical view recounts: "Stuart was the unfortunate victim of the whole thing. As Chair, he was clearly, absolutely, in the clear over all of this, but because there was this perception that the public and private interest was being confused, he had to go." Second and third inquiries followed in 2005, but in the meantime the leadership gap at the top of CABE was filled, first by Paul Finch stepping into the breach to act as interim chairman until the appointment of John Sorrell in December 2004, and second by the appointment of Richard Simmons as the new chief executive from September 2004. Together they steered the organisation through some choppy waters and into the next stage of its journey. Their first job was to sort out the mess CABE had

been landed in by some of its rather lax internal governance arrangements.

Before that, the House of Commons Select Committee on the Office of the Deputy Prime Minister (2005) decided to hold a hearing into the effectiveness of CABE, and this was followed by a Royal Town Planning Institute disciplinary hearing. The latter followed accusations of professional misconduct levelled at Adrian Dennis, the Croydon councillor (and chartered planner) who had brought the original complaint against Lipton, and who then repeated it in Parliament (to the Select Committee).[24] This proved a short-lived affair as the RTPI quickly dropped the case following advice that it was in danger of breaching parliamentary privilege.[25] The Select Committee hearing was more significant, with the Committee strongly supporting the complete rethinking of CABE's governance arrangements. In essence these aimed at establishing governance arrangements to meet the highest standards of probity in line with those set down by the Committee on Standards in Public Life (2005), arrangements that (by the time it reported) CABE's new leadership was already implementing following the AHL review. The Committee also supported a plan to put the organisation on a proper statutory footing and urged a complete review of CABE's design review arrangements.

As well as the cases of South Kensington and Croydon, the Select Committee heard from a variety of other witnesses about CABE's design review function. Most notably, this included the planning and property correspondent for the *Evening Standard*, Mira Bar-Hillel, who, claiming the support of CABE's former chief executive (Jon Rouse) for her views, argued passionately that design review at CABE should be ended. As she saw it, design review suffered from "unaccountability, lack of transparency, cliquism, groupism, stylism and back to unaccountability and lack of transparency" (Select Committee on the Office of the Deputy Prime Minister 2005: question 113). Others spoke eloquently in defence of the function, including CABE's new chief executive and its acting chair, and in the end the Committee came down on the side of retaining design review, but making it more rigorous (dropping the lighter-touch weekly desktop sessions), more transparent (opening sessions to the public), and better managed (with clearer criteria and more attention to context).

In its response, the government largely backed CABE's design review practices, whilst arguing that they could be made more open for educational purposes (although not to the general public) (ODPM 2005: 9). It is notable, however, that in the years following, the numbers of reviews fell back sharply to around 350 schemes per annum chosen from amongst the more than 1,000 cases submitted annually for review (CABE 2006c: 24–25). The Committee had helped to put quality, rather than quantity, of activity back to centre stage at CABE, and this provided a useful reminder to the organisation about its role as it moved forward to embark on the next stage of its journey.

Mature CABE—2006–2011

Institutionalising CABE

The departures of Rouse and Lipton and the distraction of the Select Committee which followed marked the close of a chapter for CABE. Once the dust had settled, and under its new leadership, CABE was effectively relaunched as a new legal entity. CABE continued to operate as an arm's-length agent of government, but from 6 January 2006 became a statutory body when the Clean Neighbourhood and Environment Act 2005 changed its status from a limited company. The move marked a final transition from the agile new kid on the block to a mature and embedded pillar of the national governance scene.

CABE's functions were now clearly established under Part 8 of the Act, which defined them as: "The promotion of education and high standards in, and understanding and appreciation of (a) architecture, and (b) the design, management and maintenance of the built environment". The steps[26] designated for CABE to discharge these duties fell into four areas of practical action:

1. Providing advice and developing and reviewing projects.
2. Providing financial assistance.
3. Carrying out or supporting the carrying out of research.
4. Commissioning or assisting in the commissioning of works of art.

This statutory position strengthened the legal basis for CABE and was vaunted by DCMS at the time as a great increase in the organisation's prestige and authority:

> CABE has important public duties including provision of practical support and advice on design quality to a wide range of clients in both public and private bodies. This will confirm CABE's status as the champion for architecture and the design of public space in England. Having achieved so much in its first five years, putting CABE on a statutory basis is a strong sign of our confidence in its abilities and future.
>
> (DCMS 2004)

However, it did not endow CABE with any legal powers of sanction or impose any obligations on third parties. The first area of activity did give CABE a notional 'right to review' projects deemed nationally significant whether or not it was requested to do so (a power the RFAC had previously enjoyed), but did not raise CABE to the position of 'statutory consultee';[27] or require others to cooperate with it; or endow CABE with 'call-in' powers[28] equivalent to those held by, for example, English Heritage in relation to heritage matters. Therefore, individual developers were not legally obliged to assist CABE in its processes of review by attending panels or providing materials, and local planning authorities did not have to consult CABE before determining relevant planning applications.

Generally these legislative changes were poorly understood, and as early as June 2006 government felt it needed, via Circular 01/2006, to 'urge' local authorities to "consult CABE at the earliest opportunity where they consider a proposal raises, or is likely to raise, significant design quality and access issues" (DCLG 2006a: para 76).[29] The move to a statutory status was also widely misinterpreted as a means to guarantee CABE a long-term future, as demonstrated in a typical comment from a senior staff member: "Being a statutory body was, I believe, intended to ensure that if you wanted to abolish CABE, you would have to have an Act of Parliament to do it and that might delay things. As it turned out, you didn't need to do that, you just stopped funding them." In fact, section 90 of the

Act explicitly provided for the secretary of state to dissolve the new 'corporate body' of CABE, and those powers were used just six years later in January 2012.

Likewise the notion that CABE had previously lacked legitimacy as a publicly funded body in the form of a company limited by guarantee was incorrect. As one CABE director recalled, "I think that was a technicality; its status up to that point had been technically illegal—which was really the reason for making it a statutory body." Official records of the time reveal that public accountability was at the heart of this concern. Thus commentary on the proposed Act from the House of Commons Library states that the change "fulfilled a Government undertaking given in response to the Sharman Report that in future all executive Non Departmental Public bodies should be audited by the Comptroller and Auditor General" (2005: 63). As this could only be done if CABE was fully part of the public sector and not a company limited by guarantee, the change to CABE's status represented a relatively minor adaption in order to allow the significant flow of public funding to continue.

A New Culture

Tony Blair won his third and final election in May 2005, but his popularity ratings soon plummeted due to accusations of misleading Parliament over the decision to support the invasion of Iraq in 2003, and in June 2007, he handed over the office of prime minister to Gordon Brown, who remained in power until May 2010. The final five years of New Labour witnessed numerous cabinet reshuffles with John Prescott also handing over his responsibilities at the ODPM to the newly formed Department for Communities and Local Government (DCLG), first under the leadership of David Miliband, then Ruth Kelly, Hazel Blears, and finally John Denham, none of whom had the same concern for the built environment that John Prescott had repeatedly shown, nor were they in office long enough to significantly shape the agenda.

The change in CABE's status also appears to have exacerbated the tension that existed between its two funding departments, who continued to have very different expectations of CABE. Whilst DCMS continued to value the original challenging nature of CABE,

DCLG was far more focussed (in the words of one insider) on "'What are you doing to support ministers?'" and took the organisation to task when it dared to criticise design in relation to particular government programmes or initiatives. As this dynamic continued, the relationship with DCLG became more fractious, with CABE increasingly seen as an effective agent for policy delivery rather than an agent provocateur for design. New priorities were being set under Gordon Brown linked to a far more controlling and reporting processes so that even the hiring and firing of staff was linked to specific 'Service Level Agreements' (SLAs). In addition, the new ministers were often less well advised on the design agenda than previously (perhaps because their interest had waned), resulting in a number of misjudgements. A senior figure within CABE reported: "One of the things that really hurt CABE was the time when Margaret Hodge [then a minister in DCMS] decided to clamp down on organisations that had regional structures, and, unfortunately, her policy advisor at the time had been to Manchester, and she'd seen the architecture centre in Manchester, and it had a 'funded by CABE' sign on it, and she had incorrectly assumed that it was CABE's regional office, so as a consequence we were given a cut in that year's budget." This was part of a larger drive for more accountability across government and an extension of the earlier concern for 'delivery', but it was also wasteful and imposed a centralising culture that undermined CABE's ability to be challenging or outspoken in its work. As a long-standing member of the 'CABE family' noted, "you started overwhelming the organisation, so something that was relatively small, light on its feet, and which could be quite critical of government, became too much an instrument of government."

Even without the sort of fulsome government commitment that it had previously enjoyed, CABE continued to operate across the country, now under the leadership of John Sorrell and Richard Simmons, who would steer CABE through its most stable years (2006–2009), and, in the case of Simmons, loyally to its bitter end. By all accounts, as a response to the challenges of managing a larger and (reflecting its new status) more heavily scrutinised organisation, these men brought a new approach to management that was lower key and more collaborative and measured. In the words of a CABE director, "As CABE grew and it got more public money, it had to be more accountable, there had to be more forms filled in, and you had to talk to more people, so it did slow down a bit, it wasn't quite as fun." New Labour's political buoyancy was wearing off, and as a senior staff member who worked across the period put it, the Labour government as a whole "became more anxious and gripped their public agencies tighter and so it became less easy to be, what was interesting, to be a public agency with a campaigning remit".

In this period, therefore, CABE was much more akin to a branch of the civil service than it had been in its pioneering days. This shift in the character of the organisation was very clear to those on the outside. As an institutional leader observed, "Well, by the time Richard had taken over . . . there was a general feeling in our community that CABE had become less lean, less assertive and rather more bureaucratic."

Clarity and a Little Confusion

The new environment within which CABE operated sat uncomfortably with some of the design governance tools that the organisation had deployed up until then, and ambiguities surfaced over others. For example, the need for campaigning still existed, but the potential for it was now much reduced, whilst the extent of CABE's powers around design review continued to be questioned. On this latter concern, the overriding argument amongst CABE's directors (until almost the very end) was that it was not practicable to extend the powers of review, since the necessary rigidity for defining when to call in schemes was hard to relate to design: when was a scheme 'significant' and when was it not? In December 2006, a letter from DCLG's chief planner tried to clarify the matter, and, whilst accepting that "Significance is difficult to define precisely because it is not necessarily related to the size of a project, its location or type" (Hudson 2006), the letter clearly set out (or restated) the basis for how such judgements should be made.[30] Local authorities were reminded about criteria first laid down in 2001 (see Chapter 9), and were advised that CABE would judge whether a submitted scheme should be subject to national design review.

There was also the worry that a command-and-control culture on design review would create a backlash. As a director commented: "The question [of call-in powers] came up reasonably often and we always said 'no, we didn't want them.'" He recalls a comparison that was frequently made with English Heritage, who, as a statutory consultee, had the right to see relevant heritage proposals: "We thought the impact of English Heritage, as a statutory consultee, was more heavy handed and more resented and therefore less heard than CABE." Amongst practitioners, the non-statutory nature of CABE's advice was also generally seen as a benefit since its recommendations always remained advisory, for local authorities and developers alike. As one practitioner said: "If there was something that said, 'you have to do this,' then the danger was that you end up with terrible design by committee."[31] Right at the end, however, views were changing within CABE, and in response to a national consultation on improving the engagement of statutory and non-statutory consultees in the planning system in March 2010, Richard Simmons argued that "CABE would like to see either a formal strengthening of its remit to include call-in or provision of greater clarity about the [2005] Act in this regard, perhaps through Ministers."[32] This represented a major change in position for the organisation and reflected a wish for CABE to further formalise its position in the light of the difficult times it knew were ahead.

Beyond CABE, a lack of clarity about the reach of CABE's review powers persisted throughout the period, a common misperception being that it had statutory powers within the planning system. As a design review director recalls, "After CABE got put in an Act, it became a statutory body, but it remained a non-statutory consultee in the planning system. . . . I'm not sure many people really understood that." Indeed, while review powers were minimal on paper, when combined with misunderstandings around its role, they had a much more significant effect on practice than they otherwise might have had. There is strong evidence, for example, that CABE's design review judgements were increasingly taken as statutory, and for some this led to questions around accountability and public accusations of unfair practice. One of the most strident was David Lock's (2009) damning criticism of CABE published in *Town & Country Planning* magazine:

'Design review' is a dreadfully shallow process. People likely to be total strangers to the designer are selected by CABE staff by unknown processes. Their appropriateness professionally or technically is unexplained, and too often is obviously quite inappropriate.... It is difficult to speak up [against the practice], because no-one wants to draw the wrath of CABE and so 'get a bad review'. That fear indicates a kind of corruption, because it puts CABE beyond criticism, and has allowed it to develop working practices that can be unprofessional and shallow and which rarely add real value. It is also sad to note that the concept of a 'bad review' misses the whole cultural point: design review should be a constructive part of the design process. It should not be an examination or trial, and, if it was, I'd want properly qualified examiners, a proper jury system, public scrutiny and full accountability!

Whilst particularly forceful, Lock's criticisms were neither new (comparable complaints about the RFAC had beset its later years—see Chapter 3) nor atypical, as similar views were fairly regularly aired in the letters pages of the architectural press (and elsewhere, e.g. at the 2005 Select Committee, see earlier) and had been throughout CABE's existence. A senior figure in the property sector described the situation as an "almost quasi statutory position, which their actual constitution and practice didn't really live up to ... if you're going to have that constitutional weight, you've got to have the right sort of transparency, the right of appeal, and the right to question how it's written up". Yet the Commission fought its corner with vigour, and in a pithy rebuttal to the Lock critique, Richard Simmons (2009b) argued, "CABE's support gives planning officers the backing to stand up to developers and demand better places for the public.... Of course the panels' more robust comments are sometimes controversial and not always well received. But that's why you keep ... a watchdog." He added, "The vast majority of designers welcome the respect we show by using people who take such care when they review designs."

Interestingly, however, the use of 'satisfaction with design review' as a key performance indicator for CABE

was only used once (see earlier) and was rapidly dropped when the target was missed by a wide margin. Instead, measures of quantity as opposed to quality continued to be used (e.g. numbers submitted for design review and numbers of schemes reviewed), although performance indicators for the 'openness of the process' (numbers of external observers hosted—CABE 2009b: 19) and 'improvement in design quality through design review' were experimented with in 2008/09 and 2009/10, respectively. The last of these demonstrated that 70 per cent of the 112 schemes seen more than once in that year improved between their first and second reviews (or were already good and maintained that quality). How rigorous that assessment was and who made it was not specified (CABE 2010c: 17).

Undoubtedly, design review was the headline service for CABE, but also the thorn in its side, often obscuring, through its prominence, all the other work CABE did. Through this means, CABE made many enemies, and this counted against it in its hour of need, but it also had a major impact on the design of development across the country, including on the delivery of such major projects as the 2012 Olympics (4.12), the masterplan for the redevelopment of Battersea Power Station, Crossrail in London, the Stonehenge Visitors Centre, Leeds Arena, the Cooperative Headquarters in Manchester (4.13), New Street Station redevelopment and the Eastside City Park in Birmingham, Liverpool Central library, an extension to the British Museum, major urban extensions and brownfield redevelopments across the country, and a host of Building Schools for the Future projects (4.14). The list goes on and on.[33]

Figure 4.12 The Olympic Park in games mode; CABE played a major role in shaping the design of the 2012 Olympic buildings and venues

Source: Matthew Carmona

Figure 4.13 The new Headquarters for The Co-operative Group in Manchester has been compared to a sliced egg, but achieved the best ever BREEAM rating for a commercial building

Source: Matthew Carmona

Figure 4.14 Building Schools for the Future projects up and down the county were systematically reviewed; here Crownwoods School

Source: Matthew Carmona

Negotiating the Limits

During this period, the government was firmly focussed on the supply side of regeneration and housing development, and now it intrinsically linked CABE to the delivery of its housing agenda. A key liaison officer in DCLG described the evolution of this role. "In the early stages, it was about helping to achieve more sustainable communities, so we were looking at much wider objectives, whereas later it started to get much more specific about 'we want housing', which became

the absolute overriding priority towards the end of the Labour government." Therefore, while CABE was still working to influence design practice generally, its activities were more tightly controlled against a more specific and measurable set of targets. This began to raise questions around the focus of CABE and whether it was being distracted too much from design and was no longer sufficiently robust. The Commission had to contend with these challenges, and did so with some success up to the end of the New Labour government in 2010.

On one hand, it was increasingly taking on the government's priorities and changing the shape of its strategy to match. For example it devoted considerable time and resources to reviewing the huge programme of rebuilding the nation's schools whilst its own educational/skills endeavours—a function of the organisation specifically laid down in the Clean Neighbourhood and Environment Act 2005—were cut back. As a senior CABE staff member described, "we moved away from offering discrete skills programmes, towards a much more integrated relationship with CABE's other programme areas, so we worked with the other directorates to deliver the skills elements of their programmes, rather than understanding what the skills needs were generically and then developing a programme which we would then promote." An exception was the Engaging Places initiative, aimed at introducing schoolchildren to built environment concerns, which was developed into a major on-line resource for children and educators, and, following a DCMS-managed pilot in 2006/07 (supported by CABE and English Heritage), was formally launched in January 2009 (see Chapter 7).[34]

On the other hand, CABE was not completely 'reined in' and sought to open up and tackle dimensions of the design agenda that it identified through its own work and that were not on the government's horizons. Examples included its work on Strategic Urban Design (StrUD) and its beauty research, both agendas that CABE pursued with some vigour towards the end of its life and that demonstrated an organisation still willing to push the boundaries and challenge conventional ways of thinking. The beauty research, in particular, represented something of a risk as aesthetics had been firmly off the agenda since the days of the RFAC, and instead a more objective, explicitly evidence-based view of design had been pursued. The return raised eyebrows in the government, and some even argue that, when it came to the crunch and the future of CABE was debated, this work played into a reawakened narrative that the pursuit of good design was a luxury and thereby dispensable.

Building Influence (or Not)

Elsewhere, however, CABE was continually repurposing its research agenda to creatively influence government, for example as a feed into the last key design-related policy initiative of New Labour: *World Class Places* (see later). Indeed, this pursuit of evidence to underpin its arguments and assertions marked a key dimension of the CABE formulae throughout. As one source from within DCLG recalls, "It was a moment where evidence based policy was really up there in big letters, and to try and get design really built into everything, we were desperate for evidence, absolutely desperate for it." For CABE, whilst initially its research had been directed at convincing developers about the value of good design, increasingly it was the national politicians who were viewed as the main audience for CABE's research. Looking back on the experience, Richard Simmons later wrote, "Over time, CABE amassed a considerable array of evidence . . . yet governmental demand did not abate. . . . Was collecting evidence useful in forming policy, or was it just a displacement activity, or a smokescreen used to justify political decisions based on more subjective foundations?" He concludes, "Evidence can be a forceful influence on policy, but the territory in which it is applied is not neutral" (2015: 409, 415). It seems government was very willing to listen to evidence on design when it reinforced what individual ministers were trying to achieve; when it did not, or when it was perceived as outside their sphere of interest, then evidence was simply ignored, discarded, or conveniently forgotten in the face of more immediate priorities and political judgements.

Like education, the delivery of research was increasingly an activity distributed across the organisation, and the function never really found a place as a distinctive service in its own right. In the words of a long-standing member of the research team, "The knowledge produced across CABE was never exactly 'codified', which is to say that it was never brought into a coherent and cogent product for CABE itself." Others criticised CABE's research as too shallow, too disparate, and too dominated by a communications as opposed to a knowledge rationale (research for a long time was a subset of the communications directorate). As a property professional put it, CABE ended up "writing things and doing websites and whatever on areas that a lot of other people were already involved in". Yet, despite the criticisms, CABE's research was very widely read and heavily used both within the organisation and outside, and alongside the website and CABE Space, represented a consistently highly regarded dimension of the CABE offer.

Like its engagement with the large and influential CABE family, CABE's research represented a key means to build and sustain credibility and influence. Some important groups, however, were always more difficult to reach (more doubting of the CABE message) than others. CABE had previously been criticised for not listening to developers, and, over time, it tried to listen more and build bridges. However, without any means to enforce its views, it often had to rely on the weight of its arguments and its reputation within the planning system to be heard. Indirect influence was also powerful, with mechanisms such as the Building for Life Awards, in which CABE partnered with the Home Builders Federation, considered effective for gently encouraging private interests to take a more design-focussed view.

The housebuilding industry was particularly hard to influence, and, at the risk of alienating developers, CABE sometimes resorted to naming and shaming to get its message across. In the case of national housebuilder Persimmon Homes, senior CABE staff reported that the developer "actually threatened any local authority that took a review to CABE that they would never build in their area again . . . because Jon Rouse had angered them by saying that in Gateshead they had built the worst designed development in Britain". Later, the publication of CABE's housing audits between 2004 and 2006 shamed the residential sector at large and carried with it the danger that housebuilders would disengage en masse from CABE's mission. However, with the arrival of Richard Simmons and his more conciliatory approach, CABE began a programme of engaging directly with individual housebuilders at a high level. Through these means, and aided by a gradual strengthening of national policy and an increasing realisation by some developers that better design both had market value and aided a smoother planning process, CABE was able to win over key players such as Barratt Homes and Berkeley Homes (4.15). This tectonic shift represented, arguably, one of the key successes of CABE's later years, even though Persimmon (amongst others) remained doggedly resistant to the design message and in interview after interview was consistently touted as the developer least receptive to the design message. As one of CABE's strong allies in government commented, "Some of the housebuilders who were less progressive just didn't get into the tent. . . . That's one of the risks of that sort of set-up, that you talked to people who were sympathetic because you had something to talk to them about. You didn't talk to people who were hostile because actually it's quite difficult."

A key means to build influence involved the energetic collaboration of the regional representatives with their localities, whilst the regional reps used their direct link to the centre to add weight to their arguments. As one commented, "The fact that we could, with some credibility . . . at least in theory, have a direct route to central government and decision makers was very powerful." The regional Architecture and Built Environment Centres (ABECs), partly funded by CABE and coordinated through the Architecture Centre Network (ACN), also helped to extend design review services and became a key part of the CABE family (see Chapters 8 and 10). By 2009/10, eight regions (all but London[35]) were covered by regional panels, many of which were hosted in the ABECs

Figure 4.15 Kidbrooke Village (phase one) by Berkeley Homes, reviewed in CABE's later years

Source: Matthew Carmona

(CABE 2010a: 17). The potential clearly existed for a comprehensive and coordinated national system of design review that, alongside CABE's enabling activities and the regional reps, further extended CABE's influence and impact across the country. This was despite the view held by at least some responsible for the national design review service in London that the regional panels "were never properly funded or supported," and as a consequence "varied in quality".

Critiques Mount

In general CABE was still extremely well regarded and well connected, but over time a number of factors subtly undermined this position. First, built environment professionals often compared this era to the earlier ones, and many felt that as CABE grew, it became more introverted and harder to build relationships with. Some, for example, felt that CABE was just too focussed on design, and failed to position that within a larger agenda around development processes and sustainability, thereby reducing the impact of its message. For example, whilst CABE was engaging more positively with developers, a view persisted that it remained too homogenous, failing to fully engage with all interested parties. On the question of sustainability, CABE certainly came late to that party, and only became interested in debates around creating low-carbon development when, in 2007, the government's interest in eco-towns took off (see Chapter 9). In this later period, CABE finally stepped up its campaigning for government action on sustainably designed buildings, with John Sorrell (2008) arguing on the eve of the Climate Change Festival of May 2008 (organised jointly with Birmingham City Council) that out of the many hundreds of reviews it conducted, the Commission had only ever "seen a handful with any serious ambition for sustainability". The following year, it launched its most ambitious (perhaps its only significant) initiative in the field, the sustainablecities.org.uk website.[36] Arguably, this was too little too late (see Chapter 7).

Second, the whiff of a clique that had proved so damaging to the RFAC never entirely went away. Again, practices in design review were often cited in this regard, and some of those involved in the national panel are clear that such participation did have its advantages: "Without doubt, if you went to one of your clients and said I or my partner is on CABE's design review panel, they would see that as a potential benefit to their project because, if nothing else, you knew the system well, and, more importantly, what they knew is it's who you know and how you use that." This perception wasn't helped by how CABE sometimes treated others. CABE Space, for example, was felt to be disinterested in work it had not instigated itself, ignoring key government-commissioned research reports such as *Living Places, Caring for Quality* (DCLG 2004) (on the management of public space), and *Trees in Towns II* (DCLG 2008). Contributors to CABE initiatives also sometimes argued that they felt side-lined when work was published or initiatives launched and their contribution was not fully acknowledged. The feeling was that everything became too subservient to the greater service of CABE, rather than to building a sense of a collective endeavour: "You would do the report, you would do all the work, and in the end you would not get recognised as having been a subcontractor. You'd read the report and it would be 24 pages of photographs that you'd taken, all the stuff that you'd advised, and it would say, this report was produced by CABE."

Third, some saw CABE falling into the mode of "large public sector organisations, in particular those who represent government, who feel they can push others around". UDAL, for example, which had been so critical to the emergence of CABE, gradually withered away through the 2000s, which some saw as symptomatic of this problem. In the opinion of one senior planning figure, "UDAL could have been, for [CABE], the gateway to the professions, but they didn't want to do that because they wanted to do it themselves." Certainly the presence of CABE in such a dominating position within the sector meant that, when CABE closed its doors, a very sizable gap remained that prior to CABE had been occupied (at least partially) by non-governmental organisations such as UDAL and the Civic Trust (see Chapter 5).

Many saw CABE as intent on extending its reach, and in the process that it had become self-aggrandising, grabbing the limelight and good ideas. In the parks world, the adoption of the Green Flag awards was a case in point. As one involved party commented: "CABE were so bloody arrogant ... they commissioned us to do this review and, simultaneously, took over the running of it. Because they were core funding the

office, they decided they owned it and could do what they liked with it—but they didn't really own it." Similar feelings existed (amongst some) in relation to Building for Life that became centrally associated with CABE (because of CABE's resources and publicity machine), although CABE was only one of the partners responsible.

A final critique had been an issue from the start and concerned the London-centric nature of CABE. CABE faced the challenge of attempting to raise design standards while at the same time needing to engage constructively with the very different realities of practice across the country. In some parts, arguments were still endemic that good design was unaffordable despite the work of CABE's enablers working in local authorities up and down the country to try and change the perception. As a CABE director argued, "You can always make an argument that something's more expensive and it's not going to make as much money, but that doesn't mean to say it's the right thing to do." Some felt, however, that such uncompromising positions portrayed a narrow metropolitan elite perspective and consequently failed to reflect the realities of practice on the ground. The initial decision, for cost and pragmatic reasons and despite the recommendations of the Urban Task Force, not to establish a regional structure undoubtedly played into this perspective. The employment of regional reps and the part-funding of the ABECs, for many, smacked of tokenism.

Two Final Reviews

Reflecting the on-going critique, but also because CABE was now officially part of the state governance machinery with the higher levels of scrutiny that implied, in the Housing Green Paper of July 2007, DCMS and DCLG jointly announced a 'light-touch review' of CABE itself (DCLG 2007: 63). There followed a nine-month delay as disagreements between the two departments over the exact remit of the review ended up postponing both the appointment of a contractor to conduct the work and CABE's planned corporate strategy. At the time, a CABE source commented: "It has been deeply frustrating, because no-one has ever really explained to us why the delay has happened. It all seems to be down to the difficulties of co-ordinating two government departments" (quoted in Stewart 2008).

Eventually the review was conducted by Richard Parnaby and Michael Short at the University of the West of England, with the reviewers asked to consider both the alignment with and relationships to CABE's funding departments and the impact and effectiveness of CABE's operations. Based on extensive documentary analysis, interviews and observations of CABE at work, the researchers concluded:

> CABE has made, and continues to make, a real difference to the quality of places and buildings in England and has the potential to be even more effective. CABE has a well thought-out set of priorities that it keeps under constant review to ensure that they are well aligned with developing government priorities. It operates effectively in a complex and constantly changing environment in partnership with many disparate bodies seeking to influence the quality of architecture and place-making across the public and private sector. It is both the government's critical friend in the contested field of design of the built environment and a delivery agency working with large departments and agencies across the country on specific policy goals.
>
> (Parnaby & Short 2008: 3)

Five recommendations followed this clean bill of health: a stronger regional strategy in order to better project the organisation's influence across the country; a stronger engagement with the planning process (an area that CABE had remarkably little engagement with up to that point); a more focussed strategy for engaging across government and with its sponsor departments; a review of its learning and dissemination strategy (perhaps reflecting a frustration voiced by some that CABE was over-publishing and needed to rein in its output[37]); and the development of an evidence-based strategy for CABE to determine its own effectiveness and that of its programmes. The review caused few ripples and, despite spending cuts on the horizon,[38] left CABE feeling confident about its position within government in the run-up to the general election of May 2010 at which New Labour looked increasingly likely to be toppled.

To add to the positive picture, CABE's own ten-year review, a year later, put a further (relentlessly) positive spin on the organisation's record, this time courtesy of a summary of its activities over the decade. CABE had:

- Reviewed more than 3,000 major development proposals at an average cost of £2,500 per review (or 0.1 per cent of construction costs), including 359 schools and 300 early learning centres.
- Reviewed schemes referred to it from 85 per cent of local authorities across the country, and 70 per cent of subsequent planning decisions were taken in line with the advice received.
- Enabled 650 projects across the county (370 housing related) and supported fifty local authorities to produce their Core Development Strategies (local plans).
- Trained 225 Spaceshaper facilitators (see Chapter 9) and 306 Building for Life assessors, and awarded 69 BfL awards (32 gold).
- Produced a new generation of state-of-the-art guidance covering planning and a wide range of design concerns, including more than seventy from CABE Space alone.
- Trained 667 local councillors, 350 green space leaders, and 600 highways professionals, and involved 230,000 young people in CABE educational programmes through the ABECs it had funded.
- Grown to a staff of 120 with a 'family' of more than 400 experts on hand for design review and enabling.

Confidence was further reinforced by the positive positions of key political parties in pre-election statements. In 2009, *World Class Places* was released, the 'Government's Strategy for improving quality of place'. Reported to have derived from Gordon Brown's concern for the poor quality of housing and schools, and largely put together in the Cabinet Office[39] with significant inputs from CABE, the strategy trumpeted CABE as first amongst its "proud track record when it comes to promoting good planning, urban design and architecture" (HM Government 2009: 6). Originally the intention had been for a white paper to be produced on place quality, but the civil servants involved recount that the difficulties raising interest and agreeing to a coherent agenda across government led quickly to its downgrading to a 'strategy' which could be published without the need for Cabinet-level approval. Richard Simmons later recalled how the initial aspirations for an ambitious relaunch of the design/place agenda were gradually undermined as the political capital of the prime minister seeped away and economic crisis came to dominate government concerns (2015: 413). The result, despite seven months of effort, was that the content was gradually watered down until the strategy contained almost no new ideas or cross-governmental commitments, and on publication it quickly sank without a trace. Authors in the Cabinet Office were even told "the built environment was 'not a vote winning issue and does not matter to the C1 (lower middle class) demographic (a key election target), so [notwithstanding the document's origins] there was no real prospect of active support from the top leadership for a raft of new policies" (Simmons 2015: 412).

Despite its fate, key sentiments were echoed in the potentially more significant pre-election statements (given the way the political wind was blowing) of the then opposition. Most notably, this included the unequivocal statement on the importance of good design in the Conservative Party Policy green paper *Open Source Planning*: "The quality of the built environment is crucial in creating liveable communities. We want to encourage the creation of buildings which are practical, sustainable, affordable and attractive, and also deliver social goals, for instance by 'designing out' crime. We must promote the highest standards of architecture and design. Not only is this a desirable end in itself, but it is an important factor in encouraging communities to support new development" (Conservatives 2010).

Of course not everyone welcomed with open arms CABE reaching its tenth birthday. Tim Evans, creative director at architects Sheppard Robson, was quoted at the time saying that the *Ten Year Review* was: "self-funded, self-directed and, quite frankly, self-satisfied" (quoted in Arnold 2009). He was not alone in arguing that CABE was doing too much, had become too unfocussed and overstretched, and had lost sight of its original intent. CABE Director of Campaigns and Education Matt Bell countered that if the objective was to move beyond one-off pieces of good design to "good, ordinary [design] everywhere", then far from being too large, the Commission was still too small (quoted in Arnold 2009). Paul Finch (by then an ex-commissioner) argued that there probably had been "some overstretch" since 2008 (with inside sources pointing most often at the Sea Change programme[40], see Chapter 10), but government demands too often left CABE "between a rock and hard place" (quoted in Arnold 2009).

A Political End

At this stage, economic policy and politics came centre stage, overshadowing a decade of investment in design governance caused by the global financial crisis that broke out between 2007 and 2008. History records that the crisis led to a severe shock in the public finances of the United Kingdom, and from this point on CABE was operating under the shadow of economic retrenchment and a technical recession from 2008 to 2009. Whilst the two core funding departments, DCLG and DCMS, continued to invest high levels of resources in these years (4.16), a DCLG official noted, "The recession was biting harder and harder and harder and

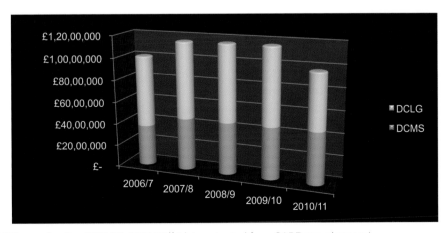

Figure 4.16   CABE's core funding 2006/07–2010/11[41] (data extracted from CABE annual reports)

trying to hang onto CABE's money was getting tougher and tougher and tougher." There were also external pressures building to reduce government intervention, and as one external observer reported: "When things started to get more difficult for house builders, just as the environmental agenda got tougher, government was under a lot of pressure from the private sector to relax everything," including design.

On top of this, and despite the warm words in *World Class Places*, government had continued to disengage from its long-term interest in built environment policy, a trajectory not helped by a review of regeneration policy which took place in CABE's last couple of years. As a senior figure within CABE recalled: "One of the things they'd noticed was that they were spending a lot of money on the built environment and that didn't appear to impact on poverty." The finding reinforced the Treasury's view that "you didn't invest in buildings; you invest[ed] in innovation and skills."

The changing context both within and outside of government meant that, irrespective of looming budget cuts, unless CABE could reinvent itself, it was likely to face a period of real turbulence. CABE's response was twofold. First, it devoted considerable resources to work with government on *World Class Places*; seconding its head of policy to assist on the report, which ultimately listed as its first action the need for CABE to once again work right across government in order to reinvigorate interest in the built environment via the Ministerial Design Champions[42] (HM Government 2009: 40). This reflected a key recommendation from the earlier Light Touch Review. Second, CABE engaged with the opposition via "a charm offensive on its potential Tory paymasters" in the hope that they could embed the idea that CABE "would be essential to deliver the Conservative plan for bottom-up 'community-led' housing design" (Arnold 2009), aka the new 'localism' agenda.

A general election was held on 6 May 2010, and the new coalition Conservative-Liberal Democrat government that emerged six days later was keen to implement large cost-cutting measures across Whitehall. A minister in DCMS at the time, reflecting on the economic situation, recalled: "It was in the middle of riots in Greece . . . so there was this overpowering need to make sure that it was clear that the Government's finances were going to be stabilised . . . every department was given a savings target, which we absolutely

had to come up with, whether we liked it or not." For CABE, despite its charm offensive, relationships at the ministerial level were not as strong as they should have been given the fact that the organisation was not universally admired. As one senior staff member suggested, "We found ourselves, sometimes, getting caught at a mid-level within the civil service from where it's much harder to break through."

The new coalition government also took a very different approach to public administration, avoiding centralised solutions, reducing the size of the state, and promoting instead a market-driven approach to urban development which the Conservative's nascent 'localism agenda' took a stage further. In this new context, there was still faith within government for the mission of improving design, but less belief that it should be designated part of the state's purpose. The new government felt that there had been a huge proliferation of quangos in the previous decade or two, and shortly after coming to power announced a review of non-departmental public bodies (NDPBs). In August of the same year, the review proposed the removal of around 200 quangos and the amalgamation of a further 120 out of the 900 the government had reviewed.[43] During this process, CABEs sponsoring body, DCMS, was experiencing intense pressure as it had proportionately more NDPBs than other Departments, and CABE was required to make the case for its maintenance and to negotiate cost-cutting measures. The leadership produced and submitted a response to this 'Public Bodies Review', which (at the request of DCMS) set out three options for the organisation (CABE 2010c):

- Continuation of CABE as a standalone public body.
- A full merger with English Heritage.
- The creation of a new regulatory body for the built environment containing English Heritage and a slimmed down and refocussed CABE.

Perhaps understandably, in view of the sometimes prickly relationship between CABE and English Heritage (although in hindsight disastrously), any form of merger between the two organisations was roundly rejected, and instead the first option was strongly favoured. It envisaged a new slimmed-down body with an annualised budget of £8.6 million (approximately a 25 per cent reduction) based on an innovative 'Open

Source CABE' model (reflecting the language of the *Conservative's Open Source Planning* green paper earlier in the year). The intention behind this was to move towards delivery of more services free online in a collaborative manner, using its own customers to critique and refine the offer. The submission stated: "The principle is that CABE's knowledge and tools can be continually improved through the inputs of people using CABE's resources. In being truly 'open source' CABE will aim to continually innovate to meet its customers' needs. As well as enabling its customers to input directly into dissemination of learning and best practice through the web, through face to face contact, and through peer to peer support" (CABE 2011f: 5).

Given the 'austerity' mandate, CABE had already been preparing for major reductions in its income, and it was on the basis of this model that CABE was moving forward prior to the Public Bodies Review. The proposed direction fed into the deliberations of the department,[44] and CABE survived the first cut of the quangos. CABE had sought to adapt to the new political climate, and until the last minute the proposals were considered viable. History nevertheless shows that the proposed solution was not nearly as radical as the situation demanded, and CABE's relief at surviving the 'cull of the quangos' was very short-lived.

The situation changed when Sir Nicholas Serota, director of the Tate Gallery (and ironically a founding CABE commissioner), wrote to *The Guardian* shortly before the announcement of the autumn spending review arguing that the government was "acting with the ruthlessness of a blitzkrieg" (Serota 2010) on cultural funding. Pressure built, and the weekend before the funding announcement, the new secretary of state at DCMS, Jeremy Hunt, decided that he was going to cut those front-line organisations slightly less than previously planned by removing the funding to CABE. As a leading commissioner recalled, "I think we were going to end up with between £2–3 million—which is really an accounting error in Whitehall terms. It was almost an accidental death which became clear when the DCLG appeared to be unaware that DCMS was cutting our money."

CABE was clearly an easy and quick cut to make, and a cut far less visible (to the public) than cuts to the sorts of high-profile cultural institutions that were the alternatives. Political expediency won out and DCMS

withdrew its funding, although initially maintained its support for CABE to remain on the books as an NDPB. This resulted in the difficult situation that CABEs sponsoring department no longer wished to fund it, whilst DCLG, which for many years had contributed half of its funding, was prepared to maintain its own much reduced contribution, but not to take over as CABE's sponsoring body. In the light of this CABE could no longer exist as a viable entity in the public sector and had to close.

Whilst, arguably there was political capital to be made by removing a body so closely associated with New Labour, by most accounts the decision to remove CABE was unforeseen and the ministers involved do not appear to have set out with the intention of closing CABE. Indeed, following the funding announcement, DCLG ministers made significant attempts to negotiate alternatives to CABE's demise. Nevertheless, the final decision to remove CABE is generally regarded as having been extremely poorly handled, and the phrase 'car crash' is often used to describe the process. While the economic mandate for change and the political ideology clearly argued for reduced spending, even with very substantial reductions in its funding CABE would have been able to continue in its all-important design leadership role. Moreover, evidence of voluntarism in CABE's history suggests that its 'family' would have quickly rallied around.

Some people felt that the writing was anyway on the wall for CABE, particularly given: "the other things that went like the Royal Commission on Environmental Pollution, which was the equivalent of burning the books really, or Planning Aid, things which had just manifestly done nothing but good for peanuts". Others felt that CABE and its family could have fought harder, but ultimately many in what might be regarded as CABE's core constituency were strongly divided on the organisation's value and demise, and this did not help its case. CABE's final chair, Paul Finch (who returned to CABE and bravely took over from John Sorrell in December 2009 just as things were starting to look bad), commented to the *Architects' Journal*: "We are bitterly disappointed. We had got through two rounds of potential quango abolitions and we thought we had done enough to survive" (Waite 2010). By contrast, the response from the architectural profession was, at best, mixed, with comments posted online that included:

"Excellent news"; "Nice to have a little sugar today to sweeten the pill"; "Some of them may even have to start designing buildings themselves instead of telling others how to do it"; or, "Well done, the only spending cut all the architects will be very happy with." Such comments reflect the erroneous perception many held that CABE amounted to little more than its design review function; a function that, as one final post reveals, still raised many of the same issues and concerns that it had done towards the end of the RFAC era ten years previously:

> CABE was an organisation which was based around the flawed theory that an overgrown architectural 'crit' could improve the design of buildings. It was filled with the self-righteous, self-important old boys and girls of the architectural establishment who could happily sit around carping about other architects' designs till the cows come home. Name another profession that openly criticises its colleagues work? No wonder we are so devalued by the rest of the industry.

Certainly the way in which the final decision was taken came as a shock to those who had been negotiating the possible options and left certain key projects in the lurch and never fully able to come to fruition. These included the establishment of a design review panel on supermarkets and the dissemination of the Strategic Urban Design (StrUD) work. On 1 April 2011, CABE was wound up as an independent body, with its final chair writing in its closing Annual Report and Accounts (CABE 2011a: 1):

> Given the country's economic circumstances, and the 2010 government review of public bodies, it was no surprise that we had been asked to reduce our size. Prior to the formal announcements of the Comprehensive Spending Review that process had started, and revised budgets for 2010–11 were agreed with our two funding departments. The ultimate decision to withdraw CABE's funding in its entirety was a shock, not least because there was no criticism of our role or the way we had carried it out over a period of eleven years.

The implied criticism was clear for all to see. He signed off, "This is a matter of profound regret for me and for all past commissioners."

Conclusion

The history of CABE has an uneven arc where CABE quickly rose to become an influential and trusted arm of government, and despite ups and downs continued to play an important role until its funding and status were abruptly cut. Early in its life, it was a radical agent with popular support, as a typical comment from a CABE supporter shows: "When it was small and it was fast, it was highly respected, it had the right people, it was incredibly exciting and influential and it did a fabulous, fabulous job." From this base it continued to punch above its weight while it gained increasing public funding, spreading its horizons into the all-important areas of local authority enabling, skills, and public/ green space. Halfway through its existence, CABE's legitimacy was suddenly called into question and necessary reform and a change in leadership gave way to a new mature, yet less agile, CABE.

As the crisis receded, government support remained strong and the reworked statutory body continued to expand its horizons in the fight for better-quality places whilst being more closely bound by its political bosses. Over time, government found ever more reasons to invest in CABE, both supporting design quality for its own sake (through DCMS) and via DETR/OPDM/ DCLG in relation to a range of more specific policy objectives that greatly expanded (and to some degree politicised) the organisation's role in design governance. The importance of design was clearly strengthened via CABE's work throughout government, local government, and industry, but its ability to provide critique of government programmes or to develop a coherent approach across its work was sometimes compromised. This tension was built into the DNA of the organisation from the start, and latterly it struggled with "how to challenge and collaborate in equal measure". Eventually, CABE fell victim to an economic crisis that, amongst its casualties, left England without design leadership for the built environment.

In the words of one high-profile commissioner, "It wasn't there to make money, it was there as education, policing, cajoling . . . it was amazing, but it took public funds and bravery to do that—a very brave government." Political support for CABE was absolutely vital throughout its history and ultimately it was a failure to adequately, convincingly, and irredeemably make the case for design amongst its political paymasters that cost the organisation its future.

Throughout, CABE was steered by a strong commission and executive that were powerful flagbearers bolstered by a committed pool of staff and a much wider CABE family. Indeed, this engagement of a large diaspora across the country in the cause of better design, often with little or no remuneration, represented remarkable value for money for the state and one of the critical successes of CABE. When the Commission had the ear of government and decision-making was less formalised, CABE was able to be very dynamic. When government funding increased, it empowered the Commission to grow its staff and thus engage more deeply nationwide, but this required a far greater formalisation of its processes. Its organisational goals also evolved from a focus on challenging the notion that architecture is a "stuck-on veneer", in the words of Stuart Lipton, to an impressively comprehensive set of built environment goals, including (reflecting the Government's preoccupation) a particular focus on housing.

The collective efforts of the CABE family enabled a proliferation of activities with regional outreach, and involved a wide range of informal design governance tools, never with regulatory force. CABE pioneered a range of new tools (see Chapters 6–10), many of which had a strong impact and helped to build an impressive reputation for CABE across the country. Despite this, from the start there was always a significant rump of naysayers who either failed to engage with or actively opposed CABE. As CABE expanded its reach, this criticism grew and the organisation was more frequently seen as overstepping its remit or acting in an overly aggressive manner. So while CABE had confidence in its public interest role, some were concerned that it increasingly appeared to colonise rather than engage other bodies and professionals acting in the same field. Beyond the professions, CABE had some intermittent success in spreading its message to wider civil society, but, despite its emphasis on campaigning, it is difficult to conclude that it convincingly took the public with it, and few outside the professions would have recognised the name. All of these factors undermined the support networks for CABE and left it vulnerable to political changes.

Whilst never admired by all, CABE represented the demise of an exceptional experiment in design governance that many still mourn. As one insider put it:

> When you look at what was lost, I would say it was a unique organisation which was widely admired across the globe, whose publications and advice are used every day by professionals, both public and private all over the world; it's one of those typical British examples of coming up with something which is a world leader, we thought of it all by ourselves, we put it into effect and, naturally, we had to destroy it. I think it was perverse for the amount of money that was saved. The leverage that £4/5million gave you in terms of being able to influence the quality of built environment was massive.

Relating CABE's work to the triad of fundamental urban governance characteristics—operation, authority, power—from Chapter 1, the organisation can be represented as:

- Ideological but pragmatic—focussed on a single core objective, the national improvement of design quality (broadly defined), but pragmatically extending and developing that agenda in line with the policy and political priorities around it.
- Centralised decentralisation—delegation from government direct to a single arm's-length organisation, but through it to a network of approved organisations and a wider family across the country.
- Publicly oriented/active—100 per cent state funded and controlled with only indirect non-directive powers, but through its considerable authority, energy, and initiative, able to set and drive a national agenda for change that public and private players alike could not ignore.

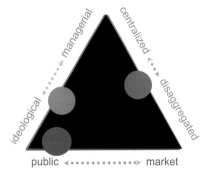

Figure 4.17 The CABE design governance model

Notes

1. DETR was established in 1997 and was succeeded in 2001 by the short-lived Department for Transport, Local Government and the Regions (DTLR) and later in 2001 by the Office of the Deputy Prime Minister (ODPM), which held the local government brief. In 2006, this became the Department for Communities and Local Government (DCLG).

2. Rouse had been the secretary to the Urban Task Force and took a major role in writing the report. At the time of CABE's incarnation, he was taking a year off to complete an MBA at the University of Nottingham, and did not arrive at CABE until it had been in existence for a year.

3. As the sponsoring department, DCMS retained formal responsibility for appointing CABE commissioners.

4. Nicholas Serota, Paul Finch, Les Sparks, and Sunand Prasad were also appointed as founding commissioners, and during the summer of 2000, Richard Feilden, Gillian Wolfe, Dickon Robinson, and John Miles were appointed.

5. For the seven months and eleven days to the end of March 2000.

6. A phrase that would appear in multiple CABE publications.

7. Where David Milliband was a junior minister and singled out for praise by all those concerned.

8. Elected in 2000.

9. English Heritage saw the intervention as very unhelpful, even though ultimately the organisation was split along very similar lines, albeit not until 2015.

10. For example in New Zealand; see Ministry for the Environment (2005).

11. The New Labour government pioneered evidence-based policy as a means to get away from what it saw as the ideology-based decision-making of the past. The 1999 UK Government White Paper, *Modernising Government,* set the scene and was enthusiastically adopted by CABE, which maintained a research unit to underpin its work throughout its life.

12. Demonstrating the increasing importance of communications to CABE, more than a quarter of these staff worked in the policy and communications directorate (which included research).

13. In the Thames Gateway area; in Ashford, Kent; in Milton Keynes and the South Midlands; and in a London-Stansted-Cambridge-Peterborough corridor.

14. Initially Jason Prior and Alan Barber, who was extremely highly regarded across the green space sector.

15. The ODPM had responsibility for the CABE Space commissioners, but the other CABE commissioners continued to report to DCMS.

16. CABE's internal Audit Committee also evaluated its annual business plans for areas of greater or lesser value for money.

17. Green Flag is the national award scheme for parks management, which from 2003 was managed jointly by CABE Space and the Green Flag Plus Partnership (see Chapter 8).

18. http://webarchive.nationalarchives.gov.uk/20110118095356/http:/www.cabe.org.uk/news/stronger-support-for-public-sector-clients

19. Organised on a regional basis and reported in 2004, 2005, and 2006, respectively.

20. Both client guides were repeatedly revised and were placed online in 2011; see: http://webarchive.nationalarchives.gov.uk/20110118095356/http://www.cabe.org.uk/buildings and http://webarchive.nationalarchives.gov.uk/20110118095356/http://www.cabe.org.uk/masterplans.

21. There were about seventy-five full-panel reviews annually with a full panel of reviewers and CABE staff and visitors (the latter to present their schemes), another seventy-five internal reviews with just the panel and staff, and the remainder were dealt with in weekly desktop reviews attended by just the chair or deputy chair of the panel and officers (ODPM 2005: 6).

22. In a second review from Sir John Egan in 2004, this time of *Skills for Sustainable Communities,* Egan had concluded there was a need for up-skilling the broad range of core and associated occupations with a role in planning, delivering, and maintaining sustainable communities. He recommended a National Centre for Sustainable Communities Skills to take on that challenge, and in February 2005, the Academy for Sustainable Communities was established (Egan 2004).

23. www.planningresource.co.uk/article/445624/cabe-audit-recommends-shake-up

24. www.publications.parliament.uk/pa/cm200304/cmselect/cmodpm/1117/1117we31.htm

25. www.building.co.uk/sir-stuart-lipton-loses-case/3048444.article

26. The full list of steps also included operational steps and is archived online at www.legislation.gov.uk/ukpga/2005/16/part/8

27. In May 2001, CABE had been given the status of 'non-statutory consultee' in the planning process, in other words, local authorities were advised to consult CABE on relevant planning applications, although there was no obligation on them to do so. This status remained until 2011. As an exception, CABE was listed as a statutory consultee on any planning application relating to vistas protected under the 2007 *London View Management Framework,* articles 10(3) and 27 of the *General Development Procedure Order* 1995.

28. Call-in amounts to the power to require that a relevant organisation see a project.

29. This 'official' reminder went hand in hand with a new national requirement that developers submit 'Design and Access Statements' with most forms of significant planning application. Whilst the idea of design

statements long predated CABE, the Commission promoted the idea to government and its adoption represented a significant achievement. In 2007, CABE authored national guidance on how to write, read, and use them.

30. "Development proposals which are significant because of their size or the uses proposed; development proposals which are significant because of their siting; or proposals that are significant in having an importance greater than their size, use or siting would suggest."

31. Although an exception was made in 2009 relating to the review of schools—see Chapter 9.

32. Letter from Richard Simmons to DCLG: http://webarchive.nationalarchives.gov.uk/20110118095356/http:/www.cabe.org.uk/files/response-improving-engagement.pdf.

33. All CABE design review decision letters were published online: http://webarchive.nationalarchives.gov.uk/20110118095356/http://www.cabe.org.uk/design-review/advice

34. www.engagingplaces.org.uk/home

35. Urban Design London (set up to offer London-focussed design training) was not allowed to join the Architecture Centre Network (ACN), which CABE indirectly supported, and had to remain as an affiliate.

36. See: http://webarchive.nationalarchives.gov.uk/20110118095356/http:/www.cabe.org.uk/sustainable-places

37. Most notoriously and unhelpfully, not long before CABE lost its funding and was told it would need to shut down, Sir Stuart Lipton and Jon Rouse complained that the organisation should ditch producing reports because no one was reading them (Rogers 2010).

38. At that time, cuts in the region of 3 per cent up to 2010 were planned across government-sponsored bodies.

39. The Cabinet Office supports the prime minister and is often the location where cross-governmental initiatives and collaborations are coordinated.

40. The Sea Change cultural regeneration programme was a £45 million grants programme aimed at small seaside resorts that DCMS Minister for Culture and Tourism Margaret Hodge requested CABE manage and deliver. Despite reservations internally about the relevance of Sea Change to CABE's core mission and the risks associated with delivering such a large programme, Sea Change was taken on and delivered internally by a small team led by Sarah Gaventa (director of CABE Space). Independent evaluations of Sea Change largely view it as a success (BOP Consultancy 2011).

41. Figures exclude income from the Sea Change programme (see Chapter 10).

42. Ministerial Design Champions were first established in 2000 after lobbying by CABE and as part of the Better Public Buildings Programme. After a first flush of enthusiasm, interest gradually waned in these roles, and by 2009, few Design Champions were truly active in the role.

43. www.bbc.co.uk/news/uk-politics-19338344. Link no longer active.

44. This exercise, called *Making the Case*, operated as a "structured and internally peer reviewed piece of research, led by the research and finance teams at DCMS, to demonstrate the impact of their various funded programmes and quangos". Comparing its submission to those from other bodies, CABE (2011) later argued that, "In the event, only CABE had the evidence base to complete the exercise and did so by including both evidence of the impact of its own activities and evidence of the impact of improved design. The final submission (unpublished) was 50 thousand words long and provided the most complete single evaluation of CABE's impact."

CHAPTER 5

Design Governance in an Age of Austerity, 2011–2016

This final chapter in Part II brings the story of national design governance in England up to early 2016, five years after the closure of CABE. It covers the winding up of CABE as a publicly funded body, the birth of Design Council CABE and the Design Network out of the ashes of the former organisation, the Farrell Review that followed, and the emergence of the Place Alliance—all attempts to positively engage with the post-2011 settlement. The period says much about CABE's impact, most notably about the huge gaps its demise left, and about the search for something new to fill them. In a context of austerity and localism, on one hand design seems more important than ever as a key local concern, yet on the other it is a concern devoid of public resources and looking instead to the market and to voluntarism as the twin means to continue a national design governance and to address that need.

Looking to the Market

Hanging on in There

During the period between 20 October 2010, when it was announced that CABE was to close, and 1 April 2011, when it did, extensive efforts were made to save key aspects of CABE's programmes. This occurred alongside processes of winding up the organisation and archiving its work of eleven years. As described in the previous chapter, the circumstances under which funding had been withdrawn were indeed peculiar, with the

Department for Culture, Media and Sport (DCMS), CABE's sponsoring department, removing funding and the Department for Communities and Local Government (DCLG) wishing to continue its support (albeit at a lower level), but refusing to take on the sponsoring mantle. Given this, CABE[1] remained hopeful that a way through the impasse could be found in order to save the organisation, or at least parts of it. As one insider to the negotiations reported, "DCLG were absolutely incandescent—they were almost not on speaking terms with DCMS—which was very difficult for us." On the positive side, DCLG, and particularly Minister of State for Housing and Local Government Grant Shapps, was keen to work with CABE to find a solution, although not necessarily at public expense.

Concurrently, the Design Council, which had been a casualty of the cull of quangos (see Chapter 4), had obtained permission from its own sponsoring department—the Department of Business, Innovation and Skills (BIS)—to continue solely as a charity.[2] Talks between the two chief executives revealed both a common cause and a potential synergy that could be exploited if a merger was to occur, a proposition that, after some haggling with respective civil servants, and the guarantee of transitional funding from DCLG, led to the incorporation of Design Council CABE as a private subsidiary[3] of the new charitable Design Council, four days before the 'public' status of both organisations ceased. The funding came in the form of £5.5 million over the accounting years 2011/12 and

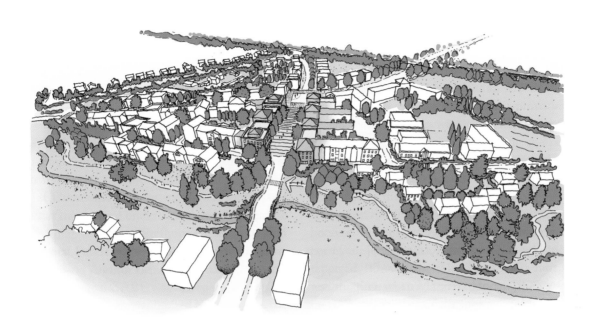

Figure 5.1 The masterplan for the proposed development at North Bicester eco-town began its design review journey in 2010 and finished in June 2011

Source: Farrells

2012/13, which was intended to allow the new organisation time to develop its own income streams,[4] most notably by commercialising its design review services, and providing support for one of the headline initiatives of the new Coalition Government, neighbourhood planning (see later). As a key protagonist within CABE recalled:

> The fact was that they [DCLG] greatly appreciated the work that we had done for them, every penny had counted, pretty much every target that had ever been set was hit, and they said, 'well, we will continue to fund you to do what you do for the next two years.' It was that which provided an opportunity for us to see whether we could salvage something from this mess.

To enable the merger, the royal warrant of the Design Council was extended with two clauses to give it a 'built environment role'.[5] Twenty of CABE's staff members (largely those responsible for design review) were transferred to the new organisation and 'Design Council CABE', as it has came to be known, began to operate as a semi-autonomous unit within the larger organisation with a remit to earn its way through commercial design review, an activity which continued seamlessly, with some projects that began their design review journey under CABE, finishing it under Design Council CABE (5.1). Few other functions from the former publicly funded CABE survived, although CABE's schools educational resource www.engaging places.org.uk was passed over to Open-City, and Building for Life was eventually relaunched as 'Building for Life 12', in which Design Council CABE maintains an interest (see later).

A New Context

Design Council CABE, like its predecessor, found itself immersed in a new context defined by two national policy agendas. First, the overwhelming drive for austerity in public services, a drive that by 2011 had reduced the national funding for its work by 75 per cent, and by 2013 (when the transitional funding came to an end) had removed it altogether. Thus at its height, CABE represented a public investment in design quality of some 0.02 per cent of the £60 billion spent on new construction each year in England, but three years of austerity had reduced this to 0 per cent (Carmona 2011b). Whilst the withdrawal of funding at the national level was dramatic, arguably of greater immediate impact was the rapid squeeze on local government finances,[6] and most notably on services relating to the built environment.[7] Surveying the urban design and conservation capacity of London's boroughs at the end of 2010 (as austerity cuts started to bite) revealed just sixty-nine urban design posts remaining across London (and a further seventy-five conservation posts) to deal with the outputs of a construction industry worth some £8 billion (on top of London's 1,000 conservation areas, 40,000 listed buildings, and 150 registered parks and gardens). This represents £120 million worth of development for each urban designer, or an investment by local government of around 0.03 per cent of the output of this industry in achieving urban quality (Carmona 2011c). The situation outside of London is likely to have been far worse, and given the non-statutory nature of such services, will have deteriorated further and substantially in the period to 2016.

A second national agenda (viewed by some as simply the politically more expedient face of austerity) was a new emphasis on localism. Whilst the coalition government itself was not always consistent in its enthusiasm for localism, it used the rhetoric of returning power to local communities to rapidly remove the regional planning tier in England when it abolished the Regional Development Agencies (RDAs) courtesy of the 2011 Public Bodies Act.[8] At the same time, the Localism Act introduced a new tier of neighbourhood planning, with local communities at the parish level (or its equivalent) given direct power to make neighbourhood plans. This process, that for two years Design Council CABE was charged to support, represented a major opportunity for the new organisation because the very tangible nature of the physical built environment for local communities meant that design issues were likely to loom large in their plans. Unfortunately, initial progress with neighbourhood planning was slow[9] (most likely because of the complexity of the process and the almost complete absence of dedicated local resources for the activity), and whilst government remained committed, the

knock-on potential to reinvigorate a new interest in design at the local level did not quickly materialise.

By contrast, the abolition of RDAs removed a set of key organisations that during the New Labour years had strongly aligned themselves with the 'Urban Renaissance' agenda of the Urban Task Force (see Chapter 4) and had, to greater of lesser extents, sought to bring a design dimension to their economic development programmes. Although these efforts were not always successful (CABE 2008b), and some criticised them on ideological grounds as simply the manifestation of neoliberal urban policy (Lees 2003), removal of this whole tier of government represented a further setback for the design agenda, not least because the RDAs had been major funders of the Architecture and Built Environment Centres (ABECs) and of design capacity generally at a regional level.

Defining a Market

Yet, despite these changes, and the seemingly almost total withdrawal of funding from urban design at the national, regional, and local levels, the Conservative-led coalition government was never ideologically hostile (as was the case in the 1980s) to the pursuit of good design through public policy; indeed, the Conservatives had recommitted themselves to this agenda in the run-up to the 2010 election. An early initiative of the new government was to streamline the voluminous planning policy (1,300 pages) that had built up over the years and replace it with a sixty-five-page National Planning Policy Framework (NPPF) published in March 2012.[10] In his forward to the NPPF, Minister for Planning Greg Clark stated: "Our standards of design can be so much higher. We are a nation renowned worldwide for creative excellence, yet, at home, confidence in development itself has been eroded by the too frequent experience of mediocrity." The paragraphs that followed laid out unequivocal support for the importance of design, with Section 7 of the NPPF under the heading 'Requiring good design' opening with the statement: "The Government attaches great importance to the design of the built environment. Good design is a key aspect of sustainable development, is indivisible from good planning, and should contribute positively to making places better for people" (para. 56).

As a whole, the new policy framework largely repeated sentiments in the Planning Policy Statements

of New Labour which it replaced, although with a greater onus on local authorities to define their own policy priorities and to establish these in an up-to-date plan (Carmona 2011d). There was, however, an important new addition to the policy that CABE and subsequently Design Council CABE had lobbied heavily for, namely that "Local planning authorities should have local design review arrangements in place to provide assessment and support to ensure high standards of design." Furthermore, local authorities "should also, when appropriate, refer major projects for a national design review" (para. 62), a service (a footnote noted) "currently provided by Design Council CABE". Coming so soon after the effective winding up of CABE as a publicly funded organisation, the inclusion of the new guidance may have seemed surprising. However, for a government aspiring to high-quality design but unwilling to support it financially, it was a logical step on the road to the creation of a market in the governance of design services, at least for the most easily commoditised tool in the kit: design review.

Design Council CABE, a Bumpy Road

About twenty CABE staff members had survived to form Design Council CABE, and led by Diane Haigh (previous director of design review at CABE), they had resources guaranteed for two years. Little did they know the torrid time the next few years would bring, particularly when faced with both the hugely challenging new economic climate, with its profound impacts on both the public and private sectors, and their own sudden loss of authority and public position. An early casualty was Haigh herself, who was encouraged to move on after just six months when David Kester (then chief executive at the Design Council) concluded that the realities of life in the market did not play to her strengths.[11] She was replaced by Nahid Majid with a brief to commercialise the product—design review—and to seek out paying clients for the service (Hopkirk 2012).

The Bishop Review

The new era began promisingly, however, with the immediate commissioning of Peter Bishop (ex-director of design for London) to conduct a wide-ranging review of the future of design in the built environment.

As Bishop commented in his introduction to the review: "In order to draw meaningful conclusions on any future role for Design Council CABE, it has been necessary to take a far broader perspective. Design Council CABE is only one element within a complex landscape of organisations and institutions all working in their own ways to change and improve the built environment." In such a context, he was clear that the fledgling organisation would need to change: "It would have been tempting to conclude that Design Council CABE could continue in its present role, albeit diminished. This is not the conclusion of this review. I believe that, although Design Council CABE still has a pivotal national role in ensuring design excellence, a new approach is required entailing a clear partnership with the industry as a whole" (Bishop 2011: 4). Bishop recommended:

- Design Council CABE needed to reignite its leadership role by engaging with other parties (the government, universities, professional institutes, etc.) to establish a research agenda and become a centre for debate, innovation, advice, and the dissemination of best practice.
- Design Council CABE should be the centre of a national system of design review in which the CABE model was effectively policed by the new organisation through a system of accrediting affiliated panels.
- Design Council CABE should build on the transitional funding it had been given to support the first wave of neighbourhood planning in order to become the national leader in the field.
- Government should facilitate payment for design review services for relevant schemes through adjusting the fees paid to local authorities for making planning applications or for pre-application discussions in relation to development proposals.
- Design Council CABE should itself continue to offer a national design review service and should set up and run a London panel as the only part of the country not covered by a member of the Architecture Centre Network (see Chapters 8 and 10).

The review itself was a difficult process, by all accounts, with Design Council CABE seemingly unwilling to let

Bishop conduct the promised 'independent' review, whilst Bishop himself grew increasingly frustrated by the interference. Perhaps because of this, but more likely because of (i) the sharp realities of the new environment within which the organisation was now operating, (ii) its failure to come to terms with them quickly enough, and (iii) government's lack of interest during these transitional years, all but the last of the recommendations were ignored. Judged in these terms, the opportunity the transitional funding provided seems to have been squandered, although the hugely difficult transition that the rump CABE needed to make should not be underestimated: one month the undisputed national mouthpiece and leader on all issues relating to design and the built environment, and the next, just one of a number of service providers in a new and profoundly difficult market.

A New Model Emerges

The realities for Design Council CABE were twofold. First, a government that was unwilling to go back on its decision to withdraw funding (or even to contemplate indirect funding as Bishop suggested) for the role. This effectively left the market and quickly dwindling local authority budgets as the only viable sources for filling the funding gap when the transitional funding ran out in April 2013. Second, operating within the market quickly revealed other more nimble and market-savvy organisations only too willing to grab a slice of the diminishing action. In 2012, for example, Design Council CABE tendered again to government to continue supporting neighbourhood planning, but lost out to a consortium of not-for-profits led by the charity: Locality. This inevitably led to a further round of redundancies and, in the same year, to a round of rapid appointments and equally sudden firings amongst the senior staff, including of its new head, Nahid Majid, and its even newer director of policy and communications, Tony Burton. Both subsequently predicted the end of the organisation (Rogers 2012). As one insider shared: "It turned out to be rougher than I think we would have anticipated . . . we got a pretty rough ride from the media in general who were more interested in whether we had a problem, rather than the principles that we were still trying to uphold, so really it was a very unsettled period."

The wobbles at Design Council CABE were clearly pre-empted by the imminent end to transitional funding for design review in April 2013, not helped by the failure (until the summer of 2012) to sign off on a business plan for a replacement commercial model for selling its services, and the initial slowness of sales relating to the plan. Yet, when in March 2013, a further round of redundancies was made, taking the staff members down to twelve (Donnelly 2012), this was a low point from which, under new leadership, both at the Design Council as a whole (John Mathers) and Design Council CABE (Clare Devine), the organisation began to stabilise.

The new model that gradually emerged was quite different to that which Peter Bishop had envisaged and one that fully embraced the new market realities, with Design Council CABE focussing only on those aspects of its operations for which income could be generated. The key strands of this new commercial model were:

- Instigation of a schedule of charges. In 2015, these were £4,000 for a 'Preliminary design workshop', £8,000 to £18,000 for a 'Phase one pre-application presentation review', £5,000 to £8,000 for a 'Phase two review', and £3,500 for a 'Planning application review'.[12]
- Recruiting a network of 250 Built Environment Experts (BEEs) from across the sector (equivalent to CABE's Enabling Panel—see Chapter 4), representing all strands of interdisciplinary expertise for the organisation to call on as and when the demand arose, in particular to sit on design review panels. BEEs were to be paid a standard rate for their involvement in projects and nothing if they were not involved.
- Revisiting the organisation's approach to design review and moving away from the purely 'public interest' design review processes CABE used in favour of a more market-sensitive and discreet model. Justifying the change, Design Council CABE repeatedly argued that the new processes could be more constructive and less confrontational whilst retaining the organisation's 'independence' in line with the charitable status and mission of the Design Council.
- A move away from reliance on general design review on an ad hoc basis to focus instead on providing a

comprehensive design review service for particular local authorities. Amongst the early takers of this service were the City of Oxford and, in London, Royal Greenwich, for whom Design Council CABE provided a tailored design review service for all major projects. The Oxford Design Review Panel, for example, is organised by Design Council CABE under its standard protocols and procedures, and meets once a month with a discounted fee paid per review by the council, which developers then reclaim.[13]

• The conduct of other activities only when fully funded by an external party, for example the Inclusive Environments Hub DCLG commissioned in 2013. This built on a long tradition within the Design Council (pre-CABE) of supporting principles of universal design, and Design Council CABE has used it extensively since to leverage other promotional and commercial opportunities, including continuing professional development (CPD).[14]

By the end of the 2013/14 financial year, its first year of operating without transitional funding from government, Design Council CABE had conducted just fifty-five design reviews and recorded an operating loss of £374,000 (Design Council 2014). The Design Council was nevertheless confident enough in the future of the new entity to incorporate Design Council CABE wholly within the operations of the main charity and to disband the subsidiary company altogether, ensuring that CABE operations were now fully integrated with the Design Council. By the close of the 2014/15 financial year, the gap between expenditure and income had risen to £671,000,[15] and the number of independent design reviews was no longer specified in year-end accounts, which instead reported that "a significant number of standalone design reviews" were conducted (Design Council 2015: 14). The team continued to proactively develop its offer of a comprehensive design review service to local authorities, seeing the certainty of the long-term income that such deals generated as a more attractive and commercial proposition than the uncertainly of ad hoc reviews from around the country.

The full incorporation of Design Council CABE into the Design Council arguably represented a weakening of the CABE brand and reflected discussions inside the Design Council about the extent to which the continued use of the name represented an asset or a liability for developing its operations. Whilst, for some, the 'CABE' brand is tarnished at home, it is thought to remain a strong brand internationally, where the Design Council now sees significant growth potential. The organisation also continues to claim the lineage of the publicly funded CABE going back to 1999 as part of its marketing pitch, despite (just five years after the merger) only one member of its staff surviving from the earlier organisation. By early 2016, the organisation seemed to have settled down with a small but more stable staff of ten and with business clearly evolving and developing in line with market opportunities as and when they arise (Rogers 2015). In 2015, it secured its first international commission for design review services, providing design review and advice for the mixed-use Al-Irfan urban development masterplan in the Sultanate of Oman. In the same year, the organisation secured the contract to provide PLACE review services for the Old Oak and Park Royal Development Corporation in London, and in January 2016, announced it had been asked to set up a design review panel for Thurrock Council in Essex.

Whilst the journey has been difficult, by its fifth anniversary, a new confidence was finally apparent in Design Council CABE. For some, the new reliance on the market had nevertheless fundamentally changed the nature and efficacy of the organisation and its services, which were no longer 'public' in the complete sense encompassed by the definition of design governance unpacked in Chapter 1. Jon Rouse remarked: "The thing about CABE is that it was set apart from the market. One anxiety I have is that the integrity of the process is not compromised by the need to charge. For a really bad scheme, if an architect or developer has paid £20,000 for the privilege [of a review], is it that easy for them [Design Council CABE] to turn around and say, 'start again, it's rubbish'?" (quoted in Rogers & Klettner 2012). The leadership of Design Council CABE counters that guarantees of independence and probity are maintained by the organisation's royal warrant and charitable status, as part of the larger Design Council, and that their mission to raise up design quality nationally remains exactly the same.

Whether independent or not, operating in the market Design Council CABE could clearly no longer afford to alienate the clientele on whom it relied for repeat business, and neither could it afford to do reviews that weren't 'useful' to those commissioning them. Given, however, that the vast majority of the organisation's work is now commissioned by and conducted for local authorities, even if paid for indirectly by the private sector, the processes undertaken still classify as design governance in the sense encompassed by this book, whilst the need for repeat public sector business may ultimately be the best guarantee of quality.

Commercialising Design Governance

If the term of the coalition government from May 2010 to 2015 saw the demise of publicly funded CABE alongside a good part of the larger design governance infrastructure that had been gradually built up across the country over the previous fifteen to twenty years, it also saw the stuttering but ultimately viable emergence of a market in at least some of these services. Underpinning this was a new bottom-up entrepreneurialism amongst service providers, many of whom had previously been able to rely on direct public funding for their existence, but which now had to learn to sink or swim in this new market.

The Design Review Market

In this market, Design Council CABE was far from the only player in town, with design review offered by a wide range of local and regional players, as well as directly by local authorities. Whilst the new landscape took a little time to emerge and settle down, the 2015 annual survey of design review capacity in London compiled by Urban Design London (2015) revealed that in London alone fourteen boroughs now had their own dedicated design review panels, with five other organisations operating panels either across the city (Design Council CABE, the Mayor's Design Advisory Group, Transport for London, and Urban Design London) or in particular localities (e.g. the London Legacy Development Corporation—5.2).[16] Amongst this group, fees paid to members of design review panels ranged from zero to £500 per session,

Figure 5.2 The London Legacy Development Corporation Quality Review Panel considers all significant proposals made within the London Legacy Corporation Planning Area (the Olympic Park and its surroundings)

Source: Matthew Carmona

and local authority charges for review services ranged from £400 to £6,000. Charges levied by Design Council CABE were at the top end of the market and compared to the average cost of design reviews conducted by publicly funded CABE, which were £2,500 per review for the 3,000 reviews of all types conducted between 1999 and 2010 (CABE 2010e).

Whilst London had quickly become the most crowded market for design review services, establishing that market had not been easy. Design Council CABE had initially used its transitional money from the government to try and pump prime the London boroughs into the pay-to-use design review habit and (as the Bishop Review had recommended) to establish the organisation's claim over this key territory. But, as one observer commented, the initiative resulted from "misreading the London situation where there is resistance to design review in important quarters . . . this was a glaring bit of inappropriate support and waste of public money". Despite the scepticism, Design Council CABE asked boroughs to sign a memorandum saying they would use the organisation's services with government money covering the first £20,000 of costs, after which developers should foot the bill.

Design Council CABE did a hard sell and made sure everyone knew what was on offer, although even with the substantial sweetener less than half of London's

boroughs signed up to the new service, and once the free sessions had been used up the number involved fell dramatically. The initiative nevertheless gave rise to the significant interest in London amongst the boroughs in setting up their own panels, with Design Council CABE securing just one of these whilst others are run by the boroughs themselves or by private companies in the small but growing 'design services' sector.

The pump priming therefore had an important impact, and even if, in the words of one commentator, "London was not proving to be lined with the design review gold that the Design Council had hoped for," the efforts largely met the government's intentions of jumpstarting a market where none existed before. Amongst local authorities who responded to the 2015 Urban Design London (2015: 3–4) design review survey, 95 per cent felt that the design review services in the capital both improved the quality of schemes and positively influenced the decisions of planning committees. This they did by:

- Providing different ideas, perspectives, and ways to improve designs.
- Encouraging the consideration of higher-quality materials and techniques.
- Providing a good platform for debate and the sharing of best practice.
- Raising the level of what is seen as acceptable design.
- Providing a forum to help resolve disputes.
- Helping to strengthen negotiations between different local authority departments and the developer.
- Providing advice on local contexts to help create schemes that are better connected with surrounding streets.
- Giving confidence to councillors that designs were acceptable.

An active market was also apparent elsewhere across England, and with London proving more of a challenge than anticipated, it was not long before Design Council CABE turned its attention more firmly to the rest of the country. Outside of London, it was competing head-on with regional providers, with local authorities that had set up their own panels, and with occasional private providers or even entrepreneurial public sector agencies. 5.3 reflects this complex typology of delivery organisations, although the relative vibrancy of the actual market varied substantially across the country. In the north-east, for example, just one organisation—NEDRES[17]—provided a design review service, whilst in the south-west of England, the South West Design Review Panel (managed by Creating Excellence) provided a regional service, Cornwall County Council maintained its own panel, and a private consortium, the Design Review Panel, operated throughout Devon and Somerset to deliver, according to its own publicity, "a cost effective" alternative.[18]

The Design Network and the ABEC Network

The diversity of providers reflects, in part, fallout from the withdrawal of funding from CABE, who in turn withdrew funding from the Architecture Centre Network (ACN). This along with the withdrawal of funding to ACN members by the Arts Council in 2012 and the failure to find other sources of funding led to the closure of the network in June 2012 as its twenty constituent architecture centres concluded that the umbrella organisation was no longer viable and their own individual survival was the priority (Fulcher 2012). By early 2013, however, two new networks had arisen from the ashes. The first, the Design Network, was a network of the eight organisations that had hosted the regional design review panels for CABE (see Chapter 4) and that, alongside Design Council CABE, had benefitted from transitional government funding until April 2013.

Covering all regions of England outside of London, the Design Network's intention was clearly to carve the country up between the eight organisations (leaving London for Design Council CABE), and in a monopolistic fashion to pursue a business model based on exploiting advice in the National Planning Policy Framework (NPPF) that design review arrangements should be put in place to support planning decision-making (Hopkirk 2013). The aspiration was quickly undermined, however, when it became clear that Design Council CABE had no intention of restricting operations to London, and was tested when, later in 2013, Shape East (covering the East Anglia region) was declared unviable and ceased to operate. The remaining seven were now joined by Urban Design

Design review provider		Operation	Example
Focus	Sector		
National panel	Third	Not for profit organisation with no geographic remit	Design Council CABE
Regional/ sub-regional panel	Public	Regional or sub-regional panel operating within the confines of its administrative area	Urban Design London, Design Surgeries; or Hertfordshire Design Review Panel (run by Building Futures a consortium of nine Hertfordshire local authorities led by the County Council)
	Public entrepreneurial	Entrepreneurial public sector trading design services to others in its region	Place Services of Essex County Council, formally part of the county's core services, but now an independent profit centre wholly owned by the council and able to sell its services, including design review, inside (to the district authorities) and outside of Essex
	Third	Not for profit organisation with a regional or sub-regional geographic remit	MADE West Midlands, providing design review (and other design services) throughout the West Midlands; or the Cornwall Design Review Panel
	Private panel for hire	Private provision of a roving panel for hire on commercial terms (so far regionally based)	The Design Review Panel, with clients that include local authorities and developers in Devon and Somerset
Local panel	Public	Local authority panel operating within the confines of its administrative area	London Borough of Lewisham Design Review Panel; or Torbay Council, Design Review Panel
	Third	Not for profit organisation with a local (usually town or city) geographic remit	Beam, providing design review (and other design services) to Wakefield; or the Greenwich Design Review Panel run by Design Council CABE for Royal Greenwich
	Private sub-contractor	Public sector organisation operating within the confines of its administrative area but with the panel management subcontracted to a private or not for profit organisation	Haringey Quality Review Panel, managed by private consultancy, Frame Projects, for the London Borough of Haringey; or the London Legacy Development Corporation Quality Review Panel managed by Fortismere Associates
	Private	Private panel organised, funded and managed by a private company to review schemes within a defined site or area	Lewisham Gateway Panel funded by MUSE Developments Ltd following a requirement within the terms of the planning permission (part of the Section 106 agreement) to review schemes
Specialist panel	Public	Public providers focussed on particular types of project e.g. transport or infrastructure	Home Office, Quality Panel, with a focus on buildings for the Police; or Transport for London, Design Review Group, with a specialist focus on roads/public realm schemes in London
	Private sub-contractor	Public or pseudo-public sector organisation focussed on particular types of project e.g. transport or infrastructure but with the panel management subcontracted to a private or not for profit organisation	HS2 Independent Design Panel, with a focus on the infrastructure and impacts of High Speed Rail 2, managed by private consultancy, Frame Projects, for HS2 Ltd
	Private	Private panel within and exclusively serving a private company	Barratt Homes' design review panel reviews all its schemes as part of an internal quality initiative designed to drive up quality across the company's developments

Figure 5.3 Typology of design review organisations operating in England in 2015

London[19] whilst the vacant eastern territory was taken over by Design South East, and with often minimal resources have continued to operate. In 2015, a key protagonist commented, "The Design Network is now a strong network and offers complete English coverage of design review panels" (5.4).

A second network, the Architecture and Built Environment Centre Network (ABEC Network) was also launched in 2013, initially with fifteen former ACN members, some of whom were also members of the Design Network. With no central funding, the ABEC Network is intended to collaborate in an informal way without the need for a central administration (Fulcher 2013). Members offer a combination of local events and exhibitions, and educational, training, participatory, design enabling, and review services. The network personifies the realities of the new context in which bottom-up rather than top-down initiative marks the progress of design governance in England. But, whilst five years after CABE's demise, many of the individual architectural centres have survived,[20] often as fragile shoestring concerns, the network itself has struggled to raise its profile, and the grouping continues to exist largely as an informal club of disparate organisations, sometimes very local and sometimes regional or sub-regional in their focus.

Reflecting on this state of provision, one prominent design review member commented: "Let 1,000 panels bloom, provided they're offering reviews of sufficient quality." For others, the demise of a central watchdog to maintain standards represented a serious concern in the face of such diverse provision, and will inevitably lead to a variety in the practices and quality of design review. As a key protagonist remarked, "Below the Design Network there are lots and lots of other local panels, some of which are good, some are not so good." In this environment, the Urban Design London design review survey concluded with the observation that even relatively vested interests operating within a commercially sensitive competitive environment "feel that the current situation would benefit from more coordination, clarity and consistency" (2015: 9).

Some limited coordination continued to be offered through the basing of much design review practice on the principles contained within the old CABE document, *Design Review: Principles and Practice*, updated by Design Council CABE (2013)[21] whilst still in

Figure 5.4 MADE Design: West Midlands, reviews projects across the region, including the Parkside Building on the new Eastside Park in Birmingham, home of Birmingham City University School of Architecture

Source: Matthew Carmona

receipt of government funding. Post-CABE, however, the document no longer has the teeth it once had when funding depended on following its rubric. As one commentator observed: "It's almost like you need the core organisation to keep everything honest, but today most review is beholden to nobody."

There is also the issue (already touched on) of how commercialisation of services impacts the essential relationship between the provider and recipient of services, and in particular the independence of the advice given. For some: "That was in the DNA of the old Commission, complete independence, you say what you think and you're beholden to nobody, which no longer exists. It means that developers, especially the bad ones, can ask that simple question, 'do I have to take the risk of taking my scheme to review and getting a stinger of a report?', because if the answer is no, why take the risk?" As an insider with experience of both CABE and post-CABE design reviews reported:

I don't think it's changed anything that we've written, but it changes the atmosphere because there's always that thing in the back of your mind which is saying, 'now on the basis of our performance at this review, never mind what we've actually said, is it more or less likely that these people would come back to us with their next scheme'?, and if you were gonna give someone a stinker, you know as you're doing it that they ain't gonna come back to you next time, whereas, under our previous guise, because we were quasi-governmental, they just had to grin and bear it if a local authority wanted a review.

Clearly the commercial imperative changed profoundly the essential relationships within design review, a reality quickly recognised by Design Council CABE, members of the Design Network, and others, many of whom subtly changed their practices to move away from the more challenging and sometimes confrontational style of old design review practices to a more supportive workshop-type activity. The impact on design outcomes of this change is, as yet, unknown, but addressing some of the reoccurring criticisms levelled at CABE (see Chapter 4) arguably has the potential to encourage developers and designers towards better design practices rather than attempting to drag them kicking and screaming.

Can't Survive by Design Review Alone

Whilst Design Council CABE and members of the two national networks were at pains to establish a range of services that extended well beyond design review, without venturing into the sorts of actual planning, design, or development services the consultancy sector offers, few of the design governance tools previously used by CABE had a ready market. By 2016, it was only design review, and conference/training (e.g. CPD activities[22]) that had gained traction as commercially viable services, and even design review remained marginal. In a continued context of national austerity following the May 2015 election and low enthusiasm within the new Conservative government to push, once again, a more holistic practice of design governance, the position looked unlikely to swiftly change. Nevertheless, building on its success signing up Oxford and Greenwich for a comprehensive design review service, in 2014, Design Council CABE launched the 'Cities' programme, aiming to bolster tailored design review with a range of 'value-adding' training, enabling, and support services for local authorities. As one commentator wryly observed: "Maybe they had learnt from CABE's busiest years; design review might be the icing on the cake, but nobody really likes icing on its own, you need cake too."

The Design Network organisations also quickly realised that without a high-profile voice such as the old CABE promoting the need for good design and design reviews, it would be hard to survive on this single product alone, and greater diversification and a more supportive offer was required, extending into community engagement, arts and culture, project support, capacity building, schools education, and professional and councillor training. But whilst each of these offered potential to extend the market and at the same time help to change local cultures and priorities on design, evidence since the withdrawal of public funding suggested that most were likely to be even more marginal than design review. To survive in this climate, organisations offering design governance services needed to be:

- Entrepreneurial with low fixed overheads.
- Sustained by local 'expert' networks that could be flexibly called on in different combinations as and when required.
- Supporting a smorgasbord of services (the more diverse the better).
- Capable of carefully tailoring their offer to local circumstances.

In this spirit, members of the Design Network were quick to adopt a final service of the former CABE that in 2012 also found a new commercial future. After a hiatus following the withdrawal of public funding, Building for Life (see Chapter 4) was relaunched as Building for Life 12, with a streamlined set of criteria (twelve instead of twenty) and a focus on a new 'Built for Life Quality Mark' as a certification of development quality (5.5). Design Council CABE retains a stake in the tool, along with partners, the Home Builders Federation (HBF) and Design for Homes, and the new model involves open access to the criteria which can be used in the design process, for constructing policy, and for negotiations between developers and planning authorities.

Whilst the new scheme was criticised by some for oversimplifying the ambition of the earlier version (Dittmar 2012), for others, the clear focus on urban design, the move away from building technology and other factors dealt with in the building regulations, the simplified assessment processes, and the move on-line, were simply smarter, and represented something for which "developers will be only too willing to pay a modest premium to benefit from" (Derbyshire 2012).

Figure 5.5 The Chocolate Works, York, 250 new units from David Wilson Homes on the former Terry's Chocolate factory site, scored well against the twelve new criteria

Source: Studio Partington

Assessment against the criteria are now conducted by Design Network members as a chargeable service, as is the actual quality mark itself, which is licenced at a rate of 0.0002 per cent of the cost of a home up to £3,000 per development.[23] By 2015, around fifty schemes had been awarded the quality mark.

Filling the Gaps with Voluntary Action

It is still early days for the commercialisation of design governance services, and their long-term viability remains to be fully tested in the market. The experience of the five years after public funding was withdrawn from CABE nevertheless suggests that some functions will never lend themselves to commoditisation. These include research, enabling, and the range of leadership functions around the production of national design guidance, campaigning, coordination across the sector, and the general advocacy of design quality. Complementing what the market can provide, a further set of activities has stepped into the gap with a strongly bottom-up provenance as driven forward by the voluntary provision of time and energy. To some degree, this mirrors the situation in the United States, where, as Dobbins recounts, influential organisations such as the Congress for New Urbanism, the Urban Land Institute, and the Project for Public Spaces (alongside the professional institutions), in the absence of national or state-led engagement with such issues, have tended to rise up from professional activism to become the undisputed leaders in the field (2009: 276).

This is not a new phenomenon in the United Kingdom either, with organisations such as the Royal Town Planning Institute (RTPI) (founded in 1914[24]), the Civic Trust (founded in 1957, succeeded by Civic Voice in 2010), the Urban Design Group (1978), the Prince's Foundation (1992[25]), and the Academy of Urbanism (2006) demonstrating a longevity of action and influence on the design agenda by finding a clear gap and a ready constituency of supporters. Others have come and gone, but have been influential whilst they lasted, for example the Urban Villages Forum (founded 1993) and the Urban Design Alliance (UDAL, founded 1997), or the Popular Housing Forum (1998). Common to all is that they emerged and gained momentum, typically during or immediately following periods when design was largely off the national agenda, and always from a sense that government and the professions, by themselves, could not be relied on to offer convincing leadership. Most recently, a similar frustration encouraged Sir Terry Farrell to convince the coalition government under the sponsorship of Architecture Minister Ed Vaizey to launch a further (low-cost[26]) review of design and the built environment.

The Farrell Review

On coming to power in 2010, Ed Vaizey, a long-term enthusiast of modern architecture, was Prime Minister David Cameron's first choice as minister for architecture in DCMS. Events required him to quickly step down from the role when another minister's conflict of interest in the communications portfolio left Vaizey swapping architecture for broadband. Returning to the architecture portfolio in 2012 to find that his predecessor had wound up CABE, Vaizey was quickly persuaded by Sir Terry's arguments that a review of architecture and design in the built environment was required. The unwritten aim was to determine what should be done to fill the glaring vacuum that, since the demise of publicly funded CABE, constituted English national policy on design and the built environment.

Following twelve months of study and wide-ranging consultation, the report shared obvious similarities with the hugely influential Urban Task Force Report, and the more recent Bishop Review (see earlier in this volume) into the future of design in the built environment, both of which Farrell referenced heavily. First, on the question of demand for good design, Farrell emphasised the importance of educating communities directly in the future of their built environments, for example through the creation of an architecture and built environment centre—an 'Urban Room'—in every town, and a programme of voluntary civic engagement amongst professional practices to 'champion the civic' and involve industry leaders in the challenges of 'everyday places'. Second, on the supply side, the emphasis in the Farrell Review was on education from the schoolroom to the workplace, with a particular focus on providing a grounding in place-making for all built environment students before they become entrenched in their professional silos. A common foundation year for built environment professionals was recommended (5.6), thus continuing an overarching theme of the review—learning to engage with places in a more holistic and joined-up manner.

Third, on questions of public sector engagement with built environment quality, here the review made important arguments around the need to rethink public procurement processes in order to give a greater emphasis to design quality (also a long-term goal of CABE), and to realign heritage and contemporary design concerns as two sides of the same 'quality coin'. Particular emphasis was also placed on the need to

move from a reactive and regulatory to a proactive and positive planning process, with the capacity for this coming from a simple (albeit somewhat naïve—Carmona 2014a: 248) switch of resources in local authorities from one to the other.

Finally, the need to bridge the divide between different disciplinary perspectives was dealt with through Farrell's most significant, yet arguably most intangible proposition: "A new understanding of PLACE" (Farrell Review 2014: 157). Here the review suggested that the term should be reinterpreted as a means to realign the professional institutes, educational processes, and built environment practices around a notion that the built environment is shaped by the core skill sets of the PLACE professions—Planning, Landscape, Architecture, Conservation, and Engineering—and that all must have a commitment to the total place. This driving idea coloured many of the most significant recommendations of the review:

- PLACE reviews, a re-branding and extension of design review to explicitly include all the PLACE professions in making judgements about the quality of development proposals, to review places in the round rather than within the red-line boundaries of projects, and incorporating the review of existing everyday places such as historic high streets as well as new developments.
- Chief PLACE advisors within government, notably a new chief architect to join the existing chief planner and chief construction advisor,[27] with a remit to advise in a consistent and coordinated manner on the built environment.
- And a PLACE Leadership Council[28] constituting private and public sector representation in order to advise on policies and programmes across government such as those relating to the creation of a more proactive planning system. (5.7)

This final recommendation was one of the most intriguing and in relation to which Farrell argued, the Council should be led jointly by government and the industry and made responsible for developing and monitoring relevant national 'place policy' across government and around the country. This was also one of the more sketchy proposals in the review, probably quite deliberately given the comparisons it inevitably

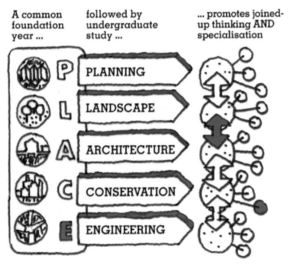

Figure 5.6 Farrell Review recommendation, a common foundation year for all built environment students

Source: Farrells

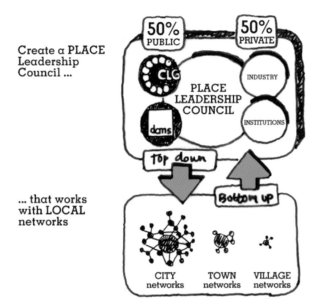

Figure 5.7 Farrell Review recommendation, create a Place Leadership Council

Source: Farrells

drew with CABE, which the coalition government had closed just three years earlier. In fact, the proposal was quite different from earlier entities. It would not, for example, do design review nor utilise any of the more proactive tools CABE had adopted to drive the national design agenda during the 2000s. Instead, a more constrained high-level policy and coordinating role was envisaged, although even this would have required a government far more willing to look beyond its own recent decisions than seemed likely at the time.

Instead, reflecting on both the Farrell proposals and the research reported in this book, Matthew Carmona put forward an alternative model at a Design Network meeting called to discuss the Farrell Review. For Carmona (2014e), the recent history of design governance in England suggested two critical things. First, the Farrell Review was correct in highlighting that the key gap left by the demise of a publicly funded CABE was one of leadership. Above all, CABE became the national voice of place design: a coordinating hand, a watchdog, and a guide. And whilst, for some, CABE was seen as too heavy-handed, its leadership role represented a gap that, for the first time since 1924, needed to be filled. Second, and departing from the conclusions of the Farrell Review, the experience of both the RFAC and CABE demonstrate that existence as an arm of or agency for government, beholden to the

waxing and waning interests of ministers and the constraints of the public purse, could be a dangerous place to be.[29] Instead, a truly independent critical friend to government, local government, the professions, and the whole development sector was required as a meeting place for people and ideas relating to design quality and the built environment. Subsequent debate of the proposition at a cross-sector BIG MEET held at UCL in July 2014 led to the establishment in October of the Place Alliance with Carmona as its chair.[30]

The Place Alliance and Other Post-FAR Initiatives

Place Alliance was set up as a confederation of individuals and organisations around a loose but shared belief that the quality of the built environment was profoundly important. They argued: "We believe that through collaboration we can create and maintain better places. To this end, we share knowledge and support each other to demand and realise buildings, streets and spaces that enhance the quality of life for all" (Place Alliance 2014a). Whilst it is too early to determine how successful the initiative will be, its defining characteristics can be summarised as:

- A belief in a broad definition of place quality—defined in terms of five Fs—Friendly, Fair, Flourishing, Fun, and Free (Place Alliance 2014a—5.8).
- A model based on a cooperative culture and a collaborative economy.
- An attempt to build an open and accessible movement rather than to construct a closed and regulated organisation.
- An independent voice beyond government and the market, harnessing volunteer skills, effort, and energy.
- A multi-polar and virtual existence rather than a fixed uni-polar one.

In its first year, Place Alliance gradually took over responsibility for advancing (through a series of working groups) a number of the strands of the Farrell Review, such as coordinating an Urban Rooms Network, and began developing distinct initiatives of its own, including a network of university hubs (Place Alliance is hosted at UCL), an Open Source Place Resource, a healthy places campaign, and, most important, a series of national and regional conversations around place quality;

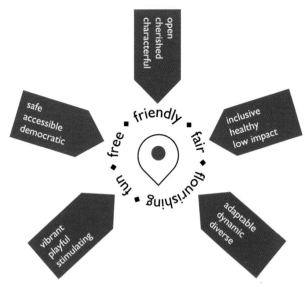

Figure 5.8   Place Alliance, the Five Fs

the BIG MEETS.[31] In its second year, it began more actively to campaign and to seek to influence national decision-makers on place-making and design, for example around the 2015 Housing and Planning Bill.

Without state resources, and based entirely on voluntary input, Place Alliance represented a new model, but one that bears analysis in the context of a further major policy initiative of the coalition government—the Big Society. The Big Society represented an attempt to reframe the role of government and move away from what some saw as an unduly paternalistic state, instead favouring the devolution of power downwards from central government to local government and ultimately to communities (e.g. neighbourhood planning), accompanied by encouragement to voluntarism, the charitable sector, and social enterprise. Others, more cynically, saw it as merely part of the rhetoric around a larger project of the political right, to shrink the state and to reduce public expenditure.

There was certainly always a fatal contradiction at the heart of the Big Society encapsulated in the desire to inspire bottom-up engagement through top-down initiative (Slocock 2015: 7), and history tells us that the initiative quickly slipped in political prominence as pressures of austerity came to dominate every action of government between the elections of 2010 and 2015, including (perversely) resources for state-led Big Society initiatives. Nevertheless, by withdrawing national government resources from non-commodifiable design

governance functions, such as those associated with coordination and leadership, Place Alliance could be viewed as an extension of the Big Society by the back door. The government simply created a vacuum and waited for something to fill it.

For its part, the government decided not to publish a formal response to the Farrell Review, preferring instead to pass the baton largely to 'the industry' to address. Rather than a PLACE Leadership Council, a Design Advisory Panel was established under the auspices of DCLG, and this quickly published a rather insubstantial guide to Starter Home Design (DCLG 2015a) before the May 2015 election,[32] and afterwards remained largely invisible within government. Just before the election, also, the government finally bit the bullet and moved responsibility for architecture from DCMS to DCLG. This directly addressed a recommendation of Farrell, and, for the first time since 1992, reunited architecture with the planning, housing, and local government functions of national government. Conservation remained with DCMS, and no new resources followed the architecture function into DCLG in order to address the brief.

At the same time, Parliament set up the first ever Select Committee on National Policy for the Built Environment within the House of Lords to scrutinise policy-making related to the built environment, and this met from July 2015 onwards, and reported in February 2016. The recommendations of both the Farrell and Bishop Reviews were early foci of this cross-bench Committee which appointed Matthew Carmona as its specialist advisor. Its report, *Building Better Places*, argued for a place-based approach to national and local policy, and for the government to better balance a concern for design and place quality with that of the quantity of development (particularly housing) and deregulation. It concluded:

> We believe it is important that the Government sets high standards for the built environment, and provides the vision, aspiration and leadership to encourage others to deliver against those standards. As a nation, our aspirations for the quality of the built environment have been routinely too low. Only the Government can set a more ambitious national path, and we urge this one to do so.
>
> (House of Lords 2016: 4)

Amongst a wealth of recommendations, the Committee argued that a number of key functions of CABE had been lost, and called for the appointment by the government of a chief built environment advisor to: help coordinate policy across departments; to publish a high-level national policy on architecture and the built environment; to head up a small strategic unit within the government to conduct, commission, and disseminate research and guidance; and to prepare an annual report to Parliament monitoring quality and delivery within the built environment and to set out priorities for research, policy, and action. Equating the model to that of the powerful chief scientific advisor, they argued this would provide both the direct access to government that the lack of national coordination and integration on built environment policy demanded, as well as the necessary degree of independence to proactively engage with the sector at large and to challenge government when required.

The report unequivocally called for a new settlement between government, design, and the shaping of place, and once again for a greater involvement and engagement of the state across all scales in such matters. This played out in recommendations dealing with, amongst other things, questions of skills and capacity in local government, national access and sustainability standards, and the use of the sorts of proactive design guidance tools discussed in Chapter 2. Whilst the Select Committee did not question the move of key design governance services into the market (or the role of voluntary action), it argued that provision was often inconsistent and fragmented with an insufficient level of activity to justify a wider investment in services. The recommended solution was more government action, this time to mandate design reviews for all 'major'[33] planning applications with the aim of driving up the volume and ultimately the quality of such activities as a means to encourage the development of a mature market in the governance of design alongside a reinvigorated public sector.

Conclusion

The five-year period from the demise of CABE as a publicly funded body to the publication of the House of Lords report in early 2016 represented a particular moment in time shaped by the confluence of two key factors:

- First, a public debt crisis leading to policies of austerity across the public sector and a consequential retrenchment of that sector (nationally and locally) from all things 'discretionary', in other words, from anything, such as a concern for design, not set down in legislation as a statutory obligation of the state.
- Second, a rapid rise of other means to fill the gaps, in part simply bubbling up in the absence of anything else, but also encouraged by the right-leaning coalition government through its long-term interest in the market and newfound concern for localism and voluntary action as alternatives to the state delivering public services.

In the design governance field, the impact of these two factors was particularly stark. On one hand, there was clearly a burgeoning of the market in areas for which a viable (even if flawed) market existed, and this has changed the relationship between many providers of design governance services and their ultimate clients, and also the nature and legitimacy of the services on offer. On the other hand, arguably, as long as CABE existed, the status of government advisor on design brought with it a position as the clear national leader on all issues relating to design that stifled local initiative of whatever type.[34] Its demise has led to a flowering of voluntary action to fill at least some of the non-commodifiable gaps in the governance of design.

In 2016, whilst some might hanker for a return to the days of bountiful public funding, others argue for positively embracing the new climate that looks likely to dominate for the foreseeable future. For the latter group, the adage "never allow a crisis to go to waste" sums up the situation. Beyond the United Kingdom, for example, the Australian Public Services Commission has argued the case for 'smarter policy', seeing "significant potential advantages for policy makers in looking beyond the traditional model of government as being solely responsible for devising and implementing policy frameworks, to one in which a range of third parties . . . play active policy roles" (2009: 19). In England, for design, this is in effect what has occurred, a move which brings with it potential advantages of extending expertise, stretching resources, and shifting ultimate responsibility for outcomes—all factors that politicians, across scales of government, might find enticing. For its part, the Young Foundation has argued that:

> Research has found strong evidence that in the public sector, innovation happens because of financial pressures—not because it is a good thing in itself. When money is plentiful people may talk about innovation and reform but inertia usually wins. When cash is tight there is no option but to get serious. The lessons of the past suggest there is a choice to be made between uncreative efficiencies and creative ones: the former freezes possibilities while the latter unblocks them.
>
> (2010: 3)

In the field of English design governance, there has certainly been significant innovation over the period covered by this chapter, but views are mixed about its impact. The market in design review, for example, is now well established, prompting one London interviewee to comment: "Competition is no bad thing, it seems, in part, to be driving innovation. In London we now have at least three organisations offering 'pay to use' design review services, in addition to the boroughs' own panels. This seems to be raising expectations, for example over how the reviews are run and could allow developers in particular to ask— what service am I actually paying for? Is it the best available?"

This, of course, is the relentless logic of the market. At the same time, if organisations in the design governance field concentrate only on the marketable elements from the design governance toolkit (see Chapter 2), then much will be lost. As one commentator argued when reflecting on the troubled transition from CABE to Design Council CABE:

> The leadership seemed to think that design review could be a profitable business. Maybe nobody saw that all the other work CABE did had helped to provide intelligence and gravitas that gave credence to the idea that the organisation really did know what it was talking about, what good design actually was and how it could be achieved. Design review without its supportive cousins of research, case study analysis, training, quality audits, policy scrutiny and

formulation etc, seemed to start to lose its gloss—quite rightly. Stripped back to a few people who think they know a lot about design offering comments on someone else's scheme, was this a product that could be bolstered enough to sell? . . . Interestingly, and to their credit, the Design Council soon widened their offer, linking design review with other types of support, training and advice.

This also seems to be a lesson that others in the market quickly learned, with members of the Design Network and ABEC Network also diversifying in the face of early disappointing returns from design review. The key conclusion from this chapter is, nevertheless, that the withdrawal of state provision from design governance services has led to a redefinition of these services through the market and voluntary provision, and to significant innovation on all these fronts; exactly as intended, except that an explicit plan to achieve this never existed (see Chapter 4). There is also a danger of overstating the positives. In reality, by 2016, the national environment for design governance echoed that at regional and local scales, with a diverse and continuing concern for design echoed in an ever more fragmented and complex picture of provision, and, whilst not hankering for a return to the pre-CABE situation, the proposals of the House of Lords were directed at addressing these challenges.

It is unknown at this stage how the market provision will develop, and whether, over the long term, it will prove sustainable, will expand its horizons further, or will retrench to design review only. It is also unclear whether the burgeoning volunteer efforts such as the work of the Place Alliance will successfully operate alongside the new market players and the public sector[35] as a stimulant to design governance. The context of supportive words from government but minimal national engagement in the design agenda, accompanied by significant energy and action in the non-governmental sector, is nevertheless reminiscent of the situation in England in the early 1990s (see Chapter 3). Whether, like the 1990s, the current climate for design governance represents a stepping-off point to something different again, only time will tell. The roller coaster ride goes on . . .

Relating the post-CABE environment to the triad of fundamental urban governance characteristics—operation,

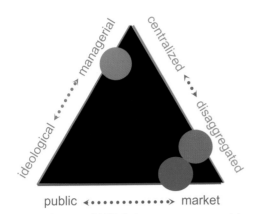

Figure 5.9 The post-CABE design governance model

authority, power—from Chapter 1 (5.9), the period can be represented as:

- Managerial—focussed on short-term austerity and minimising intervention without due regard to the consequences for long-term quality.
- Disaggregated—looking to a diversity of actors and means, national and local, to make the case (or not) for place quality.
- Market-oriented (with gaps)—reflecting the complete withdrawal of public funding from state-led design governance at the national level and the development of a market (where one is possible) and voluntary action (where it is not).

Notes

1. Particularly its chief executive, Richard Simmons, who made what some described as "herculean efforts" to safeguard key aspects of CABE's work and legacy.
2. The Design Council was founded in 1944 by Winston Churchill's wartime government as the Council of Industrial Design to promote better standards of design in British industry as it rebuilt after the war. It was incorporated as a registered charity by royal charter in 1974 under the Design Council name, but continued to operate as a Non-Departmental Public Body with broadly the same mission (http://en.wikipedia.org/wiki/Design_Council). Because the Design Council had a charitable status alongside its existence as a NDPB, it was able to attach its royal warrant to the charity and continue to exist when its existence as a quango came to an end.
3. A wholly owned company limited by guarantee, echoing where CABE began back in 1999 (see Chapter 4).
4. In fact, because CABE was effectively moving out of the public sector, EU competition rules required government to tender for these work streams which were then publicly advertised. Three other organisations (thought to be the RIBA, the Prince's Foundation, and the Architecture Centre Network) also bid for the work, each seeing the commercial possibilities of design review. CABE beat off the competition to secure two years of transitional funding.
5. These were clause 3.2: "The protection, enhancement, improvement and revitalisation of the natural and built environment (including architecture), and the advancement of the education of the public in such subjects and in subjects relating to sustainable development and sustainable living, and to promote study and research in such subjects provided that the useful results of such study are disseminated to the public at large; and clause 4.4 : "To encourage the incorporation of architecture and design education and education relating to the management and maintenance of the built environment in the national curricula, and particularly in the teaching of science, technology, engineering and maths."
6. A 40 per cent reduction in the government grant to local authorities by May 2015 (www.local.gov.uk/media-releases/-/journal_content/56/10180/6172733/NEWS).
7. For example, planning and development services were cut by 43 per cent between 2010 and 2012 (www.ifs.org.uk/budgets/gb2012/12chap6.pdf), and funding for parks and open spaces was projected to fall by 66 per cent by the end of the decade (www.local.gov.uk/publications/-/journal_content/56/10180/3626323/PUBLICATION).
8. Some of the RDA functions, including economic development, were taken on by new Local Enterprise Partnerships (LEPs), where local authorities and businesses entered into voluntary partnerships.
9. By April 2014, 1,000 communities across England had expressed an interest in preparing neighbourhood plans, but just thirteen had gone all the way through to passing local referendums. As of December 2015, this had improved, with 1,700 communities across England expressing an interest, leading to 126 referendums (DCLG 2015a).
10. http://planningguidance.planningportal.gov.uk/blog/policy/achieving-sustainable-development/delivering-sustainable-development/7-requiring-good-design/
11. He himself resigned shortly after in April 2012.
12. www.designcouncil.org.uk/our-services/built-environment-cabe
13. www.oxford.gov.uk/Library/Documents/Planning/Oxford%20Design%20Panel%20Details%20of%20the%20Service.pdf
14. www.designcouncil.org.uk/projects/inclusive-environments
15. Income into built environment-related activities was £700,000 and expenditure (including overheads) was £1,371,000.
16. During this period, the English Heritage Urban Panel had also been active in London as part of its national

programme of visiting places and offering advice to local governments.

17. Operated by the RIBA.

18. www.designreviewpanel.co.uk/#!locations/c24vq

19. Which does not offer commercial design review services.

20. In 2015, the ABEC Network had eleven English members, which have been joined by PLACE Northern Ireland.

21. In partnership with the Landscape Institute, RTPI, and RIBA.

22. Conferences and training activities generally have long had a ready market with a range of dedicated providers, particularly those licenced and publicised by professional institutes such as the RTPI to meet their CPD requirements.

23. www.builtforlifehomes.org/go/about/faqs~7#faq-ans-7

24. Initially founded, not as a professional institute, but to advance the study of town planning and civic design, and to coordinate those engaged or interested in these practices.

25. Initially established as the Prince of Wales' Institute of Architecture.

26. The review was largely funded by Sir Terry Farrell's own firm.

27. A post that was cut in 2015.

28. Modelled on the Construction Leadership Council established in government in 2013 to act as a joint government/industry forum for debating and taking forward the industrial strategy for construction.

29. Equally, the experience of UDAL (see Chapter 4) demonstrates the dangers of undue influence by the industry's professional bodies. UDAL flourished for about five years, after which some of its member organisations decided that they no longer needed to work together on urban design. After a few years of inaction, in 2010 the alliance was formally disbanded.

30. http://placealliance.org.uk/big-meets/

31. http://placealliance.org.uk

32. This contained eight suggested exemplars that the architectural press immediately dismissed as too nostalgic (Hopkirk 2015).

33. Residential sites of more than 0.5 hectare or 10 units, or sites of more than 1 hectare or 1,000 square metres of floorspace for all other uses.

34. Some argue the dominance of CABE was behind the demise of UDAL and later the Civic Trust, both of whom had their roles at least partly usurped by the state-funded organisation (see Chapter 4).

35. It is important to remember that local government remains the dominant, albeit much reduced provider of design governance services through its core regulatory roles.

PART III

The CABE Toolbox

CHAPTER 6

The Evidence Tools

In Part III, the tack of this book changes, from the theory of Part I and sweeping histories of Part II to a compendium of the everyday tools of informal design governance. This chapter is, therefore, the first of five dealing with the tools CABE used. Tools in this category are more remote from implementation and broadly refer to the sorts of background investigation that provides the knowledge to underpin more 'interventionist' tools. This chapter covers the two main activities under this category—research and audit—and is divided into three parts covering the why, how, and when of CABE's evidence activities. The first discusses why CABE employed research and audit, the second explores processes of gathering evidence and disseminating the knowledge it generates, and the conclusion briefly reflects on when these tools are best utilised within the design governance field of action.

Why Engage in Evidence Activities?

Research

From the start, evidence was fundamental to CABE's mission. It included research around particular themes of relevance to CABE and large-scale audits of development quality in order to understand 'the state of the art' of design. The early emphasis on research related to a general perception at the time that a huge gap in knowledge existed around design and the built environment and how to bridge it, and CABE saw its job, in part, as filling that gap. As discussed in Chapter 4, there was also a growing demand from government for evidence-based policy.

Reflecting this, one of the main objectives of producing research was for CABE to evidence its own activities and to make them robust in a manner that design had never been perceived to be before. This was seen as particularly important because of the intangible nature of many of the assumed benefits of good design, and because of the widespread view that such benefits were subjective and not amenable to proper rigorous research. As put by a prominent member of the advisory group set up to guide the early activities of CABE Space:

> The important thing was to set off with the intention of creating a body of evidence-based guidance because many people think of design as being a rather airy fairy and capricious activity done by self-indulgent and capricious, largely, men. So the work that was done . . . to demonstrate a connection between good design and value, whether that's financial value or how people feel about their environment, was immensely important.

Consequently, CABE's research effort, which began with *The Value of Urban Design* project (CABE 2001b), also quickly established value as its most enduring research theme. This was followed by: *A Bibliography of Design Value, The Value of Good Design, The Value of Housing Design & Layout, The Value of Public Space, The Impact of Office Design on Business Performance, Mapping Value in the Built Environment, Design with Distinction, The Cost of Bad Design, Physical Capital, The Value Handbook, Paved with Gold* (Box 6.1), and *i-Valul.*

Box 6.1   Paved with Gold

The *Paved with Gold* research project was undertaken in 2007 and published by CABE Space as part of a wider CABE programme that provided research, guidance, and case studies aimed at promoting high-quality street design (CABE Space 2007). Commissioned from consultants Colin Buchanan, the project aimed to apply established valuation methodologies in a new context by applying them to valuing design quality on a range of central London high streets (6.1). The objectives were to demonstrate and measure the economic benefits obtained with investment in the quality of street design, management, and maintenance, and to show how to calculate the extra financial value good street design contributes, over average or poor design.

Paved with Gold was conducted under the supervision of an advisory group which had as its chair a CABE commissioner (Joyce Bridges), and included

a project coordinator from CABE's research team, other representatives of the organisation, and four external experts coming from industry, local government, and academia.

The research team carried out quality assessments on ten London high streets using the Pedestrian Environment Review system (PERS), a multi-criteria analysis tool that scores the way a street works as a link, facilitating movement from A to B, and as a place in its own right (6.2). PERS was developed by consultants Transport Research Laboratory in 2001 as a walking tool to assess pedestrian environments, and *Paved with Gold* sought to link PERS scores with a range of social and economic data. Using regression analysis, they then established a correlation between design quality and the level of retail rents and residential property prices on and around each street.

The project was conceived as a demonstration project (like many of CABE's value projects) to show that the correlation between design quality and socio-economic value could be measured. As a CABE commissioner close to the project commented, "I think there was also a sense that enough had been done to demonstrate that there was something in this, and if other people wanted to take it forward, fine . . . it was giving people the material to start the argument."

According to the research findings, the value increment relating to the quality of design was

Figure 6.1   Walworth Road in London was one of the cases examined in the *Paved with Gold* research, a street that had undergone extensive public realm works to better balance the space between pedestrians and vehicles

Source: Matthew Carmona

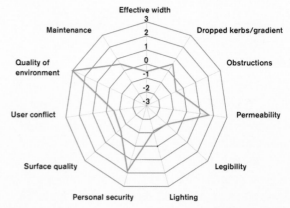

Figure 6.2   The PERS assessment of design quality for Chiswick High Road showing strengths and weaknesses across a range of variables

Source: CABE

around 5 per cent (CABE Space 2007: 7). These findings were ground-breaking because they provided some of the first econometric evidence that better-designed streets might carry an economic dividend. They also proved influential with a follow-up survey CABE conducted demonstrating that council officials used the research to support arguments for good design. In the words of one of the project directors: "Almost immediately after the work was done, it started to have noticeable effects on particular projects. So, for example, the project manager at Camden for the public realm improvements outside CABE's own offices said that he'd used the work to justify expenditure on the street."

Others argue that the work is one of CABE's research projects that "has had the most sustained resonance with users".

Despite its impact locally, the work did not have an impact on the Department for Transport (DfT), the government department responsible for roads which for most of CABE's existence remained reluctant to engage with a public realm quality agenda. As one of the consultants involved in the project noted, "We managed to get one meeting with them, and they basically said, 'We might be interested in the public realm around stations where people are walking for business. . . . Anything else, we're not interested.'"

Above all, CABE's efforts were intended to provide evidence for its claims about the nature of good design, and this required that research was conducted and presented in a usable manner persuasive to policymakers, professionals, and the development industry, as well as helping to guide the activities and initiatives of CABE itself. Indeed, throughout CABE's existence, research fed the organisation with intelligence, helped to justify its work, and opened up conversations with external parties, allowing it to talk to and persuade the doubters. Increasingly research was also used to support and underpin CABE's campaigning activities (see Chapter 8), allowing it to reach out to much larger audiences and spread the core message about the importance of place quality.

An Expanding Research Agenda

As CABE expanded its activities, so did the topics that were researched in order to continually build the evidence base. It started with a focus on the value of design—seen as an essential underpinning of CABE's work—and spread to all aspects of CABE's increasingly wide agenda. As one of CABE's directors recalled: "We used to have a matrix to track the research so we could say: 'We're doing some stuff on value, we're doing some stuff on space, we're doing some stuff on housing' and maybe a bit of research about customer interest, or industry concerns, or the market." Research projects in the main came from within the organisation in support of its identified strategic objectives and the organisation's

directorates, but were also regularly suggested by external partners, including government departments, other quangos, professional institutes, and universities. CABE had a range of relationships with these as co-funder, as delivery partner, or simply as advisor. This was a conscious strategy for the research team who, through involvement in the work of others, aimed to make its own limited resources but larger influence go as far as possible. Some, however, suggested that this external involvement increasingly represented a distraction from the organisation's own core agenda.

CABE's own research explored a broad range of subjects covering:

- The spectrum of development types (e.g. health, education, housing, public spaces, commercial properties).
- Urban scales (from strategic urban design to streets and spaces).
- Design processes (design codes, master planning, housing standards, client involvement, procurement, skills, and so forth).
- Design impacts (e.g. on health and well-being, sustainable development, inclusivity, beauty, liveability, and value).

The creation of CABE Space with its own agenda of research on parks and public spaces and their specific problems brought still another set of research topics, for example around the funding and management of parks (6.3).

Figure 6.3 Early research from CABE Space (2004) sought to learn from good practice in green space management in places as far afield as Minneapolis in the United States

Source: Alexius Horatius

CABE's research agenda was heavily guided by the needs of one of its main government sponsors, the Office of the Deputy Prime Minister (ODPM)/ Department of Communities and Local Government (DCLG), and in large part this work aimed at providing an evidence base for the Department's different policy initiatives, and shifts in the nature and approach of CABE to research were generally influenced by shifts in governmental policy and concerns to engage particular policy stakeholders. Because of this, the completion of research projects (although not their quality or impact) became one of the key performance indicators through which CABE's work was monitored in its early years.

Changes in CABE's own leadership were also reflected in the research agenda. Whilst Stuart Lipton and Jon Rouse had strongly championed the value of design agenda, the arrival of Richard Simmons as chief executive in 2004 marked a major push on the inclusive design agenda, a particular interest of his. This new body of work included research on black and minority ethnic (BME) representation in built environment professions, on design and access statements, principles of inclusive design, independent living for the elderly, sexuality and public space, and on inclusive place-making (e.g. CABE 2004f; CABE 2006d). It was supported by the Inclusive Environment Group (IEG),[1] sponsorship for which switched from ODPM to CABE in 2005, and which thereafter advised CABE on a broad range of inclusivity concerns, albeit in an arm's-length manner.[2]

The Status of Research

CABE research sometimes defined agendas, such as its work on value and, later, on beauty, but often it reacted to larger governmental agendas or to agendas already established by others. Its research on design coding, for example, followed the housing agenda set down in the 'Sustainable Communities' programme (see Chapter 4) and a visit of John Prescott to Seaside in Florida; for its first few years, the research of CABE Space largely followed the gaps in knowledge so clearly established by the Urban Green Spaces Taskforce and in subsequent ODPM (2002) policy documents; whilst research towards the end of CABE's life on Strategic Urban Design (StrUD) reflected the larger national move to a system of spatial planning. CABE's research also supported its continuous goal of injecting a 'quality' dimension into the huge upsurge in public sector building across the country during the 2000s, in: health, education, social housing, childcare, regeneration, the Olympics, and management of the public realm.

Yet whilst CABE's research programme expanded considerably over its life, the status of this part of CABE's remit did not. In *CABE: Ten Year Review* (CABE 2009a), the research role was hardly mentioned, with just four mentions of research, all relating to specific findings of projects, rather than to the holistic accomplishments of CABE in this area. Some argued that this omission reflected a tendency for research to be seen as simply the handmaiden of communications rather than a valuable service in its own right. There was also a tendency for the constituent directorates of CABE, as they grew and became more powerful, to simply take on this function themselves (e.g. enabling managed the research on design codes and design review undertook the various assessments and resulting practice guides that stemmed from their work). Arguably, this undermined the role of the central team CABE had built up, and it certainly failed to fully utilise its expertise.

At its demise, however, CABE's website was more effusive:

CABE's research programme has produced an unrivalled portfolio of research reports, policy guidance, best practice and case studies, widely available via our publications and the website. . . . This set of highly innovative resources has opened up a new field of knowledge around the impact of good design and how to create great places through better planning and design processes. CABE delivered over 80 informative and purposeful research studies, devised to address gaps in industry knowledge, with the intent of improving the understanding of the relationship between the physical quality of cities, their spaces and buildings, and the quality of life of their users. Our approach has been the robust and critical application of theory and evidence to improving policy and practice across the built environment.[3]

Audit

The other component of evidence activities were the audits CABE carried out on the quality of buildings and built spaces. These auditing activities started logically later than its research programme, as it required, first, a set of indicators with which to measure the quality of buildings and places. Whilst best known for its audits of housing for sale, CABE also conducted audits of social housing, secondary schools, childrens' centres, and green space. The various audits each had similar objectives and focussed on establishing an evidence base from which to argue for better design and to monitor progress on design quality, as well as to influence key stakeholders, including (most notably) developers, but also the general public. As many of the later audits were related to governmental capital spending programmes, those had the further objective of monitoring the quality of the outputs from these programmes.

The Housing Audits

The housing audits were based on the Building for Life (BfL) criteria (see Chapters 8 and 9), which helped to define what good design meant in a way that could be applied to existing or proposed buildings (6.4). The result was the first complete national audit of housing design quality in England, and provided a robust evidence base from which to argue for greater attention to the issue. Generally these audits revealed that the quality of housing design was not good and included important regional data allowing CABE to engage with stakeholders regionally and locally on the issues raised. Indeed, after the scale of the problem had been

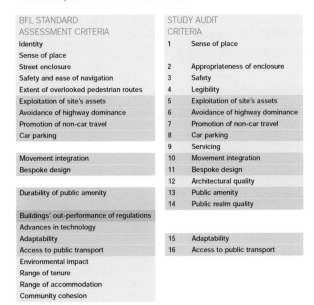

Relationship of BFL criteria to audit criteria

BFL STANDARD ASSESSMENT CRITERIA	STUDY AUDIT CRITERIA	
Identity		
Sense of place	1	Sense of place
Street enclosure	2	Appropriateness of enclosure
Safety and ease of navigation	3	Safety
Extent of overlooked pedestrian routes	4	Legibility
Exploitation of site's assets	5	Exploitation of site's assets
Avoidance of highway dominance	6	Avoidance of highway dominance
Promotion of non-car travel	7	Promotion of non-car travel
Car parking	8	Car parking
	9	Servicing
Movement integration	10	Movement integration
Bespoke design	11	Bespoke design
	12	Architectural quality
Durability of public amenity	13	Public amenity
	14	Public realm quality
Buildings' out-performance of regulations		
Advances in technology		
Adaptability	15	Adaptability
Access to public transport	16	Access to public transport
Environmental impact		
Range of tenure		
Range of accommodation		
Community cohesion		

Figure 6.4 The housing audits used a modified version of the Building for Life (BfL) criteria to assess the quality of housing developments

Source: CABE

identified, CABE devoted considerable resources to encouraging national, regional, and local governments to take the associated challenges seriously.

For CABE, the national housing audit met two further primary objectives. First, of exerting pressure directly on housebuilders in order to challenge them to up their game on design. Second, of generating a public debate and thereby exerting further indirect pressure to improve through informing and influencing customer demand. This latter objective was sometimes handled a little crudely, with CABE officials berating housebuilders in the national press and broadcast media and as a result encouraging at least some developers to dig their heels in and insist that the market knows best. Some never relented from that position, whilst others were more amendable and increasingly responded to the pressure (see Chapter 4). Carefully conducting the analysis over three phases helped by providing detailed evidence about the scale and nature of the problem that was difficult to refute, and by keeping the issue in the public eye for longer (on and off over the three years it took to do the work). The audits were heavily publicised in the national, regional, and trade press.

Looking back on the audits in its ten-year review, CABE argued: "Between 2004 and 2006, our housing audits provided a vivid insight into the kind of places that had planning permission in the period before 2003. This research established a benchmark for housing quality across England, which can now be used to measure progress over the next 10 years. The housing audit was important because it made the quality of homes as important as the volume" (CABE 2009a). The audits' real long-term benefit, therefore, was their anticipated role as part of an evidence base that would build up over time and monitor change in housing design. At the time of its first housing audit CABE (2005d), ambitiously stated: "We intend to work with the industry and with local authorities to ensure that, when we audit these regions again in a few years' time, nearly every scheme achieves a 'good' score against the CABE/Home Builders Federation's Building for Life criteria." CABE closed before the exercise could be repeated.

Beyond Market Housing

The perceived success of the housing audits led to an extension of the tool into other development remits. First, from market housing into the affordable housing sector, where the national funder of affordable housing provision at the time—the Housing Corporation—was planning to introduce Building for Life criteria into its funding regime. Consequently, in 2006, it commissioned its own social housing audit from CABE as a benchmark of quality before the new measure was introduced (HCA 2009). A concurrent audit of schools followed an intervention by John Sorrell (CABE chairman), who flagged the lack of evidence about the quality of schools being built under the national schools rebuilding programme, Building Schools for the Future (BSF). The decision to mount a review also provided an opportunity to assess the impact of the CABE enabling programme that was devoting significant resources to BSF, and ultimately helped to provide clear thresholds for an acceptable level of school design (CABE 2006e). A review of children's centres followed shortly afterwards, two thirds of the way through the first national Sure Start children's centres programme (see Chapter 10). This aimed to draw lessons for the centres still to be built and for similar capital programmes in the future (CABE 2008c).

A later review of green spaces attempted to tackle a recommendation in the Urban Green Spaces Taskforce that highlighted the need to create a single national reliable source of information about the quality of green spaces in England. Three different government departments held information on various aspects of green spaces, but this was not coordinated, making strategic decisions difficult. The aim was to understand more about the state of green space in urban England and to establish a baseline through a suite of indicators that could be used to track changes to England's green spaces. *Urban Green Nation* was published in 2010 (CABE Space 2010b) whilst a related study examined in more depth the impact of green space quality on the well-being of people in deprived areas (CABE Space 2010a).

How Were Evidence Activities Delivered?

Research

Research and policy was one of the original directorates of CABE, although research was later absorbed into policy and communications, with a head of research sitting under the director of policy and communications. Numbers of staff associated with the research function varied significantly, from just one at the inception of CABE to eight, at its height, including three research staff members located in CABE Space.

Conducting Research

From the start, therefore, CABE had a research function, and this developed into a dedicated research group within its structure, although, as already mentioned, this was not always responsible for every research project the organisation undertook. Its research programme developed from small beginnings (just one £20,000 project in its first year of operation) to a substantial programme, reaching its peak in terms of projects commissioned in 2004/05 when projects across nine themes were active, and with multiple projects in the green/public spaces area. In 2005/06, CABE's annual report identified that the organisation significantly exceeded its government performance target of publishing five evidence-based research projects (it published eight) and of commissioning a further three relating to aspects of the ODPM policy agenda (it commissioned five) (CABE 2006c: 25). Yet, despite this growth, as one of its contractors observed, "CABE never moved entirely away from the notion that research could be commissioned at high speed and on shoestring budgets, a consultancy rather than academic view of research that ensured resulting outputs were sometimes less than heavyweight."

CABE's own expertise was in the framing, commissioning, managing, steering, and dissemination of research projects which were then conducted by others, and CABE rarely conducted its own research in house. Instead, CABE worked with a wide spectrum of academics and consultants who applied a very varied mix of qualitative and quantitative methodologies. These ranged from the large-scale national housing audits reporting the actual design quality delivered by volume housebuilders, surveys assessing the relative trade-offs that consumers accept when buying a new home, to studies of planning skills in local authorities and their use of design champions. This was balanced against finer-grained qualitative explorations of more intangible issues such as how the design of homes and neighbourhoods can support an ageing population or community, perceptions of beauty, and risk and safety in public areas. CABE's research continued to explore new agendas, revisit and update old ones, and innovate methodologically until the end (6.5). For example, its beauty research, which began in 2010 under the banner of 'People and Places', involved a MORI poll on the subject, qualitative analysis of experiences in Sheffield, AHRC-funded semiotic analysis, a series of commissioned essays, and CABE's first (and last) Facebook campaign and photographic competition (see Chapter 9).

Many of CABE's own projects were relatively small scale, but its strength as a dissemination partner resulted in a wide range of relationships with academic institutions and others, and participation in a large number of advisory groups for external research projects. At the strategic level, CABE built close and influential links with the key academic research funding councils, and over time also came to manage built environment-related research for a range of government departments and other organisations, including the Department of Culture, Media and Sport, ODPM/DCLG, Department of Transport, Department of Health/

NHS, Community Health Partnerships, English Heritage, the Museums Libraries & Archives Council, Housing Corporation, English Partnerships, Higher Education Funding Council for England, National Audit Office, various regional development agencies, and the Arts and Humanities Research Council. It also undertook collaborative research with a wide range of industry bodies and professional institutions such as the British Council for Offices, Urban Buzz, Nuffield Trust, Society of Black Architects, Popular Housing Forum, Home Builders Federation, and so on.

Research projects themselves were typically constituted with an advisory or steering group, often chaired by a commissioner, and constituting experts hand-picked from academic, public, private, and voluntary organisations as appropriate. CABE also established a Research Reference Group with a varied and interdisciplinary membership tasked to monitor the research programme and to provide impartial external advice. Participants suggest that this became little more than a talking shop as detailed decisions over how to conduct its individual research projects were a matter for the research team in association with its selected contractors and project steering groups whilst strategic decisions about the direction of CABE's research largely reflected the needs of CABE's funders and the strategic priorities identified by CABE's executive and ratified by commissioners.

In 2003, for example, perhaps the largest single research theme was launched in the form of the new five-year programme of green spaces research. In this area, the Urban Green Spaces Taskforce had set the initial agenda, but CABE enjoyed considerable freedom to develop it as its own expertise and knowledge-base grew. Delivered by a dedicated research and policy team within the newly established CABE Space, the programme eventually delivered twelve research reports and ten briefings/think pieces and in so doing, provided the evidence base for many of CABE's campaigns, including the influential 'Wasted Space' (see 4.8), a national campaign launched in 2003 to find the worst wasted spaces in Britain. CABE Space's research was conceived to: first, build up evidence on the value and contribution of green spaces across economic, environmental, and social agendas, and, second, to address long-standing gaps in knowledge and ultimately improve understanding across the urban green space sector by providing a

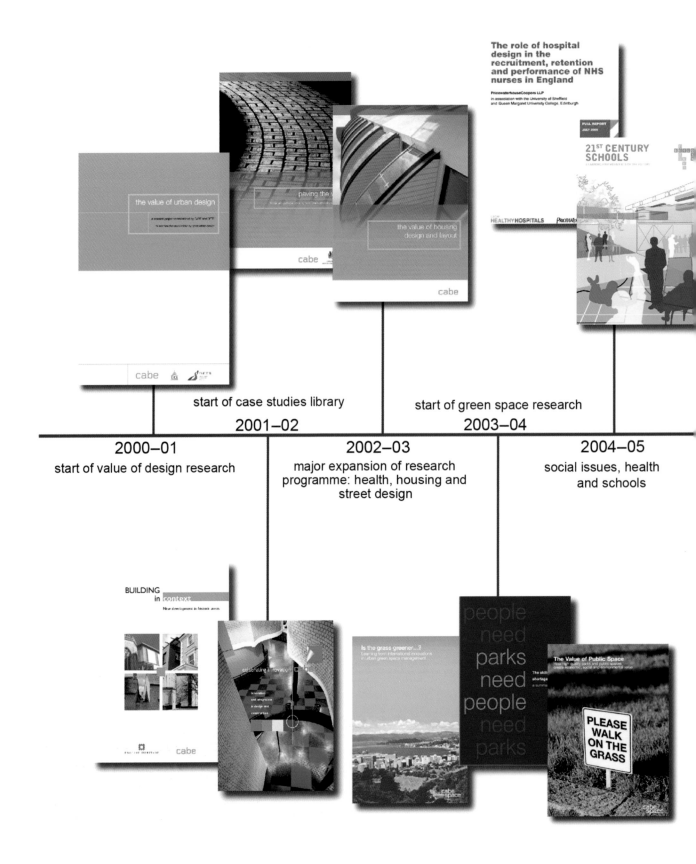

start of case studies library

start of green space research

2001–02

2003–04

2000–01

start of value of design research

2002–03

major expansion of research
programme: health, housing and
street design

2004–05

social issues, health
and schools

Figure 6.5   Timeline of CABE's research

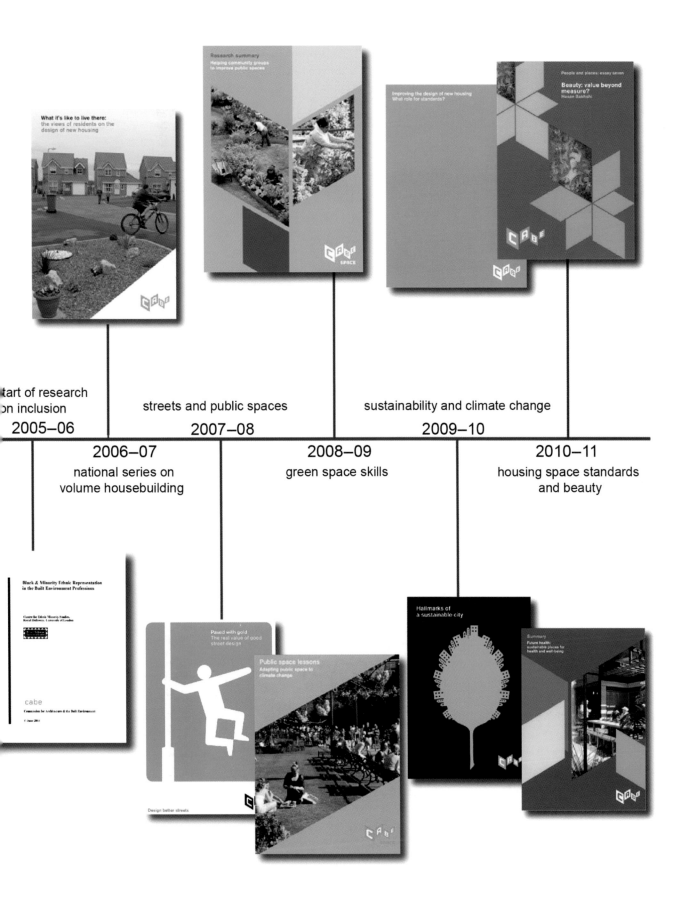

start of research
on inclusion
2005–06

streets and public spaces
2007–08

sustainability and climate change
2009–10

2006–07
national series on
volume housebuilding

2008–09
green space skills

2010–11
housing space standards
and beauty

body of work which moves forward innovation, knowledge sharing, best practice, and skills development. The programme reflected, at a smaller scale, CABE's larger goals and the importance of research.

Research for an External Audience

As the green spaces example shows, CABE's research was also part of its communication activity, and published research reports had the role of spreading the message and the findings about the importance of good design to target audiences in industry, government, and the public. Over time, this work resulted in an extensive published resource of evidence across the design and the built environment arena—work that seems to have been very well used across the sector. The evidence for this is contained in surveys CABE commissioned to assess the impact of its research with, for example, a CABE customer survey commissioned in 2009 showing that 80 per cent of a sample of 1,000 CABE stakeholders used CABE publications, 95 per cent of those found them useful, and 89 per cent had changed the way they worked as a result (CABE 2010a).

However, as might be expected, opinions about the effectiveness of CABE's research varied, with more positive views expressed among those already inclined towards CABE or who worked for the organisation, and less so from CABE's critics. For some, the usefulness of the research was in the evidence it provided, which confirmed the main thrust of CABE's message and which could be used to persuade key stakeholders to invest in design quality. As one urban design practitioner expressed it: "CABE did some research that showed that if your house looked over x amount of green space, it will eventually sell for six per cent more. . . . My reaction was, 'Oh, my God; we knew that, but here we finally have the bloody proof.'" He went on: "There was quite a lot of money spent on research, but it was really, really well thought out and I know I personally was able to use it to show planners . . . 'Come on, this is proof that this is the way we should be doing it.'" One of CABE's directors agreed: "One of the ground breaking documents that we did was called *The Value of Public Space*, which was the first time anybody had brought together, in a really clear and beautiful format, the key values of public space and what it does

for all our lives. And then we'd layer onto that some current market research, so that you could say what people thought and felt at that moment . . . It worked hugely well."

Elsewhere came suggestions that a change occurred in CABE's understanding and use of research during its eleven-year history. As put by a DCLG civil servant, "Research by CABE at the beginning was robust and useful, and helped make the case for CABE within the funding departments, but as time progressed, the proportion of research that resembled just publicity for the organisation grew." He concluded, "At the end, most of it was useless and reinforced the view of CABE within those departments, especially DCLG, as a self-obsessed luxury."

Research within CABE

CABE's research activities had important internal objectives within the organisation. Its outputs were meant to inform and shape the initiatives of other parts of CABE and make effective use of the wealth of information and data collected through its front-line tools, for example via enabling and design review. A related dimension of CABE's research activity was therefore to function as a hub for gathering knowledge about relevant research done elsewhere. As a member of the research team explained: "We became much more of a knowledge hub, and that was partly in recognition that, by 2006, we weren't just commissioning or doing research . . . it was about coming together, making sure that we knew what was happening."

How effective all this gathering of information and reflection on CABE's own practices was, was a matter of contention. As with many organisations, the different directorates within CABE tended to build their own silos, and collaboration and communication among them was not always smooth. Design review was CABE's most visible activity, and here the feedback loop between reviews conducted and design and development practice in the country at large was seen as very important, although not always consistent. As one of CABE's commissioners noted: "When a new building type emerges, let's say residential above supermarkets, you could start to pluck evidence that's coming to you from different regions, you can make an analysis of it, and then you can draw some conclusions: 'It's better if you do that,' 'It's a disaster if you do that,' and then you roll that out to every design review panel in the country."

Despite this, some suggested that design review and other front-end activities were not very good at passing data to CABE's research teams. Others felt that the boot was on the other foot and that those doing the research mostly ignored the wealth of information CABE itself generated: "I always thought that design review was where we saw things on the ground, where we were interfacing with what was actually happening, and I was always amazed that other sections of CABE, like the people who did the publications, tended to totally ignore what we were seeing. In my view, there was a crazy kind of competitiveness between the different sections of CABE that didn't communicate very well and weren't very supportive to each other."

Research was also used internally for the evaluation of and reflection on the impact of CABE's activities, although this happened more consistently in relation to some activities than others, and the research team saw part of its role as getting the rest of the organisation "to be a lot better about feedback and responses to what they were doing, so that evidence wasn't just quantitative". CABE Space, as a smaller and more focussed division of CABE with its own research team and leadership, seems to have been better at using research to guide its strategic decisions, as one of CABE's research directors explained: "CABE Space . . . was always really canny about the research that it did and how it would shape exactly what their programme should be . . . so there was a very nice iterative process." The larger, more disparate organisation found this much tougher to achieve.

Audit

The original housing audit started in 2004 as part of CABE's DCLG-funded work programme and looked at private housing schemes completed between 2001 and 2003. The intention from the start was national coverage, and this was achieved over three years, focussing on London, the south-east, and the east of England in 2004; the north-east, the north-west, and Yorkshire and Humber in 2005; and the East Midlands, West Midlands, and the south-west in 2006. The audits revealed a slightly rosier picture in London and the south-east, but very little cheer elsewhere, with the final

audit suggesting that fewer than 18 per cent of schemes could be classed as good or very good design, and 29 per cent where the design was so poor that they should not have received planning permission (CABE 2007e: 4):

[The audit] paints an uncompromising and unflattering picture of the quality of new housing built over the past five years. There is far too much development that is not up to standard—a standard that CABE has agreed with the trade body for developers—and far too little that is exemplary in design terms. In short, there is a long way to go before new housing is something of which we can be proud.

(CABE 2007e: 7)

The later audit of social housing and a specific audit of new housing in the Thames Gateway[4] demonstrated a similar picture. The first of these, for example, reviewed schemes built between 2004 and 2007 and also revealed 18 per cent in the good or very good categories, 61 per cent as average, and 21 per cent as poor. The controversy this caused within the government, with some DCLG ministers believing it might be construed as reflecting badly on them, delayed publication of the report until 2009. By this time the Housing Corporation, who had commissioned the work in 2007, had been subsumed into the Housing & Communities Agency and they slipped the research out without launch or fanfare.

CABE received various tranches of funding for its audit work. The first three housing audits were funded through DCLG core funding, and the fourth through Housing Corporation funding. Some funding from the National Audit Office was secured to review schools as a feed into their value for money review of the Building Schools for the Future (BSF) programme, whilst the Department for Children, Schools and Families (DCSF) funded the audits of children's centres.

Following the success of the audits, the 2010/11 funding agreement between CABE and DCLG featured a new indicator of CABE's success: the number of new housing schemes across the country rated as 'poor' by housing audits should halve from 29 per cent to 15 per cent (CABE 2009d: 6). Given CABE's sometimes fractious relationships with housebuilders (see Chapter 4), its ability to deliver on such a target would have been somewhat challenging. DCLG nevertheless asked CABE in the same year to conduct a second round of the national housing audit, although this was quickly cancelled when CABE lost its funding, after which interest in government relating to housing design quality all but evaporated.

The Methods

The methodology used for the national housing audit was reasonably consistent throughout its three phases (Box 6.2), although the second and third audits incorporated residents' views into the approach. Each audit compared around 100 recent housing developments (generally mixed-market homes built by the top ten volume housebuilders) against Building for Life (BfL) criteria. As a by-product, this approach helped to demonstrate the legitimacy of BfL, and led to its adoption by other organisations, including DCLG, the Housing Corporation, English Partnerships, and later the Housing and Communities Agency.

Box 6.2 The First Housing Audit

CABE undertook its first housing audit on its own initiative which looked at the quality of housing schemes completed between 2001 and 2003 in London, the south-east, and the east of England regions. As one of the commissioning directors explained, the idea stemmed from internal discussions relating to the lack of evidence around housing and concerns about whether the organisation was doing enough on the topic: "Within CABE most people were fairly bleak about it, stemming from time sitting on trains going around the country and staring out of the window and thinking 'God, what have we been building for the last twenty years and how do we get a grip on it in an evidence based way'?"

The initiative reflected the pressure for more housing nationally and the need to persuade local authorities to accept increasing housing targets, making housing probably the biggest issue the organisation would face. As one of the main consultants who worked on the audits suggested: "If we were going to force local authorities to deliver 200,000 new homes a year over the next twenty-year period, we also needed, at the same time, to try and improve the quality of those homes, to try and sweeten the pill."

The audits used the Building for Life (BfL) criteria as the tool to measure quality, a tool that (up to that point) had largely been used to award exemplary developments which ranked well against its twenty indicators. The first audit therefore needed to explore the possibility of using BfL criteria as a metrics tool for housebuilders and local authorities across all categories of quality. As one of the CABE

research advisors explained, "As time went on, we really tightened up the criteria, or the guidance on how the criteria should be applied for the assessments, and we really did a lot of work with the assessors to make sure that they were all assessing things in a consistent way. We had a very close look at things like making a record of what the weather was like when schemes were visited, and we ended up finding a difference between ones that were assessed on a sunny day and ones that were assessed on a grey day, for which we were then able to adjust for parity." This learning process continued throughout the first audit, which as a result was arguably less robust than later ones that benefitted from a tightening up of the methodology.

The first audit (like the others) showed a generally low occurrence of good or very good design and a general dominance of highways at the expense of streets and public space (6.6). It also received immediate national headlines, and, as a CABE director recalled: "The thing that caught most attention was that the quality of housing in this country is shocking and created a sense of urgency around the problem." The reaction of the industry was initially defensive, as a member of the Home Builders Federation (HBF) pointed out, "I think the audits ruffled a few feathers. The industry were clamouring to build more and then CABE arrived on the scene and we said, 'Who are these people?' Then the audit gets carried out and the message pushed out was that the majority of people were getting a raw deal . . . ultimately, that put quite a few people on the back foot."

Figure 6.6   (i) Admiralty Way (off Queens Road), Teddington, identified as an example of poor highway design; (ii) Poundbury Dorchester, praised for its careful consideration of highways and its pedestrian-friendly environment

Source: Matthew Carmona

Part of the problem was the perception of CABE among parts of the housebuilding industry, and the distance between CABE's agenda and the modus operandi and business model of large sectors of the housebuilding industry. The same member of HBF continues: "CABE was seen, very much, as a trendy, urbanite sort of organisation, not really reflecting the wider picture across the country, and I think that caused some people to think . . . essentially, they're New Labour luvvies . . . and there was nothing CABE gave them to make them feel part of the process, they were anti, anti, anti. Other housebuilders were much more enlightened and wanted to embrace it," and some already were (6.7), although, "as a generally conservative bunch, it took many a long time to warm up to the idea."

Figure 6.7   Greenwich Millennium Village, Phase One, lauded for its quality in all aspects of design

Source: Matthew Carmona

The secondary school audit was in two parts. The first surveyed the quality of recently completed schools and gathered feedback from CABE enablers and clients. The second involved interviewing CABE enablers to provide a snapshot of the design quality of BSF schemes still on the drawing board. Of the 124 schools completed between January 2000 and September 2005, CABE assessed 52. To make quality assessments, the work used a 'DQI for Schools', a tailored form of the Design Quality Indicator developed by CABE and the Construction Industry Council (see Chapter 9). The result was a new Schools Quality Assessment (SQA)

evaluation methodology based on 111 indicators presented as statements in three categories: functionality, build quality, and impact. Each school was given an overall rating by a single expert, and no attempt was made to gather user perspectives or cost data.[5] The final report, *Assessing Secondary School Design Quality*, revealed that 50 per cent of secondary schools were poorly built, badly designed, and failed to provide inspiring educational environments (CABE 2006e: 4) (6.8). The results led CABE to establish its Schools Design Panel as a dedicated design review service for new schools.

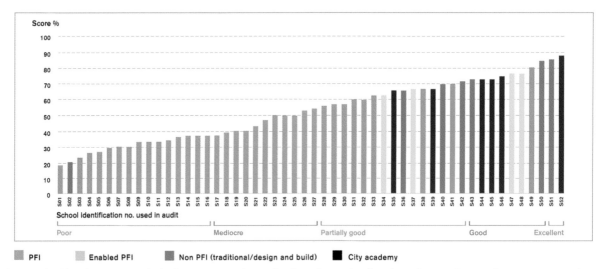

Figure 6.8   This data set provided information on where schools performed well and poorly, as well as on design process and procurement routes. The National Audit Office (2009) used the data to support findings in its own extensive report on the value for money of the BSF programme

Source: CABE

The later analysis of children's centres used post-occupancy evaluation techniques in the largest public sector project of its kind, investigating 101 recently completed schemes (CABE 2008c), whilst later still CABE's green inventory covered more than 16,000 individual green spaces over eleven categories. The resulting *Urban Green Nation* contained an estimate of size and a geographic location of each space and drew from more than seventy existing data sources covering various aspects of quantity, quality, use, proximity, management and maintenance, and the value to local people. Data was donated by partners to the research, including the National Trust, Greenspace, and Sport England (CABE Space 2010b). In contrast to the earlier audits, this exercise was done remotely without the need to visit a single site or evaluate any actual schemes. CABE was wound up before the usefulness of such an approach could be fully tested.

Whilst audits as a tool came relatively late to the CABE toolbox, their use gathered momentum quickly and the variety of large-scale audits undertaken and the various methodologies developed and successfully used demonstrate that they were both an effective and flexible means to gather and present evidence around the quality and impact of design and (in the case of parks) long-term management concerns. The results remain as a valuable baseline to which future research can compare.

When Should Evidence Tools Be Used?

This chapter has explored the first and least interventionalist of the informal tools that CABE deployed, the gathering of evidence about good design. At the heart of this category was research, focussed on understanding the problems and processes of design and development as they effect the built environment. A second tool, audit, concentrated on measuring the quality of outcomes and ultimately the impact of development on place (6.9). Whilst it did not always meet its full potential, to a significant degree evidence provided the basis on which CABE's other tools were developed, refined, and monitored.

Evidence represented a means of constructing a knowledge base that could inform government, developers, commissioners of buildings, and users but also, internally, it helped CABE to better focus its own agenda with empirical evidence. These tools evolved over the lifetime of the organisation and developed to touch almost every sphere of the built environment from construction to spatial planning, buildings to landscape, and product to process. The methods also evolved, both of its research and audit, and collectively, through its funding and enabling of such activity, CABE contributed substantially to knowledge and to establishing a capacity and know-how to undertake design-based research in the United Kingdom.

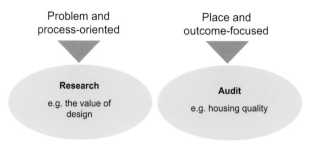

Figure 6.9 Typology of evidence

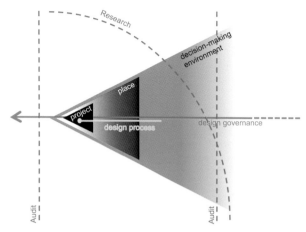

Figure 6.10 Evidence tools in the design governance field of action

Although the amount of evidence CABE produced or compiled, either through dedicated research or by collecting information from its own activities, was unprecedented in the field, its actual impact varied. As with any organisation involved in research, it is the connection with the end users of the knowledge produced that dictates impact, and for CABE, this meant a balance between defining a research agenda as a function of government priorities, following its instincts about what kind of knowledge it should produce, and being aware of the ultimate users of its research and how it would be perceived and used. For some users, CABE's research represented an invaluable source of rigorous ammunition with which to arm themselves in their battle for better design, nationally, regionally, or locally. For others, CABE quickly became bogged down in its own crusade to produce more and more (to meet government targets and to continually demonstrate its relevance), and this pursuit of quantity was not always accompanied by an equal level of attention to rigour or quality. Most agree that the experience of CABE would have been immeasurably less effective and impactful without the focus on evidence that had been a key feature of the CABE story from the start, and that was amongst the key factors that distinguished the organisation so completely from what had come before.

Placing the tools of research and audit in the design governance field of action identified in Chapter 1 (6.10) shows that CABE used audit as both a post- and

pre-development tool: as a means to revisit developments en masse after completion in order to evaluate them collectively and gauge the 'state of the art', but also as a valuable baseline of quality against which to benchmark subsequent interventions. Research, by contrast, transcended the decision-making environment and all aspects of quality from aesthetic, to project, to place and process. For CABE, evidence had the potential to inform all aspects and stages of design governance.

Notes

1. Formerly the Built Environment Group of the Disabled Persons Transport Advisory Committee (DPTAC).
2. Those involved report that the two organisations were very poorly integrated and communication was minimal, although in 2008, IEG did become the Inclusion by Design Group (IBD).
3. http://webarchive.nationalarchives.gov.uk/20110118095356/http://www.cabe.org.uk/research
4. This audit differed from others in using forty-one schemes submitted for planning approval (rather than built schemes) and applying Building for Life criteria to the results.
5. As most schools were PFI projects, this data was commercially sensitive.

CHAPTER 7

The Knowledge Tools

CABE's dissemination activities encompassed a wide range of types of action, from publication of practice guides, to the compilation of best practice case studies, to the more active provision of education and training. These activities are one step closer to intervention 'on the ground' than the gathering of evidence discussed in the previous chapter. This chapter itself is divided into three parts covering the why, how, and when of CABE's knowledge activities. The first discusses why CABE used practice guides, case studies, and education/ training, the second explores processes of garnering knowledge and of disseminating it by these means, and the third touches on when, within the design governance field of action, these tools should be used.

Why Engage in Knowledge Activities?

Practice Guides

As CABE evolved and its agenda and activities became more complex, so did its range of knowledge dissemination activities. At their most basic, they involved the preparation and publication of documents aimed at diffusing the knowledge CABE produced to an audience of practitioners, local authorities, end users, and other key players. These forms of practice guidance published by CABE came to have many purposes and to encompass a diversity of approaches, from focussed technical advice aimed at particular professional audiences, to broader messages meant for non-specialist groups, to guidance for CABE's own staff and others within the wider 'CABE family' on its own activities, including its various guides to design

review. Key users of CABE's guidance therefore included design and development professionals, public servants responsible for the procurement of buildings, and end users. Given this varied clientele, CABE's guidance was also carefully designed and articulated to speak to its likely audiences, and users came to see this as a 'CABE style'.

CABE's involvement with the production of guidance began in the early days of the organisation with its involvement in the production of *By Design: Urban Design in the Planning System: Towards Better Practice* (DETR & CABE 2000). This was the first of many pieces of guidance CABE was to publish. *By Design*, like much of the guidance CABE produced, was a joint effort in which the Department for Environment, Transport and the Regions (DETR) took the lead. The project predated CABE, and CABE was a relatively minor partner in its production, although it often got much of the credit for it, as before CABE arrived, government had been dithering and delaying over its publication (see Chapter 4). As the organisation evolved, the quantity of guidance produced increased significantly, especially in the period 2002–2004, as did the range of themes covered (7.1) and the formats used. Newsletters, for example, were introduced in this period as a regular means of communication, the first of which, *Shaping Future Homes* (with the Housing Corporation), aimed to disseminate key design messages to housing providers and ran for three issues before being merged with the *Building for Life Newsletter* that started in September 2004.

The stated goals of practice guidance reflected multiple purposes: filling gaps in knowledge, educating key players, offering specific technical information, disseminating CABE evidence, or, sometimes, simply setting out a CABE view on a particular policy proposition, for example the 2003 document *Ten Ways to Make Quality Count, Business Planning Zones*.[1] Disseminating knowledge in the context of government investment programmes was a major focus, and a large number of practice guides were produced that related directly to one or other capital spending programme such as schools or green spaces. Guidance in these cases was aimed at steering that particular injection of funding in a positive manner, enhancing their outcomes, and clarifying and developing policy. At a broader level, this form of dissemination also promoted CABE as an entity and its agenda, acting as one of the tools in CABE's larger advocacy and campaigning for better design.

The Effectiveness of Guidance

There are differing views on how effective CABE's practice guides were, but there is a general consensus that at least some of those documents became very influential because of their practical use in helping practitioners in their day-to-day work, for example CABE's 2007 guide *Design and access statements: How to write, read and use them*, on which the director of one regional Architecture and Built Environment Centre (ABEC) commented: "At the time, the document on how to prepare design and access statements was the most heavily used of all the CABE documents; it was incredible how many times that was downloaded" (7.2).

Similar views were expressed in relation to the work of CABE Space where the usefulness of guidance documents was linked to the immediate applicability of the knowledge they contained, as an urban design practitioner explained: "I think the one thing that was really valued were the publications, all the stuff that's still filling our shelves. That, in many ways, was valued more than design review or perhaps even enabling, because people just needed that stuff, they needed arguments, they needed guidance as to how to do things, and they needed that collective knowledge bringing together."

Practice guidance was also used as a campaigning tool, and notably by CABE supporters within

government to persuade those who might not have been so receptive to CABE's agenda. As a minister at the Department for Culture, Media and Sport (DCMS) put it, referring to the 2000 report *Better Public Buildings, A Proud Legacy for the Future*[2] "What I was seeking to do with that publication was to post a manifesto on behalf of the Labour Government about our commitment to good design, and to mobilise No. 10 to exercise leverage on the Treasury and DETR." He continued, "I drafted a forward which Tony Blair very helpfully was willing to sign, and there he proclaimed that it should be a hallmark of a New Labour Government that it was committed to good design.... It was as much a device for gaining traction in other parts of Whitehall, as it was proclaiming to a wider world that the government was committed to supporting good design."

Practice guides typically took the form of stylish, eye-catching publications that CABE proactively circulated and distributed. For some, however, the production of these glossy publications became an end in itself, and part of the expansionist outlook sometimes attributed to CABE. Indeed the sheer numbers of CABE publications (practice guides and research reports) became a frequent criticism of the organisation in its growing years, and by 2011, the CABE website included around 320 publications, or almost two and a half every month of the organisation's existence.

In its mature years, CABE began to show an increased sensitivity to the criticism that it was 'publishing' too much, and responded by turning its attention increasingly to web resources. Beyond its own comprehensive cabe.org.uk website,[3] CABE had started to experiment with freestanding websites for disseminating its work as early as 2002, when the buildingforlife.org.uk site was launched,[4] and in March 2009, CABE commenced its most ambitious web-based project, sustainablecities.org.uk.[5] This was the result of two years of research aimed to bridge the gap between sustainability and design by bringing together accessible and comprehensive guidance on sustainable design in one place (see Box 7.2). That year also saw the launch of the ambitious www.engagingplaces.org.uk site as a major new resource for teachers to champion the built environment as a learning

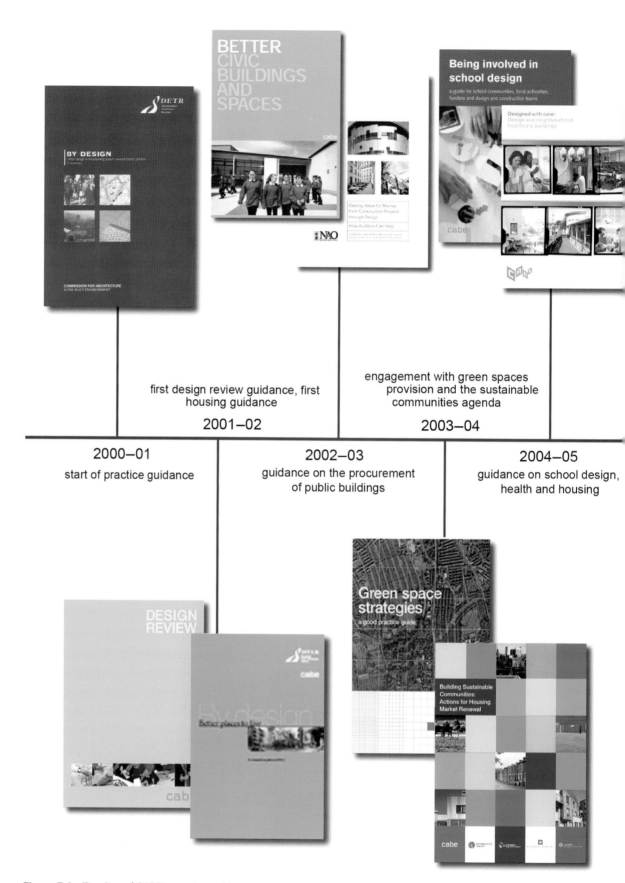

first design review guidance, first
housing guidance

2001–02

engagement with green spaces
provision and the sustainable
communities agenda

2003–04

2000–01

start of practice guidance

2002–03

guidance on the procurement
of public buildings

2004–05

guidance on school design,
health and housing

Figure 7.1   Timeline of CABE's practice guidance

masterplanning and the
new planning system
2005–06

focus on school building
2007–08

emphasis on web resources
2009–10

2006–07
guidance on design codes,
public space management

2008–09
Continuing focus on schools
and public space

2010–11
guidance on large scale
urban design

Figure 7.2   Jubilee Park, Canary Wharf Used in the popular 2007 guide *Design and access statements How to write, read and use them* as an example of how to design buildings and landscape together

Source: Matthew Carmona

Figure 7.3   Engaging Places was an initiative in partnership with English Heritage to provide educational resources for schools using the whole of the built environment to help with learning in a variety of subjects

Source: CABE

resource (7.3), whilst in 2010, CABE began to produce its freestanding guides, such as *Designing a Free School* and *School Refurbishment*, as web-based resources and no longer as downloadable PDFs. If CABE had continued, then these forms of resource and virtual practice guides would have formed a key part of the 'Open Source CABE' model which the organisation flirted with just before its resources were withdrawn (see Chapter 4).

Case Studies

Whilst being hands-off in a similar manner to practice guidance, CABE's case studies were also (to some degree) propositional in that they revealed actual examples of 'best practice' instead of just the principles that theoretically might lead to it. The compilation and dissemination of case studies represented a core activity of CABE across a wide range of its initiatives.

Case studies were used prominently in research projects, including in *Shifting Sands*, which looked at design in the regeneration of English seaside towns. In such cases, the goals went beyond simple presentation of the case study material and cases were analysed in depth to produce recommendations (CABE & English Heritage 2003). Numerous practice guides also contained case studies such as the 2009 guide *This Way to Better Residential Streets* (7.4) that vary in their depth

Figure 7.4   The streets in the early phases of Upton in Northampton were used in *This Way to Better Residential Streets* to illustrate both how to integrate green infrastructure into the street environment and how not to connect into surrounding areas

Source: Matthew Carmona

from brief illustrations to in-depth presentations of cases, typically to support particular proactive learning. Specific case studies were also chosen to illustrate best practice in the briefing papers produced for CABE enablers with the intention of disseminating key messages to the enablers and so that they in turn could use them in their training sessions and as influences to inform other projects.

Whilst case studies were used in all these ways, this chapter refers to their use as a knowledge tool in their own right through their collection into a library and their simple, passive presentation as exemplar cases. The idea of compiling case studies demonstrating best practice was conceived as early as January 2000, and a digital case study library quickly developed to provide ready examples of high-quality design across a range of development types. The initial target was to develop 100 case studies in architecture and urban design (CABE 2011g) using the digital images architects submitted for project enabling or design review, whilst the key target audience was perceived as "clients who aspire to good design but have little idea of what is possible or how to achieve quality". These ideas evolved over a two-year period into the possibility of constructing a more comprehensive library that included text introducing, describing, and evaluating the design merits and design process of each entry. The first case studies became available in October 2002 when 2,000 postcards were sent out to key recipients to publicise the new resource.[6]

The Building for Life digital library of housing schemes (in which CABE was a partner) was developed separately and eventually featured seventy case studies that were ultimately merged with CABE's larger library (7.5). The 'Building in Context' toolkit (jointly with English Heritage) also featured a series of unrelated heritage-focussed case studies.[7] The objectives of compiling these cases varied throughout the life of CABE, but broadly were intended to inspire others to emulate the exemplar cases (the initial goal of the case study library), disseminate best practice, and promote high-quality design. A later objective was to use the case studies as parameters against which to monitor and evaluate future interventions, although how this was to be done was never spelt out and may not have been feasible in any systematic way.

Figure 7.5   Newhall Harlow, one of the cases in the BfL library, praised for its enlightened landowner working within a strong masterplan and with an urban designer

Source: Matthew Carmona

Education/Training

As a response to the Urban Task Force (1999), which had underscored the lack of skills in urban design, one of CABE's core functions was education; indeed, this was later laid down in Part 8 of the Clean Neighbourhood and Environment Act 2005 that made CABE into a statutory body (see Chapter 4). CABE's education activities had three specific goals: increasing design skills; promoting urban design as part of students' education; and expanding the range of built environment professionals who understood design. Ultimately these activities focussed on creating the capacity to deliver better-designed buildings and spaces and are more hands-on than either practice guidance or case studies as they engage 'customers' directly in the learning. For CABE, this involved the preparation and provision of teaching materials and the organisation of courses, seminars, and summer schools, focussing on particular types of skills perceived as lacking among professionals in development, design, and management.

In the case of CABE Space, this emphasis on management and maintenance was particularly important, as one of its directors highlighted: "People working in parks were very de-skilled, very de-motivated and there was a huge problem with skills. . . . But it was not just about design, it was also about management and maintenance; the whole thing." CABE also sought to train a range of professionals about the role of urban design and in 2001 established the Urban Design Skills Working Group, ostensibly at the request of the Department for Transport, Local Government and the Regions (DTLR), although the idea had been CABE's who subsequently managed the initiative. The Urban Design Skills Working Group argued in favour of such "a multi-disciplinary approach to training in urban design" and for the need "to consider how local authorities might be encouraged to promote better urban design in their areas" (2001: 5). CABE subsequently focussed on establishing an appreciation of urban design across the range of built environment professions and especially within local government.

Another aim stemming from the work of the Urban Design Skills Working Group was to engage young people in the built environment. For example, CABE's initial programme of education work aimed at influencing the national curriculum,[8] and to work with schools at "unlocking the potential of the built environment as an educational resource" (CABE 2003e). This fed into the laudable long-term aspiration that the next generation would have a better awareness of design quality in the built environment and its impacts. However, given CABE's limited resources, the scale of this particular challenge, to reach the 24,000 schools in England, was quite considerable, some might even say overwhelming. This reality informed CABE's initial focus on trying to influence the national curriculum, first through campaigning for recognition of the built environment in the curriculum itself, but subsequently

(upon making little headway), via the provision of materials that could utilise the built environment as a resource through which to explore cross cutting themes already within the curriculum such as history, geography, art, and design and citizenship. In 2006/7, CABE produced one of its most successful educational outputs, *How Places Work, a Teachers Guide*, as part of the How Places Work initiative. This aimed to encourage school visits to inspiring architecture and achieved 12,000 pupil visits in the two years to 2008 (CABE 2009b). It demonstrated the impact that it was possible to achieve by providing teachers with high-quality, carefully thought through resources, and backing this up with local delivery, in this case through support provided by the Architecture Centre Network.

Across CABE and Beyond

Despite featuring as a concern of CABE, almost from the start, the position of education within the structure of CABE remained somewhat confused. Initially education activities were reported alongside research in the annual reports, but as a second tier—non-director—level responsibility, and it wasn't until 2003 that the Directorate of Learning and Development was established. Later, from 2006, the remit was split between a Directorate of Campaigns and Education and a separate Directorate of Knowledge and Skills, the second of these being wound up in January 2010. From 2002, CABE also created the 'CABE Education Foundation' (or CABE Education—Box 7.1) as a charitable arm to undertake its education work with young people.

Box 7.1   CABE Education Foundation

CABE Education Foundation was a separate entity created to deliver the organisation's educational programmes and especially its school's work. A CABE document from 2004 defined it as "A registered charity established to inspire young people to get more from their built environment. It produces curriculum resources and manages a national network for educators. The network is supported by a tri-annual magazine and a website which contains information on projects, resources and events organised by individuals across the country that

engage young people in the built environment" (CABE 2004i: 58).

Its creation as a separate legal entity from CABE reflected the importance given to education in the original remit of the organisation, but also a strategic decision to create a body that could access a different range of funding streams and, if successful, could float off and become a completely separate body dedicated to education in the built environment. The education foundation was led by CABE commissioners who became the trustees, but also worked with a good degree of independence from the main organisation.

Although its own *360°* magazine gave CABE Education a good profile amongst educationalists (7.6), it never fully succeeded as an entity in its own right and never raised the sorts of external funding (as opposed to funding from CABE) it hoped for. Those involved felt that this was because, in many instances, the organisation was competing for funding with CABE itself or with other charitable education providers who were perceived as better alternatives as they were not

Figure 7.6 *360°* magazine, addressing teachers and education professionals, was the most successful of CABE's newsletters, lasting from 2003 to 2010 with twenty-six quarterly issues

connected to a public body already in receipt of government funding.

Although to a large extent operationally independent, CABE Education also worked with the different CABE directorates in a collaborative way, for example working with CABE's research unit as part of the Building Futures work on school design. In this case the purpose was to provide examples of new school designs, and through an interactive guide dealing with alterations to an existing school, to elicit pupils' opinions about their own environment. This kind of work required some effort from CABE Education to persuade other parts of CABE to set time aside to convert experience and knowledge into the development of educational resources for children and young people.

Important also was the relationship between CABE Education and the Architecture and Built Environment Centres (ABECs) across the country, and this became the main route to giving the foundation the national profile and reach it needed. However, this relationship was complex, not least because many ABECs were already doing education work and saw CABE Education as muscling in on their turf. Moreover, as a partner, it could offer only a small amount of regular funding, and was a less attractive source of income than CABE itself. As a CABE director involved in education explained, "We tried to work with them [the ABECs] collaboratively, and this was harder than anticipated. . . . There was a defensiveness on their side and a naivety on my part for not understanding their funding situation. They saw CABE Education as competition and were suspicious of any attempt at oversight."

Towards the end of CABE's existence, CABE Education functions were absorbed into CABE proper and with the incorporation of CABE into the Design Council some functions transferred to Open-City, a charity championing excellence in design quality in the built environment.

Reflecting this confusion, a substantial part of the education agenda was actually delivered through CABE's other programmes, for example in relation to Building for Life (BfL), training for enablers, or using tools such as Spaceshaper (the tool CABE developed

to assess built environment quality—see Chapter 9), and generally this work was highly regarded. As one of CABE's regional representatives described the approach: "Building for Life and the 'accredited assessors' programme worked incredibly well because

CABE was committed to supporting local authorities to a point where at least one assessor existed in each local authority. Consequently they trained people like me to help train other people, . . . locally based, sensitive and a first port of call to come to if you were struggling with stuff."

The main generic design quality training programme run by CABE was its urban design summer school. The summer school, alongside CABE's more focussed skills delivery programmes, reinforced a perception of CABE as a design training and education hub, and this soon led to requests for training from other potential clients. In fact most of CABE's post-professional training remained quite specific, and CABE never engaged in or significantly tried to influence the professional education field. Even its summer schools were designed and delivered by external providers, and these, typically university providers, varied from year to year. There was also a strong regional dimension to delivering CABE's training programmes, and the regional Architecture and Built Environment Centres (ABECs) were instrumental here (see Chapter 8), although training in the regions was occasionally contracted out to other organisations outside the immediate 'CABE family', such as to the Civic Trust.

Like its other endeavours, CABE's education and skills initiatives were not without their critics, and the most substantial criticism related to what some saw as a timidity in CABE's education programme. Certainly education played a far less substantial role in the organisation's profile than some of its other activities. As a director of an ABEC that contributed substantially to CABE's education provision commented:

The one thing that CABE could have done was improve skills, and given the resources that they had at one time, they could have provided some substantial programmes. In terms of impact, you could argue that actually improving skills would have a greater impact than critiquing x number of developments and giving feedback on them. Maybe there are arguments that they didn't want to step on the toes of the education institutions, or the professional bodies, but I think there was a particular set of skills, largely around urban design and placemaking, which weren't particularly being covered elsewhere . . . and so I think it was a missed opportunity.

By 2008, CABE had held nearly 3,800 training sessions, and had around 1,500 people in its education network (CABE 2008a). The following year, CABE recorded a running total of 6,000 training sessions, including the urban design summer school, a CABE Space leaders programme, and strategic skills development for those in a position to embed good design within the planning system (CABE 2009b). The annual report for 2007/8 indicates that CABE was holding thirty-five training workshops a year, and from 2008a to 2010 there were forty-seven regional 'taster' sessions for Spaceshaper facilitator training. By the end of 2010, CABE records indicate that it had trained 503 local authority professionals and accredited 334 assessors in 213 local authorities to carry out formal BfL assessments, and was "on track to achieve accredited assessors in 70% of local authorities" (CABE 2011e). This was a part of CABE's activities that continued to scale up its ambition until almost the end.

How Were Knowledge Activities Delivered?

Practice Guides

Guidance publications were often produced with partner organisations, including government departments, notably DETR/ODPM/DCLG, the Treasury, Department for Education and Skills, and the Office for Government Commerce; other government bodies, such as the National Audit Office, Audit Commission, Local Government Association, English Heritage, Arts Council for England, Corporation of London, Architecture & Design Scotland, Natural England, Sustainable Development Commission, Asset Transfer Unit, and the Housing Corporation; and professional bodies and amenity societies, such as the Society of Chief Architects in Local Authorities, Society of Local Authority Chief Executives, Planning Officers' Society, Home Builders Federation, and the Civic Trust. Typically these guides were produced on the basis of underpinning research and were written by external consultants who had themselves conducted the research for CABE.

Resources for the production of guides were spread across CABE with every front line directorate publishing guidance of some type at some time. Because of this, only very large programmes such as sustainablecities.org.uk (Box 7.2) were likely to be identifiable as budget lines in resource terms. Consequently an assessment of the costs associated with this work is almost impossible to make.

Box 7.2   Sustainable Cities/Places Programme

The Sustainable Cities/Places Programme was created in the context of increasing government focus on climate change that led to the Climate Change Act 2008 and the Energy and Climate Change White Paper of July 2009. As part of this national drive to sustainability, in 2007 DCLG asked CABE to develop a programme addressing the issues from a design perspective. The programme was to be funded through CABE's core funding grant, but sponsored by the private sector, including property and energy companies: Crest Nicholson, Hammerson Places for People, Eon, Dialight, and Xeropex. The work was overseen by a CABE commissioner supported by an external advisory group, and was developed in close cooperation with the local authorities of the English core cities.[9] Whilst in development the project was located in CABE's research unit, but when fully operational was moved to CABE Space.

The programme contained two main elements. The first was a learning programme launched in 2007 and linked to a Climate Change Festival. This was developed by CABE and the University of Westminster and involved residential courses in four cities and 'sustainable design task groups' with events that engaged 127 participants of sixty-six local authorities. The second was the sustainablecities.org.uk website with guidance and best practice cases that was launched in 2009. The purpose of the website was to provide easy and accessible updates on policy, publications, consultations, and best practice examples. It was therefore conceived as the CABE 'sustainability resource', but, as with a good proportion of CABE's work, was not developed internally but was instead outsourced to professional web designers with the content commissioned and managed by Urban Practitioners, a private consultancy.

Many practitioners and researchers contributed to the contents of the site, which was peer reviewed to ensure its robustness. The cases studies it drew on were not limited to the United Kingdom, but instead came from around the world with the material grouped by themes: energy, waste, water, transport, geographical information, public spaces; and by spatial scale: building, neighbourhood, region (7.7). How this was configured changed during the project's development as the designers strived to make the resource more easily accessible and more relevant to users. As one of those involved in creating the site commented: "[In the beginning,] It was quite confusing—there was a lot of stuff. Sustainability is a massive subject but because the content developed for two years before we launched it, the web technology also changed. . . . Instead of having a traditional website with sub categories and subpages, we moved to a flat structure, where everything was tagged with the spatial scale and the various themes."

The general idea of the website as a resource was to cut through the complexity of climate change issues by separating a large problem into its constituent parts and offering advice and examples of solutions to local authorities trying to grapple with it. As a CABE source explained: "Everything may have looked so big before that they didn't

Figure 7.7 Portland, Oregon, one of the international cases in the Sustainable Places database, chosen as a good example of a city that encourages public transport, walking, and cycling through its high-quality public realm

Source: Matthew Carmona

know where to start, but the site showed how things join up. Take for example a big construction project with building materials transported by canal. That has an economic benefit, and it also takes lorries off the road, using less fossil fuels and improving air quality. One decision has many different outcomes. So the site opened minds."

Accordingly, the material was written to match the expectations of a target audience of mostly local authority leaders, senior staff, council members, and executives, whilst an educational dimension was directed towards securing a demand for the website and ensuring that that target audience would use it. Following its launch, the website and its collection of case studies was run separately from the main CABE website, although in 2010 it was merged into the main site under the heading 'Sustainable Places'. In its brief existence as a free-standing resource it seems to have been successful, attracting more than 120,000 hits by December 2010.

Alongside the formal guidance, CABE soon developed a habit of commissioning 'think pieces' and 'briefing papers' on key topics, often to mop up year-end funding, but also to kick off new lines of enquiry and/ or guidance. CABE Space, for example, commissioned twelve briefing papers between 2005 and 2010 on subjects as diverse as allotments and sexuality and public space. Sometimes these were grouped together and published, such as the essays collected together in *What Are We Scared of? The Value of Risk in Designing Public Space*, or were used to create a separate guide such as *Making Design Policies Work* (CABE 2005e), which was largely based on a paper commissioned from Matthew Carmona. These were produced quickly and cheaply with budgets of less than £2,000.[10]

During its wind-down, CABE produced a series of handover notes on all aspects of its work, and *Handover Note 47* deals with best practice guidance in the green space sector. It observes that producing a printed guide within the twelve-month funding cycle CABE was subject to for many of its projects was consistently challenging and in particular that the quality of researchers and writers was often disappointing, reflecting a scarcity of skills and a poorly developed market for analytical skills and services in design (CABE 2011h). To overcome the issue, CABE commissioned a diversity of research contractors and writers, across academic, public, and private sectors to undertake these projects. Project steering groups with representatives of key stakeholder organisations were also typically used to help shape project briefs and to ensure the desired level of quality in the product. The practice also encouraged organisations around the table to assume some level of ownership of the projects, and this in turn helped in disseminating the resulting guide.

CABE put a huge effort into disseminating its key messages, and every publication was carefully designed in the CABE style already referred to and often rewritten to ensure maximum accessibility to identified audiences. Most were published in a traditional form, sometimes by external publishers but more often by CABE itself to be given away free with simultaneous release as an electronic file on CABE's website.

Driven in large part by this content and the case studies, in 2004/05 the website was receiving around 728,000 visits a year, and by 2007/08, this had increased to 2 million visits and 384,000 downloads (CABE 2005c; CABE 2008a). By 2009/10, the website featured details of more than 200 design reviews being read by 116,000 visitors per year, whilst the most popular publications in 2009/10 were those dealing with school design, receiving 10,706 unique page views (CABE 2010a). In the same year www.engagingplaces.org.uk received 86,000 visits and sustainablecities.org.uk received 59,750 unique visits. By its demise, CABE's website had been built into a huge and unrivalled on-line resource dealing with all aspects of design and the built environment. Arguably, the reach and impact of CABE's on-line presence was much wider than anything else it did, although it relied completely on all of CABE's other work to populate its content and give it depth and credibility. As CABE was wound down, two key publications were translated into new web resources and launched in early 2011 for incorporation into the CABE archive: cabe.org.uk/buildings an on-line version of *Creating Excellent Buildings, a Guide for*

Clients;[11] and cabe.org.uk/masterplans, an on-line version of *Creating Successful Masterplans*.[12]

Over the years, CABE clearly devoted huge resources to the production of practice guidance, and, where appropriate, to updating it (7.8), and, in its

Figure 7.8   Key practice guides were kept up to date; the guidance for design review was (i) issued in 2002 and (ii) updated and reissued in 2006

ten-year review, concluded: "As the policy context has shifted in favour of design, so CABE has produced state-of-the-art guidance on how to create great places. . . . This has changed the terms of the debate. There is now a canon of practical guidance" (CABE 2009a: 18). Looking at the legacy of guidance, most still available for use via the CABE archive, this is a statement to which it is difficult to demur.

Case Studies

The case studies were an important part of this on-line success, and like visits to the website, the production of case studies quickly became part of the performance measurement regime as established for CABE by DCMS (see Chapter 4). In the 2005/06 end of year report, for example, CABE was charged to increase the number of digital library case studies championing high-quality architecture and urban design and disseminating best practice by 230 cases (in fact, it achieved 233) (CABE 2006b). In 2007/08, it was charged to increase the visits to the case study section of the website to 21,000 per week (and achieved 31,000) (CABE 2008a: 7), suggesting that more than three quarters of visits targeted that section of the site (amongst others).

Ultimately the digital library grew into a unique resource of 398 case studies, and at the time of CABE's demise, the range of case studies was listed as follows:[13]

- housing (116)
- public space (102)
- culture and leisure (66)
- regeneration (57)
- commercial buildings (52)
- educational buildings (44)
- neighbourhoods (41)
- sustainable development (41)
- parks and green spaces (36)
- historic environment (32)
- health buildings (29)
- planning (10)
- transport and infrastructure (9)
- inclusive design (8).

Geographically, thirty case studies were listed as outside of England and the remainder were split across the

Figure 7.9 A programme of rebuilding streets, upgrading public spaces, and refurbishing historic buildings features in the case study library as having helped to transform the derelict Grainger Town in Newcastle upon Tyne into a vibrant mixed-use quarter

Source: Matthew Carmona

English regions (7.9), although with a skew to London and the south-east. Some categories were focussed more on processes (e.g. sustainable development, regeneration, planning) and others more on outcomes (e.g. housing, public space, inclusive design) and over time, priorities varied depending on (and in order to support) other work programmes. For example, in 2003/04 the emphasis was on primary health care projects; in 2009, a sustainability review was undertaken to improve the case studies' focus on sustainability; in 2008/09, primary schools were added; and one of the last categories to be added, in 2009/10, was inclusive design.

Each case study has a standard format with sections covering a description of the case, the design process, an evaluation of the case, further information, and identification of the design team. Choosing case studies involved a selection of best practice from across the country, and often included projects CABE had been involved in, for example enabling their realisation. Like their practice guides, CABE's case studies were also often conceived and developed with partner organisations. These included a series of case studies looking at the impact of the design quality indicator developed with the Construction Industry Council (CIC) and a series of case studies developed with Sheffield University looking at community-led design projects.

As the library grew, the content was reviewed and amended to reflect changes in criteria, developments on the ground, and new priorities. In a few cases projects were removed from the database because featured elements proved problematic and could no longer be justified as best practice.

The development of clear internal documentation helped to streamline the case study process, including templates and writing guides for the preparation of entries, and calls were frequently put out to likely organisations to rapidly compile case studies in order to mop up any year-end unspent budget. Evaluations of the case study library were conducted in 2003, 2005, and 2009 which confirmed the on-going popularity of the resource with the strength of the photography regularly highlighted as a key asset by site users (CABE 2011g).

CABE's own website was the most effective instrument in the dissemination of this work, and a quote from a prominent urban design practitioner gives an indication of its value and the range of case study material that could be assessed through it: "If we wanted a precedent about something, if we wanted to find out about what was going on in schools in Europe, or what was the best example of a new park—CABE was the first place to go to. Everybody was out there looking for case studies, going on trips and looking. People were even doing it as a hobby, travelling at weekends, and finding, for example, the best housing development in Holland. So the website was pretty powerful."

Education/Training

The most direct knowledge tool that CABE deployed were its professional training workshops where the focus was on particular aspects of urban design and different types of associated work, with seminars, workshops, and similar events. These included CABE's urban design summer schools from 2004 onwards but also comprised other types of professional training, particularly in the last years of CABE.

Training Professionals

Each year the summer schools were held in a different location and lasted three to five days, attracting between 71 and 136 delegates.[14] These events involved hands-on pedagogic techniques that included design charrettes, site visits, case investigations, and reflective breakout sessions, often with 'live' schemes, such as those investigated around Bristol's city centre in 2009. The cost of running summer schools was covered to some extent by delegate fees and sponsorship and delegates paid between £750 and £1,095 to attend, with the price rising over time. CABE provided in-kind support, produced materials, and co-ordinated and facilitated. CABE also contributed to core delivery costs in order to create space in the budget for the appointed delivery partner to innovate in responding to the brief, although this later changed.

The first three summer schools were co-produced with the University of Westminster and CABE underwrote the running costs over and above the amount raised by delegate fees. CABE records state that the partnership with the university was highly productive and that the model was successful as it tested the concept and grew the summer school to more than 100 delegates. However, following this initial period, CABE was obliged to re-tender the work to comply with government 'best value guidelines', and the new partners were a consortium led by Birmingham City University, who delivered the following three summer schools under similar terms. In the last year, the summer schools were outsourced to a consortium led by MADE (the ABEC for the West Midlands) that included Birmingham City University. The summer school was still branded 'CABE', but did not have core subsidy from the organisation and relied on a variety of local partners. These included private businesses and government bodies, who could draw on their local knowledge to arrange site visits and secure sponsors to cover the costs of the event.

Beyond the summer schools, CABE provided continuing professional development (CPD) on many topics. These ranged from a national programme of events on inclusion and 'inclusive placemaking', to design workshops across England for planners run jointly with the Town & Country Planning Association (TCPA), to a series of 'business breakfasts' with CEOs of major construction firms CABE hosted in London. CABE also developed a programme of training for the design champions within government departments and other public bodies. There were design champions workshops run with Planning Aid, and two-day events

for the planning inspectorate's design champions held in 2009/10 together with the University of the West of England, which secured CABE a 'Lifelong Learning award' from the Royal Town Planning Institute (RTPI). These were held partly in response to the developing national policy on housing design (in Planning Policy Statement 3) and CABE's larger arguments around the need to build housing developments of better quality, also as an attempt to encourage the Planning Inspectorate to take account of these issues in public inquiries into the emerging Local Development Frameworks (LDFs)[15] of the time.

Other forms of training focussed on the use of CABE's own 'products'. Some of this focussed on instructions for the application of specific practice guides and a significant amount on particular CABE tools. This was often targeted at particular professionals, for instance training on how the government's *Manual for Streets* (DoT et al. 2007) applied to rural settlements or how to use Building for Life criteria as an assessment tool. *Building in Context* workshops were held from 2007–2010 and focussed on the toolkits CABE had produced with English Heritage. There was also training for Spaceshaper facilitators with an emphasis on using the tool to increase youth involvement in design assessment, that attracted 509 delegates to sessions in seventeen locations. Other events were linked to particular campaigns, as was the case in 2007/08, when a sustainable cities learning programme was offered that included insights into sustainable master planning.

Creating and Supplying Educational Materials

An important part of CABE Education's work was the production of education resources for school pupils on built environment issues, resources that emphasised learning about local places, placemaking, citizenship, design, and construction. Most notable amongst these were the 'safari guides'. *Getting out There*, for instance, was aimed at students aged eleven to sixteen and was described as an art and design local safari guide intended to help students learn differently, and to open children's eyes. It included five suggested local safaris covering place, routes, space, building, and public art, each with a photocopyable local resource sheet and detailed guidance for teachers about how to link the learning back to different dimensions of the national curriculum (7.10). *Neighbourhood Journeys* targeted children aged between seven and eleven years old, and introduced the idea of place as part of people's identity, linking it to literacy, dance, numeracy, and geography. The document offered suggestions for creative activities in those areas using local streets as a resource. Similarly, *Our Street* set out exercises whereby children could analyse a street in their area and judge its quality. *A Sense of Place* and *Making Better Places* both included a CD-ROM, which was advanced technology at the time.

R   Changing the streetscape: design exercise

Choose a photograph of a streetscene you have encountered on your fieldwork. A4 or A3 are good sizes to work on this.

Make a tracing of it to record all the key features.

Photo

Analytical drawing

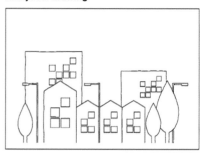

Make two further copies of the resulting analytical drawing.

On the first copy, add or change three elements to improve townscape quality.

On the second copy, add or change three elements to destroy townscape quality.

Ideas for improving townscape quality

Ways to destroy townscape quality

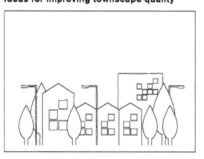
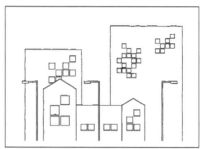

You might wish to add or remove elements, change their scale, colour or positioning, alter visual or spatial relationships.

Figure 7.10   Resource Sheet 5 from *Getting Out There, Art and Design Local Safari Guide*
Source: CABE 2006b

Briefs were prepared for these resources which were then put out to tender through a network of consultants and specialists that CABE Education identified through publicity, seminars, and events organised by the wider CABE 'family'. However, as this area of work was rather specialised, it was not always easy to find suitable specialists to produce the work, and considerable steering from CABE Education was often required to deliver the right products.

Some of these materials were aimed solely at teachers, rather than targeting areas of the curriculum. This reflected the idea that establishing protocols and resources which encouraged teachers to use the built environment in their lessons was, if anything, more important than providing a raft of instructional materials for students to absorb. The process of developing resources themselves was also seen as an educational opportunity, with, for example, *Neighbourhood Journeys* produced together with Creative Partnerships Bristol: teachers, children, and interested parties from two local schools and two local communities in Bristol (CABE Education 2004). Other resources were developed with trainee teachers, engaging them in the development of content and involving them in piloting learning and teaching techniques.

Materials were widely distributed free of charge, including a mass mailing of *Our Street: Learning to See* in 2001 as an early guide for teachers on how to use the built environment in their teaching. Recipients of this were regularly updated, up until the final version of *Our Street*, published in 2007.

Educating Leaders

The Urban Design Skills Working Group was quickly disbanded after reporting in 2001, and instead from 2002 onwards a Housing Design Task Group was formed and this supported a learning network including seminars, workshops, and other educational sessions across the country. Whilst the Housing Design Task Group was more focussed and easier to control than the earlier group (being officially a CABE initiative), this type of education was orchestrated rather than led by CABE. Events were organised thematically around issues such as community involvement, place making, sustainability, and partnership working, and CABE records indicate that there were around fifty

delegates mostly from local authorities at each event who would: "share best practice and develop a strong network of inspired people who can champion design within their organisations" (CABE 2011i).

The network had a strong focus on the government's agenda and in its early years concentrated on the housing market renewal[16] and housing growth areas.[17] These events brought key actors together to learn about quality design, with CABE organising the events. There were three housing quality workshops between 2003 and 2005, and CABE's annual report of 2004/05 argued that the initiative was helping to develop best practice and link together national agencies and the local pathfinders[18] (CABE 2005c). Later international learning events were added, including a special event in the Netherlands in 2007/08 for Housing Design Task Group delegates, and in the same year forty delegates were taken on a two-day study tour to Emscher Landschaftspark in Germany. In its justification of the Emscher tour, CABE argued that it was "not only an opportunity to learn from the Ruhr but also to learn from each other, bringing together experience from both housing growth and housing market renewal" (CABE 2007f).

CABE also offered other types of educational events for leaders. In 2001/02, for example, there were training sessions for public sector construction clients, with twelve regional 'Making Places' events which, according to the annual report for the year, "were a great success, attracting almost 2,000 local decision-makers" (CABE 2002c). From 2006, an annual CABE Space Leaders programme was introduced, designed, and run by a consultancy and supported by Natural England and the HCA Academy (the skills arm of the Homes and Communities Agency; see Chapter 4), with endorsements on the CABE archive website suggesting that these hands-on events helped to inspire participants and gave them confidence to consider quality.[19] Later CABE even developed what it characterised as "a new executive coaching programme" (CABE 2008a), including a Strategic Urban Design masterclass in Bristol in 2008. The impact of all these activities and many more is hard to quantify, but clearly acted as a constant drip reinforcing the CABE message and spreading the word about design across a range of professional groupings, many of whom may otherwise have given scant regard to such concerns.

When Should Knowledge Tools be Used?

This chapter has explored tools with a focus on disseminating the knowledge CABE acquired, knowledge gathered through the sorts of evidence examined in the previous chapter and obtained via CABE's more proactive work such as enabling and design review. They comprise practice guides aiming at a variety of audiences, but especially professionals looking for sources of advice; databases of best practice case studies to serve as sources of reference and benchmarks; and education through summer schools for professionals, specialist and leadership training, and preparation of school materials for children and young people. In this respect, they range from detached and passive tools (e.g. the case studies) to more hands-on and active tools involving the direct engagement of participants (e.g. training), although in an educational rather than practice capacity (7.11).

CABE was engaged in the production of guidance and in education initiatives throughout its history, and in case studies from very early on. Throughout this period, the strategic priorities of CABE varied, and this was reflected in its knowledge activities, with key inputs from CABE itself, but also from government bodies and partners. In the absence of formal intervention and/or delivery powers, it was logical to seek to influence those who did have such powers, and the most straightforward way to attempt to do this was through generating and disseminating knowledge that would shape their practices.

Although it is difficult to produce a final verdict on the effectiveness of CABE's knowledge tools, the practice guides in particular were clearly responsible for a large part of CABE's visibility, and many of the guides (alongside the case studies) were and still are widely consulted by practitioners five years after CABE's demise. They represent an important part of CABE's legacy. Education, as a tool, was far less visible, although the numbers of local authority officers who attended CABE training events helped to build a critical mass of design-aware practitioners, particularly within the public sector. This legacy may be more transient however, as faced with the day-to-day realities and pressures of practice, subtle lessons about design quality and its importance will be easily lost. The impact in schools and on the next generation is perhaps most difficult to gauge, as whilst CABE's interventions may have inspired a future generation (it is too early to tell), CABE's efforts may have represented something of a needle in the haystack given the sheer numbers of schools and schoolchildren it needed to reach. Without continually investing in, promoting, and renewing these resources, their on-going impact is likely to be slight.

Placing the knowledge tools in the design governance field of action from Chapter 1 (7.12) shows that, depending on their focus, practice guides have the potential to inform practice across much of the design governance remit, from helping to establish a robust decision-making environment in the first place to directly informing the project design and delivery process. Case studies, by contrast, are likely to have a more limited utility, and are typically used to inform the design process itself—offering inspiration—although

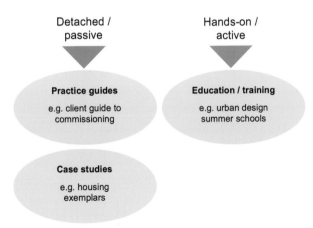

Figure 7.11 Typology of knowledge

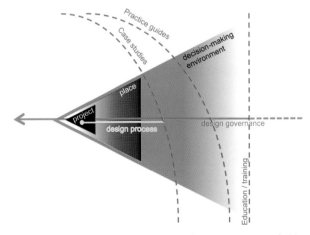

Figure 7.12 Knowledge tools in the design governance field of action

they might also impact aspirations for the decision-making environment, for example as a feed into the preparation of policies and guidance. Education and training is likely to have only a gradual impact on the quality of places, projects, or processes (particularly if directed at children) and therefore will be largely focussed on the pre-development phase and on raising skills and capacity for design decision-making over the long term.

Notes

1. This document reacted to a proposal in the 2001 Planning Green Paper to reinvigorate a policy of the previous Conservative administration that in 1987 had introduced Simplified Planning Zones (SPZs). Within these a streamlined form of planning permission was all that was required. The new proposal for Business Planning Zones (BPZs) was similar and CABE was concerned that development within such zones would be of poor quality. Whilst the government quickly dropped the idea, CABE wasted no time setting out ten principles to guarantee design quality if and when BPZs were used (CABE 2003d).
2. *Better Public Buildings* was prepared by CABE, with the drafting done by one of CABE's commissioners, Paul Finch, drawing on discussions at the Better Public Buildings Group, a cross-governmental group chaired by Lord Falconer with representation from eight departments of state and CABE. It was published as an HM Government (2000) document.
3. Partly available via the government online archives at http://webarchive.nationalarchives.gov.uk/20110118095356/; www.cabe.org.uk/
4. See: http://webarchive.nationalarchives.gov.uk/20110118095356/http:/www.cabe.org.uk/building-for-life
5. See: http://webarchive.nationalarchives.gov.uk/20110118095356/http:/www.cabe.org.uk/sustainable-places
6. In 2006, 5,000 bookmarks were produced to publicise the launch of the case study library on CABE's new website.
7. In 2015, there were thirty-seven of these: www.building-in-context.org/casestudies.html
8. The nationally defined common curriculum taught in state schools across England.
9. The major cities outside of London—Birmingham, Bristol, Leeds, Liverpool, Manchester, Newcastle, Nottingham, and Sheffield.
10. Below £2,000, projects did not need to be competitively tendered.
11. See: http://webarchive.nationalarchives.gov.uk/20110118095356/http:/www.cabe.org.uk/publications/creating-excellent-buildings
12. See: http://webarchive.nationalarchives.gov.uk/20110118095356/http://www.cabe.org.uk/resources/masterplans
13. http://webarchive.nationalarchives.gov.uk/20110107165544/http://www.buildingforlife.org/case-studies
14. 2004 Ashford (71 delegates), 2005 East Lancashire (100 delegates), 2006 Plymouth (103 delegates), 2007 Birmingham (123 delegates), 2008 Newcastle (136 delegates), 2009 Bristol (131 delegates), and 2010 Birmingham (111 delegates): http://webarchive.nationalarchives.gov.uk/20110118095356/http://www.cabe.org.uk/urban-design-summer-school/history
15. LDFs were Development Plans produced by local authorities, now known as Local Plans..
16. In 2002 there were nine of these: Birmingham/Sandwell, East Lancashire, Hull and East Riding, Manchester/Salford, Merseyside, Newcastle/Gateshead, North Staffordshire, Oldham/Rochdale, and South Yorkshire. A further three were added in 2005: West Yorkshire, West Cumbria, and Tees Valley.
17. The Thames Gateway, Luton, Ashford and Cambridge
18. The partnerships in the Housing Market Renewal areas.
19. http://webarchive.nationalarchives.gov.uk/20110118095356/http:/www.cabe.org.uk/public-space/leaders/2007

CHAPTER 8

The Promotion Tools

CABE's remit was to promote good design, and therefore campaigning-type activities played a large role in the history of the organisation. This includes the use of awards and campaigns to spread the notion of good design among the public, government, and industry and to advocate within government to influence legislation and policy. In many cases, partnership instruments were part and parcel of the promotion of good design as they allowed CABE to spread the reach of its activities either spatially or across government and industry. This chapter is divided into three parts covering the why, how, and when of CABE's knowledge activities. The first part discusses the purposes of those activities, the second looks at how they were delivered, and a final brief discussion places them within the design governance field of action.

Why Engage in Promotion Activities?

Awards

The headline goal of design awards is always to reward good practice, for example the Prime Minister's Better Public Building Award was conceived "to reward excellence in both design and procurement across the public sector" (CABE 2011c). However, awards have a second, more important goal, to raise the profile of the sectors and/or organisations that establish them and to stimulate better practices within the sectors they celebrate. For CABE, they were part of a larger drive to promote good design and its benefits, not least because of their power to attract media attention and to raise the profile of the organisation's work. It was also hoped

that awards would encourage others to follow the example set by the award winners.

CABE's involvement in awards can be separated into two categories. The first includes those that were part of long-running initiatives in which CABE came to occupy a key position, whether or not CABE actually originated them. The second encompasses occasional awards linked to specific events or short-lived initiatives to which CABE was asked to give support as the government's champion for good design.

Long-Running Awards

The first category is represented by the Prime Minister's Better Public Building Award, which ran throughout CABE's life (and beyond), at a time of massive investment in public sector building. The award applied to any public building of any size anywhere in the country and was established with the aspiration that it would motivate ministers and departments across government to work towards achieving high-quality design (8.1). A range of knock-on benefits were also perceived as helping to make public projects easier and more efficient to deliver, something that was reflected in the wide-ranging criteria covered by the award: high-quality design; efficient procurement; economic and social value; good teamwork between client, designer, and contractor; sound financial management; whole-life value for money; client satisfaction; and sustainability (HM Government 2000; CABE 2006h). From the start, it was also intended to direct attention to the quality of everyday public buildings in Britain, with the Department for Culture, Media and Sport (DCMS) announcing that: "Over the last few years Britain has

Figure 8.1 In 2003, two very different Manchester schemes were shortlisted for the Prime Minister's Better Building Award (i) The Imperial War Museum of the North and (ii) Piccadilly Gardens

Source: Matthew Carmona

benefited from a host of new landmark buildings, many of them funded through the lottery. Now we need to apply the same energy and imagination to improving the tens of thousands of everyday public buildings, which play such a vital role in our lives" (HM Government 2000).

Another award in this category was the Building for Life Award, part of the larger Building for Life (BfL) initiative. These awards aimed at recognising the private housebuilders and housing associations that had demonstrated a commitment to high design standards, good place-making, and sustainable development (CABE 2004c). BfL Awards were based on the same criteria as the BfL certification scheme (see Chapter 9), but gave both the winning schemes and the larger BfL programme much greater recognition.

The only award scheme solely owned and managed by CABE was its Festive Fives awards which for seven years (2001–2007) in the run-up to Christmas aimed to recognise five public sector organisations, five private companies, and five individuals whose forward thinking and motivation was deemed to have led to better buildings and public spaces. In some years these were themed, for example in 2006 CABE's website announced: "This year the awards focus on school design and inclusive design—two of CABE's core priorities and where the country faces some of its biggest challenges. The awards acknowledge those who understand the importance of good design for effective teaching and learning, and also major strides to create buildings and places that can be used and enjoyed by everyone."[1] Over the years the awards recognised influential civil servants, large developers such as Barratt Homes, local authorities such as Essex County Council, housing associations, architects, commissioning organisations, local politicians, and many more, and were always well covered in the professional and national press as the good news seasonal stories they were intended to be.

Occasional or Short-Run Awards

The second category (occasional awards) included both one-off schemes and awards that were intended to run for longer but for various reasons were cut short. In the field of inclusive design, for example, CABE sponsored both the CABE/RIBA Inclusive Design Award of 2007 (8.2), and the Royal College of Art (RCA) Design for Our Future Selves Award as part of the Inclusive Design Programme the RCA organised in 2007 and 2008. This engagement with inclusive design was part of the larger interest in the subject Richard Simmons pushed after his arrival as chief executive, which helped to expand the definition of inclusive design from its focus on physical access, towards a much broader range of social and economic barriers in the built environment.

The Parkforce awards run by the Local Government Association (LGA) with CABE's support also come into this category and ran in 2005 and 2006 to reward the best park workers and parks teams in local authorities. The awards focussed on a key priority of CABE Space at the time, raising skills in the parks sector, and

Figure 8.2 Portland College, Mansfield won the 2007 RIBA/ CABE Inclusive Design Award

Source: Charlotte Wood

also reinforced its campaign (launched in 2005) that pressed the case for on-site staff in parks. In a similar vein, in 2008 and 2009, CABE sponsored the APSE horticultural apprentice of the year award, rewarding excellence in new green space learners and their managers and providing role models to promote apprenticeships. In general these sorts of awards reflected particular priorities of CABE which came and went, and unlike the more generic long-run awards, the organisation's involvement in these more focussed accolades, for example as sponsor, helped to reinforce key messages at particular points in time.

Campaigns

Campaigning for design quality was a goal for CABE from its creation, the main objective of which was to raise awareness about the subject amongst those involved in commissioning and delivering buildings. A considerable part of this campaigning activity focussed on ensuring that public sector bodies, private developers, and regulatory authorities incorporated design quality more prominently into their processes and decisions. A secondary, although increasingly important part was directed at the everyday users of buildings and spaces, about whom it was believed the demand for higher standards in the built environment needed ultimately to come.

Amongst the wide array of campaigns and events that CABE promoted during its existence, some were

more formalised, involved a number of other participants, lasted for some years, and were associated with research and dissemination programmes. Building for Life, Building Futures, and Better Public Buildings might each be included in this category, as can the campaigns for better-designed hospitals and schools. Others were short-lived and related to the promotion of CABE and the design agenda it encapsulated among the general public and target audiences. This work involved CABE appearing at a huge diversity of events on a multitude of topics and countless speeches the CABE leadership made to professional audiences and relevant decision-makers. CABE's large output of publications—including its research findings and best practice cases—were also integral to its campaigning effort, and these were always produced to a very high graphic and written quality in order to extend their readership and impact.

In terms of their subject matter, campaigns and events could be classified into one of three types:

- Generic campaign activities and events carried out by CABE on its own or in partnership with other interested organisations, aimed at improving the quality of design or raising awareness in general, without aiming at particular types of buildings, spaces, or issues.
- Specific campaigns aimed at improving the design quality of particular types of buildings (especially in the public sector) or urban spaces. These were more structured and usually ran in partnership with other public bodies and organisations.
- Campaigns related to government policy programmes in a variety of policy areas, which in themselves did not necessarily have a built environment quality focus, but whose outcomes did. These were also structured and focussed campaigning activities and were undertaken in partnership with the government department or organisation responsible for the policy programme in which the CABE intervention was nested.

Generic Campaigns

Among the first type can be included general urban design quality awareness events, involving presentations to important civil society organisations by the

CABE leadership; participation in relevant discussion panels, forums, and conferences; and attempts at a wider spread of ideas through engagement with the media. For example, the compilation and publication of generic evidence relating to the *Value of Good Design* in 2002 was accompanied by events aimed at raising awareness about the issues the publication had raised. This effort continued throughout CABE's existence and included, for example, the publication of *Physical Capital* and another series of events three years later with a focus on the day-to-day public value generated by better design in the built environment.

Sometimes these initiatives focussed on particular groups, for example the professionals charged with the roll-out of the urban renaissance agenda, or, from the mid-2000s, planners engaged in the introduction of the new system of spatial planning. A separate campaigning effort aimed at Parliament—'Why Design Matters'—exhorted members to be advocates for good design and focussed on the role of CABE, what it stood for, and how such parties could raise awareness of design quality among their constituents and contacts.

Some of this generic campaigning effort was directed at influencing the public's perception of the role of design, for example campaigns amongst schoolchildren aimed at developing interest among the end users of the future. Equally, 'Building Sights', an early joint initiative with the Arts Council, was part of a larger effort to get the construction industry better engaged in communicating with communities and aimed to inspire the general public to think more deeply about the construction process. The initiative utilised decorative hoardings around building sites, as well as visitor centres and web-cams.

Specific Campaigns

The second type of campaign, focussing on specific types of buildings or urban spaces, often had a focus on improving the quality of buildings commissioned by the various branches of the public sector, such as the Better Public Buildings campaign. A key part of this campaign (which included the award already discussed) focussed on the principle that change must be client led as recommended by the Egan Construction Task force (1998). This notion led to work aimed at

improving design outcomes from Private Finance Initiative (PFI) projects, emphasising the need to ensure that public buildings produced through PFI partnerships met the expected design standards. As a government minister with responsibilities over CABE explained: the initiative "was as much a device for gaining traction in other parts of Whitehall, as it was proclaiming to a wider world that the government was committed to supporting good design . . . We even asked Tony Blair if he'd hold a reception at No. 10 for architects and designers, which he did, so we really did get that support from the very highest level of government". Spin-offs included campaigns focussed on particular building types such as 'Better Public Libraries' which aimed at reinforcing the social value of libraries and removing the deterrent effect on their use brought about by outmoded design and poor location.

Other campaigns focussed on the quality of housing, with the totality of approaches brought together under Building for Life (audits, case studies, awards, certification) forming an overarching campaign to improve the widely perceived shortcomings in housing design (CABE 2002j) (8.3). Building Futures (in partnership with the RIBA) was a similar initiative, aiming at stimulating a discussion of the built environment in the context of society's changing needs. Whilst this was largely a futures-oriented research programme, the resulting publications, such as *Housing Futures 2024* (CABE 2004b), and accompanying events were firmly

Figure 8.3 Maurer Court, part of the Greenwich Millennium Village in London, was the winner of the Building for Life Awards in 2005 for its pioneering development in terms of its technology, design, and location, and was subsequently included as a case study of best housing design in the Building for Life campaign for well-designed homes and neighbourhoods
Source: Matthew Carmona

stimulating a wider debate on the big social, technological, economic, environmental, political, and delivery factors affecting design.

Campaigning on the improvement of hospitals and other health care buildings was an early priority for CABE. This work was largely conducted in partnership with NHS Estates, underpinned by the assumption that more attention to design would lead to improvements in the diagnosis and prognosis of patients and to lower staff turnover (Pricewaterhouse Coopers 2004). Later it was expanded to include the relationship between good urban design and healthy lifestyles. A similar effort focussed on the design of schools, and, in 2003, CABE was active in setting up the Exemplar School Designs initiative and later (more prominently) was involved in the Schools Design Quality Programme (CABE 2007g). This involved a comprehensive review of recently built secondary schools and led to a larger role

for CABE that focussed on providing support to local authorities in receipt of funds from the government's Building Schools for the Future (BSF) programme.

Raising awareness of the qualities of better places was also an early priority, and the quality of streets was the subject of one of the first structured campaigns in CABE's history: 'Streets of Shame' (Box 8.1). In association with BBC Radio 4, this sought to get the public to reflect on the quality of the streets with which they were familiar and controversially included direct public involvement in naming (and shaming) the five best and five worst streets in the country. Like other areas of CABE's campaigning, the process of raising and articulating problems led to further research and guidance and to focussed enabling activity aimed at finding solutions to the particular local problems, including for some of those that were 'shamed'.

Box 8.1   Streets of Shame Campaign

Streets of Shame was conceived in the context of increasing policy interest about the quality of streetscapes, and in 2001, the Department for Environment, Transport and the Regions (DETR) asked CABE to undertake research on institutional barriers to achieving quality streetscapes. The research was carried out by Alan Baxter Associates and was published the following year as *Paving the Way*. This publication showed that the quality of streetscapes was being compromised by the rigid application of highways design standards, by an absence of a co-ordinated approach to their design and specialist skills, low levels of long-term care, and an inadequate framework for the operation of utility companies (CABE & ODPM 2002).

A MORI Poll that CABE commissioned revealed that more than twice as many people (34 per cent) thought their area had deteriorated over the previous three years compared with 15 per cent who thought it had got better (CABE 2002k), but also that many residents would be prepared to pay an extra levy on their council tax if they knew it would be spent on improving their local environment.

The main argument was made by Jon Rouse: "Streets are the living rooms of our nation and a

barometer of how we all feel. . . . They should be an expression of collective pride and not places to rush through as quickly as possible" (*Bristol Evening Post* 2002). By putting the issue of street quality very publicly in the limelight, CABE intended to highlight what people liked and didn't like about their streets and their overall condition, and to call attention to best practice in street design. CABE also hoped to inspire some rethinking by local authorities about their practices of street design, repair, and maintenance.

The initiative generated headlines in media outlets as diverse as *The Guardian*, *The Sun*, and BBC One and across the local press, whilst a listeners' poll on BBC Radio 4 saw 1,500 different streets nominated across the country in both good and bad categories. The final Streets of Shame list included: Streatham High Road in London, which topped the poll, the Cornmarket in Oxford, Drake's Circus in Plymouth, Maid Marion Way in Nottingham, and Leatherhead High Street in Surrey. Five of Britain's best streets were also named, most of which had already been subject to major high-quality regeneration schemes (8.4).

The campaign succeeded in raising the profile of street quality issues generally, and led to

Figure 8.4 Britain's best and worst streets according to the 2001 poll, respectively (i) Grey Street in Newcastle, renowned for its grandeur and elegance, and (ii) Streatham High Street in London, a busy London arterial

Source: Matthew Carmona

effective opportunities for interventions in the field by CABE and others. In Streatham, for instance, CABE lent its professional expertise to advising the local authority on its street improvement scheme, which was then put in place with help from Transport for London. In Norwich, City Hall officials were moved to secure funds for the improvement of St Stephens Street (voted the worst street in East Anglia), and in Nottingham, Maid Marion Way was improved and received a design award three years later.

Following on from Streets of Shame, a more grass-roots campaign, 'Changing Streets', also aimed to help people take charge of their own streets by bringing local people, professionals, and politicians together. As one local paper put it: "The awareness that people can and should take ownership of their streets is an outcome of the campaign" (Groves 2003). Yet the impact of the Streets of Shame was not all positive, not least because of the knock-on negative effects from publicly branding poorly performing streets. One local councillor was reported to have commented about Streatham that it was meaningless to compare a highly trafficked major London arterial road with city centre streets with little or no traffic. He argued: "Roads like this present difficult challenges, and haven't had the investment they need over many years" (*New Civil Engineer* 2002). Another complained that in naming and shaming the street, "the campaign has insulted [in equal measure] those people in the community that have worked hard for the area, against formidable odds, intransigent government funders, and reluctant partners such as Transport for London" (*South London Press* 2003).

Policy Campaigns

The final type of campaigns and events, those associated with the design quality implications of broader government policies and programmes, tracked the range of built environment-focussed policy initiatives over the course of the 2000s. Activity relating to the broad Sustainable Communities agenda (see Chapter 4) fits firmly into this third category, where CABE was seen directly by government as a key means to achieve its policy ends. Here the intention was to emphasise the role of good design in different types of

regeneration policies. The specific focus of these activities varied across the decade, but at various times focussed on issues raised by the Housing Market Renewal and Housing Growth Area programmes, the reuse of brownfield sites, the social inclusion agenda, and later the eco-towns initiative. Sustainability and climate change also became more prominent, motivated by the rise of these topics up the national political agenda and culminating, for CABE, in its 'Grey to Green' campaign which brought together organisations within and outside the public sector to lay claim to a new urban design paradigm more attuned to the natural environment.

The natural environment was a key focus for CABE Space, whose creation was accompanied by campaigns aimed at improving the design of public spaces stemming from the government's 'Cleaner, Safer, Greener' agenda with its focus on liveability and the management of green and public space. As a dedicated unit focussed on championing the design of parks and public spaces, its first public campaigns: 'Wasted Space' and the 'Manifesto for Better Public Spaces', aimed at raising awareness of the missed opportunities represented by abandoned and derelict space and generally about the quality of public space design. With its focus on parts of the built environment to which the public could directly and easily relate, the imaginative campaigns of CABE Space are widely regarded as particularly effective at raising the profile of CABE generally and the larger cause of the green space sector specifically (see 4.8).

Some of CABE's campaigning activities focussed on raising awareness of design issues in connection with particular geographically focussed policies of government, such as those associated with the Thames Gateway. In this case, activities involved seminars and presentations with the key stakeholders in the Thames Gateway area (government, local authorities, professional and local interest groups) in order to raise the profile of design; encourage a more profound understanding of the qualities and challenges of this unique landscape; and promote the creation of design frameworks to coordinate new developments in the area (CABE 2008d). Whilst ultimately all of CABE's work had direct or indirect connections back to national policy, in areas such as this the connection was particularly apparent, and increasingly brought into focus CABE's role as a delivery arm of government.

Advocacy

The Urban Task Force report of 1999 had proposed wide-ranging changes in government urban policy delivery systems, changes deemed necessary if policy was to deliver the kind of built environment the report recommended. Therefore, from its creation, an important part of CABE's role as champion of good design included advocating policy changes that would lead to the production of better-designed buildings and public spaces.

The Bigger Picture

The Planning Green Paper of 2001 was New Labour's first attempt at substantially modifying the planning system, and CABE duly reacted to it by publishing its response to the Green Paper: "What we do know is that the health of our economy and the quality of our environment is reliant on a fair, positive and efficient planning system. That is what the Government must now strive to deliver. CABE will be ready to offer support and advice through the difficult phase of transition" (CABE 2002d). In particular, CABE was active in ensuring that revised planning legislation and associated guidance would incorporate design quality issues and was often successful in these aims, although it continued to push the government to go further.

In relation to the Planning and Compulsory Purchase Bill that resulted from the Green Paper, CABE called on the government to be bolder, arguing that "CABE has a keen interest in ensuring that the bill successfully aids in the delivery of a planning process not just focused on speed and predictability, but also on the delivery of high quality environments for communities. . . . Overall however legislative changes will have little impact on an already over stretched, under skilled planning system. We need to consider further how to increase the resources and skills levels within planning authorities" (CABE 2003b).

CABE backed this up through its subsequent advocacy work relating to changes to the national Planning Policy Statements (PPSs) that accompanied the Planning Act of 2004. In all these cases, CABE aimed to emphasise the role of good design in achieving economic and social policy objectives and continually made the case for good design as an integral part of planning policy and as a key element of good planning. In doing so, it attempted to make it as easy for government to accept its recommendations as possible, for example suggesting new wording formulations for PPSs as they came forward for consultation. On the critical *PPS1: Delivering Sustainable Development*, CABE commented:

It is suggested that the importance of the design of buildings and spaces as a cross cutting objective and the interdependency between good planning, sustainable development and good design are made clearer in the PPS. This should be done within the introduction to the PPS and reinforced throughout the document. This can be achieved through the suggested wording for the design section included within this submission, and also through a more logical positioning of design policy within the PPS.

(CABE 2004a)

As the government's advisor on architecture, urban design, and public spaces, and after 2006 with a statutory duty to promote high standards in the design, management, and maintenance of the built environment (see Chapter 4), CABE also provided evidence at Select Committees. These powerful committees of Parliament, such as the 2001 House of Commons Select Committee on the Design of Open Spaces, the 2002 Select Committee on Tall Buildings, and the Select Committee on Education Outside the Classroom in 2003, fed into and informed national policy, and provided CABE with ready opportunities to both feed into the national policy formulation process and to continue spreading the word.

Projects, Plans, and Publications

CABE was also asked to provide evidence at planning public inquiries on development proposals. In fact, CABE's work in this area was limited not least because of the significant time and cost implications, for example in appointing legal representation. Nevertheless, on the occasions it did get involved, the main aim was to defend design quality in specific projects judged important enough to justify CABE's contribution, although if, and only if, CABE had previously been involved through its design review function (CABE 2011b). Consequently, despite its obvious expertise, CABE only got involved in five public inquiries, four of which related to tall buildings in London for which CABE had a statutory consultee status (CABE 2009a). In many other cases, CABE was effectively represented by its earlier design review decision letters (8.5).

CABE was also involved in the Examination in Public for the draft Replacement London Plan in 2010 and submitted written statements commenting on issues broadly related to design quality (policies on

Figure 8.5 In 2007, following six design reviews, CABE supported the design of Rafael Vinoly's 'Walkie talkie' building at the public inquiry into the redevelopment of 20 Fenchurch Street in London; in doing so, it opposed English Heritage, who spoke against the scheme

Source: Matthew Carmona

local character, public realm, architecture, tall buildings, density, and housing standards), and succeeded in having its views incorporated in the revised version of the plan. The aim was not to get involved in commenting on plans across the country, but instead to set up a precedent in terms of influencing standards for built environment quality at the local plan level that other cities and towns could follow (CABE 2011b).

Finally, CABE's advocacy work extended through its use of evidence and knowledge tools to mark out its position in relation to particular issues (see Chapters 6 and 7). Publications such as *Is the Grass Greener?* not only presented the findings of focussed investigations into identified built environment issues, but also advocated solutions later articulated in CABE's advocacy on particular policy issues and in its campaigns and partnership work. In such cases, it is difficult to disentangle this less direct advocacy work from the other functions those tools performed.

Partnerships

As an advisory body, CABE depended on others to achieve its objectives. Apart from being directly involved in various forms of promoting awareness about the role of good design, CABE also entered into partnerships, less formal liaisons, and networks with other organisations that it thought could help to deliver its objectives of raising design awareness and capacity. By these means, CABE could expand its reach and influence with minimal cost. Just before it closed, CABE argued that:

> The defining characteristic of CABE's working methods was the use of influence. CABE had no powers to demand or impose, and instead used persuasion to promote better design. Even design review, although formalised, was an entirely voluntary system. Measuring CABE's impact was therefore always a complex task because CABE did not directly deliver its objectives, but achieved them indirectly through influencing others.
>
> (CABE 2011a)

Regional and Local Champions

Part of this effort related to expanding CABE's influence in the English regions, and in the process dispelling the perception that its ideas carried a London-centric understanding of the built environment; in other words by setting up champions for its work around the country. For that, and as a direct response to DCMS targets, CABE entered into a partnership with the Architecture Foundation in 2001 with the purpose of assisting it in the creation of the regional Architecture and Built Environment Centres (ABECs) around the country. This partnership was expanded in subsequent years to include other organisations including the RIBA, the Civic Trust, and eventually the Architecture Centre Network; the network of the various centres that resulted from this initiative (Box 8.2).

Box 8.2 The Architecture Centre Network

CABE's involvement with the Architecture Centre Network (ACN) dates from 2000, with the start of its Regional Funding Programme (RFP) (see Chapter 10). The RFP was headed by a committee with representatives from the United Kingdom's nine economic regions whose job it was to establish CABE's regional strategy. This was a consequence of the service-level agreement between CABE and DCMS which specified the establishment of a network of local and regional built environment centres, but it wasn't until the Office of the Deputy Prime Minister (ODPM) began to put money into CABE from around 2003 that the initiative really took off. Before that, resources to put into local centres were very scarce. As one CABE employee commented: "I remember the Hackney Exploratory coming to us with a plea that it was about to collapse if we didn't fund it and, immediately, we had this problem—we didn't have enough money and we were being inundated with requests for funding."

Seen by many as an effort to counteract suggestions that CABE was too 'London-centric', the RFP promised to deliver on the regional dimension that had been envisaged (but not delivered) when CABE was first set up and that the Urban Task Force Report had advocated (see Chapter 4). Amongst other things, the idea was that this network could carry out regional design review functions.

In 2001, the ACN was formally established as an organisation following funding from Arts Council England although it had already been operating informally for a number of years supporting centres in Bristol, Manchester, and London. Nevertheless, it was CABE's RFP funding that transformed the network into a truly national player with a role to facilitate the exchange of good practice across English regions by sharing knowledge and innovation in respect of the quality of architecture and the public realm. It did so through advocacy, facilitation of public engagement, events, and education; receiving direct funding from CABE for this role, for example £150,000 between 2008 and 2010.[2]

In that year it represented twenty-one ABECs, the vast majority of whom had been created as a result of direct public investment through grants and contracts, with CABE grants via the RFP programme complementing funds from the Arts Council, Regional Development Agencies, English Heritage, and other bodies. 8.6 illustrates the diversity of these funding arrangements. This situation reflected the fact that the individual centres were independent organisations with different structures and funding profiles which over the years developed service agreements with various public bodies to deliver core programmes at the regional level, including (for some) design review and enabling through their contracts with CABE. For CABE, therefore, it made sense not only to support the individual centres, but also their coordination through the ACN in order to ensure that they developed into a coherent and effective network for the local delivery of design governance across the country.

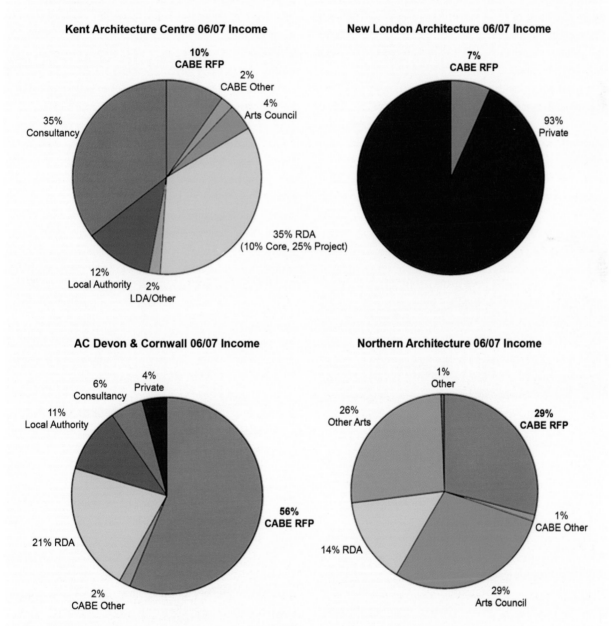

Figure 8.6 Selected ABECs, funding structure (CABE 2007j)

As CABE did not have regional offices, the ABECs were instrumental in promoting awareness of and access to CABE's messages and services across the country and to ensuring that CABE's activity was responsive to local needs. These centres were conceived as independent, locally based, not-for-profit organisations, working for the creation of better-quality neighbourhoods, buildings, and public spaces across the United Kingdom. ABECs engaged with the agendas of learning and social inclusion, regeneration, housing, culture, and heritage in their own areas, sharing the same overall agenda as CABE but developing their individual identities in response to the policy, environment, and audience in the areas they were located.

Other local-level organisations were also involved in partnerships with CABE to deal with specific local contexts. As a member of CABE's staff explained, "Beyond the architecture centre network there were other specific, more localised initiatives, that could do an important job, which, because of the specialist knowledge required, neither the regional reps nor the architecture centres could do in an effective way." An example was the East Lancashire mill towns initiative which operated in a particularly challenging economic and heritage context, but one in which design quality had an important role to play. These localised partnerships also had a role in helping to reinforce local civil society and in widening the reach of CABE's message even further, for example through the Civic Trust's Pathfinders programme that one recipient described as "a worthwhile programme of training . . . about being more effective as civic societies".

National Champions

A further vitally important partnership programme, this time national, was encapsulated in the Design Champions initiative. This early initiative of CABE was aimed at promoting the importance of design quality within public sector-commissioning organisations. It operated through the recruitment of senior employees or political representatives that were already within the targeted organisations who would then promote CABE's agenda of design quality internally amongst their colleagues. The programme was rolled out in several forms:

- Ministerial design champions
- NHS design champions
- Local authority design champions
- Design and heritage champions.

Design champions had no powers, and there were always issues around the effectiveness of the initiative. Nevertheless, their numbers grew significantly with, for example, sixteen ministerial design champions by 2002 in government departments, including those with sizable capital programmes such as Education, Health, and Justice, and others with smaller, yet high-profile programmes like the Foreign and Commonwealth Office with its remit for British embassies around the world (*Architect's Journal* 2002).

Though heavy promotion, the initiative gained early traction and was widely considered effective at spreading a design culture. However, the commitment from CABE gradually waned and in its later years rapidly declined. In part this was because success at the government level was so directly linked to prime ministerial support, and as policy attention inevitably moved in other directions, so did support for the champions. As a government minister close to CABE commented: "It seemed a good idea to have, at strategic points, someone whose role it was to remind everybody that design matters, so we hoped to have design champions—a team of ministers—across Whitehall. But they were a mixed bunch in terms of personal commitment and, at the ministerial level, I'm afraid it all rather petered out." An attempt to revive and boost the idea was included in the 2009 government strategy for place quality, *World Class Places* (see Chapter 4), but by that stage it was too late.

CABE periodically entered into partnerships with the professional institutes and other organisations, for example through the auspices of the Urban Design Skills Working Group (see Chapter 7) or the Making Places initiative, which aimed at promoting careers in the built environment professions and which was funded by ODPM (CABE 2005b). Part of this effort to work through others also involved positioning CABE within networks of organisations that were in a position to deliver CABE's key objectives. Early on, CABE recognised the limitations of what it could achieve on its own, and instead sought to establish liaisons with arts organisations, urban design groups, building commissioning bodies, and many others. A by-product was that CABE also quickly became the central coordinating and effective leadership point for design and the built environment. It was a partnership, although not necessarily always a partnership of equals.

How Were Promotion Activities Delivered?

Awards

The awards were in general not isolated initiatives, but were part of larger campaigns, and in themselves they involved a host of other activities. As a component of the pre-existing British Construction Industry Awards,[3] for example, the Prime Minister's Better Public Buildings Award connected government and the construction industry. Prime Minister Tony Blair launched the new award in 2000 with the first prize given in early 2001. CABE took over as co-sponsor of the award in 2001 (at the request of DCMS) and remained a sponsor until 2010, jointly with the Office of Government Commerce (OGC), and from 2009 with the Department for Business, Innovation and Skills (BIS).[4] Throughout, CABE was heavily engaged in the organisation and promotion of the award, seeing it as an important and continued sign of endorsement for good design from the very top of government. This included:

- Marketing and promoting the awards, using extensive national, regional, and trade media coverage of shortlisted and winning projects.
- Promotion of high-profile events linked to the awards (launches, announcements of shortlisting, announcement of winners), attended by government ministers.
- Publication of materials promoting the awards such as *Better Public Building*, or *Building and Spaces: Why Design Matters*, including a website with descriptions and images of all shortlisted projects since 2001.
- Preparation of case studies of shortlisted projects (HM Government 2000), and, in 2005, a travelling exhibition.

In 2007/08, CABE evaluated the awards to determine their impact up to that point, and decided to revise the criteria for the award to incorporate the criteria that by then had been well used and refined for Building for Life (BfL). BfL standards themselves had first been published in 2002/03, and the launch of the awards began soon after and ran until 2010. In its first five years the awards were conflated with the certification scheme (see Chapter 9) with between seven and fourteen awards given per year until 2008. However, when the BfL criteria began to be adopted as a standard by public and later private sector organisations and was developed into a free-standing certification scheme, there was a need to differentiate the awards. In its final years, therefore, the awards were used to recognise exceptional schemes from among those housebuilders that had already achieved the highest BfL standards (gold and silver) and whose commitment to design quality was most profound. In this respect, the award element became more specifically 'award-like' (e.g. awarded to the best through an expert panel) and less a set of benchmark standards. Consequently, from 2008 a much smaller number of outstanding developments were given awards (8.7). CABE co-sponsored the BfL awards as a member of the BfL Partnership with the Home Builders Federation, Civic Trust, and later Design for Homes, who was awarded the contract to coordinate the awards.

The Inclusive Design and the Parkforce Awards (8.8) were intended as temporary tools and resulted

Figure 8.7 Barking Central by volume builder Redrow Homes was one of the winners of the last Building for Life Awards in 2010

Source: Matthew Carmona

Figure 8.8 (i) Mile End Park was one of the cases of parks with dedicated park staff publicised in the 'Parkforce campaign', run by CABE Space, which focussed on the importance of park workers; (ii) The campaign included a number of awards for the best park staff and park teams in local authorities, one of which was won by the keeper of the Sunset and Moonlit Parks in Birmingham, here with its Green Flag Award flying (see Chapter 9)

Source: Matthew Carmona

from agreements with other organisations already involved in these specific areas, with CABE sponsorship providing an immediate and important authoritative weight. The Festive Fives awards, by contrast, focussed on CABE's generic agenda to raise the profile of good design, and, like all awards, was first and foremost a communications tool. The selection of organisations and individuals among the huge array of possible projects and interventions each year were often connected with other CABE activities and were increasingly carefully selected according to which areas the organisation deemed should be prioritised each year. Ultimately, however, any award scheme,

particularly a long-running one, represents a major commitment of organisational time and resources, which perhaps explains why many came and went during CABE's relatively short existence.

Long-running award schemes were also used as performance indicators for CABE and its various initiatives, with baseline figures agreed with DCMS on how many entrants CABE should try to achieve in a given year for its own awards, or how many awards outside its control should be given in certain areas. The 2001/02 Annual Report, for example, gives the target of fourteen RIBA and Civic Trust architecture and design award-winning schemes located in England's fifty most deprived areas (CABE 2002c), and in 2002/03 this target was raised to twenty-seven awards in such areas (CABE 2003a). Intended as a measure of CABE's impact, in reality as CABE was neither a commissioning authority, funder, or designer, the organisation's relative inability to influence such matters meant that this was a poor indicator and was not repeated in subsequent years. The inclusion nevertheless demonstrated the credence placed in awards as an indicator of success. Thereafter the number of applications for the Prime Minister's Better Public Buildings Award (something over which CABE had greater sway) was included (CABE 2003a), with, for example, 121 entries received in 2007/08 against a target of seventy, twenty-one of which were shortlisted (CABE 2008a).[5]

Campaigns

CABE's campaigning and events activities covered a wide array of topics and aimed at different types of audiences, professional, political, and public (8.9). From one-off seminars and conferences to long-running multidimensional structured campaigns, these efforts reached out to society at large in an effort to widen the support base for better design quality. As CABE (2004a) itself argued five years into its mission: "Since 1999 CABE has become a definitive public voice on architecture and the built environment. In its first five years CABE generated over 5,000 news articles and broadcasts and we currently average 17,000 website visits every week." As early as the 'Streets of Shame' campaign (see Box 8.1), CABE became very adept at using quick-fire polling and other means to give legitimacy to CABE positions by reaching out to the public and capturing and framing headlines through the view on the street.[6]

In 2003, a policy and communications director was appointed to take forward this work, and this signalled that as part of the larger communications mission of CABE, campaigns were to become a more important part of the remit.[7] In particular, it used campaigns that reached out to the wider public in order (over time) to build a demand for better development amongst the populace at large. For instance, the 'Wasted Space' campaign of 2003 aimed to involve the public in nominating spaces in their localities that were derelict or underutilised with the winner of the country's worst wasted space chosen from the nominations by a panel of judges. As one CABE director commented, such campaigns generated "huge amounts of press coverage that was overwhelmingly positive", and when brought together with relevant research and up-to-date market research, "It worked hugely successfully in getting key messages out." But how far this influence went is open to question. A commissioner admitted that whilst "There were constant stories that kept architecture, landscape, and urban design on telly . . . and everything would quote CABE this and CABE that, I don't think the public ever knew what CABE was." Raising public awareness and demand was always likely to be a very long-term and challenging aspiration, and few believe CABE made any real dent in this over the decade or so during which it was active.

Campaigning activities were rarely ends in themselves. Instead, they were closely linked to research work at one end (setting the parameters around which the campaign or event was conceived), and guidance/enabling activities at the other (ensuring actual change in design-related practices). For example, through its growing body of research on the value of design, generic questions about why investing in design quality was worthwhile had gradually built up and had been extensively used in CABE's advocacy work. In 2006/07, the organisation took a new angle with a specific campaign around 'The Cost of Bad Design' and in a publication of the same name argued for new methods of accounting to recognise the costs. The same year saw CABE engage in an area where these costs had become very evident and which was then preoccupying government, the Thames Gateway (8.10). CABE's role was focussed on attempting to raise the profile of design, although,

as usual, it had no power to require the multitude of actors active in that territory to actually engage with them. Its solution was a series of initiatives to encourage the coordination of efforts between parties, including: a *Thames Gateway Design Pact* published in draft form in 2008 which encouraged all parties to sign up to invest in design quality;[8] a Thames Gateway Design Task Force with associated workshops; focussed Building for Life training in the Gateway; a Thames Gateway Housing Audit (see Chapter 6); and a characterisation study—*New Things Happen* (see 10.8) which focussed on understanding the diverse character of the places that make up the Gateway and establishing ideas to inform its future planning.

Many campaigns lasted in one format or another and with varied levels of intensity throughout much of CABE's life. The value of design work, better public buildings (particularly schools, hospitals, and health buildings), housing design campaigns, design in the planning system, various public space management foci, and the role of space quality and design in urban regeneration, are all examples. Other campaigns were particularly noticeable in certain years as a reflection of changing government or partner interest in topics or resulting from internal changes in direction within CABE associated with changes in administration, for example, the emergence of sustainability and social inclusion in later years. But because campaigning activities and events were so often integrated into CABE's other activities, it is difficult to gauge the resource implications of this aspect of the organisation's work.

The tone of the campaigns also varied, with some suggesting that those directed at the development sector had a more aggressive campaigning style than when the targets were government decision-makers. Reflecting on the campaigning accompanying the launch of the housing audits (see Chapter 6), for example, one insider commented:

A big piece of campaigning went on around the headline statistic that 83 per cent of new homes weren't good enough. . . . The industry was apoplectic—we had huge media coverage and they were completely backed into a corner—and it was the first time they had been seriously challenged in perhaps twenty years about the impact of what they were producing . . . so, quite deliberately, the

start of Building for Life initiative
and associated campaigns
2001–02

new Policy and Communications
director, in charge of campaigns
2003–04

campaigns on
public space
2005–06

2000–01
campaign activity starts with
launch of By Design

2002–03
streets and public spaces and
first structured campaign
(Streets of Shame)

2004–05
campaigning for the Better
Public Buildings programme:
libraries and hospitals

Figure 8.9 Timeline of CABE's campaigns

after the Housing Audits:
campaigning for housing standards
and sustainability
2007–08

long term view of quality
2009–10

2006–07
the costs of bad design and
the Thames Gateway

2008–09
campaigning during the crisis:
space standards for housing

2010–11
winding down and reducing
the scope: focus on BfL

Figure 8.10   The very poor quality of housing design in the Thames Gateway became an increasing concern during the 2000s

Source: Matthew Carmona

campaigning there was confrontational, initially, to give them a really good kicking where it hurt.

Such an approach might seem self-defeating when viewed against the aspirations of the other tools in this chapter, creating enemies rather than partners. But those involved argue that putting the industry on the back foot then allowed CABE to be more collaborative when subsequent audits were published. A confrontational approach was never pursued with local government who arguably were often equally culpable in the poor standards of residential design.

Advocacy

CABE spent much time cultivating a wide network of contacts and relationships with organisations in government, industry, academia, and the voluntary and community sectors to maximise its impact. Its very active advocacy for design within government was something quite new in British design governance and

focussed in particular on the large commissioners of new public buildings, especially the NHS and the Department for Education. CABE utilised advocacy throughout its tenure, although arguably the period from 2000 to 2005 was the most intense. Partly this was because the job needing to be done to close the gap in understanding about design was greatest at that time; partly because of the significant changes that were occurring to the planning system and to national planning policy during this time; and partly because Sir Stuart Lipton made a particular point of engaging with the range of government departments and agencies in order to spread the message. Confirming this, one of CABE's original commissioners suggested that in the early years a lot of the advocacy work was done directly by the chairman and chief executive, drawing on their own personal connections and status: "One of the best things Stuart [Lipton] did as Chairman was his work with government. He can be very blunt . . . he was prepared to bully government a bit and made his presence fairly well known in Whitehall and he was highly critical of PFI and its shortcomings. He was the one who really took on government and said, 'You've got to be a champion for architecture,' . . . and got various Treasury people to recognise design as something which contributed to value. We all had our roles, and that was, clearly, the one that Stuart played most effectively."

Initially, also, much of this work reflected the organisation's own view of its role in implementing the principles laid out by the Urban Task Force as regards good design, or from opportunities that arose to play that role together with specific government departments, public sector organisations, professional bodies and advocacy groups. Thereafter (and increasingly) CABE also reacted to emerging government agendas and sought to secure attention to built environment quality in these, for example those relating to sustainable communities policy.

The influence on government often depended on both support from higher levels of government and the attitude of individual departments, as a government minister explained:

We got different degrees of buy-in from different departments. The first generation of PFI hospitals were a design disaster, in my personal opinion, but the Department of Health took very little persuading that it was their proper responsibility and, indeed, it was in their interests, and it would be good business practice to ensure that the next round of PFI funded hospitals were better designed. The Lord Chancellor's Department were particularly good, so we got a new generation of magistrates courts and so forth, where there really was attention paid to design. But it depended so much on the disposition of individual ministers. . . . There were some departments where the minister would arrive in a palpably grudging mood, briefed, clearly, by his officials to be as unresponsive as possible, but we tried to get this [design] culture broadened out, all the way across Whitehall.

The largest difficulty seems to have been how to reshape departmental procurement systems so that design quality variables were systematically considered. In the view of one CABE director, these were often "hugely difficult, complicated big beasts to influence", although perseverance brought success: "If I think of the school building programme, if you look at waves 1 and 2 of the Building Schools of the Future initiative, they were terrible, there were some shocking schools built there. By the time we got to wave 4, the School Design Panel and the campaigning work we had done on school procurement was having a really big impact in beginning to commission some really good schools."

Later, as the work convincing national government subsided, CABE increasingly turned its attention to the housebuilders who had been somewhat ignored in CABE's early years, and extensive efforts were made (with varying degrees of success) to engage those key players in the design agenda. To some degree, this was harder because whilst CABE rarely criticised government (the hand that fed the organisation), in the mid 2000s its housing audits and other work had been very critical of the housebuilders. Consequently, and despite some suggesting that the confrontation was necessary, the result was undoubtedly a distrust between the Home Builders Federation (notwithstanding their partnership on BfL), many of its members, and CABE, which was perceived as unsympathetic to their market imperatives. The work nevertheless continued and claimed some significant successes (see Chapter 4).

The process of advocacy in relation to changes in relevant policy and legislation was more straightforward and normally involved the production and submission of written responses to formal consultation processes. This was accompanied by public talks and articles by leading figures in CABE and by private talks between CABE and the relevant government departments. The approach was much the same for private sector stakeholders such as the housebuilders.

Partnerships

The processes involved in building partnerships were complex and varied, and following the removal of a short-lived partnerships co-ordinator who had been appointed to the senior management team between 2001 and 2003, the responsibility was broadly shared across the organisation. The degree of influence CABE was able to exert also varied. In the case of the ABECs, CABE was directly responsible for catalysing the development of nearly two-thirds of the twenty-two centres that came into existence in the period 2000–2010, mostly through a grant-funding programme that started in 2002 (CABE 2011d).

From this time, the network grew from eight unconnected centres (some of which pre-existed CABE) into a network with shared values, shared activities, and coordination through the Architecture Centre Network (ACN). Despite this, not all of the ABECs were treated equally by CABE, with only some securing roles as host to a CABE regional design review panel, and many were less than happy with the influence CABE had over their work via its various funding strands (for training, enabling, design review, etc). As the director of an independent design centre commented: "It didn't matter what region you were in, the approach was the same: 'Here's some funding to do one Building for Life training and you've got to do it exactly, exactly how we say,' and that was it, or: 'Here's some funding to do design review and here's our ten principles of how to do design review.' I think they got very dictatorial, they thought they knew it all, and they were, I suppose, justifying their existence." Whilst much of the time CABE and the ABECs worked effectively together, the situation demonstrated the challenges of partnership working when the two sides to that agreement were not equal.

By contrast, the processes involved in encouraging design champions were of a different nature, and far more detached. In essence, this initiative relied on persuading initially government organisations and later local authorities, house building companies, and others to appoint a senior person as their own champion, and thereafter that person would only have a distant relationship with CABE. The period from 2004 to 2006 saw a massive increase in the number of design champions in public bodies, and by the end of the period two thirds of local authorities had appointed a design champion, alongside 78 per cent of primary care trusts and 93 per cent of acute hospital trusts (CABE 2006c). At the cabinet level, the culture secretary, Tessa Jowell, became the government's design champion. There was also a drive to introduce champions in the building industry, and six of the eleven major volume housebuilders appointed a champion (CABE 2005a).

CABE provided some training for these champions, and at one stage, in an unsuccessful attempt to attract English Heritage funding, linked design champions to the allied but uncoordinated initiative run by English Heritage that promoted heritage champions in local authorities (8.11). CABE hosted a major conference for local authority design champions in

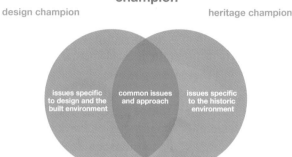

Figure 8.11 Design and heritage champion

Source: CABE n.d.

December 2006 and issued a leaflet—*Design Champions*—exhorting housebuilders to appoint champions at the board level. However, the approach never had a consistent home within CABE and commitment fluctuated. An effort to launch a new framework called 'championing design' in 2007, with a view to making the champions more effective by linking them up eventually came to nothing, and after that the initiative was allowed to wither on the vine. Because they were dispersed, independent, not beholden to CABE, and without constant input and encouragement from a single point, it proved difficult to sustain this very loose form of partnership.

Throughout CABE's work, priorities came and went, new initiatives were launched, and old ones declined. CABE's promotional tools were no different, but the sheer range of energy and innovation put into these activities and the culture change that it is widely recognised that they helped to bring about remains an impressive component of the organisation's legacy. Partnerships in particular, sometimes opportunistic and sometimes more strategic, enabled CABE to greatly extend its reach. Ultimately, faced with closure in 2011, it was to a new form of partnership (merger with the Design Council) that CABE looked to save what it could of its operations (see Chapter 5).

When Should Promotion Tools Be Used?

This chapter has explored tools which focus on the promotion of CABE's message and views, themselves often based on the knowledge CABE gathered and

Figure 8.12 Typology of promotion

disseminated through the sorts of tools discussed in previous chapters. For CABE, promotion involved four tools. First, two awareness-raising tools: awards to exemplary projects and people as a way of promoting those who adhered to CABE's agenda; and structured (and sometimes opportunistic) campaigns to promote the message of good design and its inclusion in the decision-making framework of public and private sector players and end users. Second, promotion activities focussed on particular audiences, encompassing: advocacy to shape the policies and programmes of government and the practices of key private actors, and partnership work to allow CABE to more effectively deliver its objectives in collaboration with others.

These were all activities that emerged early in the history of CABE and were formalised, consolidated, and continually invested in over time. These were also in large part entirely new tools for the British state and reflected the idea that the public sector should no longer be sitting back but should be actively and publicly making the case for good design. In this respect, CABE's work was both breaking new ground and continually developing and innovating throughout the 2000s.

As with the discussion of other tools, producing a verdict on how effective these promotion activities were is not straightforward. As the story suggests, promotion was an integral part of what CABE did and the activities discussed here were an integrated part of a larger effort to promote an agenda that cut across most of what CABE did. In totem these efforts are seen by many as a critical part of the CABE armoury and

effective in continually highlighting the significance of design, putting those messages where they mattered—in front of key decision-makers (both professional and political, public and private), and helping to raise the profile of CABE into the dominant force that it became. Whether this significantly impacted the national awareness of good design amongst the larger (non-professional) population (a key objective of CABE, especially after 2003) is doubtful (despite occasional flurries of national media interest), but such an objective would certainly be a very long-term project and whether, if CABE had continued, this might have been possible, remains an open question.

Placing the promotion tools in the design governance field of action from Chapter 1 (8.13) shows that the preponderance of these tools are focussed on the early part of the design governance remit, helping to shape the decision-making environment by raising awareness and arguing the case for good design. This is certainly the case for most advocacy work which is fundamentally about encouraging actors to put in place the right sorts of resources, skills, and processes to engage positively in design. The earlier this occurs, the more effective it is likely to be. Campaigns also largely focus on the decision-making environment, on arguing the case in order to get actors engaged and motivated around design, although of course their content and messages will focus on all dimensions of quality. Partnerships, by contrast, will ideally form early and will persevere, although different partnerships may focus on

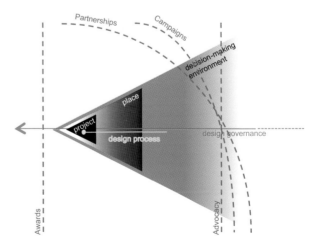

Figure 8.13 Promotion tools in the design governance field of action

different stages of design governance, and some may be far more limited than others in their scope and operation. Finally, awards, which may sometimes focus on good process, more often on place quality and most frequently on project quality, will almost always happen after the fact, looking back on the subject of a particular award in order to make judgements about success. In doing so, however, it is hoped they will influence all stages of the design and development process and will therefore also (through their impact) help to shape a better decision-making environment in the future.

Notes

1. http://webarchive.nationalarchives.gov.uk/2011011809 5356/http://www.cabe.org.uk/news/pace-setters-for-2007

2. http://webarchive.nationalarchives.gov.uk/20110118095 356/http:/www.cabe.org.uk/about/what-we-fund
3. BCIA had run the British Construction Industry Awards on a commercial basis since 1998.
4. After which they have continued to be run by BCIA on a commercial basis, with continued sponsorship from BIS and the Cabinet Office.
5. In some years, this was further refined to the number of applications from particular sectors, notably the health and education sectors (CABE 2004c; 2005c; 2006).
6. This sort of polling was typically undertaken by MORI (later Ipsos MORI), and Ben Page, its chief executive, was drafted in as a CABE commissioner from July 2003.
7. CABE's initial structure had a public affairs directorate which took charge of structured campaigns.
8. As the housing market collapsed in the same year and DCLG became distracted with the revival of the development industry rather than with the quality of its products, a final version was never published.

CHAPTER 9

The Evaluation Tools

This chapter explores some of CABE's best-known governance tools, the most high-profile of which was design review. It moves beyond previous tools explored in Part III of this book because judgements are being made on actual projects in the field on which the evaluation may or may not have had a direct impact. If, as established in Chapter 2, these are placed in order of their relative 'intervention', CABE's evaluation tools encompassed indicators, design review, certification, and competitions. This chapter is divided into three parts covering the why, how, and when of these evaluation tools. The first part discusses the rationale for these activities, the second examines the processes involved in each type of evaluation, and the third touches on when, within the design governance field of action, they should be used.

Why Engage in Evaluation Activities?

Indicators

For any organisation seeking to pass judgements about the quality of design, the first task must be to establish the criteria and means through which such an evaluation can be made in a reliable and objective fashion. In this work, CABE focussed mainly on housing and public space issues, which were government priorities, but also had interests in developing indicators around green infrastructure and tweaking existing indicators for use in the NHS and school curricula.

CABE's various dalliances with indicators attempted to rationalise the qualities and complexities inherent in making such judgements and employ them to underpin a series of tools that could be used to make

systematic and replicable evaluations of project and place quality. For instance, when launching one of these tools, the Design Quality Indicator (DQI), CABE proclaimed:

> The Roman architect Vitruvius provided us with the principles of design quality when he suggested "commodity, firmness and delight" as the key elements of a well-designed building. He was less obliging however in suggesting how we might objectively measure the largely qualitative aspects of design. A couple of thousand years later Design Quality Indicators . . . have finally given us a method for doing just that.
> (CABE 2003a)

However, such indicators were not an attempt to produce a definitive codification of design quality, but were instead an attempt to systematise the processes of design evaluation so that different players could engage with the activity and understand, discuss, and compare the results. Box 9.1 demonstrates how this was done with a second indicator tool, Spaceshaper, developed to evaluate the quality of public spaces by professionals and non-professionals alike. Through such means, CABE hoped to establish a wide recognition of the parameters of 'quality' and ensure that consistent evaluation could be made and communicated in a clear and concise manner. This underlying objective also applied to tools ultimately developed as part of more formalised programmes of quality recognition, such as Building for Life certification or the criteria underpinning design review, but their wrapping inside of a larger tool means they went further than simple indicators and are described separately later in this chapter.

Box 9.1   Spaceshaper

In February 2007 CABE Space launched a public space indicator called Spaceshaper which it had developed together with the Construction Industry Council (CIC) based on the DQI for Buildings. The tool covered eight themes—access, maintenance, environment, use, design and appearance, other people, community, and you—scored on a 'spider diagram'. Spaceshaper was used in local areas at facilitated events, involving a site visit, the computerised production of the diagram, and discussions around the results. For CABE, the Spaceshaper programme fitted in well as, in the words of one of the programme leads, whilst "CABE Space was originally set up to try and improve the quality of green space only, its remit quickly evolved into the public realm at large."

Given its growing interest in public space issues, the government was keen on the idea of developing a DQI for space, and the Department for Communities and Local Government (DCLG) funded the development and roll-out of Spaceshaper through CABE. Unlike the DQI (which aimed to be self-financing), facilitators did not pay for the use of Spaceshaper software and initially were trained free of charge.[1]

A key challenge was to identify and consider the needs of all the different users of public space, because, as one facilitator described it, "A public space is somewhere where somebody might be walking a dog, lying down, reading a book, playing an active game, lurking to do all sorts of anti-social things—it's all things to all people—and varies according to the weather, the season, the time of day and so on . . . and includes people that may never go into the space, but just value it being there." The aim was, therefore, to create a common and intuitive language for this range of participants and to develop a simple computer model in order that results could be immediately inputted and the resulting spider diagram reviewed and discussed.

CABE heavily promoted the branded indicator kit. As one staff member recalls: "What we were trying to do was to find a number of organisations who would say, 'Spaceshaper was the standard way' in which they do consultation on public spaces, and we actually paid for a number of workshops for key organisations . . . the Forestry Commission, the Woodland Trust, and so forth." This early marketing paid off, and soon organisations were approaching CABE to run Spaceshaper workshops and to train their own facilitators.

The role of facilitators was important and focussed on using the tool to get people talking. Since there was a high chance of opposing views, the role required preparation through discussions with stakeholders and good planning for inclusion. However, as one regular facilitator recalled: "The basic notion of walking around somewhere and focussing your attention on a number of criteria elicited a really useful kind of information," and often, eventually, agreement (9.1).

Critics of the Spaceshaper tool tended to focus on the diagram—typically calling it a "weird spider's web"—as one parks professional put it: "Spaceshaper was an inherently top-down patronising attempt to connect with the 'natives.'" Nevertheless, the new insights often fed into discussions about future developments and sometimes even produced instant action on design and management issues. A good example of the latter was the Lenton Recreation Ground in Nottingham, where "The parks team were horrified to understand that people didn't think that anyone was looking after the park as the dark green uniforms of staff meant they couldn't see them around. So, they gave all of the parks team visibility vests."

Figure 9.1 Spaceshaper engaged people in evaluating their local public realm and focussed on getting people talking in groups

Source: Design South East

In 2009, Spaceshaper operations transferred to the Kent Architecture Centre (one of the original ABECs—see Chapter 8), which later became Design South East and which continues to provide training and support for the tool.[2] By September 2010, around 3,500 people had attended Space-shaper workshops and there were 328 trained facilitators.

Indicators were also a design improvement tool by encouraging deliberations on design that were more systematic and structured around a holistic notion of design quality. The logic was that the systematic means of quality assessment would guide the thinking of decision-makers who were typically 'non-designers' and influence their interactions with others. Such decision-makers needed to work with multiple stake-holders who had influence, whether in the develop-ment, build-out, or maintenance of a scheme, and in that context, indicators were a measurement of quality that could provide a focus for seeking agreement. By encouraging reflection on design at the local level with key groups, CABE hoped to raise the aspirations of a wider set of actors, and more consistently aim for high standards in design.

Design Review

Design review was CABE's most high-profile service and built on the practices the Royal Fine Art Commission had established since 1924, albeit in those days typically referred to as 'enquiries' rather than 'reviews'. As discussed in Chapter 2, these processes were informal in the sense that they were not formally part of any statutory process of regulation or approval and only ever had an advisory status.

Ultimately, CABE hoped its design review pro-gramme would raise expectations of design and thus help build a culture of quality in England, and as Les Sparks (chairman of the design review panel at the time) put it, "CABE's principal aim is to inspire people to demand more from buildings and spaces. Our design review programme is a key part of achieving this" (CABE 2005a: 3). Yet the more immediate function of the design review tool was to improve individual schemes by providing advice from a pool of experts whose joint experience could be brought to bear. As explained in the publication *How to do design review*, design review "brings a breadth and depth of experi-ence that may not be available to the project team or to the planning authority; it can offer expert views on complex issues such as sustainability; and it can broaden discussions and draw attention to the bigger picture" (CABE 2006g: 5).

CABE's design reviews were intended to influence thinking within the context of the local decision-making environment, so expert judgements also had to be sensitive to both the locality and the surrounding development strategies, whilst not being too con-strained by these realities if they were proving barriers to the achievement of good design. As the organisation confirmed, "Design is a creative activity, and definitions of quality in design are elusive. It cannot be reduced to codes and prescriptions; and even in those areas where there appear to be codes—such as classical architecture—the best examples often break or tran-scend the rules" (2002f: 3). Thus the skills required were extremely broad and required a good deal of professional maturity as well as technical proficiency.

An Independent Process

CABE had several different tools that shared high-level expertise, but the distinguishing feature of design review was that it provided advice which was 'independent'; bespoke advice from experts unconnected to the schemes under review. The logic was that by maintain-ing distance, reviews could offer a new perspective that might be considered trustworthy or politically neutral. As explained in CABE's ten-year review, "Most devel-opers respect a judgement based on the opinion of professionals with no stake in the project but a great deal of experience from highly successful schemes else-where" (CABE 2009a: 12). On occasions relationships could become more established and therefore, arguably, more compromised, and when this occurred, the degree of separation was not fully maintained. As one borough officer remembered, "They had their own dedicated panel for the Olympic Park and that was great, but there was some collusion behind the scenes in the spirit of, 'Can you help us with this'?"

Design review was also supposed to be independent in its outlook, with no attachment to any particular design 'ideology' or aesthetic preference. CABE had its own set of design principles, but saw these as "a largely objective set of criteria that stress the importance of avoiding undue emphasis on matters of personal taste" (CABE 2006g: 5). In practice, also, there were some areas where CABE might espouse particular positions, although these could be tailored to particular circumstances. For example notes on a review of a sixth-form college in Worthing stated: "As a general principle CABE is always opposed to the conversion of playing fields to buildings but there may be local reasons why that view may be discounted" (CABE 2002g).

Although a huge diversity of schemes passed through the design review service, CABE was dissatisfied with much of what it saw, leading to strong criticisms of designs. Peter Stewart, the head of design review, commented: "Too much of what we see is mediocre and there are many schemes that do not come near to CABE" (CABE 2003a: 8), implying that CABE was often seeing the best of a bad lot. The hope remained, nevertheless, that improvement through review would eventually feed higher expectations into the consciousness of professionals and politicians, and encourage clients to expect better designs (9.2). What progress it made towards such a goal is hard to assess,

Figure 9.2 Design review offered an independent voice that encouraged greater ambition for major new developments such as in the case of the New Birmingham Library

Source: Matthew Carmona

particularly given that other tools often had much the same objective, and in aggregate terms it is difficult to distinguish the impact of one tool from the totality.

Certification

Certification in effect represents a further step towards formalisation as it combines evaluation with an 'official' stamp of approval. These schemes differ from awards (see Chapter 8) in that they recognise all designs that reach a certain standard and also tend to be more formalised, with explicitly published and measurable criteria for success. As one commissioner put it, "Because CABE was not the planning authority, it couldn't intervene in the private sector, but it could work with decision makers to give them the tools and the confidence so that they could say, 'This isn't good enough.' That could be done through training but also through tools like Building for Life, which certified a level of quality." Whilst published criteria for certification could be used independently, these tools operated through the voluntarily submission of schemes for assessment, with an evaluation following on from a review of the submitted information and (in the case of those CABE endorsed) a site visit.[3]

CABE became involved in two major certification programmes, Building for Life (BfL) that was development oriented, and the Green Flag Awards that focussed on open spaces. The BfL programme was established in response to the national need for housebuilding and worries over its likely quality. The first edition of the BfL Newsletter (Building for Life 2004) explicitly noted the ambition to link the criteria to the new sustainability aspirations being promoted at the time through the national *Sustainable Communities* plan (see Chapter 4), whilst CABE's own Corporate Strategy for 2002–5 clarified: "Building for Life is a three-year campaign to champion better design in house building," responding directly to "England's need for almost 4 million new homes in the next 25 years" (CABE 2002b). Similarly, the Green Flag programme was promoted as a means to deliver betterquality parks. As the minister at the time, Yvette Cooper, put it when speaking about the 2003/04 Green Flag winners: "It helps to raise standards by highlighting good practice" (CABE & Civic Trust 2004). In practice, it was also used as a management tool and a way to encourage communities to get involved (9.3).

Figure 9.3 CABE Space used the Green Flag to certify excellence in parks and to recognise park management and proactive local involvement, as well as for design and construction

Source: *Daily Echo Bornemouth* Online

BfL's certification system sat at the heart of the broader BfL programme as a defined "mark of quality" (CABE 2003a) for which scheme promoters could continually apply. Likewise, the Green Flag certification was boosted through a larger outreach programme and work to build public recognition of this quality mark. Its strong public visibility meant that Green Flag was seen as a good tool to expand the CABE Space brand and develop its work (CABE 2004g). Julia Thrift, CABE space director from 2003 to 2006, was particularly active on this front, and having worked at the Civic Trust on Green Flag in its early years (before CABE picked it up), used the tool extensively to advance the CABE cause and to build relationships (Taylor 2003).

The criteria underpinning certification offered the potential to define performance in narrow or broad terms and from design concerns to management factors. Green Flag criteria covered social and financial factors, sustainability, and community involvement whilst the twenty Building for Life criteria clustered under four headings: environment and community; character; streets, parking, and pedestrianisation; and design and construction. There were also two specialist versions of Green Flag. The first, the 'Green Pennant Award' (now known as the Green Flag Community Award), was launched in 2002 to recognise the work of voluntary and community groups in managing green spaces. The second gave 'Green Heritage' site status and was introduced in 2003 with sponsorship from English Heritage. Schemes submitted for this certification needed to have a conservation plan, although

they were judged on the full range of Green Flag factors, and not just on historical factors.

Competitions

Whilst much of CABE's work focussed on generally raising standards, the competitions tool was explicitly intended to stimulate excellence in practice. The premise was that winning teams would produce schemes of the highest possible quality through participating in a design competition with only the best schemes winning. For example, the competition for the new Turner Contemporary arts centre in Margate, on which CABE advised, demonstrated CABE's intention to facilitate the creation of exemplar buildings of 'international standard'. The brief demanded: "The bold new building should set up a welcome trend for English seaside towns—first Bilbao, now Margate" (CABE 2002c) (9.4).

CABE also hoped that through the use of competitions England would be exposed to 'world-class' winning designs that others would then emulate, thus lifting the standards more generally. In fact, competitions as a tool was under-utilised in the United Kingdom compared with some countries, and CABE used the approach sparingly. Indeed CABE itself sought to learn from countries with a much greater experience of the tool, and an Anglo-French competition was organised jointly with Direction de l'Architecture et du Patrimoine (DAPA), whose remit is to support and promote heritage, conservation, and architecture in France. In this case, the "aim was to develop

Figure 9.4 Although the Margate competition winning design was never built out, others were, such as the bold and daring Seagull and Windbreak beach huts in Boscombe, pictured here

Source: ABIR Architects

Figure 9.5 Housing by Cartwright Pickard Architects, one for two winners in the Anglo-French competition, for high standards in the design of affordable housing

Source: Matthew Carmona

international best practice and raise the architectural and urban design quality of affordable housing" (CABE 2005g: 4), with sites chosen in White City and on the Rayners Lane Estate (both in London) (9.5). Most high profile, however, was CABE's involvement in the pan-European housing design competition, where the organisation again piggybacked on the much greater experience in Europe with competitions, whilst cementing its own reputation on the international stage as the United Kingdom's pre-eminent representative on design and the built environment.

CABE often had larger social goals behind its use of competitions with the criteria established for judging competitions frequently focussed on promoting 'social value'. This extended to encouraging entrants to rate themselves and their team structure against 'socially oriented' criteria, as well as the social improvements that the resulting design would bring. Such lofty goals were not always so evident, however, and occasionally competitions (of a different nature) were used for spreading a message or publicising campaigns,

including the photographic competition—Areas of Outstanding Urban Beauty—used in 2010 as part of CABE's beauty research (see Chapter 6). In much the same way that natural areas of beauty are valued and protected, the idea in this case was to "think about the places all around us. Look at them critically. See what's special. And value it" (Etherington 2010).

More conventionally, the use of architectural competitions was driven by government building programmes in the hope that such involvement could help to deliver a positive design legacy from the significant public funding. CABE, for example, organised a competition around the Neighbourhood Nurseries initiative, which responded to the Department for Education and Skills' (DfES's) New Opportunities Fund with its budget of £203 million of revenue funding and £100 million of capital funding (2001–4) for new nursery schools. In 2007, CABE also agreed to play a key role in establishing and evaluating an ideas competition for the development of design principles and development process ideas for the government's eco-towns initiative, although this competition was later abandoned in favour of CABE establishing a dedicated design review panel to examine eco-town proposals (Hurst & Rogers 2009). This final episode revealed something of the uncertainty that always followed the use of this tool and perhaps some of CABE's reluctance to use it in favour of other tried and tested techniques.

How Were Evaluation Activities Delivered?

Indicators

CABE developed its indicators by incrementally building on existing knowledge and techniques. The DQI was instigated by the Construction Industry Council (CIC) in 1999,[4] but, seeing its potential, CABE became involved in its development and 2000 launch. CABE was also instrumental in getting the DQI written into the Treasury's *Green Book* (HM Treasury 2003), the all-important rules for funding by central government and its executive agencies, and while it was directly involved after that time, it used the learning to influence its work on Spaceshaper and on the *Achieving Excellence in Design Evaluation Toolkit* (DH Estates & Facilities 2008), the NHS version of the DQI. Similarly, in partnership with DCLG and the Civic Trust, in 2008 CABE Space produced a structured scoring system in the *Parks and Green Space Self Assessment Guide* (CABE 2008a). The ambition there was to establish a set of indicators for local authorities to use to assess their own processes for managing parks and green spaces for which the logical starting point was the criteria used to evaluate the Green Flag awards that already had a long history of successful use.

CABE also produced the *Green Infrastructure Healthcheck*, an on-line indicator toolkit for local authorities to assess not only the priority given to green spaces but also the staff and resources to manage them. The ten GI-focussed questions concentrated on priorities, but also gave local authorities feedback that rated their performance so they could identify where to make improvements. As Sarah Gaventa, CABE Space director, explained: "The GI Healthcheck is an easy way for local authorities to identify how seriously they take their green spaces. The CABE website has useful tips to help councils make the shift from grey to green if their healthcheck score reveals they need support" (*Horticulture Week* 2010).

Once available, CABE sought to empower others to take ownership of their indicator tools and Spaceshaper, for example, was taken up as a public engagement tool by the Homes & Communities Agency, British Waterways, Groundwork, Riverside Housing Association, and the Architecture Centre Network. In this way indicators were used as a key day-to-day improvement tool and as simply part of the arsenal of good design governance. They could also be used for educational purposes, as was the case when, together with Beam (the architecture centre in Wakefield), CABE secured £245,000 from the Department for Children, Schools and Families to develop a version of Spaceshaper for nine- to fourteen-year-olds (9.6). Finally, they could be used in performance management, and just before the May 2010 election CABE and DCLG worked up a project to establish a 'quality of place' indicator as part of the national indicator set to support the government's *World Class Places Action Plan* (HM Government 2009—see Chapter 4). The intention was that this would feed into future spending rounds, although it was cut when CABE itself was cut in the spending round of 2010.

Figure 9.6 Spaceshaper was used as a learning resource for nine- to fourteen-year-olds

Source: Design South East

Design Review

A wide variety of projects was submitted to CABE to review from regeneration schemes and public works related to transport and infrastructure to the full gamut of development projects, including offices (increasingly for tall buildings—Box 9.2), retail developments, buildings for sports, heritage, or cultural uses, residential developments, hotels, and master planning. Buildings from the NHS and the Department of Education for nurseries, schools, and university buildings featured prominently, as did court and police buildings from the Home Office and, after 2002, public and urban space review work became more prominent, such as the Winter Gardens in Sheffield (9.7)

Figure 9.7 Sheffield Winter Gardens, an early and prominent public realm scheme to be reviewed

Source: Matthew Carmona

and schemes to improve Manchester's Piccadilly Gardens and Trafalgar Square, as well as heritage schemes such as designs for Convoys Wharf (London) and the remodelling of St Martin-in-the-Fields. Industrial schemes became more prevalent later on, in particular for waste-to-energy proposals.

Box 9.2   Reviewing the Shard

From its inception, the commercial tower that now stands above London Bridge Station on London's South Bank was intended to be an ambitious and eye-catching building, and when built was the tallest building in Western Europe (9.8). Those involved with the property developer at the time recall how Irvine Sellar, who owned the site, had the appetite to invest in an ambitious scheme "for notoriety and for credibility" whilst Renzo Piano, the architect, was very aware of the historical importance of the scheme, taking inspiration "from the white stone towers of Wren's churches and the ships masted on the River Thames".

Given the importance of the scheme, it was submitted to four panel reviews between December 2000 and March 2003. The first meeting, by all accounts, was a nervous affair, and while CABE was meticulous about not involving Stuart Lipton, an active developer and CABE's chair, in the reviewing processes, even his presence in the offices made Irvine Sellar uncomfortable, which unsettled the presenting team. From CABE's perspective, this was a high-profile case and likely to be reported in the national press, so CABE's early institutional reputation was particularly invested in the review. Reportedly, commissioners were "particularly worried that if CABE gave full blooded support and then the scheme fell flat on its face, that would damage CABE's reputation".

In addition, the outcome of the review would necessarily affect CABE's relationships with significant organisations, particularly given the weight it would carry in the planning process. Ken Livingston, the incoming mayor of London, for example, "felt that London was in the doldrums and needed lifting out, and that required, amongst other things, a lot of inward investment inspired by world class architecture".

The panellists were not dazzled by the presenting 'starchitect' team, and across the four reviews, they delivered much the same type of critique as they did for other similar schemes. Certain critical aspects had not at first been worked up, and the review tackled these. CABE, for example, advised that a masterplan for the larger area should be commissioned since, as minuted: "The public realm proposals which have been developed for the uses for the lower five floors are diagrammatic at best; nor did we think that the proposal for public uses higher up the building (in itself welcome) was as yet convincing" (CABE 2000b). By the second review, Southwark was consulting with the mayor and was in discussions with the Shard team and Railtrack about producing a masterplan and Renzo Piano had worked up a Decalogue containing public realm and public access elements which subsequently formed the basis for a binding design agreement with the developer.

By the third review, however, the presentation (which had also been submitted to a public inquiry) no longer set the building in its master-planning context largely because the plans of Railtrack to redevelop London Bridge Station were moving forward at a much slower pace and no commitments could be made on such an uncertain basis.

Figure 9.8   The Shard as built, now a dominant feature of London's skyline, here as seen projecting behind the Tower of London World Heritage Site

Source: Matthew Carmona

At this and again in the final review letter, CABE argued for further public realm improvements even though much of what was being asked for remained outside the gift of the developer to deliver. For him, CABE's reviews that came down largely on the side of proposal, provided an on-going and significant crutch for the scheme as it moved through the planning processes, not least in helping to navigate the many objections on design received by the public inquiry, most notably from English Heritage.

In the words of a senior CABE advisor, the organisation focussed on "the totality of the scheme's relationship to London Bridge Station, the future development of London Bridge, how it hit the ground, how people flowed, and how it affected the way the wind would blow" (9.9). The perspective was distinct from that of English Heritage, which focussed on the protected view from Parliament Hill and the backdrop of St Paul's Cathedral, out of which the Shard now rises.

In addition to the direct effects on the scheme, the review also seemed to have more widely raised the bar within the Greater London Authority. As one insider confirmed, "One of the good things

Figure 9.9   The Shard hitting the ground, perhaps the major pre-occupation of CABE

Source: Matthew Carmona

that came out of this was that we moved from a very crude assessment of impact—taking photographs and sketching lines on it—into something much, much more sophisticated." The public disagreement with English Heritage also later helped the two organisations to strive to find common cause, one product being their joint *Guidance on Tall Buildings*, first published in 2003.

While a statutory body (after 2006), CABE was never a 'statutory consultee' within the planning system (see Chapter 4). It had a remit from the government, but could not oblige people to submit their schemes for review. There was, however, no difficulty in achieving large volumes of schemes to review, and in 2007/08 the organisation received 1,203 submissions, a high point (CABE 2008a). Most applications were initiated by architects, local authorities, and developers. There were occasionally community-led schemes, a large number of arts-related schemes funded by the Arts Council for England, and in later years focussed programmes of review for specific government departments. CABE responded by developing an efficient service with its own pool of reviewers and bespoke processes to cover the country.

Managing a Complex Process

In 1999, the first design review committee was formed of three members and over time a larger team grew, including employees and contracted panellists. By

2008, there were eighteen full-time staff equivalent working on design review and more than forty panellists, but despite this growth, CABE spent far less on design review than it did on other programmes. For instance, as shown in 9.10, the proportion of CABE's total expenditure for CABE Space, enabling and regional services were double those of design review as recorded in the accounts for both 2006/07 and 2007/08

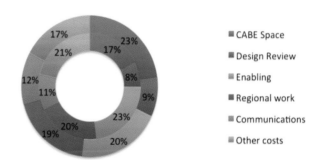

- CABE Space
- Design Review
- Enabling
- Regional work
- Communications
- Other costs

Figure 9.10   The proportion of expenditure on design review was relatively low, as compared with other programmes and typically under 10 per cent of CABE's total costs (inner ring 2006/07, outer ring 2007/08)

(although the regional budget included funds for design review conducted by CABE's regional partners).

In the first years of the design review service, senior panellists conducted all of the work under a single national design review panel (much as the RFAC had done). Subsequently appointments were made to build particular capacity, for instance in master planning, school design, and sustainability, and the pool of reviewers was constantly 'refreshed' for its balance of skills. Panellists needed to be independent, authoritative, and have recent experience in practice, and sometimes this presented challenges. It was not uncommon, for example, for panel members to cross the floor from panel to presenter or for senior experienced professionals to sit on the board of different development companies, which meant they had to declare a conflict of interest and remove themselves from the process.

CABE had the freedom to select cases for review, but the protocols hung on the concept of 'significance'. In a letter to all chief planning officers in 2001, the government stated that CABE should review projects that were significant, either because of their size, use, or location, or because they had an importance greater than their size, use, or location would suggest (Bowden 2001). There was no guidance on the criteria of 'use', but significant sites would include those which: "affect sensitive important views or are sited in such a way that they give rise to exceptional effects on their locality" (Hudson 2006); had regional or local significance; or had major public investment. Significant size was identified as including large buildings or clusters of buildings (public, commercial, and mixed uses); major infrastructure projects; major public realm works; and large-scale masterplans, policies, design codes, or other guidance. By the mid-2000s, reviews undertaken by virtue of the size of the scheme accounted for around a quarter of the total workload (CABE 2005f).

Since its selection of schemes indicated that they were 'significant' or in the national interest, CABE could appear political. For instance, reviews of casinos, health campuses, and retail-led regeneration all had their detractors and supporters. Sometimes this was avoided when cases were sifted out because their timing didn't allow CABE to have any impact, for example, if it was too late in the development process, or simply was so uninteresting or bad there was no point looking at them. CABE consistently advised that the

earlier it could view proposals, the more effective the process of review would be (CABE 2005f: 3).

CABE had three main formats for reviewing: full presentation panels; internal panels; and desktop review. For the more complex, costly, larger-scale, or higher-profile schemes, the designer or developer of a scheme would present at a full-panel review and this was generally the preferred format, even though it could be nerve-racking. As a representative from a high-profile architectural practice recalled, "There's a team that has been working day and night for a couple of weeks putting together a presentation; everybody's stressed because of the board and there's this sort of formality which makes it slightly unusual, for example they ask you to leave the room and then come back in for the verdict." Internal panels were conducted by a CABE panel, but without the presence of the applicant, as were desktop reviews, at which only the panel chair or deputy chair presided. These desktop reviews were common if a scheme was returning for a second review, but in 2005 came in for heavy criticism as too light a touch and lacking transparency (see Chapter 4). There was also a short-lived format referred to as a pin-up review, where schemes were exhibited for key panellists and commissioners without a presentation.

From 2005, thematic panels were introduced, and much of the work was transferred from the general committee to these more specialist panels. These covered: construction projects, retail, NHS, regeneration, master planning, public sector works, energy stations, development frameworks, cultural buildings, regional schemes, and eco-towns. In 2006, CABE set up a specialist panel for the London Olympics, in 2007, one for schools, in 2008, a Crossrail panel, and in 2009, two more panels to provide expertise for sustainability and infrastructure on behalf of the Infrastructure Planning Commission.

The Review and the Letter

Prior to any review, a CABE advisor would be allocated to a scheme, to liaise with the applicants, marshal the required materials, and, in most cases, to conduct a site visit. CABE gave a good deal of guidance concerning the expected types of materials and content for reviews, including with regard to visual aids, image boards, narratives from likely users, and protocol for the review

Design review also needed to be pragmatic as it needed to evaluate each case on its merits, bearing in mind the local development context and balancing optimising design potential with a sense of feasibility. For instance, records from a review of a proposed development on London's Hammersmith Road state that it was "perfectly acceptable to put a contemporary intervention onto the site. If, however, the local authority's view is that any development needs to bear more resemblance to the surroundings, the proposed façade retention is the least bad option" (CABE 2002h).

There was also the constant constraint of time, which meant that only a limited number of full-panel reviews could be conducted, leading to the introduction of internal and desktop formats. For those being reviewed in these ways, a perception existed that CABE was unduly "secretive" and "frustrating", as they could neither present to nor hear or clarify comments from the panel. Likewise some review panel chairs felt such approaches missed the chance to pose questions to applicants. These formats also required more preparation time on the part of CABE staff members, as they in effect had to present on behalf of the applicant. Full panels also had the advantage of giving applicants a sense of what to expect from the eventual letter that formally recorded CABE's advice—although this did not always work out and could lead to frustration (or relief) if the letter seemed to depart from the remembered conversation. In the words of a Greater London Authority member, "I used to come away from some of those meetings seething with anger . . . how can they be so bloody stupid! It's almost as if the voices of stupidity outweigh those of sanity, and then you get the letter and you think 'Oh, thank God; someone there has got their head screwed on.'"

Advisory letters covered a wide range of aspects from: professional competency; adequacy of the materials provided for review (both in terms of understanding the physical context and the proposed scheme); the process of design and development; an assessment of the design and advice on improving it; and advice on implementation. The design assessment could be very wide ranging, but often dealt with massing, social issues such as pedestrian access, and the relationship of a scheme to the local context, inevitably touching on planning. There were also 'X-factor' elements such as 'joie de vivre', 'innovation', elegance, and style on which

Figure 9.11 Norman Foster's Canary Wharf cross-rail station proposals were an early focus of the specialist panel, which concluded that the concept was confident and intelligent, but that the presentation was unclear and misleading

Source: Matthew Carmona

itself (CABE 2002f). In practice, submissions could include context analysis, site history, aerial photography, site plans, 3D drawings, models, and schematics, although sometimes it was a struggle to get good-quality materials and images often lacked clarity and were occasionally misleading (9.11).

The review process itself was intended to ensure a level of detachment between the presenters and the panel in order to retain objectivity, and each review included a closed discussion in order to agree on the key points that would be reflected in the review letter. Writing the letter also relied on having an exceptional individual to chair the meeting. As a long-standing head of design review put it, "Without a good chair at design review, the panel will not flourish, so it relies on getting all the comments from the panel and writing down everything that's said during the course of the meeting and then developing a really clear . . . but not necessarily a detailed, line of argument."

advice could be given, and letters also recommended, when appropriate, where design teams should have regard to CABE practice guidance, most particularly the *Guidance on Tall Buildings*.

The tone of letters also quickly evolved from the format inherited from the RFAC (see 4.11), and while maintaining strong statements about its core recommendations, its language was becoming more conciliatory and measured. For example: "We recognise our comments will be disappointing to the client and to the design team who have clearly put a lot of thought and work into the current proposal. Our advice, nevertheless, is that a fresh start is needed if the aims of the project are to be brought to a successful conclusion. CABE would be happy to advise further on how this might be done" (CABE 2001d).

After the events of 2004 and 2005 (see Chapter 4), there were calls for greater accountability for CABE's processes and particularly with regards to design review. While closed panel deliberations were a key means of drawing together independent expertise and would continue to be used for most of CABE's reviews, there were moves towards opening up reviews to public scrutiny and increasing the transparency of the design review process (CABE 2006c). Several reviews were filmed in 2006, and over the next two years, 'open access reviews' were piloted which were open to the public or invited observers. By 2008, there were performance targets to "increase openness of design review by continuing to enable appropriate groups and individuals to observe" (CABE 2009b). These, however, were minor changes, and broadly design review remained the most consistent tool as regards the manner in which it was undertaken and the position of the service within the organisation—at the forefront.

Afterwards

While CABE had no means of enforcing its advice, it had enormous power through its reputation within the industry and influence within the planning process. Importantly, it made its advice public through publishing its letters online, which were also copied to all parties and released to the press; except where a scheme had not yet been submitted as a planning application (in which case they were made available only to English Heritage and the relevant local planning authority).

The one notable exception to these informal powers of review were schools being built under the Building Schools for the Future programme from 2009 to 2010, which were formally required to reach a minimum design standard in order to secure funding. This was assessed through the dedicated schools panel.

Despite its limited powers, there was evidence from the outset that returning proposals generally took on board CABE's comments (CABE 2001a, 2001c), including some high-profile cases where aspirations were significantly raised, such as BDP's scheme for Liverpool One (CABE 2001e) (9.12). Recording this sort of impact was an important part of the work, primarily because CABE had to monitor conflicts of interest and track progress against performance targets (see Chapter 4).

Because CABE could not require an organisation to take its advice on board, for important schemes it instead pursued compliance in other ways. Simply repeating comments that had not been taken on board was rarely successful, and so in such cases CABE sought dialogue, particularly when a returning proposal was thought to be worse than it had been at an earlier panel. CABE did not shy away from controversy or from hard-hitting critique, and only very occasionally stood back from expressing a view, for example on some public art where judgements could never be more than subjective (CABE 2002i). There

Figure 9.12 Liverpool One retail development, a transformative regeneration scheme in the heart of Liverpool which CABE was keen to ensure functioned as an integrated and connected part of the city

Source: Matthew Carmona

were also instances when CABE was more nurturing or handholding, offering multiple reviews or triaging cases to its enabling services.

Sometimes complaints were received about how CABE's advice could vary on the same scheme from one review to the next, or between advice received from CABE's design review and enabling teams. Most often this related to a perceived inconsistency where panellists changed between reviews, despite the unwritten principle expressed by a panel chair that "Fundamental views expressed at a first review could not be overturned by subsequent reviews." CABE itself recognised the inconsistency and tried to deal with it by limiting the number of panel chairs and monitoring for recommendations that "went against CABE policy" (CABE 2007h). Schools had the most rigid application of consistency measures, and in 2007, the schools panel even developed a scoring mechanism for this purpose.[5] CABE's enabling staff were also told that they should advise clients head on that a successful enabling process would not automatically lead to a good design review.

Overall, CABE provided a design review service that was generally (if not universally) respected and that had a positive impact on the quality of development and aspirations for design in developments across England (9.13). Yet the national provision of review had limitations since the workload was extremely high, and CABE did not always have suitable expertise or knowledge of local areas, explaining why CABE was so interested in setting up regional panels to conduct design review. Although monitoring consistency in the quality of advice from external panels was much harder, these practices were both effective and popular and nationally did much to increase the capacity to conduct design review (CABE 2010f). For the ABECs that hosted regional panels (see Chapter 8), the advice CABE provided on the setting up and management of panels, including on: funding, staffing and administration, selecting panel members, conflicts of interest, the role of the chair, training, site visits, conducting meetings, write-up and follow-up, and on confidentiality and publicity (CABE 2006a), was invaluable.

Certification

CABE worked on its two certification schemes together with external partners from early on. BfL was initially operated through a panel chaired by Terry

Figure 9.13 Lottery-funded arts and culture projects were a mainstay of CABE design reviews including (i) Nottingham Contemporary (ii) Hepworth Wakefield

Source: Matthew Carmona

Farrell reviewing schemes against the so-called BfL 20, with Wayne Hemmingway taking over as chair in 2003. As discussed in Chapter 7, BfL had originally been devised as a web-based platform to share best practice case studies in housing design from the United Kingdom and abroad, and the BfL partners used these studies and the objectives set out in government guidance on design and the planning system, *By Design* (DETR & CABE 2000), and other key urban design texts to produce criteria to judge the quality of new housing development. Cleverly, they packaged these under their compact set of just twenty questions, providing a manageable basis for the certification scheme (Box 9.3).[6] All schemes achieving fourteen or more out of the twenty received a silver or gold standard (9.14).

Figure 9.14 Building for Life gold standard on site plaque

Source: Matthew Carmona

Box 9.3 Building for Life Standards

On the occasion of the fortieth anniversary of the Civic Trust Awards, and reflecting on the dearth of housing winners over the years, the director of the Civic Trust, Mike Gwilliam, approached the Home Builders Federation (HBF) with the idea of showcasing the best new housing. CABE was quickly brought into the discussions, and the idea evolved into a search for good cases that could serve as examples of what was possible. In particular, the aim was to spotlight high-quality but 'ordinary' schemes that did not have the advantages of exceptional circumstances such as Poundbury (much discussed at the time) with its particular stylistic emphasis and royal patronage. Although the cases were swiftly put together, they offered a diversity of location and market profile.

The diversity of the BfL consortium led to a new approach to certification. The Civic Trust's involvement brought a more user-led evaluation, and CABE appreciated that "it brought the non-architect view and kept the whole thing grounded". CABE's contribution was to provide an early focus for writing business cases and working up the basket of case studies, the web site, and creating an expert panel. Later on, when it had recruited its own housing specialist, it provided leadership to the initiative as well as the significant funding without which BfL would not have survived.

While establishing a fixed set of criteria risked a degree of reductionism, it also offered a user-friendly tool. It was useful also for local authorities as "a hook to hang a discussion on", whilst many of the case studies were chosen to 'speak' to a wider audience beyond designs specialists. In these ways, it was hoped the initiative would exert pressure on housebuilders in a manner that awards could not, with their focus on the exceptional. In the words of a commissioner with responsibility for housing, "Government expected CABE to have some influence, and the important thing about Building for Life was that it sought to join with the industry as a way of achieving that." Hence the importance of having the HBF as a committed partner. Design for Homes also played an important role in defining the criteria and providing coordination in the early days.

While BfL might have been easy to use, promoting it was initially a struggle. As one of the creators admitted: "We just never communicated clearly enough that, actually, there is a benefit to design, which is that schemes built to the standard will give least grief for the people living there and therefore, potentially, highest values for re-sell." The BfL awards did not help in this respect (see Chapter 8). They were not originally intended to be part of the scheme, and the distinction between these and the standard (certification) was not well understood. Some award judges were expecting more outstanding schemes, and the winning schemes did not always obviously convey the benefits of applying the BfL criteria. A good example was when the deputy prime minister's communications team pushed for him to be photographed in front of the BfL Gold Award–winning Abode scheme from Proctor and Matthews, and, as one CABE employee described it: "So, we raced over there, did this launch where people like Prescott were very excited to be photographed against something that looked like it was very much of the twenty-first century, and there were lots of press releases put out, . . . but the houses we were standing next to, which were selling at £430,000, had actually cost £450,000 to build—which was absolute suicide for the [BfL] message."

The difficulties were compounded by a low familiarity with the different market contexts, and by the need to peg the standards so that it was not impossible for the volume housebuilders to have their scheme represented. To quote the CABE commissioner responsible for housing, "Warm words didn't translate into very much action on the ground, particularly outside London." The working practices of developers posed the greatest challenge, and many involved admit that the public realm was often not given enough priority and was the weakest part of many high-ranking schemes. BfL was on the edge of two stools, fully connected neither to the market nor to social value.

Despite the challenges of creating meaningful categories and communicating the value of BfL to all involved, the programme garnered a good deal of backing and a simplified version, Building for Life 12, continues to be used today (see Chapter 5).

CABE heavily promoted BfL and by 2005, BfL applications had already outstripped the service-level targets, with sixty applications rather than the expected twenty-five, which led to the need to train more assessors and ensure assessments were broadly comparable (see Chapter 7). Through these means, BfL quickly became recognised as the industry standard amongst volume housebuilders, housing associations, and planning departments. So whilst BfL was initially an entirely voluntary scheme, by 2005, it had begun to be adopted as standard by public and private organisations, as well as being incorporated into the development plans of about eighty-five local authorities. In 2007, the Housing Corporation began to use BfL as a part of its funding criteria and included it wholesale in its *Design and Quality Standards*. In 2008, the criteria were refreshed, and (reflecting the poor showing of design in the housing audits) local authorities were required by government to use them to report on design quality via their development plan Annual Monitoring Reports,[7] and as core output indicators that were part of the mandatory reporting procedure back to DCLG. This took the scheme to new levels despite the decline in the national housing market.

The Green Flag certification scheme had a longer antecedence, being run by the Civic Trust from the 1990s with the first award given in 1997. When, in 2003, CABE Space became the main funding partner and began to seek to increase its use, this, alongside strong political support for the scheme nationally, drove increased uptake amongst local authorities. In 1997, only seven sites had met the criteria, but seven years on, 182 Green Flag awards were given. Like BfL, as the Green Flag scheme grew, it required, and CABE delivered, a large pool of assessors, although this led to difficulties ensuring consistent application of the criteria. As a report on the subject noted: "Given the influx of new judges and the indication that this has led to a lowering of marks awarded, it would be beneficial to provide some element of checking for consistency with a limited system of informal checks, probably carried out by one or two experienced judges" (Wood 2004).

Around 2006, coinciding with a change of leadership at CABE Space (with Sarah Gaventa taking the helm), there was also a change in the emphasis in the work of CABE Space, from an almost exclusive concern with parks to streets and other public spaces as well. As Gaventa argued: "I was appointed to move CABE Space into the broader public realm. CABE's focus will no longer be on parks" (Appleby 2006), at least not on parks alone. Nevertheless, CABE continued to support and expand the Green Flag work, and by 2007, CABE reported that "more than seven out of ten local authorities employed the nationally recognised Green Flag criteria in the management of their green spaces" (CABE 2007b). CABE's involvement with the scheme continued and only ended around the time when the Civic Trust went into receivership (2009) and the Keep Britain Tidy campaign took over management of the scheme.

Certification programmes needed to make a strong statement about quality, which was most effective when the principles were understood and considered part of professional practice. For BfL, it helped that the standards represented the centrepiece of a wider programme where other tools drew on the certification programme, most notably the awards, case study library, guidance, campaigning, and CABE's housing audits. The awards, in particular, provided a ready source of headline material for media coverage, whilst high-level events focussed on design achievements.

The number of local authorities achieving at least one Green Flag Award was included as a performance indicator for CABE in 2003/04 (CABE 2004d), and the year after these were extended to include the total number of green flags, and the numbers of local authorities using Green Flag as a management tool. The number of schemes reviewed for a Building for Life standard was also added (CABE 2005c). Green Flags as a management tool remained as the only Green Flags indicator until 2007/08, when it was dropped,[8] and the BfL indicator mutated to become the numbers of local authorities signed up to use BfL criteria to assess planning applications, and then, the following year, the numbers of trained BfL assessors (CABE 2008a, 2009b). Both schemes were clearly critical to CABE, but exactly how their success (and that of CABE) should be judged remained a moving target.

Competitions

In its early years, competitions with a focus on rethinking particular generic 'types' of development were employed on a number of occasions. In its founding year, preliminary work on the Neighbourhood Nurseries initiative (launched in April 2001) eventually led to conceptual designs for three sites in Bury, Sheffield, and Bexley. In 2002, the Designs on Democracy call asked entrants to 'reinvent' the town

hall, with a focus on Bradford, Stockport, and Letchworth town halls;[9] in 2003, the DfES asked CABE to organise an international competition and development briefs procedure for the commissioning of multidisciplinary design teams to develop exemplar school designs for six secondary and six primary schools, and in 2005, the Anglo-French housing initiative (see earlier) was launched. Up to 2005, CABE was also regularly involved in competitions for particular sites as part of its enabling function (see Chapter 10) and continued to work with councils as well as arts organisations. In December 2007, CABE even put on an exhibition at New London Architecture (NLA) with the title 'Competitions Work' to showcase this aspect of its work. On the website CABE argued:

> Competitions attract keen design teams and can unlock underused talent in big architecture practices. While in Europe competitions are routinely used for smaller-scale, everyday projects, in the UK they tend to be used for large, landmark projects. Opportunities to get the highest-quality designs for a whole range of projects—big and small—may therefore be being lost.[10]

Yet, despite this seeming enthusiasm, in its later years, this aspect of its work, which was never very prominent in the public eye, fell somewhat out of favour. CABE's declining interest in competitions was illustrated most emphatically through its involvement in Europan, the biennial competition for architects under forty years of age concerned with the design of innovative housing schemes across Europe; a key feature of which was that projects should actually be built. CABE was late to this party and first became involved in Europan 8 (2005) after the competition had already been running for sixteen years. Nevertheless, with support from DCLG, English Partnerships, and the Housing Corporation CABE identified three UK sites for participants in 2005 and followed this with a further three for Europan 9 in 2007. However, the competition struggled to gain a foothold in the United Kingdom, despite its success on the continent with only two winning schemes selected for UK sites in 2007 and just one winning scheme actually receiving planning permission in the time that CABE was involved. Whilst CABE remained officially involved, it did not put any sites forward for

Europan 10, blaming lack of interest from potential site providers, and pulled out altogether prior to Europan 11 (*Architects' Journal* 2010). This marked CABE's final significant involvement with competitions as a tool.

Where used, the involvement of CABE generally helped to demystify the competitions process, which was then seen as a useful means of encouraging transparency in procurement and of dealing with judgements that could otherwise appear subjective. The enabling role more generally could place CABE staff in an awkward position when involved in selecting teams to design a scheme (see Chapter 10), and in such cases competitions offered a way out as they constructed a demonstrable threshold of design quality that client teams could consult on and agree with CABE in advance. For example, in relation to the Canada Water Masterplan, it had not been possible to come to a judgement about which development team to select based on the proposals submitted. Creatively, the enabler proposed to the London Borough of Southwark that they "long list the 12 submissions down to eight and add a new requirement that each consortia needs to demonstrate their design approach against agreed criteria".[11] This led to a competition specifically designed to improve the selection of teams, by offering clarity and comparability through design (9.15).

In practice, competitions could entail several rounds of selections, which typically began with the rationalisation of the entrants through basic team

Figure 9.15 Canada Water Library, a critical component of the final masterplan

Source: Matthew Carmona

requirements in order to save time and effort on both sides. For instance, the Designs for Democracy competition was a two-stage call. In the first instance, brief expressions of interest from architect-led design teams were evaluated against the goal of creating 'accessible and welcoming civic places' such as public meeting rooms and debating spaces. Successful applicants from the first stage were then worked up into more comprehensive design proposals for the second round.

Nationally, competitions remained a little-used tool during the CABE years, and enablers working on competitions in England had to spend a good deal of time bringing non-design partners up to speed about their uses, utility, and pitfalls. At the same time, CABE staff working internationally (on Europan) found relations difficult and complex and the whole process protracted. Both experiences go some way to explaining why competitions as a tool never really gained significant traction in the CABE toolbox. Indeed competitions was the only tool to be used significantly less, rather than more, as the CABE experiment unfolded.

When Should Evaluation Tools Be Used?

Although CABE's evaluation tools remained largely 'informal' in their status (see Chapter 2), they nevertheless offered a range of systemised means to evaluate design quality which, they argued, were objective, robust, and holistic in their scope, and therefore could be trusted. Because, as compared to the previous tools, evaluation grappled with real developments, it also brought the governance of design into the field, with a direct and tangible impact on actual projects and places. In effect, these tools led to judgements, good or bad, about design propositions, and by implication also passed judgements, right or wrong, on the performance of the teams responsible for them, with the inevitable backlash and controversy this sometimes caused. Moreover, it did so in a variety of ways: sometimes formative, feeding into and informing the design process; and sometimes summative, evaluating the outputs from design (9.16).

It was in relation to its evaluation tools that CABE was best known, and arguably these tools helped to build CABE's reputation, but also, particularly in the case of design review, a constituency of dissenters who

Figure 9.16 Typology of evaluation

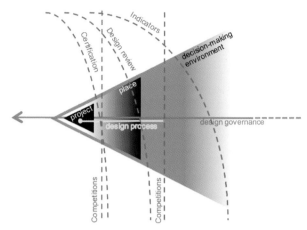

Figure 9.17 Evaluation tools in the design governance field of action

felt that 'official' judgement on design without recourse to either a democratic process or an obvious means to challenge decisions was always going to be problematic (see Chapter 4). Of course these concerns were nothing new, and whilst CABE continued to conduct design review as its 'headline' service throughout its existence, this chapter demonstrates how it also found other means to evaluate design through the use of indicators, certification, and competitions in (arguably) a less confrontational and more encouraging and aspirational manner.

By these multiple means, CABE developed its own distinctive blend of approaches, where evaluations were not just a means to measure performance but were also a way to shape urban design throughout the country, and were often part of larger packages of tools that approached the governance of design from different directions. Whilst competitions remained a relatively underutilised tool in the CABE armoury—perhaps because CABE itself was not a commissioner of projects, but also because of the inevitable costs and uncertainties associated with such processes—indicators, and particularly certification, were heavily relied on. They were also key means through which the organisation could project its aspirations for design and provided ready means through which CABE could find common cause with allied organisations.

Placing the evaluation tools in the design governance field of action from Chapter 1 (9.17) shows that evaluation tools are primarily focussed on making evaluations during or immediately following the design process. The exception are indicators whose criteria can

be used to inform the design process but also, like the Spaceshaper, to better understand the context within which design occurs. Informal design review can happen at different stages of the design process but arguably, to be most useful, should occur early on and at a time when the outcomes from the review can still be used to inform the evolution of the design. However, reviews may, and often do, occur at a later stage, as an informal feed into the formal process of determining planning consent. Certification, by contrast, will need to happen a little later when the design is settled and when a final judgement can be made on its merits and on whether it has met the requirements for certification. This might even occur post-completion. Finally, competitions by their very nature occur at the start of the design process, although this may be at the start of a larger urban design process focussed on the whole place (e.g. a masterplan), or with a more narrow focus on a particular project (typically a building), or perhaps both.

Notes

1. Once CABE had a critical mass of trained users, a one-off £300 fee was introduced and the training programme slowed down.
2. See www.designsoutheast.org/supporting-skills/space shaper-facilitator-training/
3. This is not the case with all certification schemes which often operate on the basis of submitted materials only (see Chapter 2).
4. At the time of writing it is still in use at www.dqi.org. uk/ [last accessed 24 April 2015].
5. Each panel member could give 0–4 points, with 10 panel members producing a total of 40 points: Excellent

(36–40), Good (30–35), Not yet good enough (25–29), Mediocre (25–29), Poor (0–15). In 2009/2010 there was a revised scoring system with new ratings of 'very good', 'pass', 'unsatisfactory' and 'poor'.

6. While the short set of questions was a handy simplified tool, in practice the criteria needed expansion and explanation and CABE commissioned a BfL guide (CABE 2005g). This fully explained the criteria and their application and referenced relevant government policies to give the guide greater legitimacy. 20,000 digital and print copies were distributed.

7. Annual Monitoring Reports were a requirement on local authorities introduced in the 2004 Planning and Compulsory Purchase Act.

8. As, a little later, were Green Flags from the CABE portfolio.

9. This competition was organised with the Design Council. It was one of very few collaborations between the two organisations prior to their merger in 2011.

10. http://webarchive.nationalarchives.gov.uk/2011011 8095356/http://www.cabe.org.uk/news/new-exhibition-for-design-competitions

11. Project Notes from a CABE enabler, September 2002.

CHAPTER 10

The Assistance Tools

The hands-on direct assistance CABE provided was perhaps the most directly 'interventionalist' aspect of its operations, and therefore the most immediately impactful, but it was also one of the least well-known and (arguably) underappreciated parts of its operations. In the context of English design governance, this work set the organisation decisively apart from previous attempts to influence the quality of design from the national stage. Two key tools are included here—first, direct financial assistance through the making of grants and direct resourcing of local design governance activities; second, the hands-on enabling of local design and design governance processes. This chapter is in three parts covering the why, how, and when of assistance, aka the purposes of these tools, the processes involved in their delivery, and when in the design governance field of action they should be used.

Why Engage in Assistance Activities?

Financial Assistance

Depending on the nature of the financial assistance offered, the goals were twofold: first, to facilitate the delivery of locally responsive design governance processes across the country, and second (albeit much less often), to directly fund particular design-led development/regeneration processes.

Resourcing Organisations

Taking the former first, by resourcing the work of other bodies with allied agendas, CABE could reach out to local areas across England and develop deeper networks and engagement with design than would otherwise be possible. This activity primarily focussed on establishing a network of local and regional built environment centres through a Regional Funding Programme (RFP) which aimed "to maximise opportunities for public involvement in issues relating to the built environment" (CABE 2003c). Through this means, CABE was able to provide significant financial support to bodies across the country, in particular to the not-for-profit Architecture and Built Environment Centres (ABECs) already discussed in Chapter 8, and to a few organisations with a national remit, notably the Architecture Centre Network (ACN) with its remit to coordinate the ABECs, and to the RIBA Trust.

As stated in the guidance for regional funding applications, the objective of CABE's regional policy was "to ensure that CABE's endeavours will lead to a significant improvement in the design of the built environment throughout every English region", and this was to be "led by energetic and confident local government, flourishing public debate in all our towns and cities, and delivered by skilled teams of local professionals" (CABE 2002c). To this end, CABE stated that it did "not intend to establish its own network of regional offices to achieve this objective. Instead we work in partnership with other bodies" (CABE 2003c). Consequently, CABE targeted its limited resources on existing locally or regionally based organisations and, only where none already existed, did it finance and support new ventures.

As well as representing a pragmatic response to the lack of resources, CABE believed that this form of outreach work could be delivered much more efficiently through external parties closer to its constituency of users, at a much lower cost than CABE developing its own regional infrastructure. Indeed, by

2010, it could claim that "Our regional funding programme has to date reached more than 600,000 people at an average cost of £2.65" (CABE 2010a: 11). Moreover, because much of this funding was long term, it had the potential to facilitate longer-standing and potentially more fruitful relationships. CABE regional coordinator Annie Hollobone described this mission in a press release: "We want everyone to know that architecture centres are places that are easy to access, offer interesting and enjoyable activities and are on their doorsteps."

Regional fund grants also enabled CABE to deliver 'quick wins' by leveraging the work of others. This work was often quite ad hoc and included education workshops; exhibitions; lecture/seminar programmes; programmes of visits to buildings or places; publications (including web resources); production of educational resources; and community workshops. With matched funding from CABE, new areas of activity could be easily initiated, requiring much less in-house preparatory work from CABE and speeding up promising initiatives wherever they occurred (CABE 2007i; Annabel Jackson Associates 2007).

Grants to Projects

Coming to the second financial assistance goal, one final but extremely significant funding programme, Sea Change, focussed directly on the delivery of projects. Over three years from 2008 to 2011, the Sea Change programme utilised £45 million of ring-fenced Department of Culture, Media & Sport (DCMS) funding for capital grants to seaside resorts, with the intention of stimulating urban renewal via cultural projects. CABE managed this £15 million annual investment, steering it towards activities that complemented wider regeneration programmes in those localities. As Sarah Gaventa, the head of CABE Space and leader of the programme explained, "We've favoured the light-footed and sustainable things [for Sea Change grants], which can just wake everyone up, lift the spirits and encourage further investment" (Christiansen 2010). In reality, CABE's role was more strategic than simple distribution of funds and included providing advice, managing the decision-making process, and seeking out partnerships and other sources of funding to complement the initiative and further support the wider redevelopment of the selected areas.

Figure 10.1 Sea Change granted £1 million for a range of projects on the Bexhill seafront, including creating a new series of seafront shelters and improving the setting around the De La Warr Pavilion

Source: Alastair Hazell

Whilst CABE did not deliver or even design any of the projects itself, the initiative represented a significant departure for CABE's operations in its sheer scale (larger than CABE's annual budget), but also because it placed CABE in the position of directly funding actual interventions on the ground (10.1). Unlike, for example, the Homes and Communities Agency (HCA) or English Heritage, CABE was not generally a funding agency of this type and this was the only time CABE got involved in directly funding projects. It nevertheless illustrates the potential of a more directly interventionalist type of financial assistance than the funding of third-party organisations, which was the normal practice at CABE.

Enabling

With the possible exception of directly funding projects, enabling was the most direct tool in CABE's 'informal' toolbox through its targeting of resources directly at engaging in particular development projects or place-making episodes. The unpublished Enabling Handbook (CABE 2005i: 5) listed five main areas for advice:

1. Helping the clients establish their aspirations in terms of design and function.
2. Ensuring a fair and competitive process for appointing consultants and partners contributing to the preparation of design briefs.

3. Assisting in the selection process for architects, design teams, or private sector partners.

4. Discussing the implications for design of procurement routes, for example PFI (Private Finance Initiative), partnering, and others.

5. Having an on-going role in briefing design teams, and reviewing progress of design proposals against the brief.

In fact, CABE enablers assisted on all of the strategic, management, operational, and technical aspects of developments, from financial arrangements, to bidding processes, recruitment, scheduling, drafting briefs, creating artwork, giving presentations, and with mentoring and monitoring design work and local design governance activities.

CABE constantly described this work as 'technical guidance' or 'support' with the expertise provided by commissioners and staff and a larger number of senior professionals who were contracted as enablers that could be called on as and when needed. Together they offered a significant pool of experience and "a guiding hand to the inexperienced client" (CABE 2001a), the overarching goal being to up-skill the sector and empower decision-making focussed on the delivery of high-quality design.

The enabling programme existed in an era of significant capital investment by the public sector,

Figure 10.2 CABE provided client advice to forty acute, community, and mental health trusts on 100 capital projects between 2001 and 2010, including working with the Lewisham Primary Care Trust to run a design competition for the Kaleidoscope centre for children and young people

Source: Matthew Carmona

often made via PFI contracts with their inbuilt challenges for those interested in delivering design quality (see Chapters 3 and 4). For instance, the twelve major hospital projects CABE enabled prior to 2006 had a total value of £3.086 million.[1] The scale of these public investments meant that the programme mainly targeted public sector initiatives (10.2), although on occasion there was involvement with private sector projects (CABE 2002a). It was also extremely closely tied to delivering the government's agenda and in particular the ambitious development goals of the Department for Communities and Local Government (DCLG). In the words of Richard Simmons, CABE's chief executive, "In the next 5 years we need at least 1000 skilled professionals capable of leading Sustainable Communities projects" (Housebuilder 2005).

Supporting the Good Client

Enablers aimed, in particular, to improve the performance of people in a client role, namely those who were 'purchasing' or who 'owned' the developments. While the public sector clients became the central focus, the private sector was also centrally involved as key actors within the development proposals, often designing and delivering the projects being enabled. As one enabler noted in relation to a new bridge in Torquay Harbour: "I was able to support LDA[2] and English Heritage in their preference for a less obtrusive structure. I was also able to add CABE's weight to the need for high quality appropriate detailing and the expectation that this would fit in with and complement the emerging design strategy for the Public Realm."[3]

CABE offered enabling widely, but there were some caveats around who the recipients of enabling should be. In particular the Commission sought to target enabling where there was a gap and if it thought there was potential to build a long-term shared understanding with the organisation(s) concerned. It suggested: "The project enabling panel offers advice to clients who aspire to quality but want help" (CABE 2002a: 7), so where a suitable advisor or consultant was already in place CABE would not provide enabling. Clients' skills and attitude were essential to the success of the enabling work.

Within these parameters, enablers provided bespoke advice to an impressive range of projects, from smaller one-off architectural schemes such as the Centre for Children's Books, Newcastle upon Tyne, to strategic visioning and spatial plans with multiple planning authorities. The latter, more strategic forms of enabling encompassed:

- Advising on how to ensure that regional and local policies reinforce and deliver quality.

- Assisting local authorities and other delivery vehicles (e.g. Housing Market Renewal Pathfinders (Box 10.1), Urban Development Corporations, Urban Regeneration Companies) with the development of design quality aspirations and their capacity to deliver design quality on the ground.

- Advising on how to work with development partners to ensure design quality is delivered.

- Managing forums to discuss and disseminate best practice.

Box 10.1   Enabling: North Staffordshire Housing Market Renewal

The experience of Housing Market Renewal (HMR) enabling in North Staffordshire demonstrates the complex and deeply embedded nature of CABE's involvement with the delivery of design excellence within government programmes. In 2002, the HMR Pathfinders initiative tasked partnerships[4] with local regeneration, and allocated £25 million (ODPM 2002) to nine areas in England. The Midlands, it was argued,[5] needed to tackle decaying and underused housing stock that had resulted from the flagging local economy (10.3i). The specific challenge facing North Staffordshire, as characterised by the local MP, was "how to remediate land and

properties and recycle and . . . recreate what was once an industrial place".

While investment in regeneration was extremely welcome in North Staffordshire, local designers were concerned about the interventions from 'the centre', seeing the overall HMR strategy as poorly aligned with their complex local needs. In particular, the general assumption that there was an oversupply of housing in the area was not always correct, with local suspicions quickly building around the characterisation of the HMR programme as a means of managing decline, removing housing, and erasing local communities, rather than investing in them.

Figure 10.3   (i) Rundown and abandoned Travers Street in Stoke on Trent and (ii) neighbouring Port Street, which provided a focus for regeneration efforts with its distinctive character rooted in the historic local pottery industry

Source: Matthew Carmona

In addition to the local politics, North Staffordshire had an extremely fragmented spatial development form. In the words of a Midlands architect, "You could clearly see sporadic pockets of demolition, apparently uncoordinated and certainly with no evident follow-on strategy." These deep-seated concerns had made local partners defensive and unduly focussed on 'their own turf', rather than on the larger potential. The fear was that properties that were sound or had local value might be demolished unnecessarily, with all the community erasure that would entail.

To address the HMR brief generally, CABE formed a team of staff members consisting of a programme manager and a number of advisors, one of whom was tasked with coordinating and dispatching suitable enablers to work directly with local actors in North Staffordshire. The elements of CABE's work varied, but, in order to effectively provide assistance, an essential first step was producing a strategic approach to its HMR activities and sharing it across the Pathfinders. A key dimension of this was encouragement for joint working, which in North Staffordshire meant directing the enabling team to work closely with the two councils of Newcastle-under-Lyme and Stoke-on-Trent, and with Urban Vision, the local ABEC.

This networking task involved linking people to other Pathfinder areas, as well as within the Pathfinder team, and CABE held a workshop and an overseas visit to a comparable post-industrial area, Emsher Park in Germany. Both events provided fresh input into the thinking around the issues, and Urban Vision played the critical role of local intermediary partner between CABE and the Pathfinders, with one foot in each camp.

This closer working facilitated by CABE resulted in shared strategies, such as a masterplan for the Middleport and Burslem area, and produced shared guidance, such as development briefs, which were drawn up for individual sites, including the revitalisation of Port Street (10.3ii). Through such means, specialist skills were injected in a more coordinated and targeted way, and CABE was able to successfully provide a space for negotiations between conflicting local parties and help to create a shared vision with a good degree of longevity. Aspirations were raised and a greater appreciation of the value of urban design engendered. As one local authority officer commented, "The atmosphere that was created by CABE ensured that I managed, at one point, to have not one but two urban designers on my staff."

This sort of success was critical for CABE as it had put its reputation on the line through association with a mistrusted government programme. Ultimately, however, these wins were extremely long in the making and, whilst CABE's role is widely appreciated amongst those involved, the initiative never reached its full potential following the withdrawal of national support from much urban regeneration activity from 2010.

Typically, however, CABE enablers helped clients to establish key urban design priorities and to think through critical factors such as the range of skills required in advance of investing in their projects. As with design review, enabling aimed to assist clients early in the development process, but, unlike design review, this often preceded the production of any actual scheme and frequently focussed on process. The enabler for an Arts Council England–funded Chinese Arts Centre in Manchester, for instance, recorded being involved in critical early work "establishing priorities for expenditure, including seeking cost efficiencies".[6]

Encouraging Culture Change

CABE enabling was about more than getting clients to 'perform'. More fundamentally, by honing the skills of those responsible, enabling hoped to deliver the capacity for the better management of development and design in the built environment. Enablers were expected to "encourage the project team to raise their sights and give the client team confidence to reject lowest common denominator solutions" (CABE 2006c: 2). It aimed to steer the hearts of the clients, as well as their minds, towards a long-term design-led approach to development: "to provoke interest and ambition, to inspire new ways of thinking and to promote the positive benefits of change". As an enabling manager explained, "The role of enablers and the enabling staff team was often to challenge, to offer different perspectives, new ways of thinking and working at a stage before a design is even commissioned" (CABE 2006f).

Given the public-oriented, relational, and somewhat missionary nature of the task, the role of the enabler was substantively different to that of other contractors. Technically speaking, enablers were not employees, agents, or partners in a joint venture, neither were they acting on behalf of CABE or the public sector clients (CABE 2010b); instead, they were independent advisors on behalf of CABE. As the enabler handbook recorded: "Any advice and support should be given on an impartial basis, in line with CABE's objectives, with the Enabler directly answerable to the Head of Enabling" (CABE 2002a: 13). The enablers' role differed from consultancy work not only in terms of fees (CABE paid a standardised rate to enablers for a service that was free to the client[7]), but also because it involved targeted interventions aimed at skills transfer focussed on the fundamental decisions of organisations. This was a brief and time-limited injection of expertise that, it was hoped, would leave a legacy of confidence so that the client (or at least the team) would not need to call on CABE for enabling again. From CABE's perspective, there was also a hope that a channel would be opened to CABE's other services.

Enabling was also valuable for CABE's broader mission. Through the enabling pool CABE broadened its collective skillset, and enabling work uncovered lessons that could be shared and aid the development of other programmes. In its Corporate Strategy for 2002–5, the Commission stated, "CABE will consolidate the lessons learnt in the first two years of its enabling programme and disseminate them widely" (CABE 2002b: 7), for example, through its published case studies, many of which originated in enabling (see chapter 7). Enabling thus became an important tool for the Commission, honing its understanding of current practice—"the extent to which we can learn about a project or process, to help other clients in the future" (CABE 2006f)—and giving a grounded view of national priorities based on grass-roots experience.

How Were Assistance Activities Delivered?

Financial Assistance

Early on, financial assistance from CABE mainly targeted arts-related initiatives such as the Royal Society of Art's (RSA) Art for Architecture exhibition. From there, grants gradually extended to a wider range of ad hoc projects with the regional budget established in 2002 allowing CABE's financial assistance to become more structured in support of the ambition to build a network of local activities, skills, networking, and capacity around the country. With this also came the emphasis on complete geographical coverage via the ABECs (CABE 2008e), with funding increasing from year to year in CABE's growing years, justified on the basis of the outreach potential of such funding right down to the level of local communities (CABE 2004h).

In the first two years of the Regional Funding Programme, CABE gave £1.2 million in grant funding to help establish thirteen centres (CABE 2003c), and this increased to £1.45 million for eighteen ABECs across the years 2004/05 and 2005/06. In 2006/07 and 2007/08, CABE total grants of £1.86 million funded nineteen ABECs (plus the ACN), and from this high point the same sum was given in 2008/09–2009/10 (10.4), but now across twenty-two organisations (CABE 2011d). In 2010/11, the funding fell back to £1,271,015 and vanished (along with CABE) the following year. Prior to that, however, the steady growth of CABE's external partner funding streams was fuelled by enthusiasm from the DCMS, which continually pushed an expanded programme with more money and wider reach.

Grants worth £20,000 to £80,000 per year were allocated for two-year tranches based on a scoring system for selecting applications that gave preference to organisations with co-sponsors. In 2002, for instance, the guidance made clear that CABE was looking for matched funding with a minimum of 20 per cent in financing or 30 per cent for in-kind sponsorship (CABE 2002e). In this way, CABE could make its modest resources travel further through the range of partnership structures this gave rise to.

Organisation	Region	Funding
Kent Architecture Centre	South East	110,000
Solent Centre for Architecture and Design	South East	105,000
Architecture Centre, Bristol	South West	100,000
Architecture Centre Devon and Cornwall	South West	100,000
Shape East	East of England	110,000
Create: MKSM	South East, East of England and East Midlands	80,000
Opun	East Midlands	105,000
MADE	West Midlands	105,000
Urban Vision North Staffordshire	West Midlands	110,000
Arc	Yorkshire & Humber	110,000
beam	Yorkshire & Humber	90,000
Doncaster Design Centre	Yorkshire & Humber	25,000
Design Liverpool	North West	40,000
Places Matter!	North West	40,000
Northern Architecture	North East	110,000
Architecture Foundation	London	45,000
Building Exploratory	London	115,000
Fundamental	London	80,000
NewLondon Architecture	London	25,000
Open House	London	45,000
Urban Design London	London	60,000
Architecture Centre Network	National	150,000
	Total	£1,860,000

Figure 10.4 CABE funding of ABECs 2008–2010 (CABE 2011f)

The ABECs themselves contained a diverse range of experience, with board and staff members who included: accountants; architects; artists; community development professionals; cultural professionals; developers; engineers; environmental professionals; fundraisers; educationalists and researchers; lawyers; local government members and officers; marketing and media professionals; regeneration managers; surveyors; and town planners. In two instances, CABE directly assisted in the creation of new ABECs, although it found the process politically tricky. A revealing instance was in determining the location of Create MKSM, the ABEC for the Milton Keynes and South Midlands area that CABE supported in the context of an associated Housing Growth Area that straddled three RDAs (10.5). During negotiations at the set-up phase of this

Figure 10.5 Create MKSM covered an area of high demand for new housing but with a strongly varying commitment to design, as here at (i) Newhall and (ii) Aylesbury

Source: Matthew Carmona

ABEC, CABE was clear that Oxford (the proposed location) was not appropriate given that growth was predominantly focussed on areas to the north and east of there. So whilst CABE did not wish to impose its view on the fledgling organisation, on this it had to use its weight to ensure an appropriate location in Milton Keynes.

Funding Led, not Funding Fed

The remit of regional funding required local partners that were structurally independent but strategically aligned to CABE, and, for example, CABE refused to fund organisations with similar goals but which also worked in the consultancy sector. Once an organisation was receiving a grant, CABE would continue to follow its work with frequent face-to-face meetings throughout the period of the grant. Operational discussions were not unusual, such as on personnel matters, and CABE was charged with ensuring that its resources were spent in an accountable manner that also represented value for money. Consequently, a substantial system was required for monitoring such a large and contingent work stream.

Milestones were agreed at the start of the grant period and tracked on a quarterly basis, and generally speaking all activities were accounted for under these milestones. The process was fairly uniform, with targets and work plans based on the themes from the original guidelines for funding, for example relating to skills development, quality in public buildings, awareness of the importance of urban design, developing local hubs, and facilitating public involvement. Activities needed to be recorded by the grant holder and progress reports submitted documenting activities as varied as: a peripatetic regeneration programme, continuing professional development seminars, architecture week events, work on a website, marketing, local partnerships, and lectures.

Grants were managed in-house by CABE staff who liaised with grant recipients on operations, and monitored targets and accounts. This structure was very different to other tools as it required a centralised 'hub' and multiple 'spokes' that, whilst looking financially efficient on CABE's balance sheet, to some degree hid layers of responsibility with DCLG managing CABE, CABE managing the ABECs, and the ABECs

managing projects. Other challenges were also encountered, foremost amongst which was that these devolved delivery arrangements were not conducive to interaction between the external parties and the other programmes of CABE. Some parts of CABE, for example, would have liked more communication with the grant partners and felt a sense of frustration that this was not possible. Minutes of meetings show that the design review and CABE Space teams in particular felt they did not have enough contact and "hoped that the ABECs would be incorporated into the wider CABE family so that they could be involved in other pieces of work" (CABE 2007i).

One key challenge was maintaining a balance of CABE influence and grant holder independence. CABE wanted to avoid producing a culture of funder dependency and promoted what it called a 'funding led, not funding fed' partnership. Close monitoring, however, could result in conflict over smaller decisions, and sometimes risked a more significant struggle between grant holders and their powerful benefactor. A good example of this is where updates and monitoring forms show the difficulties a grant holder faced in finding the 'right' staff, and CABE's resistance to any compromise candidate. There were also sometimes difficulties of ownership, for instance over tools grant holders had produced. This required that CABE continually worked towards a transparent common understanding with the grant holders, and in most instances this worked well.

In practice also, milestones set by CABE were difficult to reliably monitor and were often not met. Some letters to grant holders record CABE reiterating the need to monitor achievement of milestones, "as this is the means by which progress is monitored and payment is released", but in these types of cases CABE preferred to negotiate revisions to milestones rather than withhold monies. What the impact of this relaxed attitude was is not clear, but as it was a permanent feature of these relationships, it can be interpreted as part of achieving the 'balance' required.

Inevitable Tensions but Ultimate Success

Over the years, there were signs of growing tensions between CABE and some ABECs, with CABE staff suggesting at the time that "There is sometimes a

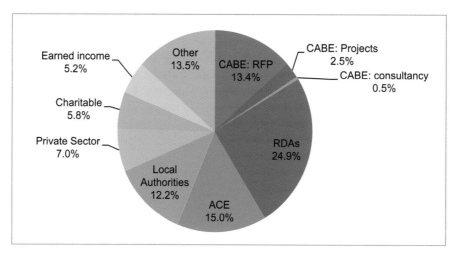

Figure 10.6   Sources of ABEC funding 2004/05–2006/07 (CABE 2007i)

perception of CABE as a 'cash cow'" (Annabel Jackson Associates 2007). It is difficult to know how widespread these perceptions were, but they were certainly misplaced. Far from being reliant on CABE, even when funding was at its highest, only around 15 per cent of ABEC funding came from CABE and the sources of the other 85 per cent were extremely varied (10.6). The money from CABE was nevertheless particularly valuable to the ABECs precisely because it could be relied on. In the words of one centre manager, "For a small organisation you need a little bit of core funding to give you the time to then bid for all the other projects."

An unpublished staff survey that CABE conducted revealed that "Most ABEC representatives were very positive, friendly and proactive" (CABE 2007c) in their relationship with CABE. Despite this, a perception of CABE as essentially heavy-handed and London-centric persisted in some quarters, and as the director of one of the northern centres put it: "We got very irritated that the London folk were trying to tell us how to run design review when we felt the collection of 30 or 40 professionals who were giving their time up to do this for us actually related to their community pretty well." A fundamental challenge was how to avoid stifling the sense of autonomous creativity whilst maintaining a clear client–contractor relationship. It was, for example, practically and symbolically important for CABE to be able to co-brand the work of its grant holders, although, in an echo of the mistrust (in the other direction) some contractors felt about the

branding by CABE of their work (see Chapter 6), this did not always happen.

Overall, CABE successfully negotiated these and other operational issues, and an external evaluation of the programme conducted in 2007 revealed that generally speaking the programme met its objectives (Annabel Jackson Associates 2007). Fundamentally it did this by ensuring that the public money at its disposal was used effectively for socially beneficial purposes and that a network of genuinely local design champions was created that decentralised key CABE programmes (notably enabling and design review) from London. Most of the ABECs it funded continue to operate today (albeit precariously) and have a track record and wealth of experience from the support and investment of the CABE years. For CABE, whilst at times it felt that the continued expansion of the ABEC network carried with it the danger that funding was being "spread too thinly" (CABE 2007i), it remained committed to the idea throughout. Thus when CABE came under pressure to make savings in its budget in the final years, it made every effort to retain funding to its regional network at the highest level possible, with savings in the cost of head office operations helping to support this objective (CABE 2010a).

Sea Change too, while to some extent an unfinished business, and having also encountered the tensions around autonomy, is generally considered a success, and was certainly a significant boon for the seaside towns that directly benefitted. As an article in *The Telegraph* confirmed, "It has left a rich legacy and serves as a salutary reminder that urban regeneration has to involve something more inspirational than mere expansion of retail space or basic facilities" (Christiansen 2010). The official evaluation of the initiative by BOP Consulting (2011: 6–10) was equally positive, with the initiative levering in £1.66 for every £1 of public money, raising skills levels in the local authorities concerned, creating 700 jobs, and improving the cultural offer of the thirty or so small seaside towns involved through a wide range of new and refurbished cultural and heritage venues and public art interventions, and the creation/improvement of 133,000 square metres of public space. The evaluators concluded that, whilst the level of innovation in the projects funded was not always up to the level originally envisaged,

> Sea Change was an effectively managed programme that has demonstrated excellent collaborative working among the national partners. The CABE team also designed the programme to be light and flexible in order to facilitate delivery, with modest reporting burdens compared to some other funding programmes.
> (BOP Consulting 2011: 6)

Although coming too late to impact CABE's future, the success demonstrated how CABE had become an extremely effective delivery agency. So whilst some argued that this and other initiatives distracted the organisation from its core mission, this was a capacity which has historically been in short supply across government, and one which is sorely missed. Whilst it lasted, the Sea Change budget, on paper, took the 'headline' funding of CABE to new heights (more than doubling it), although in fact the money was tightly ring-fenced and was quickly distributed to support the work of CABE's delivery partners. Indeed, CABE's administration of the programme took only a very low 2 per cent share (CABE 2011f) and consequently the remaining Sea Change income (the 98 per cent) is not included in the breakdown of CABE funding shown in Chapter 5.

Enabling

In its earliest years, CABE provided enabling directly through its commissioners, but proceeded swiftly to develop a substantial programme that would eventually reach into local and national authorities across the country, including some challenging areas. Indeed, by 2002, enabling was already outstripping the performance target that 50 per cent of its enabling activities should be conducted in areas of regeneration or deprivation (achieving 60 per cent—CABE 2002c: 17). The goal of providing design skills and experience to all types of projects was a new departure for English design governance, and an ever-increasing range of largely public sector clients took up the offer through an increasing prevalence of large-scale projects expanding from individual buildings and masterplans to significant building programmes and strategic planning. In this way the running total of projects enabled grew from 80 cases over the first two years to 652 by 2009 (CABE 2009a: 18), by any measure a very significant injection of design skills and expertise in places that otherwise may not have prioritised quality.

An Immediate Hit

The programme kicked off in 2000 with an initial boost from the Arts Capital Programme of Arts Council England, for which CABE provided "training on managing the early stages of capital projects" (CABE 2002a). Enabling was an immediate hit, and the caseload quickly became more diverse, reaching every region of England. To facilitate this, the pool of enablers also quickly became more expansive with eleven by the end of the 2000/01 financial year and 102 just a year later (CABE 2001a, 2002c), including "architects, urban designers, planner/masterplanners, landscape architects, project managers, engineers, property & quantity surveyors, and people working as clients for capital projects" (CABE 2002a). By 2009, the number had grown to 323 (CABE 2009a: 50). Predominantly CABE enabled local authorities, but also other national agencies (e.g. the NHS), community organisations (on specific design aspects of building), and other bodies at regional, subregional, and local scales. Usually this involved sitting and working alongside the staff, or more distantly reviewing and advising on their work, but occasionally it involved complete secondment to another organisation.

From 2002, CABE expanded the areas of enabling and as well as the Housing Market Renewal work there was a major focus on primary and acute care NHS buildings for the Department of Health, and specific panels were set up to deal with public buildings, master planning, and public space. Periodically, particular building programmes came to the fore, including an early brief from the Department of Work and Pensions (DWP) to enhance job centres and another from the Lord Chancellor's Department to look at the country's courts. Later the 'public buildings' panel expanded to encompass work on secondary schools under the

Building Schools for the Future (BSF) programme, nurseries through Sure Start (Box 10.2), and health care buildings via the Local Improvement Finance Trust (LIFT), as well as a series of investments in hospitals, police stations, fire stations, and community buildings. An Urban Design and Homes enabling team grew out of the master-planning panel with a focus on public realm projects, and this became an extremely large tranche of work.

Box 10.2 Enabling: Sure Start Enabling

From 2003 to 2008, CABE engaged in a major programme of work to enable public sector clients in the design and build of early years buildings known as the 'Sure Start' building programme; part of New Labour's larger commitment, as Tony Blair (2001b) put it, to: "education, education, education". In 1998, funding of £450 million was announced for the first three years of Sure Start, and by 2004, this had grown into a ten-year strategy for 3,500 new children's centres.

Through its strategic advice, CABE built a successful working relationship with the Department for Education and Skills (DfES), and this allowed CABE commissioners to make the case for good design as a means to build social value from capital investments with Richard Feilden, who spearheaded this area of CABE's work, being particularly vocal in lobbying for better-quality early years building design. Although DfES itself had ambition and some capacity in design, it still needed to ensure performance in local authorities across the country, and CABE became the vehicle for this.

Enablers had to work to a demanding agenda and get clients up to speed for this new area of activity. They provided direct assistance to head teachers and other local education authority clients on Sure Start projects that ranged from individual buildings to portfolios of up to forty buildings and on complexes that also encompassed facilities for pregnant women and new mothers, health services, and employment training (CABE 2006c: 18). In particular they advised on how to approach schemes or to select architects, and on procurement more widely.

The Sure Start and children's centre programmes were ambitious in scope, and the clients were often

working to very tight two-year funding time scales with 50 per cent of their funding to be drawn down by the end of the first year. Consequently, CABE needed to have early engagement and prove its value with clients who were simultaneously under pressure to deliver. To facilitate this, enablers were provided with techniques of communicating with clients, including a pre-prepared patter to initiate the relationship that emphasised the potential CABE provided "to work one to one with an experienced architect".

Perhaps because of the speed, Sure Start enablers found it difficult to engage with CABE's internal management structures and did not, for example, record case information as systematically as CABE wished. Because enabling typically finished well before construction began, such feedback also provided little data on how effective the advice had been. Partially filling this gap, in 2008, the government commissioned CABE to conduct a post-occupancy evaluation of the Sure Start capital programme, which for CABE also represented an opportunity to test whether key messages about design had been getting through to clients.

The study reviewed 101 recently completed buildings using a rating system that included questionnaire data from a lay group of staff and parents who used the buildings, and data collected on site by a team of design professionals trained in post-occupational analysis. It revealed that "Most new Sure Start children's centres are performing well and are supporting the government's aim of giving pre-school children the best start in life. However, the two-year turnaround time allowed to build them is proving very challenging for local authorities . . . [and] this is having an impact on design" (CABE 2008e: 2).

The report offered a wide range of recommendations for improvement to both designers and commissioners of children's centres, most obviously around the time needed for good design and the proper involvement amongst all interested parties. It also revealed a significant gap between the ratings of centre staff and parents, seventy-eight of whom rated their centres good to excellent (10.7i), and enablers, who rated just eight in the highest category and a quarter neutral to unacceptable (10.7ii) (CABE 2008e: 5–6). Whilst the report had nothing to say specifically on the role of CABE enabling, for the enablers involved in Sure Start the limitations on time clearly compromised outcomes and what could be achieved with clients. This was captured in the professional ratings which, arguably, are more a reflection of 'what might have been', rather than in the lay ratings which will largely have been made without the benefits of comparison. The experience shows the limitations of enabling when the fundamental system within which it is operating is flawed. Also, perhaps, that things might have been a lot worse without it.

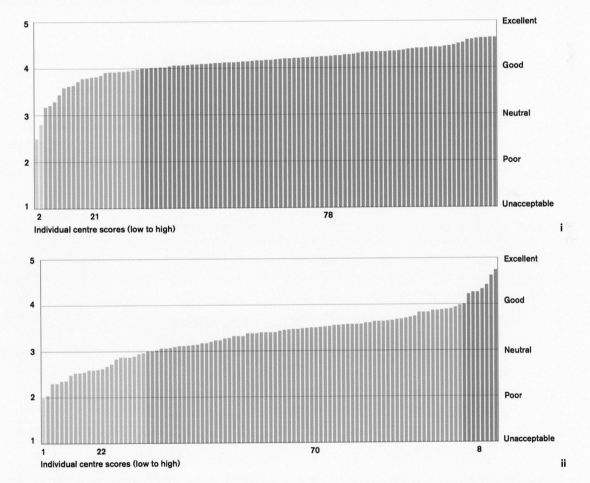

Figure 10.7 Comparison of (i) users' views and (ii) enablers' views on the quality of the Sure Start buildings (CABE 2008c)

A range of important initiatives either emerged through or were tested by enabling, including the design coding pilot programme of the mid-2000s (see Chapter 4), the Mixed Communities Initiative that aimed at long-term transformation of extremely deprived areas, work on the Thames Gateway regeneration project, and eventually the piloting of the new Strategic Urban Design (StrUD) methodology. In such cases, the diverse expertise of the enabling panel was brought to bear to discuss and debate particular issues, to share experiences, and ultimately to trial new approaches in the field through the enabling process. In the case of the Thames Gateway, for example, CABE conducted a focussed housing audit (see Chapter 6), launched Building for Life training in the Gateway, ran a series of identity and place-making workshops, created a *Thames Gateway Design Pact*, and, perhaps most significant, produced *New Things Happen: A Guide to the Future Thames Gateway*. In an area of hugely fragmented governance arrangements and an even more fragmented and complex built and natural environment, this aimed to deliver a much-needed map of the identity and character of the sub-region, and to set out some ideas to underpin local policies for places. In other words, it injected some coordination and strategic thinking into the maelstrom (10.8).

As the success of enabling led to its continued growth, issues grew around the boundaries of the work. As a leading landscape architect put it, "There were occasions when they were undertaking work which I thought should actually have been done by private consultants, rather than a government body." There was also some concern about cross-over with other government agencies, most notably with the powerful new Homes and Communities Agency (HCA), which had been formed following the merger of the former Housing Corporation, English Partnerships, and the Academy for Sustainable Communities in order to help drive forward delivery of regeneration and housing, and which had the achievement of good design as part of its statutory objectives.[8] In particular CABE was concerned to ensure that this statutory objective was taken seriously whilst it, rather than the HCA, remained the focus of national leadership on design. The solution was to seek ways to build a working relationship with the new mega-agency through its enabling team, which reported back in 2008 that: "We are in strong dialogue . . . to define what the HCA need to do in order to embed design quality in their programmes and also to establish how CABE, through all of its programmes, will support them in achieving this" (CABE 2008f: 15). With the exception of a few hiccups, such as over the audit of social housing (see Chapter 6), the relationship grew into a largely positive one.

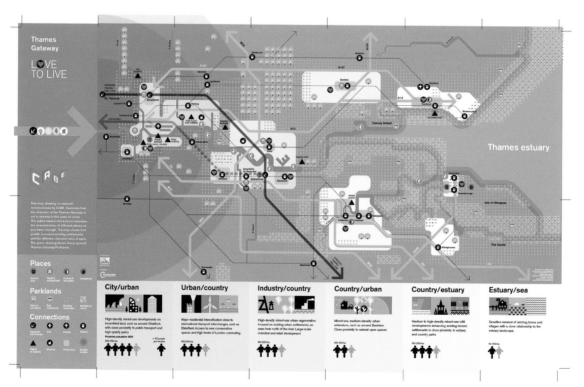

Figure 10.8 *Thames Gateway, Love to Live,* an attempt to capture the diverse and changing character of the Thames Gateway
Source: CABE

In the last years of the programme, concerns over the cost of the enabling programme became visible in the trade press, with Richard Simmons and Jon Sorrell increasingly engaged in making the case publicly for its value. One article warned that CABE needed to "move with the times" and particularly criticised the appointment of forty new enablers with a day rate of £400, presciently surmising that "The effect is to make it look spendaholic rather than thrifty, which is a dangerous position to be in." Simmons countered with the explanation that this was not an expansion of the service but of the pool of skills. He also referred to the reduced rates the enablers offered to CABE, and argued: "These people work at minimal cost because of our common interest in creating wonderful buildings and places. In a few days over a period of months, an enabler creates a capable client and improves the procurement of projects worth millions" (Simmons 2009a). Whilst effectively working behind the scenes and largely out of the 'public' eye for most of CABE's decade, towards the end even this service came under greater scrutiny.

The Processes of Enabling

Across the range of its enabling activities, CABE was acting in a support role, having direct input into the design aspects of the development work, but not taking control or ownership of any task and remaining strictly in the realm of advice. The programme of enabling was extremely complex, and, as a new realm of design governance, CABE had to develop its processes as it went along. In particular, in order to maintain coherence in the service, significant amounts of internal guidance and briefing papers were produced. This provided a common point of reference and reflection for the large numbers of enablers that was boosted further in 2004 and 2006 by two significant rounds of enabling panel recruitment and intermediate phases of 'refreshment' where the skills pool was assessed for relevance and training provided to update enablers.

Direct and continued enabler contact with a project client was a critical aspect of the tool, and in contrast to design review, enabling advice was typically given in person to a project client and always followed up. An enabler could visit the office of the client, meet a project team, or take a site visit, and then offer "hands on,

flexible, responsive advice that could take a variety of forms as appropriate: workshops, seminars, or one-to-one advice" (CABE 2010g). As such, it was always moulded to the needs of a client or programme. In design review, for example, although the same scheme could be reviewed several times, it was always a very structured process providing a snapshot of that project's progress. Enabling, by contrast, was much more about process and could occur over a range of timescales. "It might involve a short engagement at a moment in a project's life, or it could be a programme of support over several years" (CABE 2010g).

The work of an enabler also required a good deal of deskwork, which might involve reading project briefs, reviewing CVs of consultants bidding for project work, or providing comments on proposals, but personal contact was critical, particularly where tasks were sensitive, such as those relating to budgetary negotiations or critical personnel decisions. In these sorts of issues, and in helping to develop the management skills the client would need over the longer term, a good deal of trust was required, as demonstrated by the difficulties reported in enabling an arts centre project. In that case, the enabler wished to encourage capacity building to deliver the intended arts outreach programme, and noted, "I do think she trusts my judgement on this, and get the impression that today's series of meetings have helped to underscore the scale of the task she is taking on."[9]

CABE encouraged holistic involvement and advice across design procurement and delivery, and expected to be involved in projects from the start wherever possible and sometimes throughout their duration, for instance in Nottingham City Council's Old Market Square renovation by Gustafson Porter (10.9). At the same time, CABE emphasised the need for impartiality and independence and unlike the design review service, enablers were not allowed to comment on competing contractors. Therefore, conflicts of interest were always flagged to clients and recorded, although, perhaps because of the trust in established relationships, these did not automatically end an enabler's involvement with the project. By contrast, where the required working relationship never developed or when a client was unresponsive to enabling advice, enablers were allowed to withdraw services: "We would not generally persist where there was no prospect of

Figure 10.9   The Old Market Square in Nottingham with its 2004 Gustafson Porter design; the competition for the square was enabled by CABE with the winning design selected by a panel chaired by CABE Commissioner Les Sparks

Source: Matthew Carmona

making a difference to the eventual outcome in terms of design or process" (CABE 2005j).

Smaller projects at the local scale often involved assistance on a more technical level, and in such cases, enablers were a very significant resource, particularly for smaller organisations where they had no previous experience of urban design. In such cases, CABE could provide guidance on all aspects of projects, and particularly the details of procuring contractors such as architects, as well as helping to assess the quality of the emerging designs. As an enabling manager described it, at this scale, "Typical assistance might involve: brief-writing, selection criteria, evaluation of submissions, design advice/guidance, support during procurement processes, mechanisms to deliver and appraise design quality, training and capacity-building" (CABE 2006f).

Work at larger scales, such as in relation to master planning, regeneration projects, and regional strategy-making, was more layered with more partners (10.10). At these scales a good relationship with the client was vital as well as astute political and inter-personal skills, as processes often required involvement over a number of years and might also involve helping to diffuse political tensions between existing actors. The most common process for bringing actors together was holding workshops with those involved, and these were sometimes billed as skills-development events, although, unlike the sorts of educational tools described

in Chapter 7, they involved co-learning as a means to develop particular projects. For example a workshop hosted by Government Office North West in 2009 involved a panel of independent professional experts discussing the challenges and future directions of the local development strategy with officers from Warrington Borough Council.

At the largest scales, including regional and national levels, there was a raft of CABE enabling work with ministers, government departments, non-government departments, and third sector bodies. This was less direct in the type of enabling it provided and more akin to the sorts of advocacy work discussed in Chapter 8 as it involved supporting others to inject a design dimension into the policies and programmes they were working on. CABE recognised that relationship building would determine the potential impact of the service, and provided guidance to enablers. The 'how to' guides for the enabling teams and induction training, which every enabler was obliged to attend, attempted to define what the client–enabler relationship was intended to be and where its boundaries lay, and to set out common processes (10.11).

Managing the Complexity

Enabling was therefore a bespoke and complex service provided to a variety of actors across a range of scales, and because every episode was different, CABE had to deal with the fuzzy boundaries of the operation and its management across layers of governance. Consequently, managing the enabling programme, which was far from a simple outsourcing and monitoring exercise, quickly became a major work stream for CABE.

For their part, enablers on the programme were mainly contracted to CABE on a two-year framework contract, allowing work on multiple projects, and this could be renewed by letter. They were selected on the basis of their skills with the aim of maintaining a balance that matched the caseload and were organised according to the different themes of the service. By the middle of CABE's life, full enabling staff meetings were convened every twelve months, and on an ad hoc basis for thematic panels. Enablers were assigned to projects, with tasks and time scales set out in advance, although in practice a lot of liaison and negotiation was necessary as projects evolved. Before starting work, they met with

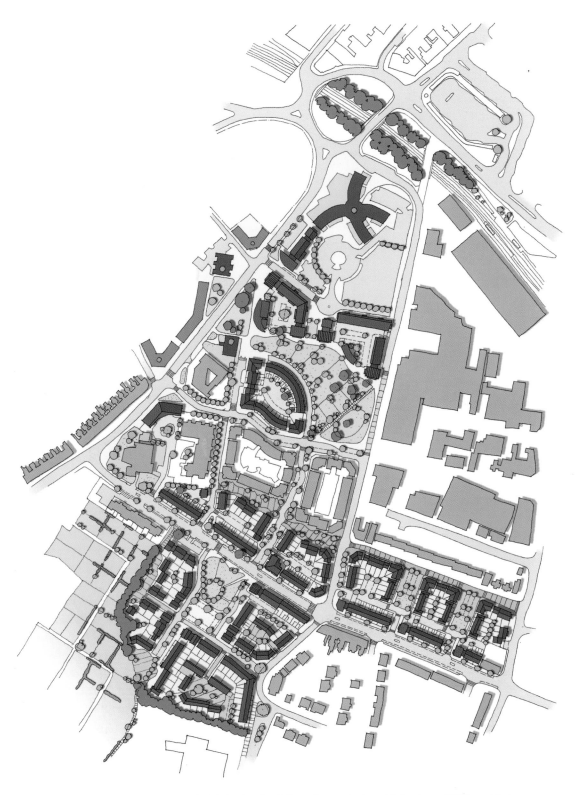

Figure 10.10 Lyng Estate masterplan by Tibbalds for Sandwell Council commissioned following a CABE-enabled processes designed to promote design quality in this deprived area

Source: Sandwell Council/Tibbalds Planning and Urban Design

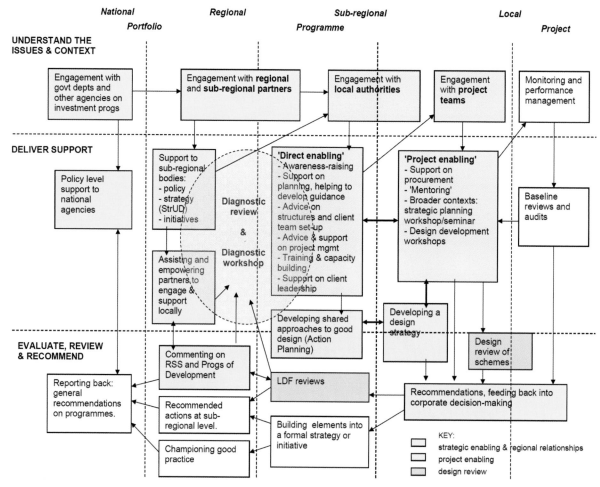

Figure 10.11 Enabling processes across the scales of involvement

Source: CABE 2011j

a CABE programme officer and were briefed about the client. Enablers would then keep the officer copied into correspondence and would formally report to CABE on a monthly basis to update on project progress and negotiate the time required for enabling a particular case. Enablers were also able to remotely communicate with CABE through an 'extranet', or members-only site, where they could access information from CABE on the case as well as best practice documents.

As the timeline of the work could be very long, progress (often gradual and painstaking) was recorded in regular enabler updates to CABE. Ultimately enablers' involvement in any case had to come to an end, and as there was no fixed procedure for withdrawal or closure, the job was simply deemed 'done' by the enabler. To assist, CABE provided a platform for

triaging and monitoring casework and had ultimate control over when, how, and over what period enablers could get involved. The enabling service advisory documentation explained: "A great deal can be achieved through enabling for relatively little investment, but only if it is well managed. We also know that a significant investment in enabler time can be made without making any impact at all, and there is therefore a constant need to select projects and allocate support in a considered manner, and to monitor and assess the effectiveness of the service" (CABE 2007d).

Internally, the enabling service sometimes presented challenges for the Commission. For instance, whilst enablers might give specific design advice, their role was distinct from design review and cases that were enabled did not always (later) get a good review (see Chapter 9). Inevitably this led to the appearance that these two arms of CABE were uncoordinated. This could result in misunderstandings around the scope of enabling externally and on whether the role was complementary to, conflicting with, or simply duplicating other services.[10] On a 2005 enabling project in Kennington (London), for instance, it was recorded that "Design reviews seem to be taking place without the knowledge of whether there is a CABE enabler on the project. It would be helpful, perhaps, to ensure that when design reviews take place, the reports of the enabler are to hand."[11]

The nature of CABE's position in relation to the enabling work could also be misunderstood. For instance, in relation to advice given on a masterplan in 2004, the local authority requested CABE 'sign-off' on the project and the enabler needed to revert to CABE to confirm that this was not appropriate.[12] In response to these misunderstandings, CABE provided clearer job descriptions for appointments to both its design review and enabling panels, and where the opportunities arose CABE increasingly sought to coordinate the activities of its enabling and design review services, for example through the strategic package of services CABE offered in 2007 to the Urban Development Corporation for West Northamptonshire.

Enabling was supported by core funding throughout, which was split between CABE's programmes, and by its third operational year this amounted to just under £500,000. In addition, service-level agreements for individual pieces of enabling work were put in place separately with the core funding departments, for example with DCLG for the Thames Gateway project and with the Department of Health for hospital enabling. The Arts Council of England remained a major source of enabling work throughout CABE's lifetime, and later English Partnerships, the Home Office, DfES, and English Heritage would invest in enabling, as did Crossrail[13] and the Olympic Delivery Authority (with their own dedicated panels) in the final years. As with other tools, the enabling budget grew rapidly and rose to a peak of £2.8 million in 2007/08, at which point it accounted for 20 per cent of CABE's total expenditure. The costs were almost exclusively staff time, either contracted enabler time or internal staff administration costs, with the bulk of internal staff time involved in recruitment of and liaison with the enablers. For enablers, a typical workload was estimated at ten days enabling for a standard project and if that rose to more than twenty CABE judged that the client ought to have been recruiting its own advisor (CABE 2007d). Training days were an extra cost in terms of administrative time and payment to enablers.

The Impact

While it is hard to directly quantify the impact of enabling, it is clear that it certainly represented remarkable value for money if for no other reason than its discounting of senior professionals' time to £400 a day, time often targeted in areas where the service added the greatest value, with the most challenging projects, and the greatest degree of knowledge transfer. The enabling programme certainly had an extremely positive reception, as substantiated by many unpublished reports from those in receipt of enabling, and elsewhere where the service was regularly singled out for praise (DCLG 2010: 103). The independent position of CABE, detached from local politics, was particularly valued as it provided a neutral space for reflection. In relation to the transformation of London's Jubilee Gardens, for example, a representative from the local employers' group recounted that CABE "spoke to each stakeholder and acted as a mirror in order for people to realise how much consensus there was, which was quite a shock" (Lipman 2003) (10.12). Local authorities, and in some instances

Figure 10.12 Jubilee Gardens, London, a rejuvenated public space enabled by CABE

Source: Matthew Carmona

communities (Bishop 2009) and developers (Hallewell 2005), also appreciated CABE's external advisory position as a source of quality assurance and certainty in the decision-making process.

The early involvement of enablers drove procurement choices and often bolstered confidence and good practice. In Shropshire, for example, the director of development in one district authority commented, "CABE's commitment is exciting for us as they are particularly interested in the early stages of strategic projects, especially those which will have a significant impact on the local environment or set standards for future developments" (*South Shropshire Journal* 2004). In Redcar, the manager of a Sure Start programme reported that enabling encouraged them to "invite five architects to present their tender to the whole community . . . [and this] created a sense of ownership right from the start" (Christie 2005). Of course not all experiences were positive and the benefits of having experienced practitioners advising on schemes sometimes could be tempered by their lack of local knowledge. On a scheme in Great Yarmouth, for example, the funding manager contended: "[CABE] came in and put much greater emphasis on quality—which comes at a price" (Smithard 2006); the implication being that this was a price the local context could not withstand.

Finally, enabling was a significant source of support and advice for other parts of CABE (and beyond), notably in the production of practice guides (see Chapter 7), or simply on giving the latest intelligence to the organisation on key building types. It also enabled others (namely the ABECs) to establish their own enabling programmes by sharing the lessons on the process of running a successful enabling service and by helping to train their enablers.

When Should Assistance Tools Be Used?

Through its assistance activities, CABE was working directly in the field and intervening in live project work and local processes of design governance. More than any others, these tools distinguished CABE from what had come before in terms of the sheer ambition of the organisation and the penetration of its governance approach across the nation. These tools allowed CABE

to get ever more involved in strategic aspects of development processes, shaping the decision-making environments of many organisations who were themselves directly influencing or actually shaping design outcomes, and influencing (early in the development process) the fundamental choices made about development. They were perhaps the most sophisticated tools of governance, allowing CABE a bespoke and direct form of intervention short of actually having design, development, or regulatory powers itself. They are consistently seen by those involved as amongst CABE's most effective design governance tools.

CABE provided assistance through two tools of financial assistance and enabling. The financial assistance CABE offered, both through organisational support and project grants, was ultimately dependent on others, outside the Commission, delivering on the objectives of these programmes; but CABE managed to carefully leverage how this occurred in order that the limited resources at its disposal were worked hard to drive design up local agendas. Enabling took the form of direct mentoring on projects of different scales provided through a pool of experts or 'enablers' and consequently depended on an external skills base and relationships built by enablers in the wider world (10.13). Because of this, the programme could sometimes appear to exist at one step removed from the Commission, but in fact was constructed and carefully steered from within CABE and became an important source of learning and development for other branches of the organisation, as well as an effective knowledge transfer programme across the country.

Placing the tools of assistance within the design governance field of action from Chapter 1 (10.14) shows that financial assistance was used in two positions. First, right at the start of the design governance process to support and mould the work of the ABECs

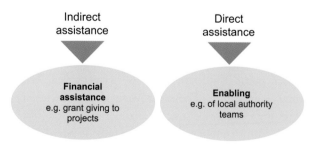

Figure 10.13 Typology of assistance

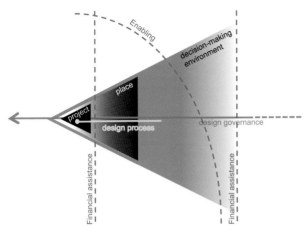

Figure 10.14   Assistance tools in the design governance field of action

and others, and thereby to maximise the potential for a positive design decision-making environment. Second, much later via grant in aid to particular design/development propositions, notably, in the case of CABE via the Sea Change programme. Enabling, by contrast, could occur across almost the entire field of design governance, from very strategic work around policy frameworks, to help in brief writing and being a good client, to hand holding during the design delivery

processes. Because of this, and because of its bespoke nature, enabling was amongst the most versatile and flexible of the CABE tools.

Notes

1. Unpublished enabling records, October 2006.
2. LDA Design, landscape designers.
3. Unpublished enabler note, March 2002.
4. "A partnership of between two and five local authorities, working with partners in the public and private sector including the Government Office, Regional Development Agency, Local Strategic Partnerships, the Housing Corporation, Police Authority, Strategic Health Authority, and lead developers" (House of Commons Committee of Public Accounts 2008: 7).
5. The ODPM's strategy started from the premise of "low demand and abandonment in parts of the North and Midlands" (ODPM 2002:13).
6. Unpublished enabler note, November 2002.
7. In the 2010 call-off contract, this stood at £400 per day or £53.33 per hour (CABE 2010a).
8. As listed in the Housing and Regeneration Act 2008.
9. Unpublished enabler note, April 2004.
10. Unpublished enabler note, December 2005.
11. Unpublished enabler note, March 2005.
12. Unpublished enabler note, October 2004.
13. The delivery vehicle for a new high-speed rail project in London and the south-east.

AFTERWORD

The Impact and Legitimacy of Design Governance

The CABE years in England defined a particular approach to the state-led governance of design. It was globally unique in its scope, ambition, and impact, yet, as Chapters 3 to 5 revealed, even in England this era could be viewed as an aberration, a departure from the normal business of design governance, which has typically been much more laissez faire. Because of its exceptional nature, we could contend that the experience is abnormal and should be ignored, but this book has shown that would be a mistake. Instead, studying the CABE experiment has revealed tangible and conceptual lessons for the governance of design that are of relevance far beyond English shores.

Many of these, for example those relating to the individual tools of design governance, have been included where relevant in the substantive chapters of Parts I to III of this book, and it is not the intention to repeat them here. Instead, in this afterword, the opportunity is taken to reflect on the research and to evaluate the governance of design in two ways. First, from the narrow perspective of CABE's impact and legacy: what worked and what did not; and what can we learn from this experiment in design governance that can inform the governance of design in the future. Second, what does the experience tell us about the nature and purpose of design governance, across governmental scales, and about the role and legitimacy of government within this most 'wicked' of policy arenas?

The Impact of State-Led Design Governance

The CABE Experiment

CABE was a product of its time and reflected trends inherent in the larger political economy. The first was a 'governmentalist' belief in the power of government

to address key areas of public policy; in England reflecting a historic tendency to take power to the centre. Through these processes, new (or greatly extended) areas of policy were developed across government and provided with a governance infrastructure in order to pursue related newly defined public policy goals. The treatment of design under the New Labour governments of 1997 to 2010 was arguably a prime example of this. The experience demonstrated a significant extension of public policy in an area that governments previously had made strenuous efforts to avoid becoming embroiled with, preferring instead that design be dealt with in the smoke-filled rooms of the largely invisible Royal Fine Art Commission (RFAC), as a local matter, or not at all.

As part of this, approaches to governance in the period borrowed heavily from the 'managerial' methods then increasingly dominant in the state's administrative practices (see Chapter 1); not just in the development of targets to drive performance (to which CABE was subject), but also reflecting a wider move from the 1980s onwards of using dedicated arm's-length agencies with focussed private sector-style missions as part of the neoliberal state. Thus CABE was charged with the role of becoming the government's advocate on matters of built environment design, a role that required it to make clear value judgements about what good design entailed and to 'take ownership' of this policy arena. This it did with great energy, and quickly came to dominate (some would say overdominate) the scene.

Whilst CABE was a child of these approaches, it also utilised them in its work, not just in the manner in which it managed its 'CABE family', but also in its belief that influence began with understanding; namely that by understanding the processes of design and development, generic principles might be derived that could be utilised to optimise the performance of players in the sector, be they developers, regulators, investors (public and private), or designers. This was central to the CABE method as, without statutory powers of its own, it had to rely on the sorts of informal tools unpacked in Part III of this book. There the key ingredients of evidence, knowledge, promotion, evaluation, and assistance were all indirect and focussed predominantly on shaping the decision-making environment within which design and its governance occurred.

Finally, as reflected in the third-way politics of the time, CABE might be seen as one attempt to marry 'popularism' with 'pragmatism'. In other words, constructing policy solutions that did not alienate key interests and emphasised what works rather than what was dogmatically prescribed in one form of politics or another. Arguably, the new focus on design did not become a priority for government in the 2000s simply because the achievement of better design was intrinsically seen as a good thing. Instead, good place-based design was viewed, first, as a means to popularise (or at least sweeten the pill of) the large quantities of new housing the nation needed at a time when community opposition had increasingly been fortified by a reaction to the generally poor quality of development that had predominated. Second, good design was seen as a necessary precondition for the pragmatic reinvestment in cities that needed to occur if the historic tendency towards sprawl was to be reversed in favour of a renaissance in urban areas whilst at the same time protecting the countryside. In essence that was the core argument of the Urban Task Force, and government signed up to it alongside CABE (see Chapter 4).

Perceptions of CABE

Whilst some of these trends predated New Labour, notably the growing interest in the importance of design in government, they strongly set the context for the work of CABE and were reflected in how the organisation saw itself and its role, and how others perceived it and whether it was effective. In this regard, an important point to make is the seemingly obvious one that CABE was by no means universally popular. Indeed, from the very start the organisation was often under fire from different players that it rubbed up against: sometimes architects (who hadn't fared well in

design reviews), sometimes national politicians (whose policies seemed to be called into question on design grounds), sometimes professional institutes (who felt CABE was encroaching on their turf), and sometimes developers (who no longer had quite such a free hand). Indeed, as one commentator suggested, only partly in jest, "By the end CABE had pretty much alienated everyone, which perhaps explained its demise."

That of course hugely overstates the case, as underpinning these tensions was a clear and seemingly popular agenda, the pursuit of design quality (aesthetic, project, place and process—see Chapter 1) that CABE pursued with great energy, initiative, leadership, and (usually) focus for more than a decade. Therefore, whilst many criticised aspects of its activities (e.g. as too heavy-handed and arrogant, as unrepresentative of its sector, or as lacking independence as simply a tool of government), the evidence points to overwhelming support for much of what CABE did and to a ready acceptance that the organisation played a very significant role in changing the perceived importance and actual delivery of design quality in England and indirectly across the rest of the United Kingdom. Yet as an organisation, CABE was never well understood in terms of its size and scope and its relationship to government, and many of the harshest critiques of its work seem to stem from this simple fact.

Whilst external perceptions were often of a monolith swallowing up huge dollops of taxpayers' money to conduct design review, in fact the organisation, at its height, was never much more than 120 strong (tiny by government quango standards), and only around a fifth of its staff was dedicated to design review where most of the headlines (and periodic controversy) derived. The remainder focussed on lower-profile but typically highly regarded and effective programmes such as its enabling work in local authorities, its research programme, its public spaces and parks work, the Building for Life initiative, or various educational enterprises. Indeed, whilst at its height CABE boasted an annual budget of around £11.6 million, increasingly large proportions of this represented annualised project funding to deliver particular programmes of government, rather than CABE's core services, most of which focussed on injecting a much-needed quality dimension into the sizable capital expenditure programmes of New Labour.

CABE, Before and After

Notwithstanding the clear antecedence of many of the governance trends in which CABE was embedded in the work of earlier regimes, its history means that CABE will always be associated with New Labour. To some degree, however, CABE found itself stuck between a rock and a hard place, courtesy of its relationship with government. Thus whilst government saw CABE as a highly competent delivery organisation and increasingly loaded it up with 'projects' to deliver, this left the organisation vulnerable to the whims of ministers, to the annualised public spending round, to perceptions that CABE was getting flabby, and arguably also diverted its attention and energies away from its own design leadership role. Moreover, whilst gaining considerable authority as, in effect, the government's design arm, its 100 per cent reliance on public money for its survival left CABE at least partially gagged and no longer really able to claim true independence. Indeed, on several occasions the organisation had its wrists firmly slapped when the increasingly control-minded ministers of New Labour's later years detected that government policy was not always fully supported by CABE's programmes.

Despite this, the subject matter of CABE's attention—better design in the built environment—has in recent years become a largely apolitical matter. So whilst some, as discussed in Chapter 1, have argued that the pursuit of better design is an elitist concern and associate its regulation with the political right, others conflate attempts to correct market failure through government action with the left and see attempts to control design as the needless imposition

of barriers to change and innovation within the free market. In both cases, design is often equated to a narrow concern for 'aesthetics' rather than with the more fundamental issues around functionality, liveability, sustainability, economic viability, and social equity that became CABE's design agenda.

In the United Kingdom, the contemporary effort (of which CABE became part) to positively address questions of design in the built environment through public policy began under the final Conservative administration of the 1990s. Acting partly on the basis of personal interest, but also in the face of the same issues around housing growth and where it should go that later confronted New Labour, the then Secretary of State for the Environment, John Gummer, transformed the policy environment in relation to design (see Chapter 3). Under him, design moved from the proscribed list (for public intervention) to the prescribed one and urban design, instead of aesthetic control, became the new focus for policy. This move provided a firm basis for the equally decisive elevation of design even further up the political agenda in the New Labour years, and gave the lie to arguments that CABE was, by necessity, a project of the left.

Comparing the different models of state-led design governance deployed in England since 1924 (A.1), in many respects the CABE experience can be viewed as a middle way. Thus whereas the RFAC was ideological in its outlook and often uncompromising in its advice, albeit easily side-lined behind its single largely closed door in London's Mayfair, the design governance landscape of the post-CABE austerity years provides a disaggregated cacophony of provision and views (or none) out of which little commonality or coordination

	RFAC	CABE	Austerity
Operation	Ideological	Ideological but pragmatic	Managerial
Authority	Centralised	Centralised decentralisation	Disaggregated
Power	Publically-oriented/passive	Publically-oriented/active	Market-oriented (with gaps)

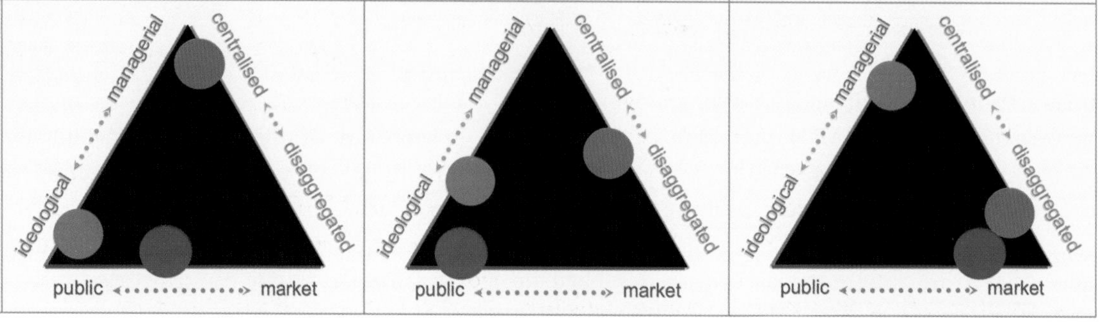

Figure A.1 National design governance models compared

prevails. By contrast, the CABE years offered a clear national leadership, but one responsive to the diversity of contexts (political and geographical) within which it operated, and coordination through a coherent regional network of design governance providers that reached out across the country. Moreover, whilst both the RFAC and CABE had in common that they were public functions of the state with a clear orientation towards the public sector, contrasting with the market-led approaches and voluntarism that dominate in the post-CABE years, they also enjoyed central funding and experienced vulnerability to the winds of political change because of it. CABE had in common with the post-CABE era that it was highly active in its advocacy for design and fully exploited the range of tools available to it. Likewise, the market is highly active in selling the services it now provides, flexibly seeking business wherever it can be found, and this is complemented by voluntary action that, with little or no resources, seeks to fill the gaps.

CABE's Impact

Turning from its modus operandi to its achievements, many of those interviewed for the research reported in this book commented that impact was a particularly difficult issue to get a handle on and even more difficult to measure. In part this may be because many of CABEs impacts were so diffuse in nature, focussed on influencing the decision-making environment for design (the processes of quality), rather than on making specific and tangible interventions in projects or places. Consequently, when compared with more focussed organisations,[1] people could readily see the costs, but not always the benefits, thus helping to explain the widespread negative perceptions about the size and cost of CABE amongst built environment professionals.

Despite this, a detailed examination of CABE's work and legacy reveals a number of profound and tangible impacts, and so whilst CABE's mission was cut short, many of these impacts, categorised in A.2, are still apparent five years after CABE's demise.

Making the Case

As a small organisation (by governmental standards) CABE undoubtedly punched above its weight,

demonstrating in the process how, despite its diminutive size, such an organisation might operate within and across government. But CABE also had to regularly make the case for its existence and the 'value it added', and as an unpublished Handover Note on the subject revealed (CABE 2011a), CABE was evaluated around twenty times during its existence,[2] most notably as a feed into the Comprehensive Spending Reviews of 2004, 2007, and 2010.

In its final and most comprehensive self-examination—*Making the Case*—CABE submitted a 50,000-word case to the Department for Culture, Media & Sport (DCMS) that in its own words made "a compelling case for CABE's impact" (CABE 2010e). The evidence was indeed extensive and varied, and ranged from the quantifiable, such as an assessment that CABE's design review services resulted in users benefitting from expertise with a market value of £684,450 per annum, provided at a cost to the public purse of only £163,800, to the unquantifiable, such as the impact of CABE's work on the life choices of the thousands of schoolchildren who came into contact with CABE's educational materials; and from the highly tangible, for example that satisfaction surveys revealed 88 per cent of users found CABE's enabling advice useful and 84 per cent found that enabling advice changed what they did, to the intangible, such as the ultimate impact of the green space strategies prepared by the 180 councils CABE worked with on those tools. In this and other documents, CABE made regular and extensive use of its own research, as well as that conducted by others (internationally), to make the case that better design could have a positive impact on health, education, well-being, the economy, safety, levels of crime, and environmental sustainability, amongst other factors.

Such evidence remained convincing as long as politicians were committed to CABE and were open to the case CABE regularly made. History shows, however, that when resources ran short, political expediency simply dictated that the evidence was ignored (see Chapter 4).

The Use of Multiple Overlapping Informal Tools and Commitment to the Cause

Where CABE differed decisively from what came before and after is in the sheer scale of activities its

CABE impacted on	CABE impacted through	But despite its impact
… politicians	… convincing a generation of politicians in national government about the importance of design, in particular that design was not all subjective and inconsequential but could be objectively assessed and delivered with a real and positive impact on the economy and society	… CABE spent less time than it should convincing opposition politicians, who (when they came to power) weren't sufficiently convinced of CABE's value to support it in the face of completing claims on a diminishing public purse
… the professions	… building on pre-existing efforts to bring the built environment professions together and for a some time they sang from the same hymn sheet about the importance of design, and particularly urban design	… CABE failed to tackle the 'tyrannies' described in Chapter 1 or the tendency of the built environment professions to revert to type and to the narrow pre-occupations of their members once CABE ceased to exist
… the public	… successfully raising the built environment onto the national consciousness through its campaigns and publicity machine	… CABE failed to change the national culture and debate, and design quickly slipped back into a specialist concern of the few and / or a passing preoccupation of those afflicted by poor quality development proposals
… policy	… its very significant influence on policy, particularly planning and regeneration policy (and latterly highways policy) where design became an overarching theme that infused the Government's guidance which directly influenced practice on the ground	… CABE some argued that CABE too easily bent with the wind and was too keen to involve itself in every latest policy fad, and by losing focus never truly moved design to become a policy focus in its own right instead of an adjunct to something else
… public building	… positively shaping the range of public building programmes that stretched through the 2000s, and was successful in ensuring that design quality became a central consideration in many of them	… CABE was less successful at institutionalising these changes, most of which were ad hoc, and so when the financial crisis came programmes like Building Schools for the Future where quickly dismissed as too expensive because of the bespoke design solutions they promoted
… private developers	… positively influencing private developers about the value of design, and whilst this influence on the volume housebuilders was late in coming and varied considerably, the organisation had significant successes in convincing some about the importance of design, impact that persists today	… some larger developers were alienated by the CABE message and its methods, and never came around to its way of thinking
… skills and capacity	… its work on professional skills and capacity, care of its knowledge and assistance tools. By all accounts, this influence played a significant role in widely changing local cultures around the importance of and priority given to design, particularly in local authorities around the country	… these skills were quickly hollowed-out when austerity began to bite, and CABE never engaged with professional education and had no impact on its continued organisation in professional siloes
… the next generation	… the wide range of innovative resources that were prepared for use by teachers and school children which, because of their engaging and creative nature and the large numbers who used them, will have had a long-term impact on at least some career choices	… given the sheer numbers of children that CABE needed to reach and the complexity of the educational field, the challenge facing an organisation of CABE's size clearly militated against it having an impact that was anything other than transitory
… specific projects and places	… its design review panels that had a direct and tangible impact on projects and places, seeing in excess of 3,000 schemes over its life of which, according to CABE (2010d), 81% were changed as a result. In doing so CABE moved design review from a marginal national activity to a significant national, regional and local one which, more than any other tool, has survived (albeit in a piecemeal fashion) the cuts in public expenditure	… by making the process so public and adversarial CABE, like the RFAC before, ultimately contributed to its own demise through the enemies it created and the consequential absence of friends when the organisation needed them most

Figure A.2 CABE's impacts

CABE impacted on	CABE impacted through	But despite its impact
... thought leadership	... the sheer quantity of its research and advocacy work, and became the natural focus for thought leadership in the field, a role that even extended internationally where CABE was increasingly regarded as a node of innovation and best practice	... ultimately CABE relied on the volume of its output more than the quality of individual pieces which only occasionally had the depth, rigour and originality needed to define the field or to convince sceptics, such as The Treasury about the real value of design
... day to day practice	... its numerous practice guides, case studies, research studies, its audits, websites and toolkits, that practitioners of all types, even if they had no contact with CABE, could draw on and utilise in their day to day practice to assist with particular tasks or to help make the case for design	... the sheer quantity of its published material was often a cause for complaint, that practitioners felt swamped with material that they rarely had time to digest
... mainstreaming design	... turning around the culture for design so that the pursuit of design quality was increasingly seen as a mainstream aspiration of planning and development and increasingly went without question by built environment professionals (of all types), and by politicians and developers alike	... CABE's influence was not the same everywhere, and CABE found it much harder to influence the hard to reach places, both those that geographically and culturally felt a long way from London, and those where economic and social challenges predominated
... the general standard of design	... improvement by degrees, with successful schemes that had been influenced by CABE setting the precedent for schemes that came after, whilst schemes that weren't up to quality were more often abandoned either directly or indirectly as a result of CABE's influence. Sometimes these changes were small scale and additive, for example the improvement in housing design gradually seen through the Building for Life tool or through enabling work that enhanced the confidence and capacity to address design challenges locally. Sometimes they were dramatic, such as CABE's work on the 2012 Olympics with its galvanising impact on East London. The ultimate impact is as much about what is not seen today as what is	... CABE can't take all the credit as the policy turn in favour of design had begun long before CABE came on the scene, in the mid 1990s, whilst government policy and non-governmental initiatives such as the Urban Design Alliance (UDAL) were also influential
... the CABE family	... its enduring influence on the people who passed through the organisation as its employees, many of whom are still working in and shaping the field in the UK. As one CABE officer commented: "It did bring together the most extraordinarily set of talented and committed people ... for younger staff CABE was the most amazing springboard job before something else, and that is still raising standards"	... CABE's demise and the austerity that followed drove many of CABE's former employees to work outside the built environment or overseas
... creating today's market for design governance	... the impact it had on the regional partners that CABE supported and which continue to survive (albeit hand to mouth) alongside Design Council CABE which CABE established as a final act, and, having weathered some very difficult times, is now gaining momentum as a premium supplier of design review services. All these players (and others, private and public) are now operating in the market that CABE, through its growth (creating the demand) and sudden demise (creating the opportunity), facilitated	... the dominance of CABE during the 2000s also led to unintentional casualties, through the sideling and eventual demise of formally influential non-governmental players such as the Urban Design Alliance and the Civic Trust – see Chapter 5

Figure A.2 (Continued)

significant public funding allowed, and, over time, the ability that gave the organisation to proactively reshape the landscape for design governance in England. Love it or loath it, CABE undoubtedly had a big impact, and most see that impact as a positive one if measured against its core objective of improving the standard of design in the built environment. As one insider commented, "CABE didn't lead the profligate life, it was relatively tightly funded, but it had a meaningful sum and it had a sum where it could have an impact beyond the individual schemes that it saw," both cumulatively (project by project and on larger places) as well as on the larger national demand for better design as encapsulated in political priorities.

In its early years, CABE was sometimes referred to as an unconventional organisation within and funded by government, but not in a governmental mould. Instead it was able to agitate, innovate, and shake things up, and exploit tactics not usually associated with the public sector to influence those not previously receptive to or interested in its messages about the significance of design. Whilst, as the organisation grew and matured this 'guerrilla' phase of its evolution came to an end (indeed had to end), CABE remained a very determined unit and one unusually effective at responding to the changing political context within which it found itself.

In part, this seems to be because of the persistence of a culture that emphasised continued learning and innovation and the flexible application of its

knowledge and practices to the range of challenges the organisation addressed. It also reflects the fact that the sorts of 'informal' tools at its disposal were particularly adaptable and not subject to the stifling rigidity of being defined in statute or circumscribed by government policy. Its tools also lent themselves to use in combination so that particular challenging problems, such as the design of volume built housing, could be confronted from different angles and with different combinations of evidence, knowledge, promotion, evaluation, and assistance, depending on the need.

A key lesson from CABE is therefore that despite the limitations of its individual powers, its ability to spread its messages on multiple fronts and through a diverse and continually changing toolkit made it a very effective organisation. As the periods both pre- and post-CABE reveal (see Chapter 3 and 5), the over-reliance on a single tool (namely design review) will only ever have a limited impact and eventually, as happened with the RFAC, those limitations will come to define (and undermine) the whole process of governing design. Instead, the CABE experiment powerfully demonstrated that multiple overlapping informal design governance tools not only cover the design governance field of action more comprehensively (because of their flexibility) than formal ones (A.3), but ultimately can decisively shape the decision-making environment within which the formal tools operate, in turn enabling them to operate more effectively.

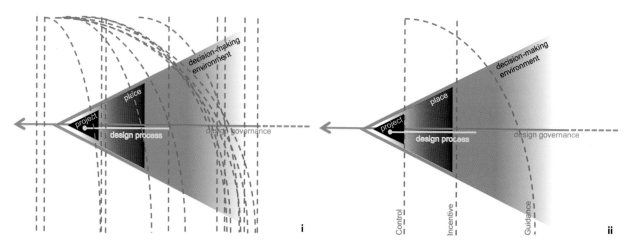

Figure A.3   Diagrammatic comparison of (i) the informal tools and (ii) the formal tools within the design governance field of action

The Legitimacy of Design Governance

The Design Governance Conundrum

This book would not be complete without a return to the conundrum set out in Chapter 1 that concerned the larger legitimacy of design governance. The question was asked: *Can state intervention in processes of designing the built environment positively shape design processes and outcomes, and if so, how?*

At the close of this book, having spent several years interrogating the experience of CABE, the final conclusion to the first part of this question has to be 'yes', the state has potentially a valuable role to play in intervening in the design of the built environment in order to deliver the sorts of place quality benefits that, throughout its existence, CABE used to justify its funding. More than that, used intelligently and with determination (as CABE generally did) and at a large enough strategic scale (e.g. nationally), processes of design governance can have a dramatic impact on the decision-making environment within which decisions about the built environment occur so that a culture of better place-making, as opposed to individual episodes of design, begins to emerge.

New Labour was a pragmatic experiment immersed in the 'third way' philosophy of 'if it works, back it' (see Chapter 4), rather than on the basis of dogmatic belief systems (perhaps explaining why it was, and still is, despised by so many). Considered in its own purely pragmatic terms, the CABE experiment must be judged a success: an investment by the state of the equivalent of 0.02 per cent of the construction industry in England (Carmona 2011b) with very significant impacts on the culture and practices of development nationally and on design governance processes locally, leading to a new sensitivity to and interest in design.

Turning to the second part of the conundrum—*if so, how?*—the CABE experiment quite clearly represents just one approach to state-led design governance and its successes should not be taken to imply either that such an approach would be suitable everywhere, or that all (other) forms of intervention in design by government and its agencies are necessarily effective; Chapter 1 demonstrated that this is far from the case and that poor design governance is often as bad, or perhaps worse, than none at all. Moreover, not

everything CABE touched was a success. Some tools, such as the use of design competitions, never got any momentum, whilst others, notably design review, were often mired in controversy, although ultimately had a significant positive impact.

Consequently, the answer to the question of how design governance should be conducted is rather inconclusively that 'it depends': it depends on the context within which it is being conducted, over what scale, by whom, with what intentions, and with what resources. However, whatever the environment within which it is being conducted, analysis of the CABE experiment has forcefully revealed that those responsible should fully embrace the informal as well as formal modes of design governance and should consider such processes part of a long-term and necessary societal investment in place (A.4).

Multifarious Critiques

A range of theoretical problematics of design and its governance were set out in Chapter 1, and CABE was accused of all of those (and more) during the course of its existence. During the research on which this book is based, these multifarious critiques, many of which are contradictory, were frequently and often compellingly restated. Summarising these, CABE was accused of being:

- A neoliberal pro-development tool: simply sweetening the pill of otherwise unpalatable and inequitable projects that offered little to society at large—"They were just very focused on the message that any kind of work with the built environment and green space should add profits."
- A poodle of central government: too nervous of upsetting its sponsors and therefore lacking the ability to confront government when necessary— "It was the government's little toy to help it do some things that it was easier to do at arm's length."
- London-centric: because that was where the money, politics, and biggest projects were—"It became evident that they were a London based coterie of chums, all the way down, the agenda, the menu, the interest is London luvvies, they were not interested in the rest of England."
- Preoccupied with 'shiny urbanism': reflecting the recipes of the 'urban renaissance' and the

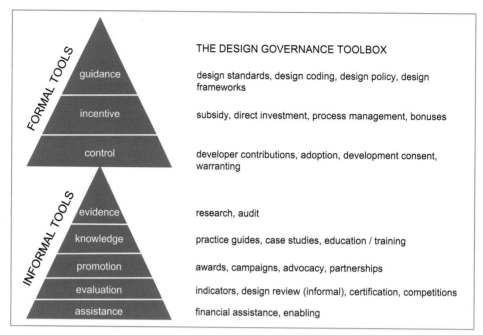

Figure A.4 The complete design governance toolbox (formal and informal)

metropolitan fascination with 'starchitects', rather than the challenges of suburban England where most wanted to live—"The town cramming, high density, mixed use, ban cars, café culture and all that vision that Lord Rogers foisted upon people, that was their agenda."

• Too unfocussed: expanding too readily into different agendas and getting distracted from its core mission—"CABE was so bound up delivering these Service Level Agreements for government; we couldn't see the wood for the trees, we were doing too much."

• Elitist in multiple ways: organisationally elitist (assuming that CABE should lead and others would follow); professionally elitist (because architectural design is inevitably so); exclusionary (only engaging positively with those already in the clique, aka the 'CABE family'); elitist in its processes (particularly the 'closed shop' of design review)—"Elitism, dear God, yes. They were going to produce standards and guidance, which the rest of us would be obliged to follow."

• Not elitist enough: failing to bring the powerful architectural establishment on board as key supporters of the organisation—"They should have had somebody who was much more embedded in the central London chattering classes of architects, who knew those people, who could talk to them."

• Scared of aesthetics: determined to see design in purely objective terms whereas, in reality, it was not—"Sometimes something would come into design review and nobody would say 'that is incredibly ugly' because everything was based on facts and figures to avoid design being seen to be a matter of taste."

• Style biased: with an in-built bias towards contemporary design and against traditional architecture—"It was certainly pro-modernist . . . they thought that anything that might be a classical design was basically pastiche and therefore couldn't be dealt with and was rubbish."

• Inconsistent in its advice: because much was intangible and not everything or everyone could be boiled down to a simple set of objective criteria—"You had some completely opposing views from some of the CABE commissioners. If you got the wrong one on your committee, then you knew you were in for trouble."

• Too powerful and undermining freedom: by imposing a state-sanctioned view on design that often ventured into matters of detail (aesthetic and functional) that should rightfully be a matter for the scheme promoter—"You might find that CABE stifled as many good buildings as it encouraged, and who are they, or who are we, to judge whether those are good or bad buildings ultimately?"

- Too weak: because it worked through influence rather than compulsion and therefore influenced those who wished to hear the message and not those who didn't—"If they'd ever found a way in which they could actually get the housebuilders in a headlock, that would be fine, but they didn't."

- Insensitive to professional responsibility: by failing to take account of the professional standing and perspective of those it sought to advise—"You spend seven years in training, then a lot of time gaining experience and, actually, that should be enough, then an outside organisation such as CABE takes the responsibility away from the architect . . . there's a kind of emasculation if you like."

- Insensitive to the market: lacking market nous by being often divorced from the commercial concerns of the different markets in which it was offering advice—"When you're considering a scheme in an affluent area of west London, and you're doing one in a regeneration area, you have to look at things differently . . . so cutting your cloth accordingly is very important and CABE didn't quite understand that."

- Overbearing and arrogant: by stealing the work and initiatives of others without giving sufficient credit and by being insufficiently supportive and too condescending to those it dealt with—"It was almost like you were at school . . . You know, the sort of school 'teachery' thing 'I know best, stop talking, shut up and listen to what I'm saying and don't question it.'"

- Too verbose: pronouncing too much and producing too much guidance—"Ultimately, there's only so much guidance you can read—it just gets put on shelves."

- Obsessed with communication: believing that being heard was more important than what was said—"They brought in lots of people [who] had nothing to do with the built environment, they became increasingly interested in media output, as opposed to actually serious, proper information and guidance."

- Too flabby and over-managed: growing too large with too many managers and not enough workers—"CABE had got bigger and bigger and bigger and more and more more bureaucratic."

- Subject to conflicts of interest: conflicts that were more perceived than real but nevertheless at key times damaging to CABE's credibility and its standing within the sector—"We were told by the then permanent secretary that . . . 'CABE's in the pocket of the developers isn't it?'"

Those interviewed during the course of the research typically took either a positive or negative stance towards CABE. Noticeably those critical of the organisation tended to take an overwhelmingly negative (sometimes vitriolic) perspective across the board, whilst those (a significant majority) who took a predominantly positive stance were more willing to entertain a degree of truth in many of the critiques, recognising that CABE was far from a perfect organisation.

Most of the latter type were sanguine that such criticisms were par for the course, and that the same critiques, a little differently, would have been made about any other organisation in a similar field.[3] As one commissioner concluded: "It would be hugely naive to imagine that the kind of glory years, if I can put it like that, when you're brand shiny and new, will last. There's nothing unexpected, or unusual about that. You wouldn't find a public body, or public agency in the world where people aren't saying it's too this, or too that, or too big, or too small, or too powerful, or too weak. That just goes with the territory."

A Simple Case for Intervention

So given the inevitability of the critiques, and their partial legitimacy, what is the moral/societal case for continued intervention in this area? Ultimately that will be a political judgement. Pragmatically the CABE experiment has shown widespread, tangible, and positive results, leading to a long-term legacy of better projects, places, and processes than would otherwise have been the case, and with positive impacts across England on local populations, the environment, and society at large (see A.2). This is in exchange for, what by any standard, was a very small national investment in the field, almost an "accounting error" in governmental terms as one interviewee described it.

Yet this will need to be set against other costs, beginning with the unknown but certainly much larger investment by private and/or public actors by dint of simply engaging with services of design governance, such as those CABE provided: for example through getting involved in processes of enabling, attending a training event, or turning up to a design review and afterwards amending a scheme. Also, beyond the financials, there are other costs, notably accruing to those whose freedoms to design (well or badly) have been curtailed by such processes, or to the fragile professional egos that find even constructive criticism difficult to take. Finally there will be costs in the mistakes that from time to time even the most sophisticated and carefully run processes of design governance will inevitably make (A.5).

Morally politicians will need to decide where their priorities lie. The CABE experiment shows that, despite the cost, the case is weighted very heavily on the side of intelligent light-touch intervention through the full range of design governance tools. When we know what good design means and the benefits it brings, and when we know how to design good places

Figure A.5 One of CABE's mistakes as widely recognised by those involved, as one influential insider commented "The Walkie Talkie is more elegant, believe it or not, as a consequence of CABE's reviews of it, but obviously, there will always be projects like that where we could and should have done more." (See Chapter 8)

and how to facilitate those processes, politicians will have to explain why we still fail to do so, and why they don't care enough to learn the lessons and start to turn the situation around.

Forgetting to Remember (and to Constantly Remind Ourselves)

Following the passage through the Houses of Parliament of the statutory instrument that formally dissolved CABE, John Penrose, the tourism and heritage minister at the DCMS who signed the order, commented in the House of Commons:

> CABE did a lot of good work and much of it will continue in different places. The organisation may be coming to an end under the order, but its work and the principles that it embodied will continue. I hope and expect that the public sector's commitment to good design in our built environment will continue, too.[4]

A CABE employee stated: "We always used to joke that CABE was working towards its own demise, and that the subject matter would be so mainstreamed that it wasn't necessary anymore and, possibly, it achieved that. . . . It's still out there, its messages, its lessons, its teachings, its ideals are still run of the mill to a certain extent." Equally, it could be argued that CABE failed to sufficiently make the case for design and so, faced with choices about where to make spending cuts, the Coalition government of 2010–15 decided the axe would fall on CABE. For others, the seeds of CABE's demise were sown when CABE became a statutory organisation and 'came into the mainstream'. As one commissioner argued, "If you take the terrorist out of the organisation, you remove the agitation and when you remove the agitation, it's very easy to remove the organisation." Another contended: "The criticisms were either that CABE wasn't doing enough, or it was doing too much, which is probably a sign that it was doing about right."

The situation post-CABE has also revealed that, as a nation, we have quickly forgotten the difference CABE made, and instead have focussed on making cuts in the areas that are politically easiest (where opposition is least vociferous) and that are least tied up in statutory obligations. These include discretionary services relating to design. Again, this was arguably a failure of CABE (despite its stated intentions); a failure to adequately reach out to a larger constituency beyond the built environment professionals who were already convinced, and to create a demand for good design within the population at large. There was also a failure to take advantage of the opportunities that came CABE's way to make the case for underpinning its activities (notably design review) with a formal and statutory status that would have tied them into the non-discretionary machinery of the state. Whilst it was in existence, CABE undoubtedly changed the culture for design and played a critical role in driving design up the political agenda, both nationally and locally. But this was a culture change built on sand, and when CABE was no longer around to remind us of the importance of good design, we quickly forgot.

The situation after 2011 has shown that, unlike, for example, health, defence, or education, the quality of the built environment is simply one of those areas we need to keep on reminding ourselves has value and should be a prime concern of the state. As, in England, the cost of poor design mounts, sooner or later we will need to remember. When we do it is hoped that the evidence collected in this book will assist us in the process, as well as the many others around the world that, for the brief time it existed, did not have the benefit of the unique, innovative, and impactful organisation that was CABE.

Notes

1. For example the Heritage Lottery Fund.
2. Sometimes externally and sometimes internally, but excluding its own annual reports.
3. For example about The Arts Council or English Heritage.
4. www.gov.uk/government/news/commission-for-architecture-and-the-built-environment

Research Methods

A Pump-Priming Phase—Towards an Analytical Framework

The importance of seizing the moment before the resources, evidence, and collective memory of those involved in the CABE experiment was lost was recognised by CABE itself, which, in the last months of its existence, funded a quick-fire pump-priming project to i) explore the possibility of a larger study and ii) if feasible, to assist in making a research application to one of the UK research councils. During this period, a UCL researcher was located within CABE for a period of twenty-five days and had unprecedented access to CABE's personnel and archives. The intention of this phase was to:

- Work with a team from the UK National Archives in order to identify and safeguard key resources as part of an evidence base for subsequent research.
- To begin the process of mapping key programmes, outputs, people, and responsibilities before the organisation closed and the collective memory was lost.
- To begin conversations with key stakeholders that have shaped the CABE experiment and whose experience needed to be captured as part of the evidence base.

The nature of this work was rapid and exploratory and largely focussed on ensuring that a subsequent in-depth evaluation of the CABE experiment would be both possible and productive through establishing contacts, safeguarding evidence, and constructing a draft analytical framework for the research proposal. This phase was completed in April 2011 with a research application submitted in November and approved nine months later.

The Substantive Research Phase—Multidimensional Inductive Analysis

The substantive research phase, funded by the Arts and Humanities Research Council, ran from January 2013 to August 2014 and is completed with the publication of this book. It employed an inductive research methodology that sought to learn from the specifics of practice and apply that to an integrated theory of design governance. The essence of the approach was a multidimensional impact analysis of CABE's work, allowing rich empirical evidence to be applied and related to the research questions posed in this book's Preface.

Five research stages were followed.

1. Analytical Framework

This stage of the project focuses on establishing a comprehensive understanding of the international design governance literature with a particular focus on:

- Understanding the dynamics of design within public policy, development, property market, and political contexts and within wider urban policy.
- Tracing the CABE story (and that of the RFAC) in the professional/academic literature and in the press (for example reviewing more than ten years worth of press clippings), and tracing evidence of the methods and impact of any comparator organisations, internationally.
- Developing and deepening an analytical framework (the tools framework discussed in this chapter) as a means to structure the analysis of the CABE experience in order to address the fundamental research questions via the preparation of a coordinated and coherent set of research tools.

2. Organisational Interrogation

On the basis of documentary analysis (of 2,868 source documents) using NVivo software, a second stage involved the in-depth review of all key policy, programme, project, and performance management documents produced by CABE (and its sponsor government departments), as well as those produced by the periodic external reviews of the organisation. The aim was to understand the drivers and barriers to the CABE experience and to trace CABE's history against the wider political and urban policy context. Key outputs included:

- A series of working organisational maps of how CABE developed over its history and of how its work responded to external political priorities and pressures.
- The first full account of the range of CABE tools, programmes, projects, people, and relationships.
- A comprehensive review of the key outputs from CABE's various programmes, with a comparison, as far as possible, against the resources dedicated to different streams of work.
- An understanding of how the organisation itself operated, established priorities, allocated resources, measured success, etc.

3. Firsthand Opinions

Utilising the findings from Stage 2, a range of in-depth structured interviews (thirty-nine in total) were conduced with two key audiences. First, those both from within and outside of CABE (including in government) centrally involved in establishing and developing the organisation and its approaches, and eventually in shutting it down. This included both professional and political players. Second, interviews with key opinion formers on record as supportive and/or critical of CABE at various stages in its history. The intention was to:

- Test the accuracy of the Stage 2 outputs.
- Understand the political, organisational, resource, professional, and practical drivers and barriers for CABE; to get under the skin of the organisation with the benefit that distance will give to players once intimately, but now no longer, involved.

- Understand the common critiques of CABE and its programmes and how these developed over time.
- Identify the critical episodes in CABE's work for potential further analysis during Stage 4.

4. The Reunions

A full understanding of CABE's work and tools over its eleven years enabled the selection of a range of key episodes within each tool for further analysis. Rather than pepper-potting across all aspects of every tool, this stage focussed on particular sets of activities, for example: design reviews relating to master planning; research projects focusing on value arguments; enabling in the parks sector, etc. This allowed a better understanding of process, problematics, and impact through the comparison of related work episodes rather than trying to draw conclusions from across each and every disparate episode. The selected 'episodes' represented the broad sweep of CABE's engagement with design, but also those which stakeholders in the third stage judged most significant in how they have shaped (positively or negatively) the design agenda. In this regard, it was important to understand the bigger picture and what had worked and what had not, but also the detailed practices.

The intention will be to trace impacts in terms of processes, influences, and wider impacts in built projects and/or design proposals, and, as far as possible, understand the range of tools CABE utilised. The stage constituted a series of small focussed seminars— 'reunions'—bringing together key stakeholders/protagonists involved in each episode from within CABE, amongst its partner organisations, and amongst the recipients of its work; followed by more focussed individual interviews as and when required. The reunions (twenty-four events in total) were structured by considering the aspirations, processes, and outcomes from each episode. The free and open discussion between parties was recorded and later transcribed before conclusions were drawn out about the effectiveness of key programmes and tools and how they might or might not be reinterpreted in the post-CABE world.

5. Synthesis

With multiple analytical techniques, it was important to carefully and individually document each stage of the research before attempting a full synthesis and evaluation against the fundamental research questions. The data was subjected to the standard qualitative techniques of data reduction, display, analysis, and deduction, with the analytical framework (refined during the course of the research) used to structure this process through devising a series of related pro-formas through which to conduct the analysis and subsequently summarise and display the data. The diverse methodological approaches were written up separately, before triangulating the evidence as a means to draw out common findings. The diversity of approaches helped to overcome known potential weaknesses with each one in order that a more rounded and coherent view of the CABE experiment could be revealed.

The final stage involved telling the CABE story (this book) and in the processes using the analysis to re-theorise design governance, using the empirical research as the basis for a fundamental and critical review of the value, means, and purpose of design governance. In this respect, the study has been prospective as well as retrospective, looking to offer lessons for the wide range of organisations that continue to pursue the design agenda in England, the United Kingdom, and internationally.

References

Adams D & Tiesdell S (2013) *Shaping Places: Urban Planning, Design and Development*, London, Routledge.

Al Waer H (2013) "Improving Contemporary Approaches to the Masterplanning Process", *Proceedings of the ICE—Planning and Urban Design*, 167(1): 25–34.

Annabel Jackson Associates (2007) CABE ABEC Evaluation, Bath, Annabel Jackson Associates Ltd.

Appleby M (2006) "CABE Space Director to Focus on Streets Rather than Parks", Horticulture Week, 14 September, www.hortweek.com/cabe-space-director-focus-streets-rather-parks/article/791767.

Architect's Journal (2001) "School Sheds Out as CABE Seeks Better Class from PFI", 25 October, www.architectsjournal.co.uk/home/school-sheds-out-as-cabe-seeks-better-class-from-pfi/184935.article.

Architects' Journal (2002) "Ministerial Design Champions Set Goals for Public Buildings", 24 January, www.architectsjournal.co.uk/home/ministerial-design-champions-set-goals-for-public-buildings/172750.article.

Architects' Journal (2010) "Europan Faces Axe in UK as CABE Withdraws Backing" Architects' Journal, 5 March, www.architectsjournal.co.uk/home/-europan-faces-axe-in-uk-as-cabe-withdraws-backing/5215043.fullarticle.

Arnold D (2009) "CABE at Ten: Is It Doing Too Much" *Architects' Journal*, 11 September, www.architectsjournal.co.uk/news/daily-news/-cabe-at-10-is-it-doing-too-much/5207922.article.

Australian Public Service Commission (2009) Smarter Policy: Choosing Policy Instruments and Working with Others to Influence Behaviour, Attorney-General's Department, Barton ACT.

Baer W (2011) "Customs, Norms, Rules, Regulations and Standards in Design Practice 1" in Banerjee T & Loukaitou-Sideris A (Eds) *Companion to Urban Design*, London, Routledge.

Baldock H (1998) "Architecture Commission Set to Replace RFAC", Building, CCLXIII(49): 11.

Ballieu A (1993) "Architecture: The Mandarins Meet Their Match: When the Royal Fine Art Commission Decrees, Governments Defer. But in Paternoster Square It Is Being Spurned", *The Independent*, 3 February, www.independent.co.uk/arts-entertainment/art/news/architecture-the-mandarins-meet-their-match-when-the-royal-fine-art-commission-decrees-governments-defer-but-in-paternoster-square-it-is-being-spurned-corrected-1470519.html.

Banerjee T & Loukaitou-Sideris A (Eds) (2011) *Companion to Urban Design*, London, Routledge.

Barker K (2004) "Review of Housing Supply, Delivering Stability, Securing Our Future Housing Needs", http://webarchive.nationalarchives.gov.uk/20080107210803/http://www.hm-treasury.gov.uk/consultations_and_legislation/barker/consult_barker_index.cfm.

Barnett J (1974) *Urban Design as Public Policy, Practical Methods for Improving Cities*, New York, Architectural Record.

Barnett J (2011) "How Codes Shaped Development in the United States, and Why They Should Be Changed" in Marshall S (Ed) *Urban Coding and Planning*, London, Routledge.

Baumeister M (2012) "Development Charges across Canada, an Underutilized Growth Management Tool", IMFG Papers on Municipal Finance and Governance, www.munkschool.utoronto.ca/imfg/uploads/201/imfg_no.9_online_june25.pdf.

Beckford J (2002) *Quality*, London, Routledge.

Ben-Joseph E (2005a) *The Code of the City: Standards and the Hidden Language of Place Making*, Cambridge, MA, MIT Press.

Ben-Joseph E (2005b) "Facing Subdivision Regulations" in Ben-Joseph E & Szold T (Eds) *Regulating Place, Standards and the Shaping of Urban America*, New York, Routledge.

Bentley I (1999) *Urban Transformations: Power, People and Urban Design*, London, Routledge.

Biddulph M (1998) "Choices in the Design Control Process, Learning from Stoke", *Town Planning Review*, 69(1): 23–48.

Biddulph M, Hooper A, & Punter J (2006) "Awards, Patronage and Design Preference: An Analysis of English Awards for Housing Design", *Urban Design International*, 11(1): 49–61.

Bishop D (2009) "Someone to Watch Over Me", *New Start*, 1 June.

Bishop P (2011) *The Bishop Review, the Future of Design in the Built Environment*, London, Design Council.

Blackler Z (2004) "Bias Allegation Hits CABE", *Architects' Journal*, 18 March, www.architectsjournal.co.uk/home/bias-allegation-hits-cabe/656648.article.

Blair T (2001a) "Address Groundwork Seminar", 24 April, Croydon.

Blair T (2001b) Full Text of Tony Blair's Speech on Education, 23 May, www.theguardian.com/politics/2001/may/23/labour.tonyblair.

Booth P (1999) "Discretion in Planning versus Zoning" in Cullingworth B (Ed) *British Planning, 50 Years of Urban and Regional Policy*, London, The Athlone Press.

BOP Consulting (2011) "Sea Change Evaluation, Final Report", www.integreatplus.com/sites/default/files/sea_change_evaluation.pdf.

Bowden C (2001) "Letter to Chief Planning Officers from Christopher Bowden, Head of Division, Addition of Commission for Architecture and the Built Environment to the List of Non-statutory Consultees", 15 May, London, DETR, www.publications.parliament.uk/pa/cm200304/cmselect/cmodpm/1117/1117we03.htm.

Bristol Evening Post (South Gloucestershire), Monday, 23 September 2002, p. 18

Brown P (2004) "Architecture Body Chief Quits Ahead of Report", *The Guardian*, 17 June, www.theguardian.com/society/2004/jun/17/urbandesign.arts.

Building Design (2013) "Anonymous Comment Posted about Lee Mallett (2013) 'The Planner as Urban Visionary'", 18 December, www.bdonline.co.uk.

Building for Life (2004) Building for Life, Newsletter 01 Sustainability, September, London, CABE.

CABE & Civic Trust (2004) Green Flag Award Winners 2003/4, London, CABE.

CABE (2000a) Commission for Architecture and the Built Environment, Financial Statements for the Period Ended 31 March 2000, London, CABE.

CABE (2000b) Minutes of the Design Review Committee, 20 December, London, CABE.

CABE (2001a) CABE Annual Report and Accounts 2001, London, CABE.

CABE (2001b) *The Value of Urban Design*, London, Thomas Telford.

CABE (2001c) Minutes of the Design Review Committee, 12 November, London, CABE.

CABE (2001d) Minutes of the Design Review Committee, 7 November, London, CABE.

CABE (2001e) Minutes of the Design Review Committee, 25 July, London, CABE.

CABE (2002a) CABE Enabling Handbook (Unpublished), London, CABE.

CABE (2002b) Corporate Strategy 2002–2005, London, CABE.

CABE (2002c) CABE Annual Report and Accounts 2001/2002, Sense of Place, London, CABE.

CABE (2002d) Design and Planning: Response to the Planning Green Paper and Associated Consultation Papers, London, CABE.

CABE (2002e) Regional Programme Funding Guidelines 2002–04, London, CABE.

CABE (2002f) Design Review: Guidance on How CABE Evaluates Quality in Architecture and Urban Design, London, CABE.

CABE (2002g) Minutes of Sift Meeting, 17 May, London, CABE.

CABE (2002h) Minutes of Sift Meeting, 30 April, London, CABE.

CABE (2002i) Minutes of Sift Meeting, 14 June, London, CABE.

CABE (2002j) *Building for Life: An Introduction*, London, CABE, HBF and The Civic Trust.

CABE (2002k) Streets of Shame: Executive Summary, London, CABE.

CABE (2003a) CABE Annual Report and Accounts 2003, London, CABE.

CABE (2003b) Planning & Compulsory Purchase Bill: Outline of CABE's Position, London, CABE.

CABE (2003c) Regional Funding Programme Guidelines for the 2004–6 Round of RFP (Unpublished), London, CABE.

CABE (2003d) *Ten Ways to Make Quality Count, Business Planning Zones*, London, CABE.

CABE (2003e) *360° Magazine*, September 2003, London, CABE.

CABE (2004a) Draft PPS 1 Creating Sustainable Communities: Response to Consultation Draft by Commission for Architecture and the Built Environment, London, CABE.

CABE (2004b) *Housing Futures 2024: A Provocative Look at Future Trends in Housing*, London, CABE and RIBA.

CABE (2004c) Building for Life Newsletter 01 Sustainability, September 2004.

CABE (2004d) CABE Annual Report & Accounts 2004: Our Buildings, Our Spaces, Our Lives, London, CABE.

CABE (2004e) *Creating Successful Masterplans: A Guide for Clients*, London, CABE.

CABE (2004f) Architecture and Race: A Study of Minority Ethnic Students in the Professions. Executive Summary: Research Outcomes 6, London, CABE.

CABE (2004g) *Corporate Strategy for 2004–2007: Transforming Neighbourhoods*, London, CABE.

CABE (2004h) "CABE Announces New Investment in Architecture Centres", CABE Extra Newsletter 10, 9 February.

CABE (2004i) *Being Involved in School Design: A Guide for School Communities, Local Authorities, Funders and Design and Construction Teams*, London, CABE.

CABE (2005a) *Design Champions*, London, CABE.

CABE (2005b) *Making Places: Careers Which Shape Our Cities Towns and Villages*, London, CABE.

CABE (2005c) Whose Place Is It Anyway, CABE Annual Report & Accounts 2005, London, CABE.

CABE (2005d) *Housing Audit: Assessing the Design Quality of New Homes in the North East, North West and Yorkshire & Humber*, London, CABE.

CABE (2005e) *Making Design Policy Work: How to Deliver Good Design through Your Local Development Framework*, London, CABE.

CABE (2005f) *Design Reviewed*, Issue 2, London, CABE.

CABE (2005g) *Winning Housing Designs: Lessons from an Anglo-French Housing Initiative*, London, CABE.

CABE (2005h) *Delivering Great Places to Live: 20 Questions You Need to Answer*, London, CABE.

CABE (2005i) CABE Enabling Handbook (Unpublished), London, CABE.

CABE (2005j) Appraisal of CABE Enabling Panel by Enabling Programme Officer, December.

CABE (2006a) *Design Review, How CABE Evaluated Quality in Architecture and Urban Design*, London, CABE.

CABE (2006b) *Getting Out There, Art and Design Local Safari Guide, a Teachers Guide to Using the Local Built Environment at Key State 3 and 4*, London, CABE.

CABE (2006c) *CABE Works, Here's How, Annual Review 2005/06*, London, CABE.

CABE (2006d) *The Principles of Inclusive Design. (They Include You)*, London, CABE.

CABE (2006e) Assessing Secondary School Design Quality: Research Report, London, CABE.

CABE (2006f) Responses to the Enabling Panel Manager Questionnaire 'Appraisal of Existing Panels' (Unpublished), London, CABE.

CABE (2006g) *How to do Design Review: Creating and Running a Successful Panel*, CABE, London.

CABE (2006h) *Better Public Building*, London, CABE.

CABE (2007a) *Design and Access Statements, How to Write, Read and Use Them*, London, CABE.

CABE (2007b) *CABE Annual Report 2006/07, Financial Statements and Accounts*, London, CABE.

CABE (2007c) Staff Survey 2007 (Unpublished), London, CABE.

CABE (2007d) How to Set up an Enabling Panel (Unpublished), London, CABE.

CABE (2007e) *Housing Audit: Assessing the Design Quality of New Housing in the East Midlands, West Midlands and the South West*, London, CABE.

CABE (2007f) *Design Task Group Report Design Task Group—Emscher Landschaftspark 30 September–2 October 2007*, London, CABE.

CABE (2007g) *CABE Schools Design Quality Programme: Building Schools for the Future*, London, CABE.

CABE (2007h) *Minutes of CABE Operations Committee, 4 May*, London, CABE.

CABE (2007i) *Evaluation of Architecture and Built Environment Centres (ABECs) Funded under CABE Regional Funding Programme 2006/8*, London, CABE.

CABE (2007j) Commission Paper, 18th July, London, CABE

CABE (2008a) CABE *Annual Report 2007/08, Financial Statements and Accounts*, London, CABE.

CABE (2008b) "Memorandum Submitted by CABE", www.publications.parliament.uk/pa/cm200809/cmselect/cmberr/89/89we32.htm.

CABE (2008c) *Sure Start Children's Centres: A Post-occupancy Evaluation*, London, CABE.

CABE (2008d) *The Thames Gateway Design Pact: Making New Things Happen*, London, CABE.

CABE (2008e) CABE Commission Paper, 18 July (Unpublished), London, CABE.

CABE (2008f) Urban Design & Homes Annual Review 2008 (Unpublished), London, CABE.

CABE (2009a) *CABE Ten Year Review*, London, CABE.

CABE (2009b) CABE *Annual Report 2008–09: Financial Statements and Accounts*, London, CABE.

CABE (2009c) "Better Buildings and Spaces Improve Quality of Life Says the Public", http://webarchive.nationalarchives.gov.uk/20110118095356/http://www.cabe.org.uk/news/better-buildings-and-spaces-improve-quality-of-lifeCABE.

CABE (2009d) *Shape the Future: Corporate Strategy 2008/09–2010/11*, London, CABE.

CABE (2010a) *CABE Annual Report and Accounts 2009/10*, London, CABE.

CABE (2010b) Enabling Framework Call-off Contract Template (Unpublished), London, CABE.

CABE (2010c) CABE and the Public Bodies Review (Unpublished), London, CABE.

CABE (2010d) *People and Places, Public Attitudes to Beauty*, London, CABE.

CABE (2010e) Making the Case, Unpublished Evidence Submitted by CABE to the 2010 DCMS 'Value for Money' Assessment of Its NDPBs (Unpublished), London, CABE.

CABE (2010f) *Helping Local People Choose Good Design, Design Review Network Annual Report 2009/10*, London, CABE.

CABE (2010g) How to Set up an Enabling Panel (Unpublished, Revised Version), London, CABE.

CABE (2011a) Handover Note 10: CABE Evaluation (Unpublished), London, CABE.

CABE (2011b) Handover Note: Local Policy, CABE Submission to Examination in Public (EiP) of the Mayor of London's Draft Replacement London Plan (Unpublished), London, CABE.

CABE (2011c) Handover Note 76: Prime Minister's Better Public Building Award (Unpublished), London, CABE.

CABE (2011d) Handover Note 32: Innovation, Creativity and Learning. Regional Funding Programme for Architecture and Built Environment Centres (Unpublished), London, CABE.

CABE (2011e) Handover Note 56: Building for Life (Unpublished), London, CABE.

CABE (2011f) *Annual Report and Accounts 2010/11*, London, The Stationery Office.

CABE (2011g) Handover Note 66: Case Studies, Case Study Library (Unpublished), London, CABE.

CABE (2011h) Handover Note 47: Green Space Best Practice Guides, Management and Skills Team (Unpublished), London, CABE.

CABE (2011i) Handover Note 20: Design Task Group (Unpublished), London, CABE.

CABE (2011j) What Is Enabling (Unpublished), London, CABE.

CABE (n.d.) *Local Authority Design Champions*, London, CABE.

CABE & DTLR (2001) *Better Places to Live by Design: A Companion Guide to PPG3*, London, DTLR.

CABE Education (2004) *Neighbourhood Journeys: Making the Ordinary Extraordinary*, London, CABE Education Foundation and Creative Partnerships Bristol.

CABE & English Heritage (2003) *Shifting Sands: Design and the Changing Image of English Seaside Towns*, London, English Heritage and CABE.

CABE & ODPM (2002) *Paving the Way: How We Achieve Clean Safe and Attractive Streets*, Tonbridge, Thomas Telford.

CABE Space (2004) *Is the Grass Greener . . . ? Learning from International Innovations in Urban Green Space Management*, London, CABE.

CABE Space (2007) *Paved with Gold: The Real Value of Good Street Design*, London, CABE.

CABE Space (2009) *Helping Community Groups to Improve Public Spaces*, London, CABE.

CABE Space (2010a) *Not So Green and Pleasant? Measuring and Mapping the State of English Urban Greens Space*, London, CABE.

CABE Space (2010b) *Urban Green Nation: Building the Evidence Base*, London, CABE.

Cabinet Office (1999) *Modernising Government*, London, Her Majesty's Stationary Office.

Campbell & Cowan (2002) *Re:Urbanism: Challenge to the Urban Summit*, London, Urban Management Initiatives.

Cantacuzino S (1994) *What Makes a Good Building? An Inquiry by the Royal Fine Art Commission*, London, RFAC.

Carmona M (1996) "Controlling Urban Design—Part 1: A Possible Renaissance", *Journal of Urban Design*, 1(1): 47–73.

Carmona M (1999) "Reinventing Residential Urban Design", *Town and Country Planning*, 68(2): 54–57.

Carmona M (2001) *Housing Design Quality, through Policy, Guidance and Review*, London, Spon Press.

Carmona M (2009a) "The Isle of Dogs: Four Waves, Twelve Plans, 35 Years, and a Renaissance . . . Of Sorts", *Progress in Planning*, 71(3): 87–151.

Carmona M (2009b) "Design Coding and the Creative, Market and Regulatory Tyrannies of Practice", *Urban Studies*, 46(12): 2643–2667.

Carmona M (2009c) "Sustainable Urban Design: Definitions and Delivery", *International Journal for Sustainable Development*, 12(1): 48–77.

Carmona M (2010) "Decoding Design Coding" in Clemente C and De Matteis F (Eds) *Housing for Europe, Strategies for Quality in Urban Space, Excellence in Design, Performance in Building*, Rome, Tipographia Del Genio Civile.

Carmona M (2011a) "Decoding Design Guidance" in Banerjee T & Loukaitou-Sideris A (Eds) *Companion to Urban Design*, London, Routledge.

Carmona M (2011b) "CABE R.I.P. . . . Long Live CABE", Town & Country Planning, 80(5): 236–239.

Carmona M (2011c) "Shaping Local London", *Urban Design*, 18: 32–35.

Carmona M (2011d) "Design and the NPPF", *Town & Country Planning*, 80(10): 456–458.

Carmona M (2012) "As-of-Right—Is the Time Right?", *Town & Country Planning*, 81(2): 104–107.

Carmona M (2013a) "Planning, Beirut-style", *Journal of Space Syntax*, 4(1): 123–129.

Carmona M (2013b) "The Design Dimension of Planning (20 Years On)", www.bartlett.ucl.ac.uk/planning/centenary-news-events-repository/urban-design-matthew-carmona.

Carmona M (2014a) "'Our Future in Place'—Or Is It?", www.bartlett.ucl.ac.uk/cross-faculty-initiatives/urban-design/urban-design-matters/farrell-review-urban-design-matters.

Carmona M (2014b) "The Place-shaping Continuum: A Theory of Urban Design Process", *Journal of Urban Design*, 19(1): 2–36.

Carmona M (2014c) "Investigating Urban Design" in Carmona M (Ed) *Explorations in Urban Design, An Urban Design Research Primer*, London, Ashgate.

Carmona M (2014d) "London's Local High Streets, The Problems, Potentials and Complexities of Mixed Street Corridors", *Progress in Planning*, www.sciencedirect.com/science/article/pii/S030590061400039.

Carmona M (2014e) "Towards a Place (Leadership) Council for England", www.bartlett.ucl.ac.uk/cross-faculty-initiatives/urban-design/urban-design-matters/Urban-Design-Matters-43.

Carmona M (2014f) *Explorations in Urban Design, An Urban Design Research Primer*, London, Ashgate.

Carmona M, Carmona S & Gallent N (2003) *Delivering New Homes: Processes, Planners and Providers*, London, Routledge.

Carmona M & Dann J (2006) *Design Coding in Practice, An Evaluation*, London, Department for Communities and Local Government.

Carmona M, de Magalhães C & Edwards M (2002) "What Value Urban Design?", *Urban Design International*, 7: 63–81.

Carmona M & Giordano V (2013) "Design Coding, Diffusion of Practice in England", www.udg.org.uk/publications/udg-publication/design-coding-diffusion-practice-england.

Carmona M, Marshall S & Stevens Q (2006) "Design Codes, their Use and Potential", *Progress in Planning*, 65(4): 201–290.

Carmona M & Sakai A (2014) "Designing the Japanese City—An Individual Aesthetic and a Collective Neglect", *Urban Design International*, 19(3): 186–198.

Carmona M & Sieh L (2004) *Measuring Quality in Planning, Managing the Performance Process*, London, Spon Press.

Carmona M, Tiesdell S, Heath T, & Oc T (2010) *Public Places Urban Spaces, the Dimensions of Urban Design*, Oxford, Architectural Press.

Carmona M & Wunderlich F (2012) *Capital Spaces, the Multiple Complex Public Spaces of a Global City*, London, Routledge.

Case Scheer B (1994) "Introduction: The Debate on Design Review" in Case Scheer B & Preiser W (Eds) *Design Review, Challenging Urban Aesthetic Control*, London, Chapman & Hall.

Chipperfield G (1994) *Financial Management and Policy Review of the Royal Fine Art Commission by Sir Geoffrey Chipperfield*, London, Department of National Heritage.

Christiansen R (2010) "Sea Change: Tide of Change That Has Swept Our Seaside Towns", *The Telegraph*, 6 September, www.telegraph.co.uk/culture/art/architecture/7984338/Sea-Change-tide-of-change-that-has-swept-our-seaside-towns.html.

Christie S (2005) "The Building Blocks of Success", *Community Practitioner*, October.

Clover C (2004) "Quango 'Wanted to Destroy Listed Buildings'", *The Telegraph*, 21 June, www.telegraph.co.uk/news/uknews/1465035/Quango-wanted-to-destroy-listed-buildings.html.

Committee on Standards in Public Life (2005) "Getting the Balance Right, Implementing Standards of Conduct in Public Life", www.gov.uk/government/uploads/system/uploads/attachment_data/file/336897/10thFullReport.pdf.

Conservatives (2010) *Open Source Green Paper*, London, The Conservative Party.

Construction Task Force (1998) *Rethinking Construction (the Egan Report)*, London, Department for Trade and Industry.

Cullen G (1961) *Townscape*, London, Architectural Press.

Cullingworth B (1997) *Planning in the USA: Policies, Issues and Processes*, Routledge, London.

Cuthbert A (2006) *The Form of Cities*, Malden, MA, Blackwell Publishing.

Cuthbert A (2011) *Understanding Cities, Methods in Urban Design*, London, Routledge.

DCLG (2004) *Living Places: Caring for Quality*, London, RIBA Enterprises.

DCLG (2006a) *Circular 01/2006: Guidance on Changes to the Development Control System*, London, DCLG.

DCLG (2006b) *Preparing Design Codes, Practice Manual*, London, DCLG.

DCLG (2007) *Homes for the Future, More Affordable, More Sustainable*, London, DCLG.

DCLG (2008) *Trees in Towns II, A New Survey of Urban Trees in England and their Condition and Management*, London, DCLG.

DCLG (2010) "Evaluation of the Mixed Communities Initiative Demonstration Projects", Final Report, www.gov.uk/government/uploads/system/uploads/attachment_data/file/6360/1775216.pdf.

DCLG (2015a) "Starter Homes Design", www.gov.uk/government/uploads/system/uploads/attachment_data/file/419212/150330_-_Starter_Homes_Design_FINAL_bc_lh_pdf.pdf.

DCLG (2015b) "Notes on Neighbourhood Planning", Edition 17, www.gov.uk/government/uploads/system/uploads/attachment_data/file/488024/15121_Notes_on_Neighbourhood_Planning_II.pdf.

DCMS (2004) Press Notice 162/04, Clean Neighbourhoods and Environment Bill: CABE to Become a Statutory Body, 8 December, London, DCMS.

Delafons J (1994) "Democracy and Design" in Case Scheer B & Preiser W (Eds) *Design Review: Challenging Urban Aesthetic Control*, New York, Chapman & Hall.

Derbyshire B (2012) "Building for Life 12, A Smarter Approach", Building, 8 October, www.building.co.uk/building-for-life-12-a-smarter-approach/5043907.article.

Design Council (2014) *Design Council Annual Report and Accounts, for the Year Ending 31 March 2014*, London, Design Council.

Design Council (2015) *Design Council Annual Report and Accounts 2014–2015, for the Year Ending*

31 March 2015, We Improve People's Lives through the Use of Design, London, Design Council.

Design Council CABE (2013) *Design Review, Principles and Practice*, London, Design Council.

DETR & CABE (2000) By Design, Urban Design in the Planning System, Towards Better Practice, London, DETR

DH Estates & Facilities (2008) "Achieving Excellence Design Evaluation Toolkit (AEDET Evolution)", http://webarchive.nationalarchives. gov.uk/20130107105354/http://www.dh.gov.uk/ prod_consum_dh/groups/dh_digitalassets/@dh/@ en/documents/digitalasset/dh_082086.pdf.

Dittmar H (2012) "Design Council CABE Stalls at the Lights", Building, 22 May, www.building.co.uk/ design-council-cabe-stalls-at-the-lights/5043745. article.

DNH—Department of National Heritage (1996) *Financial Management and Policy Review of the Royal Fine Art Commission, Summary of Conclusions and the Department's Response*, London, Department of National Heritage.

Dobbins M (2009) *Urban Design and People*, Hoboken, NJ, Wiley.

DoE—Department of the Environment (1987) *Circular 8/87, Historic Buildings and Conservation Areas—Policy and Procedures*, London, HMSO.

DoE—Department of the Environment (1997) *PPG1, General Policy and Principles*, London, the Stationary Office.

Doern G B & Phidd R (1983) *Canadian Public Policy: Ideas, Structure, Process*, Toronto, Methuen.

Donnelly M (2012) "CABE Confirms Latest Redundancies", 27 March, www.planningresource. co.uk/article/1176393/cabe-confirms-latest-redundancies.

DoT, DCLG & Welsh Assembly (2007) *Manual for Streets*, London, Thomas Telford Publishing.

Egan J (2004) *The Egan Review, Skills for Sustainable Communities*, London, ODPM.

Elkin S (1986) "Regulation and Regime, a Comparative Analysis", *Journal of Public Policy*, 6: 49–72.

Ellin N (2006) *Integral Urbanism*, London, Routledge.

English Heritage & CABE (2002) "Building in Context, New Development in Historic Areas", http://web archive.nationalarchives.gov.uk/20110118095356/

http://www.cabe.org.uk/publications/building-in-context.

English Heritage & CABE (2007) *Guidance on Tall Buildings*, London, CABE.

Etherington R (2010) "Areas of Outstanding Urban Beauty Photographic Competition", *Dezeen Magazine*, 6 September, www.dezeen. com/2010/09/06/areas-of-outstanding-urban-beauty-photography-competition/.

Fairs M (1998) "Rogers Blasts RFAC", *Building Design*, 2 October, 1367: 2.

Fairs M & Lewis J (1998) "Architecture Council Begins to Take Shape", *Building Design*, 22 January, 1379: 6

Falk N (2011) "Masterplanning and Infrastructure in New Communities in Europe" in Tiesdell S & Adams D (Eds) *Urban Design in the Real Estate Development Process*, Chichester, Wiley-Blackwell.

Farrell T (2008) "Twelve Challenges for Edinburgh", *Prospect*, 130: 2–43.

Farrell T (2014) "The Farrell Review of Architecture + The Built Environment, Our Future in Place", London, www.farrellreview.co.uk/downloads/The Farrell Review.pdf?t=1454326593.

Ferris H (1929) *The Metropolis of Tomorrow*, New York, Ives Washburn.

Fischer J & Guy S (2009) "Re-interpreting Regulations: Architects as Intermediaries for Low-carbon Buildings", *Urban Studies*, 46(12): 2577–2594.

Fisher J (1998) "Architecture: The Country's Architectural Enforcer", *The Independent*, 21 August, www.independent.co.uk/arts-entertainment/ architecture-the-countrys-architectural-enforcer-1173032.html.

Flint A (2014) "Braving the New World of Performance Based Zoning", www.citylab.com/ housing/2014/08/braving-the-new-world-of-performance-based-zoning/375926/.

Fulcher M (2012) "Architecture Centres 'Abandoned' as Umbrella Organisation Shuts Down", *Architects' Journal*, 19 April, http://m.architectsjournal. co.uk/8629258.article.

Fulcher M (2013) "Resurrected Architecture Centre Network to be UK-wide", *Architects' Journal*, 3 January, www.architectsjournal.co.uk/news/daily-news/resurrected-architecture-centre-network-to-be-uk-wide/8640696.article.

Garreau J (1991) *Edge City: Life on the New Frontier*, London, Doubleday.

George R V (1997) "A Procedural Explanation for Contemporary Urban Design", *Journal of Urban Design*, 2(2): 143–161.

Gordon P, Beito D & Tabarrok A (2005) "The Voluntary City, Choice, Community and Civil Society" in Ben-Joseph E & Szold T (Eds) *Regulating Place, Standards and the Shaping of Urban America*, New York, Routledge.

Grover P (2003) *Local Authority Conservation Provision in England, Research Project into Staffing, Casework and Resources*, Oxford, Oxford Brookes University.

Groves P, *Birmingham Post*, Tuesday, 21 January 2003, p. 11.

Gummer J (1994) DoE Press Release 713: More Quality in Town and Country, 12 December, London, Department of the Environment.

Hall AC (1996) *Design Control, towards a New Approach*, London, Butterworth.

Hall P (2014) *Good Cities, Better Lives, How Europe Discovered the Lost Art of Urbanism*, London, Routledge.

Hall S (2003) "New Labour Has Picked Up Where Thatcherism Left Off", *The Guardian*, 6 August, www.guardian.co.uk/politics/2003/aug/06/society.labour.

Hall T (2007) *Turning a Town Around*, Oxford, Blackwell Publishing.

Hallewell B (2005) "Initiative Looks into Home Plan", *East Anglia Daily Times*, 12 January.

Hansen B (2006) *The National Economy*, Westport, CT, Greenwood Press.

Held D, McGrew A, Goldblatt D, & Perraton J (1999) *Global Transformations: Politics Economics Culture*, Cambridge, Polity.

Hester R (1999) "A Refrain with a View", *Places*, 12(2): 12–25.

HM Government (2000) *Better Public Buildings, A Proud Legacy for the Future*, London, DCMS.

HM Government (2009) *World Class Places, the Government's Strategy for Improving Quality of Place*, London, DCLG.

HM Treasury (2003) *The Green Book: Appraisal and Evaluation in Central Government*, London: TSO www.gov.uk/government/uploads/system/uploads/attachment_data/file/220541/green_book_complete.pdf.

Hood C (1983) *The Tools of Government*, Chattham, Chatham House Publishers.

Hopkirk E (2012) "Design Council CABE Appoints New Director", 19 January, www.bdonline.co.uk/design-council-cabe-appoints-new-director/5030745.article.

Hopkirk E (2013) "Design Network Rises from Ashes of Architecture Centre Network", *Building Design*, 2 January, www.bdonline.co.uk/design-network-rises-from-ashes-of-architecture-centre-network/5048115.article.

Hopkirk E (2015) "Government's Starter Home Exemplars Dismissed as 'Missed Opportunity'", 31 March, www.bdonline.co.uk/governments-starter-home-exemplars-dismissed-as-missed-opportunity/5074690.article.

Horticulture Week (2010) "Green Infrastructure 'Health Check' Launched by CABE", *Horticulture Week*, 28 January, www.hortweek.com/green-infrastructure-health-check-launched-cabe/article/980142.

Hou J (2011) "Citizen Design, Participation and Beyond" in Banerjee T & Loukaitou-Sideris A (Eds) *Companion to Urban Design*, London, Routledge.

Housebuilder (2005) "CABE Expands Advisory Team to Boost Quality", *Housebuilder*, January/February.

House of Commons Committee of Public Accounts (2008) *Housing Market Renewal: Pathfinders, Thirty-fifth Report of Session 2007/08*, London, The Stationery Office.

House of Commons Library (2005) *The Clean Neighbourhoods and Environment Bill (Bill 11 of 2004–05)*, London, House of Commons.

House of Lords (2016) *Building Better Places, House of Lords Select Committee on National Policy for the Built Environment*, London, House of Lords.

Housing & Communities Agency (2009) *Affordable Housing Survey: A Review of the Quality of Affordable Housing in England*, London, DCLG.

Hubbard P (1994) "Professional vs. Lay Tastes in Design Control—An Empirical Investigation", *Planning Practice and Research*, 9(4): 271–287.

Hudson P (2006) "Planning Applications: Arrangements for Consulting Commission for Architecture and the Built Environment as a Non-statutory Consultee", www.gov.uk/government/uploads/system/uploads/attachment_data/file/7978/

061206-Letter_to_Chief_Planning_Officers-_ Arrangements_for_Consulting_CABE_as_a_ Non-Statutory_Consultee.pdf.

Hurst W & Rogers D (2009) "Design Competition for Eco-Towns Mothballed", *Building Design*, 24 July, www.bdonline.co.uk/design-competition-for-eco-towns-mothballed/3145561.article.

Imrie R & Street E (2006) "The Codification and Regulation of Architects' Practices", Project Paper 3, in *The Attitudes of Architects Towards Planning Regulation and Control*, London, Kings College London.

Imrie R & Street E (2009) "Regulating Design: Practices of Architecture, Governance and Control", *Urban Studies*, 46(12): 2507–2518

Imrie R & Street E (2011) *Architectural Design and Regulation*, Chichester, Wiley-Blackwell.

Kavanagh D (2012) "Lord St-John of Fawsley: Flamboyant Politician Who Fell Foul of Margaret Thatcher", www.independent.co.uk/news/obituaries/lord-stjohn-of-fawsley-flamboyant-politician-who-fell-foul-of-margaret-thatcher-7537625.html.

Kayden J, New York City Department of City Planning & Municipal Art Society of New York (2000) *Privately Owned Public Space, the New York Experience*, New York, John Wiley & Sons.

Kent E (n.d.) "Toward Place Governance: What If We Reinvented Civic Infrastructure around Placemaking?", www.pps.org/reference/toward-place-governance-civic-infrastructure-placemaking/.

Kropf K (2011) "Coding in the French Planning System: From Building Line to Morphological Zoning" in Marshall S (Ed) *Urban Coding and Planning*, London, Routledge.

Lang J (1996) "Implementing Urban Design in America: Project Types and Methodological Implications", *Journal of Urban Design*, 1(1): 7–22.

Lang J (2005) *Urban Design—A Typology of Procedures and Products*, Oxford, Architectural Press.

Lascoumes P & Le Gales P (2007) "Introduction: Understanding Public Policy through Its Instruments—From the Nature of Instruments to the Sociology of Public Policy Instrumentation", *Governance: An International Journal of Policy, Administration, and Institutions*, 20(1): 1–21.

Lees L (2003) "Visions of 'Urban Renaissance': The Urban Task Force Report and the Urban White Paper" in Imrie R & Raco M (Eds) *Urban Renaissance? New Labour, Community and Urban Policy*, Bristol, Policy Press.

Lehrer U (2011) "Urban Design Competitions" in Banerjee T & Loukaitou-Sideris A (Eds) *Companion to Urban Design*, London, Routledge.

Leinberger (2008) *The Option of Urbanism, Investing in a New American Dream*, Washington, DC, Island Press.

Levitt R (2013) "Why Tsars and So Popular with this Government", www.theguardian.com/society/2013/oct/15/why-tsars-popular-government.

Lewis J & Blackman D (1998) "New Body Replaces Arts Commission", *Planning*, 18 December, 1299: 4.

Lewis J & Fairs M (1998) "Architects Need Not Apply", *Building Design*, 18 December, 1377: 1–2.

Linder S & Peters G (1989) "Instruments of Government, Perceptions and Contexts", *Journal of Public Policy*, 9(1): 35–58.

Lipman C (2003) "No Cause for Jubilation", *New Start*, 14 February.

Lock D (2009) "Rules for the design police" Town & Country Planning, July/August, 308–9.

Lonsdale S (2004) "Urban Chic Finds a New Home in the Countryside", *The Telegraph*, 27 March, www.telegraph.co.uk/finance/property/new-homes/3323279/Urban-chic-finds-a-home-in-the-countryside.html.

Loukaitou-Sideris A & Banerjee T (1998) *Urban Design Downtown: Poetics and Politics of Form*, Berkeley, University of California Press.

Lung-Amam W (2013) "That 'Monster House' Is My Home: The Social and Cultural Politics of Design Reviews and Regulations", *Journal of Urban Design*, 18(2): 220–41.

Lynch K (1976) *Managing the Sense of a Region*, Cambridge, MA, MIT Press.

Mantownhuman (2008) "Manifesto, towards a New Humanism in Architecture", www.mantownhuman.org/manifesto.html.

Marshall S (2011) *Urban Coding and Planning*, London, Routledge.

Mayor of London & Newham London (2011) *Royal Docks Spatial Principles*, London, Mayor of London.

McDonnell L & Elmore R (1987) "Getting the Job Done: Alternative Policy Instruments", *Educational Evaluation and Policy Analysis*, 9(2): 133–152.

Ministry for the Environment (2005) "The Value of Urban Design, The Economic, Environmental and Social Benefits of Urban Design", www.mfe.govt.nz/publications/towns-and-cities/value-urban-design-economic-environmental-and-social-benefits-urban.

Ministry for the Environment (2006) "Urban Design Toolkit, Third Edition", www.mfe.govt.nz/publications/towns-and-cities/urban-design-toolkit-third-edition.

Nasar J (1999) *Design by Competition: Making Design Competitions Work*, Cambridge, Cambridge University Press.

Natarajan L (2015) 'Socio-spatial learning: A case study of community knowledge in participatory spatial planning', *Progress in Planning*.

National Audit Office (2009) *The Building Schools for the Future Programme: Renewing the Secondary School Estate*, London, The Stationery Office.

New Civil Engineer, Thursday 26 September 2002, p. 7.

Office of the Deputy Prime Minister (ODPM) (2002) *Living Places: Cleaner, Safer, Greener*, London, ODPM.

Office of the Deputy Prime Minister (ODPM) (2003) *Sustainable Communities, Building for the Future*, *London*, ODPM.

Office of the Deputy Prime Minister (ODPM) (2005) *Government Response to the ODPM Housing, Planning and Local Government and the Regions Committee Report on the Role and Effectiveness of CABE*, London, The Stationary Office.

Parnaby R & Short M (2008) "CABE, Light Touch Review", http://webarchive.nationalarchives.gov.uk/+/http://www.culture.gov.uk/reference_library/publications/5787.aspx/.

Paterson E (2012) "Urban Design and the National Planning Policy Framework for England", *Urban Design International*, 12(2): 144–155.

Pierre J (1999) "Models of Urban Governance: The Institutional Dimension of Urban Politics", *Urban Affairs Review*, 34(3): 372–396.

Place Alliance (2014a) "Our Purpose", www.bartlett.ucl.ac.uk/placealliance/pa-content/vision.

Place Alliance (2014b) Place Matters, friendly, fair, flourishing, fun & free, http://placealliance.org.uk/wp-content/uploads/2016/02/Place-Matters.pdf.

Plater-Zyberk E (1994) "Foreword" in Case Scheer B & Preiser W (Eds) *Design Review, Challenging Urban Aesthetic Control*, London, Chapman & Hall.

PricewaterhouseCoopers (2004) *The Role of Hospital Design in the Recruitment, Retention and Performance of NHS Nurses in England*, London, CABE.

Punter J (1986) "A History of Aesthetic Control: Part 1–1909–1953, the Control of the External Appearance of Development in England and Wales", *Town Planning Review*, 57(4): 29–62.

Punter J (1987) "A History of Aesthetic Control: Part 2–1953–1985, the Control of the External Appearance of Development in England and Wales", *Town Planning Review*, 58(1): 351–81.

Punter J (1999) *Design Guidelines in American Cities, a Review of Design Policies and Guidance in Five West Coast Cities*, Liverpool, Liverpool University Press.

Punter J (2003) "From Design Advice to Peer Review: The Role of the Urban Design Panel in Vancouver", *Journal of Urban Design*, 8(2): 113–35.

Punter J (2007) "Developing Urban Design as Public Policy: Best Practice Principles for Design Review and Development Management", *Journal of Urban Design*, 12(2): 167–202.

Punter J (2010) "Reflecting on Urban Design Achievements in a Decade of Urban Renaissance" in Punter J (Ed) *Urban Design and the British Urban Renaissance*, London, Routledge.

Punter J (2011) "Design Review—An Effective Means of Raising Design Quality?" in Tiesdell S & Adams D (Eds) *Urban Design in the Real Estate Development Process*, Chichester, Wiley-Blackwell.

Punter J & Carmona M (1997) *The Design Dimension of Planning, Theory, Content and Best Practice for Design Policies*, London, E & FN Spon.

Reade E (1987) *British Town and Country Planning*, Milton Keynes, Open University Press.

Richards JM (1980) *Memoirs of an Unjust Fella*, London, Weidenfeld & Nicolson.

Roger Evans Associates (2007) *Delivering Quality Places, Urban Design Compendium 2*, London, English Partnerships & Housing Corporation.

Rogers D (2010) "Government to Wind Up Sea Change Programme: Building Design", 23 July, www.bdonline.co.uk/government-to-wind-up-sea-change-programme/5003113.article.

Rogers D (2012) "Axed Director Predicts End of CABE", *Building Design*, 7 December, www.bdonline.co.uk/axed-director-predicts-end-of-cabe/5047081.article.

Rogers D (2015) "Design Council on Hunt for Architecture Deputy", *Building Design*, 8 May, www.bdonline.co.uk/design-council-on-hunt-for-architecture-deputy/5075315.article.

Rogers D & Klettner A (2012) "CABE Prepared to Become Self-funding Consultancy", *Building Design*, 7 March, www.bdonline.co.uk/cabe-prepares-to-become-self-funding-consultancy/5033049.article.

Rowley, A (1994) 'Definitions of Urban Design: The Nature and Concerns of Urban Design', *Planning Practice & Research*, 9(3) 179–97.

Rowley A (1998) "Private-Property Decision Makers and the Quality of Urban Design", *Journal of Urban Design*, 3(2): 151–73.

Royal Fine Art Commission (1924a) Minutes of the Fine Art Commission, 22 February, London, RFAC.

Royal Fine Art Commission (1924b) Minutes of the Fine Art Commission, 8 February, London, RFAC.

Royal Fine Art Commission (1924c) Minutes of the Fine Art Commission, 4 April, London, RFAC.

Royal Fine Art Commission (1924d) Minutes of the Fine Art Commission, 1 May, London, RFAC.

Royal Fine Art Commission (1924e) Minutes of the Fine Art Commission, 5 June, London, RFAC.

Royal Fine Art Commission (1926) The Royal Fine Art Commission Second Report, London, HMSO.

Royal Fine Art Commission (1928) The Royal Fine Art Commission Third Report, London, HMSO.

Royal Fine Art Commission (1943a) Minutes of the Fine Art Commission, 19 May, London, RFAC.

Royal Fine Art Commission (1943b) Minutes of the Fine Art Commission, 11 August, London, RFAC.

Royal Fine Art Commission (1943c) Minutes of the Fine Art Commission, 15 September, London, RFAC.

Royal Fine Art Commission (1945) Observations on the City of London's Report on Post-war Reconstruction, London, HMSO.

Royal Fine Art Commission (1950) The Royal Fine Art Commission Tenth Report, London, HMSO.

Royal Fine Art Commission (1951) Minutes of the Fine Art Commission, 11 April, London, RFAC.

Royal Fine Art Commission (1952) The Royal Fine Art Commission Eleventh Report, London, HMSO.

Royal Fine Art Commission (1958) The Royal Fine Art Commission Sixteenth Report, London, HMSO.

Royal Fine Art Commission (1962a) The Royal Fine Art Commission Eighteenth Report, London, HMSO.

Royal Fine Art Commission (1962b) Minutes of the Fine Art Commission, 11 April, London, RFAC.

Royal Fine Art Commission (1962c) Minutes of the Fine Art Commission, 14 November, London, RFAC.

Royal Fine Art Commission (1968) Minutes of the Fine Art Commission, 9 October, London, RFAC.

Royal Fine Art Commission (1971) The Royal Fine Art Commission Twenty-First Report, London, HMSO.

Royal Fine Art Commission (1980) Building in Context, London, RFAC.

Royal Fine Art Commission (1985) The Royal Fine Art Commission Twenty-Second Report, London, HMSO.

Royal Fine Art Commission (1986) The Royal Fine Art Commission Twenty-Third Report, London, HMSO.

Royal Fine Art Commission (1990) Planning for Beauty: The Case for Design Guidelines, London, HMSO.

Royal Fine Art Commission (1994a) What Makes a Good Building? An Inquiry by the Royal Fine Art Commission, London, RFAC.

Royal Fine Art Commission (1994b) The Royal Fine Art Commission Thirty-Second Report, London, HMSO.

Royal Fine Art Commission (1995) The Royal Fine Art Commission Thirty-Third Report, London, HMSO.

Royal Fine Art Commission (1996) The Royal Fine Art Commission Thirty-Fourth Report, London, HMSO

Royal Town Planning Institute (RTPI) (2014) *Making Better Decisions for Places, Why Where We Make Decisions Will Be Critical in the Twenty-First Century*, London, RTPI.

Rybczynski W (1994) "Epilogue" in Scheer BC & Preiser W (Eds) *Design Review: Challenging Urban Aesthetic Control*, New York, Chapman & Hall.

Salamon L (2000) "The New Governance and the Tools of Public Action, an Introduction", *Fordham Urban Law Journal*, 28(5): 1611–1674.

Salamon L (Ed) (2002) *The Tools of Government, a Guide to the New Governance*, Oxford, Oxford University Press.

Schneider A & Ingram H (1990) "Behavioral Assumptions of Policy Tools", *Journal of Politics*, 52(2): 510–529.

Schuster M (2005) "Substituting Information for Regulation, in Search of an Alternative Approach to Shaping Urban Design" in Ben-Joseph E & Szold T (Eds) *Regulating Place, Standards and the Shaping of Urban America*, New York, Routledge.

Schuster M, de Monchaux J & Riley C (Eds) (1997) *Preserving the Built Heritage: Tools for Implementation*, Hanover, NH, Salzburg Seminar/ University Press of New England.

Select Committee on Office of the Deputy Prime Minister: Housing, Planning, Local Government and the Regions (2005) "Fifth Report", www.publications.parliament.uk/pa/cm200405/cmselect/cmodpm/59/5903.htm.

Serota N (2010) "A Blitzkrieg on the Arts" *The Guardian*, 4 October, www.theguardian.com/commentisfree/2010/oct/04/blitzkrieg-on-the-arts.

Sherman (2003) "Prescott Wants £500 Million Facelift for Slums and Curbs on Landlords", *The Times*, 27 January, www.thetimes.co.uk/tto/news/uk/article1905732.ece.

Siegan B (2005) "The Benefits of Non-Zoning" in Ben-Joseph E & Szold T (Eds) *Regulating Place, Standards and the Shaping of Urban America*, New York, Routledge.

Simmons R (2009a) "Rules for Achieving Design Standards", *Town & Country Planning*, 78(9): 349.

Simmons R (2009b) "No Duplication", *Building*, 15 May, www.building.co.uk/no-duplication/3140548.article.

Simmons R (2015) "Constraints on Evidence-based Policy: Insights from Government Practices", *Building Research & Information*, 43(4): 407–19.

Slack E & Côté A (2014) "Comparative Urban Governance, Future of Cities: Working Paper", www.gov.uk/government/uploads/system/uploads/attachment_data/file/360420/14–810-urban-governance.pdf.

Slocock C (2015) "Whose Society, The Final Big Society Audit", www.civilexchange.org.uk/wp-content/uploads/2015/01/Whose-Society_The-Final-Big-Society-Audit_final.pdf.

Smithard T (2006) "Red Tape Blame over Facelift", *Great Yarmouth Mercury*, 13 January.

Solesbury W (2001) *Evidence Based Policy: Whence It Came and Where It's Going: Working Paper 1* London, Centre for Evidence Based Policy and Practice.

Sorrell J (2008) "Time to Leave the Comfort Zone", http://news.bbc.co.uk/1/hi/sci/tech/7410305.stm.

South London Press (Friday), Councillor Brian Palmer, Friday, 14 February 2003, p12.

South Shropshire Journal (2004) "Chance to Have Say on Home Design", 30 January.

Stamp G (1982) "Official Aesthetics", *The Spectator*, 13 November: 28–30.

Stewart D (2008) "CABE 'Light Touch' Review Finally Launched", www.building.co.uk/cabe-%E2%80%9A%C3%84%C3%B2light-touch%E2%80%9A%C3%84%C3%B4-review-finally-launched/3112575.article.

Stille K (2007) "The B-plan in Germany", *Urban Design*, 101: 24–6.

Syms P (2002) *Land, Development & Design*, Oxford, Blackwell Publishing.

Szold T (2005) "Afterword, the Changing Regulatory Template" in Ben-Joseph E & Szold T (Eds) *Regulating Place, Standards and the Shaping of Urban America*, New York, Routledge.

Talen E (2011) "Form-based Codes vs. Conventional Zoning" in Banerjee T & Loukaitou-Sideris A (Eds) *Companion to Urban Design*, London, Routledge.

Talen E (2012) *City Rules, How Regulations Affect Urban Form*, Washington, DC, Island Press.

Tang Y (2014) "A Review of Large-scale Urban Design in China", *Urban Design and Planning*, 167(DP5): 209–20.

Taylor D (2003) "Park Life", November, www.architectsjournal.co.uk/home/park-life/147167.article.

The Herald (1949) "Royal Fine Art Commission", *The Herald*, 31 December, https://news.google.com/newspapers?nid=2507&dat=19421230&id=OQ01AAAAIBAJ&sjid=m6ULAAAAIBAJ&pg=4201,6373543&hl=en.

Tibbalds F (1991) "Planning—An Architect's View—Grasping the 'Nettle' of Design", The Planner TCPSS Proceedings, 13 December, 71–4.

Tiesdell S & Adams D (2004) "Design Matters: Major House Builders and the Design Challenge of Brownfield Development Contexts", *Journal of Urban Design*, 9(1): 23–45.

Tiesdell S & Adams D (2011) "Real Estate Development, Urban Design and the Tools Approach to Public Policy" in Tiesdell S & Adams D (Eds) *Urban Design in the Real Estate Development Process*, Chichester, Wiley-Blackwell.

Tiesdell S & Allmendinger P (2005) "Planning Tools and Markets: Towards an Extended Conceptualisation" in Adams D, Watkins C & White M (Eds) *Planning, Public Policy and Property Markets*, Oxford, Blackwell Publishing.

Tolson S (2011) "Competitions as a Component of Design-Led Development (Place) Procurement" in Tiesdell S & Adams D (Eds) *Urban Design in the Real Estate Development Process*, Chichester, Wiley-Blackwell.

TSO (2008) "Housing Market Pathfinders Report to the House of Commons Committee of Public Accounts", 9 June 2008 www.publications.parliament.uk/pa/cm200708/cmselect/cmpubacc/106/106.pdf.

UN Habitat (2010) State of the World's Cities 2010/11: *Bridging the Urban Divide*, London, Earthscan.

Urban Design London (2015) "UDL's Design Review Survey Report January 2015", www.urbandesignlondon.com/wordpress/wp-content/uploads/UDLs-Design-Review-Survey-2014-2-2.pdf.

Urban Design Skills Working Group (2001) "Report to the Minister of Housing, Planning & Regeneration DTLR", http://webarchive.nationalarchives.gov.uk/20110118095356/http:/www.cabe.org.uk/files/urban-design-skills-working-group.pdf.

Urban Greenspaces Taskforce (2002) *Green Spaces, Better Places*, London, DTLR.

Urban Task Force (1999) *Towards an Urban Renaissance*, London, Spon Press.

Vabo S & Røisland A (2009) *Tools of Government in Governance—The Case of Norwegian Urban Government*, Madrid, EURA Conference.

Van Doren P (2005) "The Political Economy of Urban Design Standards" in Ben-Joseph E & Szold T (Eds) *Regulating Place, Standards and the Shaping of Urban America*, London, Routledge.

Vedung E (1998) "Policy Instruments: Typologies and Theories" in Bemelmans-Videc M, Rist R, & Vedung E (Eds) *Carrots, Sticks & Sermons, Policy Instruments and Their Evaluation*, New Brunswick, Transaction Publishers.

Vedung E & Van der Doelen F (1998) "The Sermon: Information Programs in the Public Policy Process—Choice, Effects and Evaluation" in Bemelmans-Videc M, Rist R & Vedung E (Eds) *Carrots, Sticks & Sermons, Policy Instruments and Their Evaluation*, New Brunswick, Transaction Publishers.

Vischer J & Cooper Marcus C (1986) "Evaluating Evaluation: Analysis of a Housing Design Awards Program", *Places*, 3(1): 66–85.

Waite R (2010) "Spending Review, CABE Closed Down"*Architects' Journal*, 20 October, www.architectsjournal.co.uk/news/daily-news/spending-review-cabe-closed-down/8607174.article.

Walters D (2007) *Designing Community, Charettes, Masterplans and Form-Based Codes*, Oxford, Architectural Press.

Wates N (2014) *The Community Planning Handbook: How People Can Shape Their Cities, Towns & Villages in Any Part of the World*, London, Routledge.

Webster C (2007) "Property Rights, Public Space and Urban Design", *Town Planning Review*, 78(1): 81–101.

Wood A (2014) *Interview: The Contribution of Urban Design Panels to Auckland's Urban Story*, Auckland, Beatnik Publishing.

Wood M (2004) *Trend Analysis Report for the Civic Trust on The Green Flag Award Scheme in England*, London, Heawood Research Limited.

Young Foundation (2010) *Innovation and Value, New Tools for Local Government in Tough Times*, www.youngfoundation.org/wp-content/uploads/2012/10/Innovation-and-value-new-tools-for-local-government-in-tough-times-March-2010.pdf.

Youngson A (1990) *Urban Development and the Royal Fine Art Commissions*, Edinburgh, Edinburgh University Press.

Web Resources

http://en.wikipedia.org/wiki/Design_Council

http://hansard.millbanksystems.com/commons/1936/dec/08/royal-fine-art-commission

http://planningguidance.planningportal.gov.uk/blog/policy/achieving-sustainable-development/delivering-sustainable-development/7-requiring-good-design/

http://planningjungle.com/consolidated-versions-of-legislation/

http://webarchive.nationalarchives.gov.uk/20110118095356/http://www.cabe.org.uk/buildings

http://webarchive.nationalarchives.gov.uk/20110118095356/http://www.cabe.org.uk/design-review/advice

http://webarchive.nationalarchives.gov.uk/20110118095356/http://www.cabe.org.uk/masterplans

http://webarchive.nationalarchives.gov.uk/20110118095356/http:/www.cabe.org.uk/news/stronger-support-for-public-sector-clients

http://webarchive.nationalarchives.gov.uk/20110118095356/http:/www.cabe.org.uk/files/response-improving-engagement.pdf

www.academyofurbanism.org.uk/awards/great-places/

www.building.co.uk/sir-stuart-lipton-loses-case/3048444.article

www.builtforlifehomes.org/go/about/faqs~7#faq-ans-7

www.designcouncil.org.uk/our-services/built-environment-cabe

www.designreviewpanel.co.uk/#!locations/c24vq

www.dtpli.vic.gov.au/planning/urban-design-and-development/design-case-studies

www.engagingplaces.org.uk/home

www.ifs.org.uk/budgets/gb2012/12chap6.pdf

www.gov.uk/government/collections/planning-applications-statistics

www.gov.uk/government/uploads/system/uploads/attachment_data/file/39821/taylor_review.pdf

www.legislation.gov.uk/ukpga/2005/16/part/8

www.local.gov.uk/media-releases/-/journal_content/56/10180/6172733/NEWS

www.local.gov.uk/publications/-/journal_content/56/10180/3626323/PUBLICATION-Local Government Association funding outlook for councils

http://londonist.com/2012/05/londons-top-brutalist-buildings-London's top Brutalist buildings

www.open-city.org.uk/education/index.html

www.oxford.gov.uk/Library/Documents/Planning/Oxford%20Design%20Panel%20Details%20of%20the%20Service.pdf

www.parliament.uk/business/publications/research/briefing-papers/SN05687/local-authorities-the-general-power-of-competence

www.placecheck.info

www.planningportal.gov.uk/planning/planningpolicyandlegislation/currentlegislation/acts

www.planningresource.co.uk/article/445624/cabe-audit-recommends-shake-up

www.pps.org/reference/what_is_placemaking/

www.pps.org/training/

www.princes-foundation.org/content/enquiry-design-neighbourhood-planning

www.publications.parliament.uk/pa/cm200304/cmselect/cmodpm/1117/1117we31.htm

www.rudi.net/books/11431

www.telegraph.co.uk/news/obituaries/9124613/Lord-St-John-of-Fawsley.html

Index